THE
Steamboat *Bertrand*
AND
Missouri River Commerce

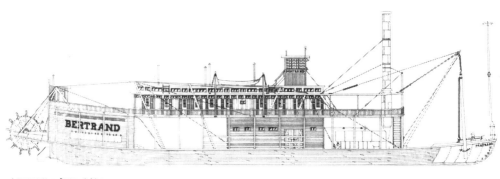

Artist's reconstruction of the architecture of the steamboat *Bertrand*
based on scale drawings and photographs. *Drawn by Jerry Livingston,
Staff Illustrator, Midwest Archeological Center, Lincoln, Nebraska.*

THE
Steamboat *Bertrand*
AND
Missouri River Commerce

By
Ronald R. Switzer

University of Oklahoma Press : Norman

ALSO BY RONALD R. SWITZER

Tobacco, Pipes, and Cigarettes of the Prehistoric Southwest (El Paso, Texas, 1969)

The Origin and Significance of Snake-Lightning Cults in the Pueblo Southwest (El Paso, Texas, 1972)

The Bertrand *Bottles: A Study of 19th-Century Glass and Ceramic Containers* (Washington, D.C., 1974)

THIS BOOK IS PUBLISHED WITH THE GENEROUS ASSISTANCE OF THE KERR FOUNDATION, INC.

LIBRARY OF CONGRESS CATALOGING-IN-PUBLICATION DATA

Switzer, Ronald R.
  The steamboat Bertrand and Missouri River commerce / by Ronald R. Switzer.
    pages cm
  Includes bibliographical references and index.
  ISBN 978-0-8061-5193-9 (paper) 1. Bertrand (Steamboat) 2. Missouri River—Antiquities. 3. Underwater archaeology—Missouri River. 4. Excavations (Archaeology)—Missouri River. 5. Shipwrecks—Missouri River—History—19th century. 6. Frontier and pioneer life—West (U.S.) 7. River steamers—Missouri River—History—19th century. 8. Steam-navigation—West (U.S.)—History—19th century. I. Title.
  F598.S95 2013
  978'.01—dc23

2013001314

THIS BOOK IS DEDICATED TO JEROME E. PETSCHE,
ARCHAEOLOGIST, EDITOR, MENTOR, AND FRIEND

Contents

Illustrations

ALL ILLUSTRATIONS OF THE *BERTRAND*, THE EXCAVATION OF the steamboat, and the artifacts mentioned in the text are courtesy of the National Park Service Midwest Archeological Center, Lincoln, Nebraska, and the U.S. Fish and Wildlife Service *Bertrand* Conservation Laboratory and Museum, De Soto National Wildlife Refuge, Missouri Valley, Iowa. Photographs of the crew members and passengers, when known, are credited in the appropriate figures.

Preface and Acknowledgments

ONCE IN A VERY GREAT WHILE, A TREASURE TROVE OF artifacts comes to light that provides insight into the development of industry, trade, and commerce in the United States during a particular period. The discovery of the steamboat *Bertrand* in a cut-off meander of the Missouri River in 1968 and its subsequent excavation yielded a cargo of thousands of artifacts reflecting the life and times of mid-nineteenth-century America. The cargo gives us a glimpse of the importance of steamboat navigation and trade on the Missouri River at a time when Americans were pushing the frontier westward across the plains and mountains to the Pacific Coast. It also offers an ideal opportunity to investigate the technology, economy, and character of the Trans-Missouri West in the 1860s.

Because the 300,000 or more artifacts recovered from the *Bertrand* have stories to tell, one main purpose of this book is not simply to categorize and describe them, but to capture the invention, manufacturing, marketing, distribution, and sale of these products and to trace something of the measures taken to get them to the frontier mining camps of Montana Territory. Chapter VI includes an annotated catalogue of the artifacts and what has been discerned of the histories and personalities associated with each kind. While the numbers and relative rarity of some types of artifacts are impressive, this is not about numbers, but about what can be learned when each artifact type is researched to its fullest. This treatment is not perfect, and much remains to be done to document the rest of the cargo. Any errors in identifying the types, numbers, or descriptions of some artifacts are mine.

A second purpose is to capture new information about the private and social lives of the officers, crew, passengers, and consignees to whom the cargo was being shipped, and to say something of the passengers' motivations for traveling to the relatively uncivilized mining towns of Montana. In the process of research, much has been learned about these men, women, and children and their genealogies, each of which is unique and engaging. In some cases, fairly extensive biographies and family histories were found, but in most instances, because of the paucity of information, only thumbnail sketches are provided. In some cases, the information was reconstructed from letters and documents compiled by the late Jerome Petsche, and there are no other attributions other than references to private correspondence or materials in the possession of the families he contacted.

A third purpose of the book is to place the steamboat *Bertrand* in the context of its time and to examine its intended use and some of the technology and industry involved in its manufacture. The *Bertrand* was one of the many light draft steamboats used in the Upper Missouri trade to deliver essential goods that would contribute to the development of mercantilism and commerce in Montana Territory in the mid-1860s. But, like so many other steamboats on the Missouri River, it foundered, and its cargo never made it to its intended destination at Fort Benton. There is no intention to replace the previously published accounts of the engineering and architecture of the boat by Jerome Petsche. Rather, this book supplements those accounts and, wherever possible, fills in a few small gaps in the history of the *Bertrand*.

Voluminous material has been accumulating for the better part of the past forty years regarding the *Bertrand* and its officers, passengers, and crew. Most of it was collected by the author and the late Jerome E. (Jerry) Petsche, who was the principal archaeologist and historian responsible for the excavation of the boat and its cargo. It was our mutual desire to publish our research in a more definitive work on the *Bertrand*. Unfortunately, in our quest to secure just a few more details, we became overly protective of our research, and that inhibited its publication. Neither of us recognized that we were getting older and that the time had come to stop. Unfortunate as well, my friend Jerome Petsche died on May 19, 2008, at Hot Springs, Arkansas, at the age of seventy-seven. I will miss Jerry. He contributed much to my knowledge of the *Bertrand* and of the genealogy of the people associated with it. After his death, his daughter, Mrs. Cathy Liberty, gave me Jerry's research files, illustrations, notes, and books so that I could continue our mutual effort to document the *Bertrand*. It is to Jerry that I dedicate this manuscript.

I first met Jerry in 1969, when I was appointed by the National Park Service as laboratory director and museum specialist to conserve and curate the *Bertrand* cargo at De Soto National Wildlife Refuge near Missouri Valley, Iowa, where the steamboat was found. Over the next few years, Jerry became my mentor and friend, and he edited nearly everything I wrote about the *Bertrand* cargo, including *The* Bertrand *Bottles: A Study of 19th-Century Glass and Ceramic Containers*, published by the National Park Service in 1974. A native Nebraskan, Jerry served in the U.S. Air Force during the Korean conflict and later graduated from the University of Nebraska with a bachelor's degree in journalism and a master's in archaeology. After working at several jobs on newspapers and at the university, he became the editor of archaeological salvage papers for the Smithsonian Institution River Basin Survey Office in Lincoln, Nebraska. In the late 1960s, the National Park Service assumed responsibility for the surveys from the Smithsonian and transformed the office into the Midwest Archeological Center of the National Park Service with a broader archeological mandate. Jerry became an employee of the National Park Service. He was a brilliant, meticulous editor and a good archaeologist whose talents surfaced when he was assigned as supervisory archaeologist on the excavation of the steamboat *Bertrand* in 1968. This large project had several setbacks and pitfalls over the better part of the following two years, but he never wavered in his enthusiasm, in his exact measurements of the steamboat, or in recording the removal of the cargo. He later published two significant works about the project: "Uncovering the Steamboat Bertrand" in *Nebraska History* in 1970 and *The Steamboat Bertrand—History, Excavation and Architecture*, published by the National Park Service in 1974. The latter will remain the definitive work on the subject.

During the time that I worked to conserve the *Bertrand* cargo and some of the architectural components of the boat, I took extensive personal notes and made numerous photographs of objects. When I left the Bertrand project, I asked for and received additional records and photos from the National Park Service with the intention of writing more about their history at a later time. The information in this book comes from those notes and photographs, supplemented by historical research. The record is imperfect but represents a starting point from which other research can be undertaken. My notes cannot be fully corroborated by the files at the Bertrand Museum and Laboratory at De Soto National Wildlife Refuge, but continuing curation and cataloguing of the cargo will undoubtedly produce more accurate artifact counts and descriptions that will complement this book.

During the years that Jerry Petsche and I collaborated on our research, Annalies Corbin published an intriguing work, *The Material Culture of Steamboat Passengers: Archaeological Evidence from the Missouri River,* in which she describes artifacts salvaged from the steamboats *Bertrand* and *Arabia* and discusses the class and other social aspects of various persons on the boats relative to their possessions. While interesting and comprehensive in their specific subject matters, the three publications by Petsche, Switzer, and Corbin only begin to capture the full story of the steamboat *Bertrand.* They do not compete with, but rather complement, each other.

No one could accomplish the task of preserving and conserving the enormous cargo of the *Bertrand* without the help of a lot of people. I would be remiss if I did not say to whom I owe my thanks. Among them is the original staff at the Bertrand Conservation Laboratory who plowed ahead on their own initiative at times to preserve as much as possible of the rapidly deteriorating *Bertrand* cargo in the late 1960s and early 1970s. Some techniques for the preservation of artifacts recovered from freshwater did not exist at the time. With the help of the Smithsonian Institution Department of Underwater Archeology, the Leather Research Laboratory at the University of Cincinnati, the U.S. Department of Agriculture Forest Products Laboratory at Madison, Wisconsin, and Corning Glass Works and Museum at Corning, New York, many experiments were tried, some of which worked and some of which did not.

My thanks to Barbara Daniel, who established the first temporary conservation laboratory in a garage bay at De Soto National Wildlife Refuge in 1968 to begin processing *Bertrand* materials as they were excavated. Subsequently, she assisted me and the refuge staff in closing off and insulating several more garage bays, building shelves, installing evaporative window air conditioners, and moving cargo to safer storage conditions. During this time, I worked with the new Refuge Manager, James Salyer, to obtain funds for a permanent treatment laboratory, and with Jim's help, the U.S. Fish and Wildlife Service design team at Fort Snelling, Minnesota, designed and built the first climate-controlled conservation laboratory. This would not have been possible without Jim's persistence and determination. Subsequently, staff was hired and trained to do the exhaustive work of accessioning, cataloguing, photographing, and preserving a rapidly deteriorating cargo of huge proportions. The staff for this pioneering effort included my secretary Valerie Reiley (Meyer), Supervisory Laboratory Technician and Procurement Clerk

Russell Rochford, Museum Curator Mary Dorinda Partch, Laboratory Technicians Maia Sorenson, Kermit Hanson, David Evans, Paula McCrary, and Nancy Aiken, and Curator Edward Dodd and his staff at the Midwest Archeological Center in Lincoln, Nebraska.

My subsequent publications about the *Bertrand* were supported by Midwest Archeological Center Staff Illustrator, Jerry Livingston, who worked hundreds of hours on illustrations for those published in my works and in the works of Jerome Petsche. In addition, Wayne Nelson, staff photographer at the center, contributed hundreds of photographs of the excavation, cargo removal, and treatment, some of which are contained here. Thanks go too to my former boss and chief of the Midwest Archeological Center, the late Dr. Wilfred D. Logan, to Assistant Center Chief, the late Jackson "Smokey" Moore, to the Chief Archeologist of the National Park Service, the late Dr. John Corbin, and to Washington staff archeologist George Fisher.

It has been said by my contemporaries and reviewers that I am an archeologist first, a historian second, and a writer third. I fully admit this flaw because my professional background sometimes leads me to a pedestrian and categorical treatment of my work rather than a romantic and captivating story as most historians are wont to do. I am not a teller of tales, nor am I one to weave historical facts and fiction into a story that compares with the novelistic talents of other historians. That being said, I will attempt to take the readers of this book on the ill-fated journey of the nineteenth-century steamboat *Bertrand*. Perhaps tracing the history of the boat and its cargo and illuminating the personas of the crew and passengers will serve as yet another example of the role Missouri River steamboats played in American frontier expansion and commerce. I hope it will provide some additional insights into the social backgrounds and behaviors of the men and women who helped civilize the west and in so doing brought the American frontier to a close. The journey may be a bit challenging, but in the end I hope the story is satisfying.

One cannot accomplish work of this kind without the support and understanding of his family. My wife, Deborah, has endured nearly forty years of my efforts on this project and of helping me cart my library and voluminous research files around the country as I changed duty stations with the National Park Service. Her patience with this imperfect effort has been exceptional.

Enid, Oklahoma
April 2012

I

The Steamboat *Bertrand*

IN THE EARLY SUMMER OF 1864, GEORGE FELLER AND THOMAS C. Reed of Wheeling, West Virginia, and their partners George Laing, Lewis W. Cochran, and Jeremiah W. Cochran of neighboring Monroe County, Ohio, contracted with Wilson, Dunlevy, & Co. of Wheeling to construct a light-draft steamboat in the boat-building yards of the first ward. They named the boat the *Argiota*.[1] Although the kinds of river trade the boat was to be used in is uncertain, she was built pretty much to the design trends and practices of the time for boats used on the Ohio River. However, a few of her features apparently were new adaptations in the evolutionary development of steamboats of her day. How she eventually came to be part of the Upper Missouri River trade is not altogether clear, but given the growing need for steamboats to transport mining and agricultural equipment, tools, groceries, and other supplies to the mines and booming communities in Montana Territory, it is not surprising that she was bought by several St. Louis entrepreneurs looking to monopolize transportation to that frontier.

Wheeling, West Virginia, was an important boat-building center strategically located on the Ohio River near abundant supplies of hard, flexible, water-resistant white oak for building steamboats and near steel mills and iron foundries with furnaces capable of turning out steamboat engines, boilers, and other components. Here the hull and keelson of the *Argiota* were constructed on beaching timbers and calked with pitch and oakum.[2] She was then towed to Pittsburgh, where her cabins were

---

[1]*Wheeling Daily Register,* November 17, 1864.

[2]A keelson is an interior longitudinal wood structure, running above and fastened to the keel of a boat, that strengthens and stiffens the framework.

constructed by Isaac Gullett of Allegheny City. Her furnishings were provided by J. and G. Mendel, and she was painted by James Stewart, both of Pittsburgh.[3] After her cabins and furnishings were completed, the *Argiota* was towed back to Wheeling, where the boilers and machinery were installed by the A. J. Sweeney & Son iron foundry.[4]

Apparently the machinery (engine(s), etc.) had been salvaged from the steamboat *A. J. Sweeney*, a sternwheel packet boat built by and named for Andrew J. Sweeney in 1863. This boat, captained by George Hill of St. Louis, hit a bridge pier on the Cumberland River on March 9, 1864, and burned and sank at Clarksville, Tennessee.[5] It was believed by *Bertrand* steamboat archaeologist and historian Jerome E. Petsche that while A. J. Sweeney & Son produced and installed the boilers, mud and steam drums, and other machinery on the *Argiota*, Wilson, Dunlevy, & Co. assisted in trussing the vessel from bow to stern with hog chains and beams in a suspension system resembling the upper works of a bridge.[6]

Very little biographic information has been recovered about the builders and outfitters of the *Argiota* except for Andrew Sweeney. Peter Dunlevy was a master carpenter, shipwright, and joiner respected for building fast and light boats. Some vessels that were copied after his designs were given such names as the *Arabia* and *Desert Queen*. River pilots, who often were fond of good jokes and masters of primitive literary similes, would submit that all you had to do to launch a Dunlevy boat was to pour a keg of beer over the bow. Some said with a grin that it would, in fact, float on the foam. Certainly the *Wheeling Daily Intelligencer* supported this notion, saying that the *Bertrand* (*Argiota*) was "a nice trim little steamer, and it sits upon the water like a duck."[7] The only thing known

---

[3]*Wheeling Daily Intelligencer*, November 26, 1864.

[4]Earl Chapin May, *Principio to Wheeling, 1715–1945: A Pageant of Iron and Steel* (New York: Harper and Brothers, 1945), 159.

[5]Ibid. See also W. Craig Gaines, *Encyclopedia of Civil War Shipwrecks* (Baton Rouge: Louisiana State University Press, 2008), 5.

[6]Some components of steamboats such as pitmans and hog chains required shipwrights and iron workers to work together. Pitmans were iron-strapped connecting rods between the flywheels and paddle wheels, and hog chains were iron-strapped oak timbers or iron rods that held boats together. Because steamboats were long in proportion to the depth of their hulls, they would sag were it not for hog chains connected to the heavy timbers fore and aft that were supported by braces on the keelsons along the length of the boats. It is logical to assume that Wilson, Dunlevy, and Company assisted Sweeney & Son to install the hog chains and stabilizing beams, but there is no direct proof of this. Petsche's notes, provided to the author after his death, do not confirm for this notion.

[7]*Wheeling Intelligencer*, November 26, 1864.

about Isaac Gullett is that, according to the Mormon archives, he was born April 11, 1817, and died April 17, 1899.

A good deal more is known about Andrew J. Sweeney and his family. The Thomas Sweeney family came to Wheeling from Pittsburgh in 1830, when Thomas purchased the shops and property of the North Wheeling Manufacturing Co. He was married to Rosanna Matthews, by whom he sired four children: Andrew J., Rebecca, Thomas Campbell (T. C.), and Robert H. Andrew was the eldest; he entered his father's business as a partner in 1858 and succeeded him in 1874.[8] Thomas Sweeney and his brothers and sons produced engines, mill machinery, foundry castings, and steamboats. After Andrew assumed control of the business, he took his son John M. Sweeney as a partner and expanded the company line of products.[9]

Apparently A. J. Sweeney was a natural leader. He held the office of mayor of Wheeling between 1855 and 1881 and served as a colonel of militia during the Civil War. He also was appointed by President Grant as a commissioner to the Vienna Exposition in 1873 and served again as commissioner to the Centennial Exposition in Philadelphia in 1876. His leadership and progressive outlook was again demonstrated when he brought electric lights to four Wheeling businesses on September 13, 1882. Sweeney died at Wheeling on February 14, 1893.[10]

When construction of the *Argiota* was complete, the steamboat's master, Captain Benjamin F. Goodwin, inexplicably enrolled the boat at Wheeling on November 25, 1864, as the *Bertrand*. Her enrolled capacity was 251 61/95 tons. She was 161 feet long, 32 feet 9 inches in beam, with a 5 foot 2 inch mean depth of hold.[11] It is uncertain whether changing the name of the steamboat from the *Argiota* to the *Bertrand* signaled a change in ownership, but this seems unlikely because Jeremiah Cochran, who was the clerk on the steamboat and part owner, was on board when the *Bertrand* left the port of Wheeling on her maiden voyage. Whatever the case, the *Bertrand* left Wheeling for St. Louis on November 26, 1864,

---

[8]Although James Morton Callahan is shown as the author of *History of West Virginia Old and New in One Volume and West Virginia Biography in Two Additional Volumes by Special Staff Writers*, the biography for A. J. Sweeney on pages 26 and 27 of Volume 2 was written by staff writers (Chicago: American Historical Society, 1923), Vol. 2, 26–27.

[9]A good biography of A. J. Sweeney is "A. J. Sweeney & Son," *Wheeling Daily Intelligencer*, September 14, 1886.

[10]Special Staff Writers, "A. J. Sweeney," *History of West Virginia Biography*, 26–27.

[11]Record Group 41, *Records of the Bureau of Marine Inspection and Navigation* (Washington, D.C.: General Services Administration, National Archives and Record Service). See also *Wheeling Daily Intelligencer*, November 26, 1864.

with Captain Goodwin at the helm.[12] Although her cargo was composed mainly of 6,000 kegs of nails, she had other freight and also stopped briefly on November 30 at Cincinnati to pick up several hundred cases of Hostetter's Bitters.[13] After her arrival at St. Louis in December, the boat may have been chartered to the Merchants and Peoples Line, a group of twenty-two vessels including the *Paragon, Lillie Martin,* and *Sultana* that are known to have been operating on the Mississippi River.[14] Apparently this company chose not to keep the *Bertrand* idle, and she made trips to Cairo, Paducah, and Nashville. On the sixth of January, the *Bertrand* headed to New Orleans, returning by the end of the month. Suddenly, in early February, the original owners sold the *Bertrand* to Captain James A. Yore and John E. Yore for $40,000 cash, whereupon they sold part of their interests to the newly formed Montana and Idaho Transportation Co., the largest firm then engaged in Upper Missouri transportation of freight.

The Montana and Idaho Transportation Company was organized in 1864 and included John J. Roe, John G. Copeland, and Captain James A. Yore.[15] These men and a much larger group were investing in the gold rush in Montana Territory, and the *Bertrand* was to be part of Roe's

[12]*Wheeling Daily Intelligencer,* November 26, 1864.

[13]The stop at Cincinnati is recorded in Jerome Petsche's notes, but there is no specific attribution. There are two possibilities as to how the two varieties of bitters were contained in the *Bertrand* cargo. It can be speculated that the Hostetter's Bitters picked up in Cincinnati were already consigned to merchants in Montana and they were off-loaded to a warehouse in St. Louis pending shipment to Montana on the *Bertrand* when spring navigation opened on the Missouri. If this is so, it may indicate that *Bertrand* was already destined for the Upper Missouri River trade when she made her maiden voyage to St. Louis. The cargo also contained several cases of Drake's Plantation Bitters that probably were bottled in Louisville, Kentucky, across the river from Cincinnati. Did the *Bertrand* also stop at Louisville to pick up Drake's tonic, or was it warehoused in St. Louis awaiting shipment on the *Bertrand*? Perhaps it will never be known whether there were one or two stops on the Ohio River, or whether the bitters were already consigned and stored for shipment at St. Louis. Questions like these underscore the challenge to finding incontrovertible answers.

[14]William A. Lass, *The History of Steamboating on the Upper Missouri* (Lincoln: University of Nebraska Press, 1962), 42–43.

[15]Little has been found in historic records about the partners in the Diamond R Freighting/Transportation Company except for Col. Charles Broadwater. Broadwater was a native of Missouri. After his involvement with the company, he became a prominent politician in Montana and built the famous Broadwater Hotel and natatorium in Helena. He also was associated with several railroads, including the Montana Central Railway. Glimpses of Broadwater's life are found in his obituary: "Col. C. Broadwater Dead," *New York Times,* May 25, 1892. More information is found in Patricia C. Spencer, *Images of America: Helena Montana* (Chicago: Acadia, 2002), 9.

transportation company. John Roe and his son-in-law John G. Copeland owned several other mountain steamers including the *Benton, Yellowstone, Fanny Ogden,* and the *Deer Lodge.* They were also engaged in overland freighting with other partners, Captain Nick Wall, Matthew Carroll, George Steele, E. G. McClay, and company superintendent Col. Charles Broadwater. The overland freighting business operated under the name Diamond "R" Transportation Company and was organized about 1863 specifically to monopolize overland freighting between Fort Benton and the gold fields at Helena.[18] In addition, Roe owned a lucrative pork-packing business in St. Louis under the name John J. Roe & Co. and later had extensive interests in insurance and banking.[16] He also derived profits from a wholesale and retail business in Virginia City, Montana.[17]

To keep the *Bertrand* productive until the spring rise of the Missouri River, she made trips to Boonville, Brunswick, Lexington, and Kansas City (more probably to Fort Leavenworth with munitions for the army).[18] In late February 1865, the first of several newspaper advertisements announced the *Bertrand's* impending trip to Fort Benton in Montana Territory. By March 10, 1865, the *Daily Missouri Democrat* was heralding the trip.[19] Sometime between late February and March 10, the *Bertrand* changed hands and was then destined to become a mountain-class freighter in the fleet of the Montana and Idaho Transportation Line.[20]

Additional research begins to close in on the dates between which the *Bertrand* was sold and when she was advertised as leaving St. Louis for Fort Benton. The *Tri-weekly Missouri Democrat* for February 22, 1865, advertised the *Bertrand* as being readied to leave the St. Louis levee for Fort Benton, Montana, with Captain James A. Yore as master. The article exalted the *Bertrand* as "of light draught, with good carrying capacity and most excellent cabin accommodations, insuring to freighters and passengers that speed and safety so essential on a trip of this kind. Shippers may rely upon this being one of the first boats to Benton."[21] By March 10, newspapers were definitely announcing ownership by the

---

[16]Thomas J. Scharf, *History of St. Louis* (Philadelphia: Everts & Co., 1883), Vol. 1, 616.

[17]*Daily Missouri Republican,* March 18, 1865.

[18]There is no specific attribution for this information. This notion was found in Jerome Petsche's notes that were left to the author. Petsche was meticulous in keeping track of his sources, but this note and a few others, although probably correct, have no attribution.

[19]*Daily Missouri Democrat,* March 10, 1865.

[20]Ibid.

[21]*Tri-Weekly Missouri Democrat,* February 22, 1865.

Montana and Idaho Transportation Line.[22] Taking on a crew and cargo on March 16 and 17, the *Bertrand* left the St. Louis levee on March 18 with as many as forty passengers and 250 or more tons of cargo bound for Montana Territory.[23] She was accompanied by five other Montana and Idaho Transportation Line boats, including the *St. Johns, U. S. Grant*, and the *Converse*, in addition to three other boats owned by competitors.[24] St. Louis must have been a bustling port that spring because twenty steamboats arrived at and thirty-three departed from the docks in March alone.[25]

Because shipping on the Upper Missouri was at its height in the mid-1860s and competition was fierce, steamboat captains and crews were paid very well. According to the *St. Louis Evening News* for April 18, 1866:

OFFICER'S SALARIES
(PER MONTH, INCLUDING ROOM AND BOARD)

Pilot	$725
Captain	400
First Clerk	250
Second Clerk	125

CREW MEMBER SALARIES (PER MONTH)

First Mate	$225
Second Mate	100
First Engineer	225
Second Engineer	125
Carpenter	150
Watchman	60
Steward	100
Cabin Boys	30
Firemen	55
Chambermaid	30
Roustabout	50
Cook	300[26]

[22]*Daily Missouri Democrat*, March 10, 1865.

[23]*Daily Missouri Democrat*, March 17, 1865.

[24]Ibid.

[25]George H. Morgan, *Annual Statement of the Trade and Commerce of St. Louis for the Year 1865 Reported to the Union Merchant's Exchange By Geo. H. Morgan, Secretary* (St. Louis: H. P. Studley and Co., Printers, 1866) 15.

[26]*St. Louis Evening News*, April 18, 1865.

Cooks were usually paid a lump sum out of which they hired as many assistants as they needed. There is reference to removal of the cook's stove from the boiler deck to shore in Willard Barrows's account of the sinking of the *Bertrand*, but the crew that has been identified does not include a cook. According to steamboat historian William Lass, the average mountain boat going upriver to Fort Benton employed about thirty-eight officers and crew.[27] It is obvious that the roster of officers and crew identified on *Bertrand* falls far short of Lass's figure by more than half.

Jeremiah Cochran, who was the first clerk on the *Bertrand*, was also part owner. Apparently it was not unusual for steamboat clerks, who essentially were the business managers on boats, to share in their ownership. According to steamboat historian Louis C. Hunter, a steamboat clerk was freight and passenger agent, "soliciting cargo, fixing rates, bargaining with shippers, making out waybills, checking cargo, and the like. He also purchased fuel and supplies, handled the payroll, shared in the hiring and dismissal of ordinary crew members, and performed a variety of other functions related to the management of the boat."[28] In addition to the fact that Cochran was on board the *Bertrand*, there is some indication that the boat was originally intended for use between Wheeling and St. Louis, where goods would be trans-shipped to the Upper Missouri and bring handsome profits to Ohio River business-men and boat owners. This speculation is supported by the fact that the *Wheeling Daily Intelligencer* for November 26, 1864, unequivocally states the *Bertrand* was on her "first" trip to St. Louis.[29]

Although the architectural and engineering differences between the *Bertrand* and other boats may never be known, a little is known about some unusual features of the boat. Petsche, Allen L. Bates, and Bert Fenn all agree that in most respects, the *Bertrand* resembled a light draft Ohio River boat. She was constructed with a flat-bottom "carvel-built" hull with bottom and side planks meeting flush at the seams and had a "model bow" as opposed to boats that were constructed for the Upper Missouri River trade with "spoon-bill bows."[30] It had an unusual rudder assembly that was relatively new for steamboats—two master rudders articulated with a slave that extended under the paddle wheel and the

---

[27]Lass, *History of Steamboating on the Upper Missouri River*, 50.

[28]Louis C. Hunter, *Steamboats on the Western Rivers: An Economic and Technical History* (New York: Dover Publications, Inc., 1949), 383.

[29]*Wheeling Intelligencer*, November 26, 1864.

[30]Correspondence between the three experts, Petsche, Bates, and Fenn, is on file at the Bertrand Museum, De Soto National Wildlife Refuge, Missouri Valley, Iowa.

stern rake of the hull.[31] Eventually, steamboats evolved to have three, and even four, articulated rudders.[32] In addition, the stern paddle wheel was not set in a recess in the hull and extended beyond the stern by a system of trusses. The cast-iron wheels themselves had thirteen arms or spokes supporting the paddles or buckets, and the complete wheel extended beyond the width of the boat to a total length of twenty-eight feet. The wheel shaft was round as opposed to the hexagonal shafts on most boats of the day.[33] While the *Bertrand* probably had bull rails to contain live-stock on the main deck, none were found during the excavation. Only the sockets were in evidence, indicating there may not have been live animals onboard and that the deck space was given to additional cargo.

Only a few engine parts and machinery were recovered from the boat during the excavation, indicating that the salvage crew probably removed whatever was of value. However, the *Bertrand* almost certainly was equipped with two boilers 18 feet in length, 42 inches in diameter, with seven 8-inch flues. Its cylinders were 16 inches in diameter, with a 4 1/2 foot stroke. These features would have been fairly typical for boats of this size and time. Cylindrical high-pressure boilers of this type are described in detail by John Wallace in his 1865 treatise on modeling, constructing, and running steamboats.[34] The *Bertrand* differed because it had two horizontal ash troughs under the boilers. The *Bertrand*'s driv-ing mechanism was probably similar to the classic horizontal example depicted by Louis Hunter.[35] The valve and cam system recovered from the *Bertrand* shows that it probably employed an adjustable eccentric or cut off mounted on the shaft of the paddle wheel that allowed the engineer to close the steam valve at any desired point in the stroke of the cam. This allowed for economical use of steam under normal conditions.

---

[31]Jerome E. Petsche, *The Steamboat Bertrand—History, Excavation, and Architecture*, Publications in Archeology 11 (Washington, D.C.: National Park Service, U.S. Department of the Interior, 1974), 80–81. The rudder assembly is depicted in a photograph in Jerome E. Petsche, "Uncovering the Steamboat Bertrand," *Nebraska History* 51, no. 1 (1970): 83.

[32]Norman Russell, "On River Steamers," *Transactions of the Institution of Naval Architects*, Vol. 2 (London: Institution of Naval Architects, 1861), 106.

[33]Petsche, *The Steamboat Bertrand*, 82

[34]John Wallace, *The Practical Engineer: A Treatise on the Subject of Modeling, Construct-ing and Running Steam Engines, Containing Also Directions in Regard to the Various Kinds of Machinery Connected with Steam Power, Prepared with Special Reference to the Needs of Steamboat Owners, Captains, Pilots and Engineers, and Also Connected with Stationary Steam Engines, On Land and Water*, 2nd ed. (Pittsburgh: W. S. Haven, 1861), 20–26 and 103–109.

[35]Hunter, *Steamboats on the Western Rivers*, 140.

Full stroke and exhaust cams were found on the deck near the stern during excavation.[36]

There is some conjecture about the number and arrangement of cabins for passengers and crew on the *Bertrand*. According to Louis Hunter, by the time of the Civil War, most steamboats were built with stacked decks: a main deck, boiler deck, and hurricane deck with a texas rising above it.[37] In all likelihood, the *Bertrand* had no texas. When the hull depth fell below six feet (as was the case with the *Bertrand*), a good amount of cargo was stored on the main deck, and the boiler deck was raised in height to accommodate even more cargo. The upper deck, which was usually narrower than the main cabin and shorter in length, became known as the "texas." On early steamboats, the texas was a simple box-like extension of the pilot house that rose from the hurricane deck and provided cabin space for officers and crews. Later, the texas was extended about one-third the length of the vessel from the chimneys aft and provided accommodations for officers and passengers.[38] No extension of this type was found during the excavation of the *Bertrand*, but it is likely that anything protruding above the waterline after the sinking was salvaged to make temporary shelter for the crew and salvage operators. A reconstruction of the boiler deck and cabins indicates the *Bertrand* could have had passenger cabin space for forty-five to fifty cabin passengers.[39]

The *Bertrand* was equipped with four-foot wide main deck extensions on either side of the boat that were called guards. These could be used to carry light cargo such as cotton that could be stacked there nearly up to the uppermost deck. Guards were originally built to guard the paddle wheel(s) from snags and to provide bracing for the outer ends of the wheel shafts.[40] The *Bertrand*'s builders even took the precaution of limiting the length of the guards just short of the points in the bow where spars could be run down her sides to spar, lever, walk, or "grasshopper" the vessel across sandbars. "Grasshoppering" over sandbars was accomplished by planting the spars in a sandbar on either side and ahead of the bow pointing downstream and attaching them by cables or ropes to capstans on either side of the deck just behind the bow. When the paddle wheel was put in reverse, river water was dammed up and forced ahead of the

---

[36]Petsche, *The Steamboat Bertrand*, 39.
[37]Hunter, *Steamboats on the Western Rivers*, 91.
[38]Ibid.
[39]Petsche, *The Steamboat Bertrand*, 87.
[40]Hunter, *Steamboats on the Western Rivers*, 91–93.

boat, thrusting it over/across the bar.[41] It is clear from her construction that this packet boat was meant to be as much at home on narrow channeled shallow waters in mountain country as on deeper channels of the Ohio or Mississippi Rivers. Although it is not certain, application of protective metal plating on the wheelhouse may have been accomplished at St. Louis prior to *Bertrand*'s departure for the Upper Missouri.

[41]Ibid., 254.

II

Economics of the
Upper Missouri Steamboat Trade

VERY SOON AFTER THE DISCOVERY OF MAJOR PLACER GOLD
deposits in Montana Territory in 1862, eastern merchants and
river transportation companies saw opportunities for huge profits
supplying mining machinery, equipment and tools, groceries, dry goods,
and other needs of fledgling frontier camps and towns, military posts,
and Indian agencies. In addition, transportation companies provided
economical means of travel for all sorts of emigrants going west, and
periodically they were called upon to transport Indians to newly established reservations.

The end of the Civil War was near in the spring of 1865, and an
ever-increasing number of miners, adventurers, merchants, farmers, and
other emigrants were flooding west in search of new beginnings. Indian
depredations caused by emigrants' transgressions on their lands also
brought a shift in Union military forces from the eastern fronts westward
to protect travelers as they moved through the territory. The need was
great to supply the tide of humanity that crossed the western plains and
mountains. Farming and ranching were in their infancy in much of the
Rocky Mountain West and could not supply the needs of the growing
emigrant movement. Granville Stuart, one of the early settlers in the
Gallatin Valley of Montana, wrote an astute analysis of the demand
for agricultural products and flour in 1865. In his notes, he described
the fifteen-mile-wide valley as "unexcelled" for farming and ranching.
He also forecast the presence of a new flouring mill in the valley in the

spring of 1866 that would produce flour at "fifty dollars a barrel, [and] maybe considered a dead thing for a rise, or in other words a sure card for a fortune," alleviating some of the flour shortage in the region. He also forecast the prices of wheat and fresh produce, "with wheat at from five to eight dollars a bushel, potatoes twelve to fifteen cents a pound, onions fifteen to eighteen cents a pound, cabbage twenty cents per pound, and other vegetables in proportion; melons of any kind a dollar and fifty cents each, barley twelve to fifteen cents per pound, and oats the same. If the farmers can't make their 'piles' at these prices, *in gold, remember,* they had better sell out to somebody that can."[1] In addition to the shortage of agricultural products, there were no industries of note in the west to provide machinery, tools, and equipment for mining and agriculture, so eastern manufacturers quickly re-tooled, re-structured, and expanded their product lines to keep up with the demand.

Examination of post–Civil War economics has been much debated among historians, but suffice it to say that as Americans moved west during and after the Civil War, their needs mostly had to be provided by the east. The Ohio, Mississippi, Missouri, Red, and Arkansas Rivers were the best avenues of commercial transportation of machinery, tools, groceries, and other needs, and many astute eastern businessmen invested in steamboat transportation companies to ensure economical movement of goods to keep up with the demands of their customers.

Although statistics are scattered and unreliable, it appears that pre–Civil War southern agriculture, based on slave labor, concentrated on production of cotton, hemp, sugar, tobacco, and other bulk commodities, while northern agriculturists produced vegetables, fruits, livestock, and grains that could be turned into canned, bottled, and packaged commodities for the war effort. The north was already tooled to provide woolen goods, leather boots and shoes, wagons, agricultural and mining tools, and groceries when the expanding western economy needed them the most. There were no manufacturers of these goods in the south, making the northern segue to profitability one of supplying the west's insatiable appetite for all manner of things.

Between 1831 and 1860, the design and manufacture of steamboats also experienced dramatic changes, an evolution that resulted in steamboats designed for use on specific river systems. By the mid-1860s, this

---

[1]Granville Stuart, *Montana as It Is; A General Description of Its Resources, Both Mineral and Agricultural, Including a Complete Description of the Face of the Country, Its Climate, Etc.* (New York: Arno Press, 1973), 72.

evolution gave rise to shallow draft "mountain" boats that extended commercial navigation farther and farther up the Missouri River. Historian William Lass divides the extension of commercial navigation on the Missouri into two parts. Between 1831 and 1853, steamboat navigation was extended from St. Louis to the hub of the fur trade at Fort Union, but keelboats and mackinaws were still used extensively on the river. Between 1853 and 1860, commercial navigation was extended from Fort Union to Fort Benton.[2] Although navigation of the Missouri River above St. Louis was fraught with risks, and numerous boats are known to have sunk, large profits compensated transportation companies and merchants in considerable measure for their bravery. No matter what the motivation was to go west, the Missouri River was a blessed and often cursed avenue of trade. The *Sioux City Register* in 1868 captured a bit of the uncertainty of steamboat transportation, saying, "Of all the variable things in creation the most uncertain are the action of a jury, the state of a woman's mind, and the condition of the Missouri River."[3]

Growing river commerce brought competition over freight rates. Steamboat freight costs in 1865 were ten to eighteen cents a pound to Fort Benton, but competition quickly drove them down to between six and nine cents a pound. Passenger fares averaged $150 one way up the river, compared to $350 plus meals by stagecoach. As a result of these reasonable transport fees, about three-fifths of Montana's groceries, dry goods, and equipment came up the Missouri on steamboats, and five-sixths of the Montana gold yield went down the river by mountain packets between 1865 and 1867. Some steamboats returning downriver literally became treasure ships. The *St. Johns* carried $200,000 in gold dust and 100 bales of furs and robes downriver from Fort Benton in 1865, and the *Yellowstone* carried $250,000 in gold dust and 3,000 buffalo robes from Fort Benton the same year. The next year, six boats leaving from Fort Benton transported at least $1,188,675 in gold and a minimum of 860 bales of robes and furs.[4]

Steamboat transportation companies took profits wherever they could, and government contracts to supply army posts on the Upper Missouri were like gifts from heaven. The army needed substantial provisions and supplies for the soldiers, and the transport of wagons, arms, ammunition, and construction tools and supplies added to the tonnage of steamboat companies. In addition, soldiers and dependents often took passage on

[2]Lass, *A History of Steamboating on the Upper Missouri River*, 8.
[3]*Sioux City Register*, March 28, 1868.
[4]Lass, *A History of Steamboating on the Upper Missouri River*, 52.

steamboats, increasing passenger trade. Between 1856 and 1867, the army garrisoned or built no less than nine posts on the Upper Missouri, all of which were supplied by river transportation companies. In 1867, steamboat companies transported 6,098.8 tons of freight to these posts. As the military presence on the Upper Missouri increased, the army tried to supply its Upper Missouri posts in the spring of the year, but steamboats were at a premium during that season and freight rates were exceedingly high. The only way the government could expedite supplies to its river posts in the spring months was to pay exorbitant rates of $530 to $600 per day for steamboats.[5] By 1866, the high cost of chartering boats in the spring led the army quartermaster at St. Louis to adopt season-long contracts with lower fees, especially later in the season. In 1865, freight rates from St. Louis to Fort Benton were generally ten to twelve cents a pound, with some rates as high as eighteen cents a pound, so military contracts during this period amounted to bleeding the government. After 1865, competition drove rates down to eleven cents a pound in 1866, and to between six and ten cents a pound in 1867. An Upper Missouri newspaper in 1873 said the average rate in 1867 was nine cents a pound.[6]

The speed at which cargoes could be delivered to Fort Benton during the spring rise or runoff period on the Missouri perhaps too often governed the amount of risk transportation companies were willing to take with their boats, cargoes, and passengers. Fast, light draft boats with nearly flat bottoms and great width in proportion to their length and captains who pushed the high-pressure engines and boilers to their limits to be the first at Fort Benton were likely to reap profits for their companies and the merchants whose goods they carried to the winter-starved mining camps. Some historians believe that most boats were not loaded to capacity so that they would only draw two or three feet, making passage through shallow river hazards less risky.[7] Nevertheless, with high profits at stake, overloading and underinsuring boats and cargoes may have been more prevalent than was reported. Whether the *Bertrand* exceeded its gross tonnage has yet to be determined, but if she did, she could have carried as much as 376 tons, assuming most available deck space was utilized. When the boat was excavated, no bull rails were in evidence on the main deck, indicating the *Bertrand* was not carrying livestock, so deck space may have been used for additional cargo.

[5]Ibid., 55.
[6]*Union and Dakotian*, November 11, 1873.
[7]Lass, *A History of Steamboating on the Upper Missouri River*, 109.

With increasing competition to get cargoes to Fort Benton early in the year, the risks of loss increased proportionately. Steamboat wrecks, boiler explosions, faulty equipment, piloting errors, and other calamities contributed to the alarmingly high rates of loss. Although insuring boats was expensive and rates commonly exceeded 10 percent of a boat's value, it was necessary to protect owners' and clients' interests. Insurance costs, however, had to be weighed against profitability. According to historian William Lass, one method of defraying insurance liability was to distribute ownership of steamboats among several investors so that it was impossible for any one owner to lose his total investment if one of the boats was lost.[7] Although there are few records, it is suspected that some boats going up the Upper Missouri in the spring and mid-summer flushes were overloaded and under-insured, with the risks being the owners' burden. One or two trips either way on the river could more than compensate for the $20,000 to $25,000 construction cost of most mountain boats.[8]

Nevertheless, to keep down insurance rates, there had to be improvements in steamboat safety. It was not that Congress turned a blind eye to this problem because as early as 1838, it tried to deal with wrecks and explosions that were the direct results of officer negligence or faulty equipment. Because steamboats were engaged in interstate commerce, the public demanded more control over the industry and got it with the passage of a steamboat inspection law on July 7, 1838 (5 Stat. L.304). The law created the Steamboat Inspection Service in the Treasury Department. It required that a sufficient number of competent engineers be employed on steamboats and that boats carry safety equipment such as fire pumps, hoses, signal lights, and lifeboats. It further required steamboat owners to apply to U.S. District judges for hull inspections every twelve months, and for boiler inspections every six months.[9] Judges were supposed to appoint experienced inspectors who would be paid by boat owners, not the federal government. This, of course, left the door open for political favoritism and fraudulent inspections. To improve this situation, the Steamboat Inspection Act of 1852 required even more rigid control of the steamboat transportation industry. Notably, the act divided the Steamboat Inspection Service into nine districts, each with a supervisor and inspectors who were to meet once a year to work out schedules and regulations.[10] The act required written examinations for

[8]Ibid.

[9]Ibid.

[10]Lloyd M. Short. *Steamboat-Inspection Service, Its History, Activities, and Organization* (New York: D. Appleton & Co. 1922), 2.

pilots and engineers prior to licensing. Oddly, it did not require examinations for captains and mates. It was not until 1871 that captains and
mates were required to pass written examinations. Therefore, in 1865,
boats supposedly were inspected, but the law remained mute on regulat-
ing the captains and mates who operated them. Whether the *Bertrand*
was inspected by the Fourth District inspectors at St. Louis prior to its
departure up the Missouri River is not known.

During winter, mining camps ran short of several commodities, notably bacon, vegetables, coffee, sugar, and especially flour. The importance
of freighting food commodities into the frontier is highlighted in an
account of what happened in Virginia City during the particularly bad
winter of 1864–1865. Granville Stuart, one of the major consignees of the
Bertrand's goods in Deer Lodge, Montana, recounted in his journals
that several wagon trains of flour and other supplies from Salt Lake
City broke down near Virginia City in Beaver Canyon, and when the
oxen died, the freight, including the flour, perished.[11] Flour was in very
short supply, and, according to historian Paul Phillips, the price shot
up to $150 for a 100-pound sack. It was rumored in Virginia City that
people were hoarding flour and there might be violence if it did not stop.
Stuart described how a group of five hundred vigilantes from Nevada
searched every business and house in Virginia City, confiscating 125 sacks
of flour and storing it in Leviathan Hall for safekeeping. Following the
seizure of the flour, the vigilantes imposed a rule that merchants could
sell available flour at no more than $27 to $30 per hundred pounds, and
that a single man could only purchase twelve pounds at a time. Married
men could purchase double that amount or more if they had children.[12]
In December, the stock on hand in St. Louis was about 80,000 barrels.[13]
Thus, while there was an abundance of flour on the market, insuffi-
cient quantities were being shipped to the frontier to meet the growing
demand. Shortages drove frontier prices beyond acceptable limits.

Omaha banker Joseph H. Millard, whose wife was a passenger on the
Bertrand, figures in a convoluted but amusing story having to do with
the "flour riots" in Virginia City. It seems that a leading financier in Des
Moines, Iowa, named B. F. Allen heard of the placer gold discoveries in

[11]Granville Stuart, *Pioneering in Montana: The Making of a State, 1864–1887*, ed. Paul C.
Phillips (Lincoln: University of Nebraska Press, 1925), 28.

[12]Paul C. Phillips, ed., *Forty Years on the Frontier as Seen in the Journals and Reminiscences
of Granville Stuart*, Vol. 2 (Lincoln: University of Nebraska Press, Bison Books, 1957), 27–28.

[13]Morgan, *Annual Statement of the Trade and Commerce of St. Louis for the Year 1865*, 19–20.

Montana in 1863, and partnered with Millard to open a gold exchange in Virginia City. Millard went there to oversee construction of a one-story stone building to house the business. In September 1863, the building opened for business, and the partners advertised they were "dealers in coin, gold dust, treasury notes and foreign and domestic exchange." Their gold scales were capable of handling $5,000 of gold dust at a time. Their fireproof safe was brought up the Missouri River by steamboat and hauled by ox team to Virginia City. Unfortunately, the doors to the safe were not shipped with the box. However, Allen and Millard did not want to lose the trust of depositors, so they placed wooden doors on the safe and painted them black to resemble iron doors. Bank customers were escorted so they would not get too close to the fake doors. In 1865, after the iron doors were installed, flour was in very short supply, and rumors had it that Allen and Millard were secretly storing flour in their safe. The vigilantes who searched the town for contraband flour threatened to break into the bank. Millard calmly informed them they could form a committee and look inside the safe. When they found no flour, the crowd outside the bank melted away. Allen and Millard sold their interest in the gold exchange the next year to Hussey, Dahler, & Company, and Millard apparently returned Nebraska with 100 pounds of gold, ostensibly in a trunk of his wife's clothing.[14] This roughly corresponds to the time Mrs. Millard returned to civilization in Omaha after her trip up the Missouri on the *Bertrand* and the *General Grant* to join her husband.

In their rush to the gold fields, emigrants at first took with them only the necessities. Merchants who followed them could not afford to stock their stores with luxuries and items that did not sell because the cost of shipping outweighed returns on their investments. They supplied what their customers needed, but not necessarily what they wanted. However, this situation changed as steamboat transportation became more competitive and lower shipping costs made it possible for merchants to carry a wider variety of goods. Luxury items like the brandied peaches and cherries, wines, champagnes, and tinned oysters recovered from the *Bertrand* became more available, the retail prices of which seemed not to have been much of a factor in securing them. This did not mean that were no seasonal shortages of some products such flour and other necessities.

[14]Anonymous, "Virginia City Was Site of First Bank," *Your Banks . . . Historical Sketches of Montana Banks and Bankers* (Helena: Helena Branch of the Federal Reserve Bank of Minneapolis, 1946), 8.

Other materials in short supply were iron and steel, which were available in the east but too heavy to ship up the Missouri River at a profit.

Finally, complicating commercial matters a bit further, Indian uprisings during this period spread from Minnesota across Dakota Territory north of the Missouri River and spilled out onto the northern plains into the Powder River Basin and Teton Sioux country, making overland travel and shipment of goods by teamsters extremely dangerous. These events began during the early 1860s, when Dakota settlers who established themselves in the path of the shortest and most practical routes to the Montana gold fields hoped to benefit by becoming outfitting points for the influx of miners heading west. Businessmen in Minnesota and northwestern Iowa pressed Congress for better overland routes to the mines, and by March 3, 1865, the government authorized construction of three wagon roads through Dakota. Of the three roads, the Sioux City–Fort Randall road was most promising and beneficial to Dakota, especially after the Big Sioux River was bridged in July of 1867 and the Vermillion River was bridged a few months later. Even though there was no attempt to extend the road from Fort Randall to the Cheyenne River, construction of this road and the failed ingress into the territory by the other two roads transgressed Indian lands. Indian resentment over the passage of roads through their lands finally evolved into open warfare between 1862 and 1868, starting with the Santee Sioux uprising on August 18, 1862. Federal troops were rushed to the Santee Reservation to quell the revolt, but many Santees fled west toward the Missouri River, carrying the Yanktonnais Sioux with them into the bloody conflict in Dakota Territory. President Lincoln called for volunteer troops to protect the settlements along the Missouri River, and by September 1862, the Santee stampede westward was on the wane. The army maintained camps between Brule Creek and the Yankton agency near Greenwood and built forts on the James River at the mouth of Firesteel Creek and at Fort Dakota on the present site of Sioux Falls to serve as protective buffers against further Indian hostilities from the north. During 1863 and 1864, the army stepped up its campaign against the Indians and garrisoned troops at Forts Union, Berthold, Rice, and at Fort Wadsworth at Kettle Lakes.

All the while, the Indian wars spread to the Teton Sioux country and drew Chief Sitting Bull's warring Hunkpapas of the Powder River into the fray. The government responded in kind against the hostile tribes, stepping up protective measures along the Bozeman Trail, but the bloodshed continued as the fugitive Santees fled into the badlands of the Little Missouri River. Hostilities flared again when the government opted to put a wagon road through the Powder River country and the Oglala Sioux revolted under Chief Red Cloud to protect their hunting grounds. Although the military was ultimately successful in putting down open warfare between the Indians and white settlers, and the Edmonds Commission of the 1860s was effective in making treaties and placing Indian tribes on reservations, sporadic Indian outbreaks continued.

Even with government efforts to patrol and maintain safe passage to the gold fields along western overland routes, Indian hostilities left the Missouri River as the only means of relatively safe travel from the east to Fort Benton. Adding to this situation, businessmen in Missouri River towns like Yankton were not sure they wanted Indian hostilities to end because the unrest brought them handsome profits from military contracts for supplies, building materials, and equipment.[15] By 1865, many steamboat and transportation companies were operating on and along the Missouri. The steamboat era was in full swing by the time the *Bertrand* was registered and placed in service on the Upper Missouri. Profits were high, competition was fierce, and risks were enormous.

---

[15]A complete discussion of the survey and construction of roads and the ensuing Indian uprisings across Dakota Territory is found in Herbert S. Schell, *History of South Dakota* (Lincoln: University of Nebraska Press, 1961), 80–88.

III

The Fateful Voyage and
the First Salvage Attempt

C APTAINED BY JAMES YORE, THE *BERTRAND* BORE A LARGE
cargo, a crew, and twenty-five to forty passengers when she left
the St. Louis levee on Saturday, March 18, 1865, at 10 A.M. She
apparently stopped at Versailles, Missouri, to board Mrs. Walton and
her children, and made a second unspecified stop at Fort Leavenworth.

Putting in at Omaha on the night of March 31, the *Bertrand* had a
relatively pacific trip to the city from St. Louis. The next day, Captain
Yore left the boat, intending to return to St. Louis, and Captain Horace
Bixby was at the helm of the *Bertrand* when she left the port of Omaha
the following day. By three o'clock on that clear, warm first afternoon
of April, the *Bertrand* was nearly twenty-five miles north of Omaha at
Portage La Force near De Soto Landing in Nebraska Territory when
it struck a submerged snag amidships on the larboard side (port or left
side facing forward) and began to sink in ten or twelve feet of water. The
downstream force of the river and upstream force of the boat caused it
to rend or warp around the snag. Bixby ran the boat to the shallows on
the Nebraska side of the river, but it began to take on water. When the
Bertrand beached itself on a sandbar not far from the bank, some of the
passengers apparently jumped overboard and swam to shore. After the
crew made the *Bertrand* fast in her position in a yawl, they moved the
stage (loading plank) aft and swung it ashore so the remaining passengers
could begin making their way off the boat. There was no loss of life, but
within ten or twelve minutes, the steamer *Bertrand* was history in more

than just a figurative sense. Apparently, some of the passengers were boarded at a hotel in the nearby community of De Soto, and arrangements were made for them to continue their journey on the *General Grant*, which was following the *Bertrand* upriver a few days behind.

Others, including some of the officers and crew, made their way to Omaha, where they took lodging at the Herndon House hotel. The Herndon House register provides some additional information about who stayed there after the *Bertrand* sinking, including the identities of some of the crew. Reputed to be "the best" in town, the hotel had been built in 1858 on city-donated land with a loan of $16,000 to Dr. George L. Miller, Lyman Richardson, and George Bride. It was named after a naval hero named Lt. William Lewis Herndon. Anyone of any importance who passed through the city stayed there to enjoy its accommodations and fine menu, including General William Tecumseh Sherman, Major General Grenville M. Dodge, Major General S. R. Curtis, railroad men Thomas C. Durant and H. M. Hoxie, circus man P. T. Barnum, and Arbor Day creator J. Sterling Morton. Guests of March 29, 1865, included the delegation of Henry Fontanelle, Joseph LaFleche, Indian leaders Little Chief, Omaha Chief Standing Hawk, No Knife, Young Crane, Winnebago Chief Little Hill, and others bound for Washington to see the president.

Interestingly, the front of the register was used as advertising space, informing travelers of the departure of steamers and their destinations: "Steamer Deer Lodge for Fort Benton, March 27, 1865, 2 p.m." or "Steamer Montana for St. Louis, March 26, 1865, 4 p.m." Some years later, the hotel was named the International Hotel, and in 1870, the building was leased by the Union Pacific Railroad as its general headquarters. The railroad left the building in 1911, and it was used as a storehouse until it was torn down in 1922.[1] A few of the passengers from the *Bertrand* were taken to the Herndon House in Omaha sometime in the afternoon of April 2.[2]

---

[1] The *Herndon House Register* is recorded on one reel of microfilm at the Nebraska State Historical Society, Lincoln, Nebraska, classified as RG3034.AM: Herndon House (Omaha, Neb.) Register: 1865–1866, Omaha, Douglas County, Neb.: Hotel-Size: 1 reel of microfilm containing 1 volume. The entries date from March 28, 1865, to June 1866. The volume was loaned for microfilming by the society in 1966. The Nebraska State Historical Society does not hold the original volume. The *Herndon House Register* for March 31, 1865, shows the registration of Captain Yore, but not of any other crew members or passengers. This implies that the others remained onboard the *Bertrand* that night.

[2] The *Herndon House Register* for April 2, 1865, contains the names of several crew members and passengers: Thomas Owens, Jno. W. Noye, H. E. (Horace) Bixby and Lady and

Eyewitness accounts testify to the confusion that began immediately after the boat hit the snag. Although furnishings were tossed around immediately on impact, and the structural integrity of the upper cabins, skylights, and the salon were compromised, it appears that most of the cabin passengers were well cared for and that their personal belongings, except for those in the hold, were saved. Passengers made their way upward through the decks as the boat slowly sank, but most of the deck cargo was probably already floating down the Missouri in the opposite direction of its intended destination. The best of three surviving eyewitness accounts was written by passenger Willard Barrows, a surveyor and entrepreneur accompanying his daughter, Mrs. Joseph Millard, and her two children up the Missouri to Fort Benton and Virginia City to join her husband Joseph. Barrows wrote:

> We left [Omaha] at daylight. And at three o'clock in the afternoon, when about fifty miles above by water and twenty-two by land, our boat, the new and pretty little Bertrand, struck a snag on her larboard side and in less than five minutes went down in twelve feet of water. The most of the passengers at the time were lounging on their berths, or sitting about the boat, reading and conversing. Thus in a moment as it were, our peaceful little home was changed into fright, confusion, and almost despair, our plans for the future were all changed, and each was eager to save himself from the muddy waters of the Missouri. It was a beautiful afternoon, and we were sailing along in hopes of a quick passage, not even dreaming of disaster, but in five minutes, some had lost their all, and others such articles as were indispensable for the trip.
>
> The Missouri River, from its constant changes in its channel and the caving of its banks, carrying with it trees whose roots soon become fastened in the sands on the bottom, is a river of snags. The tops of the trees are soon worn and broken so that they become pointed. And always lying with the current, they are elevated in general to the surface. Sometimes the whole tree becomes submerged and out of sight. This was the case with the one that the Bertrand struck. It was a submerged log. The scene

Servant, Albert Rowe, J. C. Burns, Capt. James Yore, John T. Murphy, W. (H.) Pim, and J. D. Lucas. It is very likely seven additional names on the register with addresses in St. Louis also were crew members who roomed together. These names have not been researched, but include T. B. Patterson, Wm. Boyd (room 24), H. McCue, F. Bronson (room 2), John Thornton, John McKeever (room 19), and Jim Lorn. Additional references to the registration of Captain Yore are found in Charles W. Martin, "Herndon House Register, 1865–1866," *Nebraska History* 48, Spring: 31; and William H. Gallaher in James E. Moss, ed., "Ho For The Mines of Montana, Up the Missouri in 1865—The Journal of William H. Gallaher," *Missouri Historical Review* 57, no. 2 (1963): 163.

on board for a time was very exciting. Ignorant of the depth of the water in which the boat lay, and the depth to which she might go, all were at a loss what to do. She soon struck bottom and commenced to career over into deep water, when the chairs, tables and other furniture of the cabin were thrown to one side; glass ware, crockery, skylight windows, and glass doors of the cabin were broken and creaking, the laboring vessel was parting and straining her timbers in rolling over. The screams of women and cries of children for a time passed description, and can be understood only by those who have experienced such a disaster. Many jumped overboard and swam for the shore, others made their way as best they could for the hurricane deck and pilot house, while others stood in mute despair, speechless and powerless.

The scene was soon over, and the boat rested on a ridge of sand in water twelve feet deep running off into twenty feet on the starboard side, being about thirty feet from shore.

The boat's yawl was got ready immediately after she struck, and a line made fast on the shore, when it returned and commenced taking off passengers, who had gathered upon the bow of the boat. The gang planks were soon floated to the stern, and a staging made from the guards of the ladies' cabin to the shore, when all were taken off in safety, and landed on a sandy beach, four miles from any inhabitants or shelter. We were on the west, or Nebraska side of the river. The little town of De Soto was some five miles distant. A runner was sent for teams to convey passengers to a place of shelter for the night, while others were soon engaged in erecting temporary shelter for such as obliged to remain.

A few of the ladies and children were sent off before night, but a greater number of the passengers remained upon the ground. The crew of the boat were soon at work removing freight from the wreck, out of which the walls of rooms twenty feet square were soon made and covered with tarpaulings. Carpets and furniture of the boat were brought on shore, and bedding from the state rooms, some stoves set up, and the people made comfortable for the night.

A cook house, being on the boiler deck, was not submerged, and its stoves and fixtures soon erected on shore and in full operation. There were ample boat-stores saved, and a good supper was smoking upon our dining table before the sun set.

No goods stored on the boiler deck or in the ladies' cabin were wet, except such as rolled off when the boat careened; but the freight on the main deck, and in the hold of the vessel, about two hundred and fifty tons, mostly groceries, was nearly a total loss. The boat, valued at forty thousand dollars, was partially insured, and the freight generally. All was turned over to the Underwriters on Insurance, who must have lost two hundred and fifty thousand dollars.[3]

Insurance underwriters must have had a busy time processing claims from wrecks on the Upper Missouri River in 1865. Of twenty steamboats that left St. Louis that year, only six made it to Fort Benton, and at least three boats were wrecked. The *Yellowstone* and *Deer Lodge* arrived in May, and the *Deer Lodge* made the trip twice more in early June. The *Effie Deans* arrived in June, and the *Deer Lodge* made another trip later in the month. The *General Grant*, the *Twilight*, and the *St. John* also made it to Fort Benton in June. Because of low water, other boats ascending the river had to discharge their cargos below Fort Benton for freighting overland or for transfer to lighter shallow draft boats. This may account for several landings of the *Deer Lodge* at Fort Benton that season because it could not have made many trips from St. Louis in one season. She was probably kept on the Upper Missouri below Fort Benton as a lighter to transfer cargos to the fort.

Farther down on the Missouri, the *Bertrand*, *Cora*, and *A. E. Stanard* wrecked in the snag-infested waters between Florence and De Soto within a stone's throw of one another. As feverish work to salvage the cargo and machinery of the *Bertrand* got underway, another company boat, the *Cora*, hit a snag and sank in six feet of water near Florence, Nebraska, on May 4, 1865. This site was about two water miles from the *Bertrand*. Work on the *Bertrand* stopped abruptly, and salvagers rushed to work on the *Cora*. Hiram Upham, a passenger on the *Twilight*, wrote that the *Cora* and its cargo were lost, and the *Twilight* took on the *Cora*'s passengers.[4]

Shortly afterward, on May 19, 1865, the *A. E. Stanard* wrecked in deep water at De Soto Bend. She was carrying a large cargo of mining supplies and went down in five minutes. The *Omaha Weekly Republican* reported the news and in the same article supported an article that had appeared that same day in the *Council Bluffs Nonpareil* calling for putting snag boats on the river between Omaha and Fort Randall. The *Weekly Republican* proposed in addition that the legislatures of Iowa, Nebraska, and Dakota provide funds to cut down all the timber along the banks of the Missouri for a distance of 100 yards on either side to

[3]Willard Barrows, "Three Thousand Miles up the Missouri by Willard Barrows, Esq., Davenport, Iowa," *The Boston Review* 5, no. 29 (1865): 445–46.

[4]Hiram Upham, "Upham Letters from the Upper Missouri, 1865," *The Frontier: A Magazine of the Northwest* 13, no. 4 (1933): 311–13.

prevent snags from accumulating in the river.[5] Everyone, it seemed, was tired of losing boats and cargos to the muddy Missouri. Even so, the six boats that made it to Fort Benton in 1865 carried 6,000 tons of freight. Freight going down the river that year amounted to 362.5 tons, including 29,000 buffalo robes and a fair amount of gold.[6]

The *General Grant* stopped at De Soto to board some *Bertrand* passengers on April 9, but the trip upriver was not uneventful. The boat was attacked or harassed several times by Indians, and in early June, a Santee Sioux war party attacked four of her crew and the pilot as they were sounding the channel from a yawl. Three of the crew were killed, and one crewman and the pilot escaped, although injured, and made their way through dense brush back to the steamer, which was then about one-half mile below where the incident occurred.[7] The *General Grant* finally arrived at Fort Benton in late June. Although the *General Grant* made four trips up the Missouri in 1864 and 1865, she was wrecked by ice on March 18, 1866, three miles below Bellevue, Nebraska, with 172 tons of freight bound for Fort Benton.[8]

Subsequent to the sinking of the *Bertrand*, an attempt to salvage the boat machinery and cargo may have been made by one of the salvage companies in which Captain James Buchanan Eads of St. Louis had retained an interest. Even though Eads may not have been directly involved in the salvage effort, his influence on steamboat salvage during this period was considerable. Eads was born on May 23, 1820, at Lawrenceburg, Indiana. He was an architect and inventor who designed bell boats, sometimes referred to as submarines, from which salvage divers could be put down on sunken steamers. He later built large salvage boats that could raise entire steamboats with their cargos. Interestingly, F. W. Switzer, who worked for Eads, designed the centrifugal pumps used on Eads's salvage boats. Whether this man was a relative of the author is unknown.

In 1842, Eads, Nelson, & Case built one of the first successful bell boats for salvaging steamboat cargos. The company name changed briefly in 1847 to Nelson, Eads, & McDowell and then reverted to Eads & Nelson in 1848 when McDowell withdrew. During the 1840s and 1850s,

[5]*Omaha Weekly Republican*, May 20, 1865, 1.

[6]Joel F. Overholser, "Commerce of Missouri Big In Fur Trade, Boat Years" (Fort Benton, Mont.: The River Press, August 8, 1979).

[7]*Montana Post*, July 1, 1865, 6.

[8]Personal correspondence between the author and Missouri River historian John Kouwenhoven, June 11, 1974. Correspondence is in possession of the author.

Eads was principal owner of the salvage company of Eads & Nelson, which was pretty much out of the salvage business by the end of the decade. However, Eads is said to have retained stock in the Western River Improvement & Wrecking Co. he organized in 1857 with capital of $250,000. After 1860, Eads put most of his energy into the invention and promotion of gun carriages and steam-operated gun turrets and the building of ironclad gunboats and river monitors at Carondelet, Missouri, under the name James B. Eads & Co. About 1866, his interest seems to have shifted to bridge building, and between 1867 and 1874, he designed and built the famous Eads Bridge over the Mississippi River at St. Louis at a cost of more than $10,000,000 and the loss of ten workers. The bridge consisted of three spans, the center one being 520 feet long, and the other two spans reaching 500 feet, all resting on limestone piers anchored to bedrock. Eads is also credited with devising a method for keeping the Mississippi River open for shipping through South Pass, above New Orleans, that involved constructing a series of parallel jetties to deflect the deposit of sandbars.[9] James Buchanan Eads died at Nassau, Bahama Islands, on March 8, 1887.

[9] The best biographical information on James Eads, exclusive of his work engineering the Eads Bridge at St. Louis, is found in E. W. Gould, *Fifty Years on the Mississippi River; Or, Gould's History of River Navigation* (St. Louis: Nixon-Jones Printing Co., 1889), 483–88. The most complete descriptions of the design and construction of the Eads Bridge are found in C. M. Woodward, *A History of the St. Louis Bridge Containing a Full Account of Every Step in Its Construction and Erection, and Including the Theory of the Ribbed Arch and the Tests of Materials* (St. Louis: G. I. Jones and Company, 1881). Yet another fine detailed account of the construction of the Eads Bridge is found in John A. Kouwenhoven, "The Designing of the Eads Bridge," *Technology and Culture* 23, no. 4 (1982): 535–68. A more obscure biography of James Buchanan Eads containing a good description of the engineering and construction of the Eads Bridge and the jetties at South Pass can be found in William Sellers, "Memoir of James Buchanan Eads, 1820–1887," 59–79. Read before the National Academy of Sciences in April 1888 (Washington, D.C.).

IV

Officers, Crew, and Passengers

BERTRAND ARCHAEOLOGIST AND HISTORIAN JEROME E. Petsche, the author, and several other researchers have tried over the past three decades to piece together a comprehensive list of the steamboat's crew and passengers. Their life stories and what motivated them to work on or take passage on the *Bertrand* contribute to understanding the personalities involved in western expansion in mid-nineteenth-century America. Some of the families represented were or would become movers and shakers in western expansion. Others were ordinary people but of no less interest. Petsche devoted a good part of the last years of his life to researching family histories and genealogies, and many of his notes are now in the author's possession.

Without a doubt, Samuel Clemens, better known as Mark Twain, was one of the most interesting and heralded riverboat captains in American history, but he was just one of a long line of rivermen. Riverboat captains were a unique fraternity. For the most part, they were highly intelligent, educated, ambitious individuals who learned river geographies well and who passed on their knowledge and skills to succeeding generations of steamboat officers. They were forgiving of mistakes, but not usually more than once. They were strong-willed men who ruled their boats and crews with absolute authority, but who could be suave, charming, and socially adept, especially in the presence of ladies. They could be cunning and persuasive in situations that engendered economic or political gain from men of means and influence. Their knowledge of steamboat design and engineering, their knowledge of the rivers, and their business acumen enabled them to command high salaries and use their resources to buy or build their own boats. Several, such as Captain Henry Shreve, and the masters of the *Bertrand,* Horace Bixby and James Yore, piloted many boats during their careers and built or owned their steamboats.

Steamboating on the Upper Missouri River was risky. The list of environmental hazards was long, and included swift, changeable currents, shoals, and rapids, sandbars, snags, and floating debris, high winds or tornadoes, and scarce burnable fuel. Mechanical problems plagued the boats, not the least of which was the collection of mud in the boiler tubes, paddle wheel failures, and broken hog chains, trusses, and cables. Additionally, Indian attacks on boats and on wooding and sounding crews were a constant menace. Perhaps as important as all other hazards combined was bad judgment or pilot error caused by lack of knowledge about the rivers or just plain arrogance. To conquer the rivers, captains and pilots had to know hundreds of landmarks along the shores, how to find and steer for slack water, and the shapes of the rivers at night so well that they did not need to see landmarks because there were no buoys or lights. In addition, they had to know the depth of the water at various places when last read by poles and soundings under the bows and under the sterns. A course followed one day when the water was at one elevation could be perilous when the water was lower the next time at the same spot. They constantly had to relearn the river and to memorize the transient obstacles and channels. In the final analysis, what made good captains and pilots was not just their knowledge of the rivers, but good judgment in the exercise of their knowledge and skills and the courage to apply them despite the risk of error.

Steamboat captains were sometimes characterized as notorious risk-takers, but those who beat the odds and got their boats to Fort Benton with large cargos in the spring collected the largest returns for their bravery. Carrying extra tonnage that was not underwritten against loss could mean even larger profits if they made it safely to the head of navigation on the Missouri to Fort Benton. Most steamboat historians, however, do not believe this was a common practice because overloading boats made them sit lower in the water, increasing the risk of grounding and running into other hazards. It took a peculiar breed of men to brave the Missouri River and to overcome its potential perils, but they did so for decades during the settling of the west. Success came from being at the right places at the right times, and these men knew well how to play the odds. Thus, it was not surprising to find the likes of captains Bixby and Yore and river pilot John Jacobs on the *Bertrand* at the height of commerce on one of the longest of the nation's westernmost navigable waterways.

What motivated *Bertrand* passengers to board a steamboat bound for the most northwestern reaches of the Missouri River or to endure the hardships of the mining frontier in Montana Territory? Given the social and economic conditions in the west in the 1860s, some answers are not too surprising, but some are a little puzzling. No matter what their origins, and they came from all walks of life, they shared the rugged individualism that enabled the taming of the frontier. They were brave, strong, independent individuals, some with a streak of foresight and entrepreneurial genius. Some were adventurers seeking their fortunes by the easiest means, and some were criminals or military deserters trying to escape eastern justice. Some were craftsmen, tradesmen, and farmers who established their professions and provided services and products necessary for the survival and growth of young communities. Finally, there were successful eastern businessmen who saw opportunities as merchants in the west, where they could profit by selling groceries, clothing, tools, and equipment that could not be obtained locally or that were needed by the military. Indeed, in Montana Territory and elsewhere in the west in the mid-nineteenth century, it was said an entrepreneur could have a go at something he had never tried before if he had an idea in his head and a dollar in his pocket with which to start.

Among the male passengers on the *Bertrand* were two successful merchants from Virginia City, Montana, John T. Murphy and George Pool Dorriss. A respected surveyor and Omaha businessman, Willard Barrows, was also on board the boat. Another man who traveled with quizzical motives was William Wheatly, a craftsman who apparently shipped some of his tools and materials in a barrel in the cargo and traveled as a cabin passenger. In all likelihood, Wheatly was not without means because he was accompanying sawmill equipment upriver that he and a partner owned, but he took his tools along in case things did not work out. A lingering question has to do with the fact there was a variety of carpenters' tools in the cargo that do not seem to have been associated with any specific lots of merchandise. Whether these were the possessions of the *Bertrand*'s carpenter John C. Burns is not known, but it is likely.

The adult women who took passage on the *Bertrand* had a variety of motivations. Two they shared was the need to join their husbands who had gone to Montana ahead of them and to preserve the unity of their families. They could have stayed in the "civilized" east, but they chose not to do so. Were they were bored with eastern society and seeking something new, or were they altruistic and truly dedicated to being helpmates to their husbands, or both? From one standpoint, these ladies were doing what might have been expected given their circumstances, but there are some speculative observations with regard to their collective motivations that are interesting in themselves. They took with them on the *Bertrand* possessions reflecting eastern Victorian civility and gentility, probably in an attempt to bring some comforts to their new surroundings. The facts that some of their personal possessions were shipped in the cargo hold and that they traveled as cabin passengers testify to their social status. They were not traveling alone or as single women; they were traveling together or were accompanied by children or a family member. Seldom in histories of western expansion are there accounts of women traveling alone.

Although these women may have been pure in their motives for going west, these were women of conviction who may not always have been obedient or passive, and as such defined their own personalities. Although the Atchison, Millard, and Walton women all came from relatively well-to-do backgrounds, they were wise enough to realize they could reap additional personal and social rewards from their husbands' entrepreneurial successes. Mrs. Millard seems to have wanted to help in her husband's endeavors, but frontier life was more than she could bear, and she soon returned to eastern civilization in Omaha, leaving her husband with the directive that he should come home too. The Campbell sisters, Annie and Fannie, were schooled in gentility, but later put their energies to productive labor, teaching and ranching and helping their husbands in pecuniary ways. Taken as group, these women did what they did in the interest of self-preservation, without losing their sense of family or sacrificing their own identities. It is fortunate that some of the artifacts from their personal baggage survived to provide glimpses of their personalities.

BERTRAND OFFICERS

Captain Horace Ezra Bixby

Horace "Lightning" Bixby was no stranger to steamboating and was an experienced captain on the Mississippi and Missouri Rivers. This wiry, dynamic captain spent the better part of his life on the rivers, and during

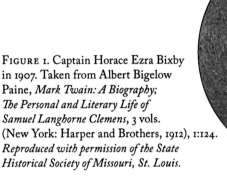

FIGURE 1. Captain Horace Ezra Bixby
in 1907. Taken from Albert Bigelow
Paine, *Mark Twain: A Biography;
The Personal and Literary Life of
Samuel Langhorne Clemens*, 3 vols.
(New York: Harper and Brothers, 1912), 1:124.
*Reproduced with permission of the State
Historical Society of Missouri, St. Louis.*

thirty-six of those years, he apparently was never ill. Bixby attributed his long life to "temperate habits," to "cultivating a cheerful state of mind," and never allowing himself "to worry about difficulties that he could not remedy."[1] He had the power to teach his cub pilots both judgment and courage by setting the example. He was a hard taskmaster and although gruff at times, it was his example, not his manners or preachments, that made him powerful. Horace Bixby possessed all of the larger-than-life attributes of a riverboat captain and apparently was not afraid of much of anything.

Bixby was generally accompanied by a "cub pilot" or assistant steerman, but it has not been determined if one was on the *Bertrand*. Samuel Clemens was one of the earlier cub pilots on his boats. Clemens eventually wrote many works about his life on the Mississippi River. One of his works, *Life on the Mississippi*, captures a good deal of the history of the river and serves as a partial memoir of his experiences on the "Big Muddy." Samuel Clemens had a permanent ambition from childhood to be riverboat pilot, but as he grew into adulthood, the dream drifted farther away. However, things took a different turn when he boarded the *Paul Jones* on a trip from Cincinnati to New Orleans in 1857. Samuel intended to embark from New Orleans for the Amazon River to seek his fortune in the cocoa trade. It was on the *Paul Jones* that he met Captain

---

[1]"Mark Twain's Tutor," *Waterways Journal*, March 22, 1902, reprt. from *Cairo Telegram* (Cairo, Mississippi), March 22, 1902, 80.

Bixby and convinced him to take him on as a cub pilot for $500, with $100 in advance and the balance from future wages. Clemens had to learn 2,000 miles of the ever-changing Mississippi River and hundreds of landmarks along its course during eighteen months of study under Horace Bixby and others. He finally received his pilot's license on April 9, 1859.

During his apprenticeship, Clemens worked on the steamboat *Pennsylvania* between September 27, 1857, and November, 26, 1857, and again between February 17, 1858, and June 5, 1858. In February 1858, while working on the *Pennsylvania*, he arranged for his younger brother Henry to work on the boat in an unpaid starting position as a mud clerk. The position of mud clerk got its name from the fact that the clerk often had to go ashore in the mud to perform administrative duties such as checking bills of lading and receiving payment for cargo. The elder Clemens apparently had a good relationship with Captain John Klinefelter, but despised the boat's pilot William Brown, whom he pummeled for abusing and striking his brother in an earlier disagreement. Klinefelter was sympathetic, offering to fire Brown and take Samuel on as pilot. Samuel left the *Pennsylvania* on June 5 and took passage on the *A. T. Lacy* to New Orleans. He was to assume his new position with Klinefelter on the next trip upriver from New Orleans on the *Pennsylvania*. Eight days later, on June 13, 1858, while Henry was at work on the *Pennsylvania*, the boilers exploded at Ship Island, six miles below Memphis, Tennessee, killing 250 people. It was rumored that Captain Klinefelter was cavorting with some ladies and was not in the wheelhouse at the time of the calamity. Henry was blown overboard, his lungs and skin were badly scalded, and his wounds were not dressed until he arrived at Memphis fifteen hours after the incident. He died June 21, 1858, with his brother Samuel at his side.[2] Young Clemens returned to the river as a steerman for George Ealer, and on September 9, 1858, obtained a full license as Mississippi River pilot. Bixby had taken leave of the river, but came back at this time, and they were again together on the *Crescent City* and later on a new steamboat called the *New Falls City*. When Bixby returned, his old chief took him on as full partner, a reflection of Bixby's respect for Clemens.

---

[2]Among the best accounts of Samuel Clemens's life is Mark Twain, *Life on the Mississippi* (New York: Harper & Brothers, 1901). A good description of Samuel Clemens's hatred for William Brown is found in Albert Paine Bigelow, "The River Curriculum," *Mark Twain, A Biography, 1835–1910, Complete; The Personal and Literary Life of Samuel Leghorne Clemens,* Vol. 1 (New York: Harper & Brothers, 1912), 127–32. A complete description of his brother's death is found in chapter 26, "The Tragedy of the *Pennsylvania*," 139–45.

Captain Horace Ezra Bixby was born May 8, 1826, in Geneseo, New York, to Sylvanus Bixby and Hanna (Barnes) Bixby. Horace ran away from home at the age eighteen and became a mud clerk on the Ohio River steamboat *Olivia*, and two years later he worked his way up to become the boat's pilot. He left the Ohio River in 1858 to become the captain of the *Paul Jones*, where he began training Samuel Clemens as assistant steerman. On March 9, 1853, in New Orleans, he married Susanna Weibling, by whom he had several children who died in infancy.[3] His one surviving daughter, Edwina, married Dr. Louis Tousard Pim on July 9, 1901. Pim was a member of a well-known steamboating family, and he had two children from a previous marriage, Pelagie Berthold Ladd and Horace Bixby Ladd.[4] Thereafter, Bixby spent his life piloting just about every kind of steamboat, as well as ironclad gunboats for the Union Naval Forces during the Civil War. Bixby is said to have been the pilot of the gunboat *Benton* under Commander Andrew Hull Foote in the Union Navy's Western Gunboat Flotilla, but in James B. Eads's "Recollections of Foote and the Gun-Boats," there is no mention of Bixby among the officers.[5]

Bixby was probably no different in many respects from a lot of riverboat captains of the middle and late 1800s. He was one of those fierce competitors bound to have successes and a good dose of failures. After the Civil War, Bixby returned to private work and took employment with Captain David H. Silver. Eventually, Bixby invested heavily in the St. Louis & Vicksburg Packet Co. By 1883, when the company merged with the Memphis & St. Louis Packet Co. to become the Anchor Line, Bixby owned more stock than any other company employee.[6] While he was employed with the Anchor Line, Samuel Clemens made a trip up the river with him between New Orleans and St. Louis on the company boat

[3]Allen Johnson, ed., *Dictionary of American Biography*, Vol. 2 (New York: Charles Scribner's Sons, 1929), 305.

[4]Albert Nelson Marquis, *The Book of St. Louisans: A Biographical Dictionary of Living Men of the City of St. Louis and Vicinity*, ed. Albert Nelson Marquis (Chicago: A. N. Marquis & Company, 1912), 475. William Pim was second clerk on the *Bertrand*, and it seems likely that he was connected with the Pim family through Horace Bixby and his daughter.

[5]James B. Eads, "Recollections of Foote and the Gun-Boats," *Century Magazine* 29 (January 1885), 419–23, quoted in John Mills Hanson, *Conquest of the Missouri* (Chicago: A. C. McClurg, 1909), Bixby is said to have been a pilot under flag officers Admiral Andrew Hull Foote and Commander Charles Henry Davis (71). It may not have been a coincidence that Albert Rowe, who helped install the engines on the *Benton*, was also the first engineer on the *Bertrand* because of his acquaintance with Horace Bixby.

[6]"Mark Twain's Tutor," 80.

Baton Rouge, making the trip in a lightning fast time of four days, fourteen hours, and twenty minutes, giving rise to the name "Lightning Bixby."

Horace Bixby's light showed bright until the night of December 12, 1890, when his boat *Baton Rouge* sank in an accident at Hermitage Landing near Nashville, Tennessee. Bixby was found at fault because he was not in the wheelhouse at the time of the accident. He was relieved of command and assigned to pilot the *City of Hickman*. Unfortunately, still more trouble was to follow. On the night of September 22, 1892, after the *City of Hickman* made port at Vicksburg, Bixby injured a passenger in a fight. To avoid a damage suit, Bixby was assigned to other boats in the Anchor Line. He remained with the Anchor Line until it folded in 1887 and thereafter worked for the government at St. Louis on snag boats.[7]

Bixby's first wife Susanna (Weibling) was the daughter of William G. and Susanna Weibling of Cincinnati. Born in 1834, she was thirty-one years old when she and an as-yet unidentified servant accompanied her husband on the ill-fated voyage of the *Bertrand*. Susanna died at the family home in St. Louis in 1867 and was interred at Bellefontaine Cemetery.

Two years after Susanna Bixby died, Horace married Mary Sheble at St. Louis. Mary was the daughter of river Captain Edwin G. Sheble. Bixby partnered with Sheble, Edwin A. Sheble, Jr., and W. Mason in 1872 to buy the sternwheeler *City of Alton* from the Memphis & St. Louis Packet Co. for $36,000. Bixby became its captain the next year, and was its managing owner and master in 1878. Bixby's career was extensive, and as late as April 29, 1907, he was re-licensed as master and pilot for a period of five years. When he died at 86 on August 1, 1912, at Maplewood, Missouri, he had spent sixty-eight years on the Mississippi River and its tributaries and was still in federal service, operating the snag boat *Horatio Wright*. He was buried at Bellefontaine Cemetery in St. Louis on August 3, 1912. His wife Mary died in 1921 and was buried at Bellefontaine Cemetery.[8]

Captain James A. Yore

Although not as well-known as Horace Bixby, Captain Yore also was an experienced riverman and pilot, one of several brothers who plied the waters of the Mississippi and Missouri Rivers and who operated

---

[7]Ibid.

[8]There are a number of articles in St. Louis newspapers about Horace Bixby: *St. Louis Post-Dispatch*, February 4, 1892; *St. Louis Republican*, February 5, 1892; *St. Louis Globe Democrat*, February 5, 1892; and *Tri-Weekly Missouri Democrat*, February 22, 1865.

out of St. Louis. Yore was part owner of the *Bertrand* and accompanied the boat from St. Louis to Omaha, where he left it, intending to return to St. Louis on business almost immediately. After the *Bertrand* sank, Yore stayed to assist with salvage operations and lodged at the Herndon House in Omaha on April 1 and 7.[9] Yore's involvement with the *Bertrand* was described in a 1927 journal article.[10]

James Yore was born in 1829 in Dublin, Ireland, and came to the United States with his parents and his brothers Patrick and John when the boys were quite young. In his late teens, he had been up the Missouri River several times, working on boats involved in the fur trade. Yore partnered with J. P. and William Fitzgerald to buy the steamer *War Eagle* and owned several other steamboats in his lifetime, including the *Luminaire, Pauline, Carol,* and the *Henry S. Turner,* in succession.[11] In the mid-1860s, he also became associated with John J. Roe, a wealthy St. Louis entrepreneur, and with Roe's son-in-law James Capelin in several financial ventures. Roe, Capelin, Yore, and several others established the Montana and Idaho Transportation Co. about 1864 to outfit shallow draft mountain steamboats to transport goods up the Missouri River to the Montana mining camps.

Among their associates was Captain Nick Wall, a colorful entrepreneur who built and commanded a number of steamboats on the Mississippi, Missouri, and Illinois Rivers after about 1836, his last boat being the *Prairie Bird* a little before 1850. Wall was born near Alexandria, Virginia, in 1820, and came to Galena, Illinois, about 1836. In 1850, he became a steamboat agent in partnership with Captain Joseph Widen in the St. Louis firm of Wall & Widen. He went to Montana in 1862, where he became a grocery merchant, and a contracting and merchandising representative for John J. Roe & Co. of St. Louis. Wall had a good stock of general merchandise, and as prices boomed, he became quite wealthy and influential.[12]

It was at about this time that the Diamond R Transportation Co. came into existence in Virginia City, Montana. A young bookkeeper who worked for Wall named Edward G. McLeay noticed that the company had many wagons and livestock that had been taken in payment of

---

[9] *Herndon House Register,* April 1 and 7, 1865.

[10] W. J. McDonald, "The Missouri River and Its Victims," *Missouri Historical Review* 21, no. 2 (1927): 455–80.

[11] *St. Louis Daily Globe-Democrat,* February 5, 1892.

[12] "Death of Capt. Nick Wall," *Helena Daily Herald,* October 11, 1889, 3.

debts. He suggested to Wall that they put a line of freight teams on the road and turn this surplus into a working asset. Wall agreed, and sometime in November, 1863, a business was established as the Diamond R Transportation Co., the "R" in its diamond-shaped logo standing for the principle owner of the business, John J. Roe. It was a little slow getting started, but in April 1864, McLeay loaded a lot of goods and hides and drove them to Helena. The hides would be sent down the Missouri to St. Louis, but the goods were sold to Major Boyce and Colonel Vaster at a handsome profit. A year or two later, the business branched out from Fort Benton at the head of commercial steamboat navigation to Missoula, Virginia City, Helena, Bozeman, Deer Lodge, and Walla Walla, taking points in Utah into its routes. In 1868, the Diamond R was bought by Edward McLeay, George Steele, and Matthew Carroll from Nick Wall and J. Roe & Co. The headquarters were established at Helena. The company retained superintendent Col. C. A. Broadwater, who became a partner and stayed with the company until 1879. Although the logo was retained, the company officially became E. G. McLeay & Co. By this time, the company was reputed to have 850 head of livestock, 300 wagons, and other assets totaling $250,000.[13]

In 1865, the Diamond R Transportation Co. acquired the assets of La Barge, Harkness & Co. at Fort Benton after its demise at the hands of Harkness. The company bought a large number of oxen for its overland freighting business between Fort Benton and the mines. After acquiring La Barge, Harkness & Co., John J. Roe reorganized it and used the oxen to upgrade the holdings of the Diamond R to 1,200 mules, 400 oxen, and a large number of horses. Feed for the livestock was obtained locally, much to the profit and delight of local farmers.[14]

[13]Two accounts of history of the Diamond R Transportation Company are found in "How Noted Old Freight Outfit, Diamond R, Came into Being as Biggest Firm in State Related," *Helena Daily Herald*, March 1, 1937, and "Diamond R Freight Line Rated as Territory's Biggest Single Business," *Great Falls Tribune*, November 30, 1858. Included in these accounts is more biographical material about Col. C. A. Broadwater. Broadwater became a very influential leader in Helena, and in 1883, he founded the Montana National Bank and built the famous Broadwater Hotel and natatorium a few miles outside the city at a cost of $700,000. By 1879, the Utah and Northern Railroad and the Northern Pacific Railroad were displacing Diamond R Transportation Company's business monopoly. Broadwater bought surplus Diamond R equipment and began lucrative contracting with the government to supply building materials for construction of Fort Assiniboine and Fort Maginnis. Thereafter, he established profitable trading posts at the forts and immersed himself in the construction of other railroads, including the Great Northern and the Montana Central Railroad from Havre to Butte.

[14]Hiram Martin Chittenden, *Steamboat Navigation on the Missouri River—Life and Adventures of Joseph La Barge*, Vol. 2 (New York: Francis P. Harper, 1903), 329–30.

By 1869, the business was so strong that it had a virtual monopoly on overland freighting, but freight rates and competition made overland freighting from Fort Benton to Helena expensive. Tolls were high, and the road was generally in poor repair. At this time, there were two principal routes to Helena from the Missouri River. One was the Helena to Fort Benton wagon road, and the other went past Virginia City to its terminus at Corinne, Utah. Both roads were seasonally unreliable, especially the former because the shipping season on the Upper Missouri was sometimes unpredictable owing to low water. Helena merchants wanted a cheaper, more direct route to the Upper Missouri, and Matthew Carroll of the Diamond R Transportation Co. was more than happy to oblige. A landing was established in 1874, 166 miles below Fort Benton and thirty-eight miles above the mouth of the Mussel Shell River, and a route was laid out from there to Helena that followed an earlier military survey.

The route eventually became known as the Helena to Carroll Wagon Road, and the landing became the bustling town of Carroll, Montana, which thrived until the late 1870s, when steamboat transportation on the Missouri began to fade. Because Helena was a main source of supplies for the mining towns, the road benefited by providing a reliable route with low freight rates. Soon, more wagons and stock were added to carry freight from Corinne, Utah, to points in Montana. Every wagon and cover, every head of stock and piece of harness, and even some of the drivers were branded with the Diamond R logo. There were "Diamond R" hotels, saloons, and "Diamond R" dance halls in Helena and at other towns along its several routes.[15] This extended story is typical of the symbiotic business and personal relationships that developed in Upper Missouri River and Montana country during the boom times of the 1860s and 1870s. It seems that everything was related to everything else, and thus it is not surprising that Captain Yore had some financial interests in the Diamond R Transportation Co., or that at least one case of canned oysters from the *Bertrand* cargo was marked with the Diamond R logo. One has to wonder if the first piano brought upriver and taken to Helena by the Diamond R in 1866 was that of *Bertrand* passenger Fannie Campbell.

The enigmatic Captain James Yore also piloted for and owned an interest in the St. Louis & Omaha Packet Line, sometimes referred to as the "O Line." This company was headed by Captain S. Joseph Nanson

---

[15]"How Noted Old Freight Outfit, Diamond R, Came into Being as Biggest Firm in State Related."

of St. Louis, and in addition to running tri-weekly packets between St. Louis and Omaha, it operated a number of steamboats to Fort Benton, including the *William J. Lewis, Henry Turner* (*H. S. Turner*—J. A. Yore, captain), *Kate Kinney, Columbian, Glasgow, Virginia,* and *Peoria City*.[16]

In his early sixties, James Yore was still active as a pilot and master of his steamboat *Jay Gould*, which was owned by the St. Louis & Mississippi Valley Transportation Co. He died on the steamer's deck on February 3, 1892, while giving orders to the pilot and crew who were attempting to free the boat from a sandbar fifty miles below St. Louis.

Yore was married and had two children, a daughter who married Franke Liebke and a son, James A. Yore, Jr.,[17] who was was born in St. Louis on August 27, 1859. As a young man, he worked with his father in steam navigation on the Mississippi River before establishing a grocery house in St. Louis, which he ran until 1876.[18] That year, he went to Helena, Montana, and did business with Murphy, Neele, & Co. at Fort Benton. Three years later, he established a 160-acre ranch and engaged in sheep ranching.[19]

John M. Jacobs

Captain John M. Jacobs was born in 1842, but the identity of his parents and the place of his birth are not known. His wife Anna Wallace is equally obscure, but it is known that Jacobs had several children, including Annie, John M. Jacobs, Jr., Louis, Frank, James, George, Walter, and William. Jacobs's role in the *Bertrand* saga is equally muddy. At twenty-three years of age, he was a newcomer to the river. It has been speculated that he was to replace Yore on the *Bertrand* as master when Yore left the vessel to return to St. Louis the day before the sinking. Other views have it that he served along with Captain Bixby as the pilot. Whatever the case, Jacobs's name appears in the Herndon House Register in Omaha along with other officers and crew.[20] Even though he was quite young by river master standards, he had considerable experience on steamboats and on the Upper Missouri River in particular. Ironically, he was one of the investors in the Montana & Idaho Transportation Co. that owned the *Bertrand*. Jacobs died on June 16, 1902, at St. Louis.[21]

[16]"Death of Capt. J. A. Yore," *St. Louis Daily Globe-Democrat*, February 5, 1892.

[17]Chittenden, *Steamboat Navigation on the Missouri River*, 329–30.

[18]*St. Louis Daily Globe-Democrat*, February 5, 1892.

[19]*History of Montana 1739–1885* (Chicago: Warner, Beers & Company, 1885), 1030.

[20]*Herndon House Register*, April 1 and 7, 1865.

[21]*St. Louis Post-Dispatch*, June 17, 1906.

BERTRAND CREW

William F. Boyd

William Boyd was the *Bertrand*'s mate and stayed at the Herndon House hotel in Omaha following the sinking.[22] Boyd is listed in St. Louis directories between 1864 and 1867 as a "river mate," living on Gay Street on the St. Louis waterfront.

Thomas Owens

Owens is another elusive crewman. He apparently was the first clerk on the *Bertrand* and is identified as such by passenger James Lucas. Interestingly, there is a note on the Herndon House Register to the effect that billing for *Bertrand* passengers was to be made to him.[23] In St. Louis directories for the mid-1860s, Owens is listed as a riverman or clerk.

William Pim

William Pim was undoubtedly related to several families of Pims who engaged in steamboating on the Missouri River, and he may have been a relative of Dr. Louis Pim, husband of Captain Bixby's only surviving daughter. Pim was second clerk on the *Bertrand* and roomed with passenger James Lucas at the Herndon House the day after the sinking.[24]

Albert Rowe

Albert M. Rowe was one of the most highly regarded professional steamboat engineers of his time and was the first engineer of the *Bertrand*. He took lodging at the Herndon House on April 2, 1865, the day after the *Bertrand* sank.[25] Rowe was born to John and Hanna B. (Morrow) Rowe near Pittsburgh, Pennsylvania, on November 5, 1832. His father was a foundry man and builder of steam engines, so it was no surprise that Albert followed in his father's trade. The family moved to St. Louis in 1850, and Rowe apprenticed in the foundries and shops near the waterfront, where he remained six years. His father died of cholera in 1852, and young Albert became the sole supporter of the family. He met and

---

[22]*Herndon House Register*, April 1 and 7, 1865.
[23]Ibid.
[24]*Herndon House Register*, April 2, 1865.
[25]Ibid.

FIGURE 2. Albert M. Rowe.
Reproduced from *History of St. Louis County*,
Vol. 2 (1911).

married Caroline Stewart in St. Louis in 1857, and the couple had two
children, Edgar M., who became a farmer on his father's property, and
Ella, who married Dr. R. D. Moore of St. Louis County.[26]

During the Civil War, Albert Rowe became well known for installing
engines on Union Navy gunboats and for refurbishing old steamers as
gunboats. As his reputation grew, he was chosen by James Eads to assist
in installing the engine(s) on the refurbished gunboat *Benton*. He also
transformed the steamer *Alexander Scott* into a Union gunboat and then
became its engineer. Albert Rowe is listed as first assistant engineer on
the armored ram boat *Lafayette*, which was commissioned at Cairo on
February 27, 1863, and sent to blockade the Mississippi River and protect
Union troops at Vicksburg. In addition, he served as engineer on the boat
used by General Nathaniel Lyon to transport a contingent of troops up
the Missouri to Fort Randall. Caroline Rowe died in June 1910 at the
age of seventy-four. Albert Rowe retired from the river business in 1888,
but the place and date of his death are not known.[27]

---

[26]William L. Thomas, *History of St. Louis County, Missouri*, Vol. 2 (St. Louis: S. J. Clarke
Publishing Co., 1911), 330, 335.

[27]Henry Walke, *Naval Scenes and Reminiscences of the Civil War in the United States on
the Southern and Western Waters during the Years 1861, 1862, and 1863 with the History of the
Period* (New York: F. R. Reed & Co., 1877), 347.

John C. Burns

Not much is known about John Burns other than he was the ship's carpenter. Throughout the 1860s, he was listed in St. Louis directories as a "ships carpenter." After the sinking of the *Bertrand*, Burns roomed at the Herndon House in Omaha with the *Bertrand*'s engineer, Albert Rowe. He also stayed at the Herndon House other days in April, probably because he was assisting the salvagers in removing cargo from the boat.[28]

M. H. Hoffman

Listed as a "riverman" in 1865 in St. Louis directories, Hoffman was probably a crewman on the *Bertrand*. He checked into the Herndon House on April 7, 1865, along with other crewmen, including captains Jacobs and Yore and other officers.[29]

T. B. Patterson

It is speculated that Patterson was a *Bertrand* crewman. During the mid-1860s a "Thomas Patterson" was listed as a "riverman" in St. Louis directories. After the sinking of the *Bertrand*, he roomed with William F. Boyd, the *Bertrand*'s mate.[30]

BERTRAND PASSENGERS

The Atchison Family

Mary S. Atchison and her two children, Charles H. and Emma, were aboard the *Bertrand* when it sank in April. They were going to Montana to reunite the family. The head of the Atchison family was John J. Atchison, born at Galena, Illinois, on December 13, 1835.[31] The federal census of 1860 for the Second Ward at Winona, Minnesota, shows him as being thirty-six years of age and having been born in Illinois. The census also shows that he was married to twenty-one-year-old Mary S. Atchison of the District of Columbia, and that the couple had a three-month-old

---

[28]*Herndon House Register*, April 2, 1865.

[29]*Herndon House Register*, April 7, 1865.

[30]Ibid.

[31]"One of Helena's First Bankers, 94, is Guest of Honor," *Independent Record*, December 24, 1929.

son, Charles H. Atchison, born in Minnesota. The notation goes on to say that John owned $2,000 in real estate and $500 in personal property.[32]

Nothing more has been found about John Atchison until 1864, when in an unverified account, the Society of Montana Pioneers says he traveled overland to Montana, arriving in May.[33] In September 1864, Atchison was appointed notary public at Virginia City by Governor Edgerton.[34] At about this time, he apparently partnered with or became associated with Joseph Millard, president of the Omaha National Bank, and with B. F. Allen of Des Moines, to establish a gold exchange near Alder Gulch in Montana Territory. Within a year, they sold their interest in the exchange and established a bank in Helena under the name Allen and Millard Bank. A local newspaper column said, "Messrs. Allen and Millard will open a bank at Helena. John S. Atchison will run the concern."[35] There also is an interesting interview between an author named Tom Stout and "Senator Millard" that refers to Governor Edgerton granting a charter for the Virginia City & Summit City Wagon Road Co. to Joseph H. Millard and B. F. Allen on January 27, 1865. The company was to provide service to Alder Gulch from Virginia City. A W. C. Burton of Des Moines may also have been associated with the Allen & Millard Bank and the wagon road company.[36]

Sometime shortly before or after establishing the bank in 1865, John Atchison moved to Virginia City to take up his new position and await the arrival of his family on the *Bertrand*. Atchison boxes found in the cargo hold of the *Bertrand* contained personal possessions and were marked "TO J. S. ATCHISON, V. City," and "TO ATCHISON, VIRGINIA CITY, MT." Among these items are women's shoes, children's gloves, picture frames, mirrors, a wicker sewing basket, a blue dressing gown, almonds, wall lamps, curtains, small lettered toy blocks, and a

[32]United States Federal Census Bureau, *Federal Census, Schedule 1—Free Inhabitants in Second Ward, City of Winona, 30 June, 1860*, 622–23.

[33]James U. Sanders, ed., "John S. Atchison," *Society of Montana Pioneers—Constitution, Members, and Officers, with Portraits and Maps . . .* , Vol. 1, Register 131 (Helena: Society of Montana Pioneers, 1899). This entry reads: "John S. Atchison. Route traveled, across the plains; arrived in Montana in May, 1864. Occupation: banker. Last address: Helena."

[34]*Contributions to the Historical Society of Montana; with its Transactions, Officers and Members*, Vol. 3 (Boston: J. S. Canner and Company, Inc., 1966), 349; see also *Montana Post*, September 17, 1864.

[35]*Montana Post*, August 5, 1865.

[36]Tom Stout, *Montana, Its Story and Biography*, Vol. 1 (Chicago and New York: The American Historical Society 1921), 285.

cast-metal toy horse cart.[37] Although it has not been confirmed, it is possible that Mrs. Millard and Mrs. Atchison became acquainted prior to their voyage on the *Bertrand* owing to their husbands' mutual business interests.

John Atchison appears again in the federal census for Montana Territory in 1870. In the entry, the ages of John, Mary, and Charles are not consistent with the 1860 Winona census, but the census was correct in showing that John was born in Illinois and that he was a banker. Mary is listed as a housewife. Charles is shown as being ten and Emma as nine. The census states that the Atchisons had $25,000 in personal property as well as a twenty-five-year-old domestic servant from Prussia named Barbara Newman, but it is not known whether she was a passenger with Mrs. Atchison and the children on the *Bertrand*.[38] Sometime after 1870, and more likely about 1881, John Atchison may also have been the owner of a mercantile and saloon six miles south of Fort Maginnis.[39] This may have been in the town of Overland, 126 miles northeast of White Sulphur Springs. Neither Fort Maginnis nor Overland is in existence today.[40]

It is not known exactly when John Atchison moved from Montana to Mentone, California, to live with his son Charles, but it was after the death of his wife Mary and may have been as early as 1884 or 1885 because he is known to have lived at Mentone for about thirteen years before he died at age ninety-seven. He was interred at Mentone's Hillside Cemetery.[41] No additional information has come to light about Mary Atchison or her family from records in Maryland and the District of Columbia.

The Millard Family

Caroline Grover (Barrows) Millard was traveling on the *Bertrand* with her two children. Her husband Joseph was a respected banker and community builder and one of the founders of Omaha. He also established

[37]Petsche, *The Steamboat Bertrand*, 71. A more definitive inventory appears in Annalies Corbin, *Material Culture of Steamboat Passengers—Archeological Evidence from the Missouri River*, Archaelogy Series (New York: Kluwer/Plenum Press, 2000), 29–50.

[38]United States Federal Census Bureau, *Federal Census for Helena, Montana Territory*, 1 June 1, 1870, 9.

[39]*River Boss*, February 1, 1882.

[40]Michael A. Leeson, ed., *History of Montana 1739–1885* (Chicago: Warner, Beers & Co., 1885), 602.

[41]"Atchison," *Redlands Daily Facts*, May 20, 1933.

the Omaha National Bank, and for fifteen years, he was a director of the Union Pacific Railroad. Caroline died in 1901, the same year Joseph became a United States senator. The Omaha suburb of Millard is named after Joseph Millard.

Caroline Barrows Millard was an interesting and magnetic figure in her own right. At the age of twenty-two, she already had two children, Jessie, age twenty-two months and Willard, age three. Caroline "Carolyn" Barrows was born in Newark, New Jersey, in 1837 to Willard Barrows and Ann H. Williams Barrows and came to Davenport as a child, where she grew to womanhood. It was in Davenport that she met and married Joseph Millard on November 27, 1860.[42] This genteel lady went to Omaha shortly after marrying, and she quickly became involved in charity and social work in the community. Given her background, it is not too surprising that she distained the Montana frontier and the rough and dirty mining camp of Virginia City.

Caroline was considered "a woman of culture and the influence of her character was appreciated by all those with whom she came in contact." She helped establish Clarkson Hospital and was its largest contributor. In addition, she was a liberal giver to the Old Ladies Home, Flower Mission, the Associated Charities, her church, and other charities. Caroline Millard died on January 3, 1901.[43]

Considerable information about Caroline and Joseph's son Willard Barrows Millard has been found in three principal sources.[44] Born in Davenport, Iowa, on September 13, 1861, he was not quite four years old when he accompanied his mother and sister to Montana. In adolescence, he was educated at Greylock Academy in Williamstown, Massachusetts, and as a young man he worked for a time at the Omaha National Bank, founded by his father.

Willard seems to have been stricken with wanderlust after that because he went to western Nebraska and worked for several years as a cowboy on the Keith and Barton Ranch near North Platte. There he met and married Frances "Frankie" Barton (daughter of Guy Barton) on November 27, 1883, and by her he fathered four sons, Barton, Joseph H., Henry

---

[42]*Omaha Bee*, January 4, 1901; *Omaha World Herald*, January 14, 1922.

[43]*Omaha Bee*, January 4, 1901, Ibid.

[44]Portions of the Millard Family Papers in the possession of Joseph H. Millard III of Anaheim, California, were copied for use in Jerome Petsche's research on the *Bertrand*. These notes are now in possession of the author. The other two principal sources are *Davenport Gazette* (Davenport, Iowa), April 13, 1865; and *Tri-Weekly Missouri Democrat*, April 16, 1865.

FIGURE 3. Caroline (Carolyn) Millard.
The source of this photograph is unknown.
It was given to the author by Jerome Petsche's
daughter, Cathy Liberty, after his death in 2008.

Ray, and Willard Barrows, Jr. In the ensuing years, Willard Millard's restless nature resurfaced. He pursued the fruit commission business, worked for a loan and trust company, and then returned to work as a director and vice president at the Omaha National Bank in 1890. Living at Fort Calhoun, Nebraska, Willard even tried his hand at farming. Not satisfied with a banker's life, he again left Nebraska in 1898 for Montana. There he and his son Joseph operated the Kennot Mine near Virginia City for five years and finally gave up when the low-grade ore assayed at only $5 a ton. Father and son then bought up numerous claims at the head of Alder Gulch and started the Kearsarge Mine, seven miles from Virginia City. They brought in a sixty stamp mill about 1900, and the mine showed a profit for the first few years, but finally petered out. Then the mine was struck by a disastrous fire, and the resulting lawsuits brought by the families of nine dead miners put an end to the Millard mining ventures.

When his wife Frances died, Millard left the mining business and moved to Chicago to run the Great Northern Hippodrome with his partner, Omaha businessman William R. Bennett. In Chicago, he married Bennett's daughter Louise in November 1916, and a few years later, the couple moved to California. Willard Barrows Millard died at Berkley, California, on September 26, 1931.

The youngest passenger on the *Bertrand* was Jessie H. Millard, born on June 28, 1863, to Joseph and Caroline at Davenport, Iowa. Jessie died at Omaha on May 15, 1950, and much of what is known about her comes from the Millard Family Papers and two obituaries in the *Omaha World Herald* and *Tri-Weekly Missouri Democrat*.[45] Although Jessie never married, she was a potent and driving force both in her father's affairs and in church and welfare work. As a young adult, she served as her father's secretary. When her mother died in 1901, Jessie began traveling with her father, who had just been elected to the United States Senate.

Throughout Joseph's time in Washington, D.C., Jessie kept house and entertained his guests. She was a consummate helpmate to her father and became a close friend of many of his political allies, including Senator Francis E. Warren of Wyoming, General John J. Pershing, and President Taft and their wives. During World War I, Jessie organized canteens and auxiliaries, and when she died on May 15, 1950, she left much of her estate to hospitals and religious institutions.

The head of the Millard household was Joseph Hopkins Millard. He was born on April 20, 1836, to J. K. Millard of Massachusetts and Elizabeth Hopkins Millard of New Jersey on his parent's farm in Hamilton, Ontario, Canada. When the family returned to the United States, they relocated in Sabula, Jackson County, Iowa, when Joseph was fourteen. Joseph remained until the age of eighteen and then began clerking in a store in Dubuque. Two years later, in October 1856, Joseph went to Omaha, where he began working as a real estate dealer, locating settlers on tracts of wild land nearby in Nebraska Territory. He soon joined his brother Ezra and became part of the land agency of Barrows, Millard, & Co. The business operated successfully, and in 1860, Smith S. Caldwell was taken in as a partner. Two years after that, Millard withdrew to start his own business. In 1860, Millard married Caroline Barrows, becoming Willard Barrows's son-in-law. When new banking laws went into effect in 1866, Ezra Millard organized the Omaha National Bank, and the following January, Joseph Millard became cashier. Joseph later became the bank president and chairman of the board.[46]

In 1863, a successful young Iowa financier named B. F. Allen learned of the gold discoveries in Montana and envisioned a business opportunity. He quickly partnered with Joseph Millard to open a gold exchange in a stone building at Alder Gulch near Virginia City under the name Allen & Millard Bank.

[45]Millard Family Papers; *Omaha World Herald*, January 14, 1922, and May 16, 1950; *Tri-Weekly Missouri Democrat*, April 16, 1865.

[46]"Former U.S. Senator Joseph H. Millard," *The Bankers Magazine*, 106: 429.

FIGURE 4. Jessie Millard.
The source of this photograph is unknown. It was given to the author by Jerome Petsche's daughter, Cathy Liberty, after his death in 2008.

Allen and Millard were not without competition. In the summer of 1864, Ben Holliday of New York and W. L. Halsey of Salt Lake City began their exchange in Virginia City, paying the highest rates for gold dust and specie and offering cash for government vouchers. They also sold drafts from principal cities in the east as well as postage and revenue stamps.[47] The fate of this bank has not been researched, but their offices in connection with the Overland Stage Line quit advertising in the spring of 1865.

Joseph must have been a busy fellow in Virginia City in 1864–1865, and probably looked forward with great anticipation to the arrival of his wife and children. Unfortunately, Mrs. Millard had no taste for the Montana frontier, and after two weeks, she returned to the east. Most assuredly when it came to a choice between business and family, Joseph decided the latter was more important. Allen and Millard sold the business in 1866 to Hussey, Dahler, & Co., and Millard returned to Omaha with 100 pounds of gold in his wife's clothing trunk. Thereafter, the bank changed hands several times before it closed in 1922.[48]

After becoming the cashier of the Omaha National Bank in 1866 or 1867, Millard became one of the incorporators of the Omaha & Northwestern Railroad. He served as mayor of Omaha in 1870–1871. He organized the South Omaha National Bank and served as its president. In

[47]Ibid.
[48]Ibid.

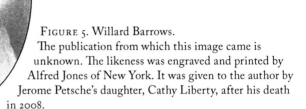

FIGURE 5. Willard Barrows.
The publication from which this image came is
unknown. The likeness was engraved and printed by
Alfred Jones of New York. It was given to the author by
Jerome Petsche's daughter, Cathy Liberty, after his death
in 2008.

addition, he was a director of the Union Pacific Railroad Co. for fifteen
years, six of those as a government director overseeing railroad business.[49]

While there was much support for Joseph Millard to run for political
office, he did not do so until 1871, when he was elected mayor of Omaha.
About 1876, he became a member of a syndicate of five capitalists who
built the Millard House Hotel in Omaha.[50] Following that, he fought
a protracted battle for the United States Senate seat for Nebraska in
1901. Millard was elected on March 28 to the Senate as a compromise
candidate and served until 1907. Thereafter, Millard resumed banking
in Omaha and died there on January 13, 1922. He was buried at Prospect
Hill Cemetery.

Willard Barrows
Although Willard Barrows came from humble beginnings, by intelli-
gence, strength of character, and hard work, he became one of the most
important and influential men in Iowa. A Davenport, Iowa, newspaper
hailed him in his obituary, saying: "Friend Barrows was a man universally beloved. Genial in character and kind hearted in the fullest extent,

---

[49]A small biography of Joseph Millard containing this information is found in "Millard,
Joseph Hopkins (1836–1922)," *Biographical Directory of the United States Congress 1774–Pres-
ent*, House Document No. 108-222 (Washington, D.C.: Congress, Joint Committee on
Printing, 2005).

[50]*Omaha World Herald*, January 14, 1922, 2.

he made friends wherever he went."[51] Barrows was born on September 25, 1806, near Monson, Massachusetts. As a youth, he attended Worcester Academy for three years and sawed wood at night to pay for his books. In 1828, he moved to Elizabethtown, New Jersey, where he studied Latin, geometry, and trigonometry under a tutor and also was employed as a teacher. He met Ann H. Williams in Elizabethtown and married her there in 1832. From this union, three children were born, Sarah, Caroline, and Benjamin H. Barrows.[52]

In 1853, Barrows moved to New Orleans, where he was awarded a government contract to survey lands in Mississippi that were part of the Choctaw Indian lands purchase and later the swamps of the Yazoo River. After a short stay in St. Louis, in April 1837, he relocated to Davenport, Iowa, where he did surveys of the Blackhawk Purchase on the Cedar and Wapsipinicon Rivers. In 1838, he took his family to the new town of Rockingham, Iowa, and in 1840, he surveyed the islands in the Mississippi River between the Rock River and Quincy. In 1853, he made a careful study of northern Iowa and drew a comprehensive map of the state that was published by Doolittle and Munscom of Cincinnati in 1854 as the "New Map of Iowa, with Notes." He also assisted in surveying the boundary between Iowa and Minnesota.[53] In 1850, Barrows traveled overland to California, where he worked as a land claims surveyor. Then he toured Central America and Cuba before returning to Davenport in 1851.[54]

In 1856, Willard Barrows partnered with Ezra and Joseph Millard to establish land agencies (real estate offices) along the Missouri River under the name Barrows, Millard, & Co. Ezra ran the office in Sioux City, and Joseph went to Omaha City to manage agency affairs there, but Willard is not mentioned until after the bank panic of 1857, when the firm consolidated its business at Omaha to compete with other companies offering to enter claims, make out papers for pre-emptors, and protect established claims from claim jumpers and trespassers. To strengthen their position, Millard became a notary public and gained a reputation for "entering land, faithfully and promptly." In 1857, they were advertising their services in Omaha City, Nebraska City, and De Soto. Omaha was

---

[51]*Daily Davenport Democrat*, January 6, 1868.

[52]The Millard Family Papers also contain biographical information about other members of the extended Millard family, one of whom was Joseph Millard's father-in-law, Willard Barrows. The notes are not numbered and include only the names of persons and subjects as headers in capital letters, in this case, "WILLARD BARROWS."

[53]Ibid.

[54]*Daily Davenport Democrat*, January 6, 1868.

incorporated in 1857. Business flourished through the summer of 1857, and trading in land rights was at an all-time high. More than a million dollars' worth of real estate changed hands during the first nine months of the year. At this time, some interest rates on loans went as high as two percent.[55] Word of the land rush quickly spread to the eastern states of Ohio, Pennsylvania, Michigan, and New York, and the *New York Daily Times* in May 1857 said: "Building of every description goes on as rapidly as the supply of material will permit, and it is safe to say that Omaha will double her importance this summer. Lots are held at $75 per foot and claims within five miles of the city, in cases where Government title is obtained, cannot be bought for less than $10 to $15 per acre."[56]

There were many pre-emptors, people who staked illegal claims and occupied tracts on public lands illegally. When the government open public lands for sale, pre-emptors began buying the rights, and many of them authorized Barrows, Millard, & Co. to sell their lands to the highest bidders as soon as title came from the government. These negotiations required so much money that Nebraska's chartered banks printed their own currency and Omaha issued $50,000 in city script backed by the inflated values of city-owned real estate.[57]

Then the bubble burst. There was a bank panic and business downturn in America in the fall of 1857, and it hit the land market in Omaha hard. Lots selling for $1,000 dropped to $100, and by 1860, only $200,000 worth of real estate changed hands. Chartered banks closed their doors, and what was left of the financial business in Omaha went to a few banking companies such as Barrows, Millard, & Co. After that, lots of land warrants were still available that had been issued to veterans of America's wars dating back to 1812. These were rights to public lands that could not be redeemed in Nebraska until the lands were open to public sale. In this currency-starved environment, the lands warrants started trading and circulating as tender, whereupon they were discounted and formed the bulk of the initial large deposits made to the banking house of Barrows, Millard, & Co.[58]

[55]Among the files of the late Jerome Petsche is a copy of part of a chapter from an unidentified textbook bearing this information. It includes a reproduction of an Omaha newspaper ad for the "Nebraska Land Agency." The chapter is titled "Here Was New Land." Unfortunately there is no other attribution, but the information is captivating. This file is in possession of the author.

[56]"Here Was The New Land."

[57]"Omaha's Prospects, 1857," *New York Daily Times*, May 29, 1857.

[58]Willard Barrows, Esq., "Three Thousand Miles Up the Missouri," *Boston Review* 6, no. 36: 442–47. See also Williard Barrows, Esq., "To Idaho and Montana; Wanderings There, Returning," *Boston Review* 5, no. 26: 118–33, 269–85.

In 1860, the company converted to a banking house with Smith S. Caldwell as partner. At this point, Barrows wanted to withdraw and pursue other interests, but because of his well-known name and reputation, the other partners persuaded him to stay on. In June 1860, Joseph Millard traveled to Davenport and married Caroline Grover Barrows, the younger daughter of Willard Barrows.

Gold was discovered at Alder Gulch in Montana in 1863, and the town of Virginia City grew up quickly the following year. Sometime in 1864, Willard Barrows partnered with Joseph Millard and Iowa entrepreneur B. F. Allen to establish a land brokerage, bank, and road development company in Virginia City. Barrows seems also be have been involved in the mercantile business because he assembled a group of four men, four horses, ten mules, light and heavy wagons, and a stock of goods and started overland for Montana, reaching Virginia City 106 days later. Having satisfied his appetite for adventure, Barrows returned to Iowa. However, owing to his partnership with Joseph Millard, he made another business trip to Virginia City in 1865, accompanying his daughter Caroline Millard and her two children on the *Bertrand*. There are two versions of what transpired with Barrows and the Millards after the *Bertrand* sank. One unsubstantiated version has it that Mrs. Millard and children continued to Montana on the *General Grant* a few days after the *Bertrand* sank, and Willard Barrows returned home to Davenport, where he made plans to reach Montana on the steamboat *Roanoke*. The second version, which comes from the Barrows's account of the *Bertrand* accident, says:

> We [we assume this meant Mr. Barrows] returned to Omaha with the ladies and children in our charge, where they remained with friends until we returned to St. Louis, purchased another stock of goods, and shipped them on the steamer *Roanoke*, with nearly the same officers and crew that were on the *Bertrand*. She left St. Louis on the 2nd of May, and on the 13th we all took passage again at Omaha for Fort Benton.
>
> On this boat we have some thirty passengers, with a freight of about two hundred and fifty tons.
>
> We passed the wreck of the *Bertrand* this afternoon, May 14th, and also the wreck of the steamer *Cora*, snagged five days since, and a total loss; though no lives were sacrificed.
>
> We passed the wreck of another steamer today, the 15th, the *E. O. Stanard*, snagged yesterday, and took off some of the passengers, of which she had about forty.[59]

---

[59] "Death of Willard Barrows," *Daily Davenport Democrat*, January 6, 1868.

While the second version seems more likely, it remains unclear whether Mrs. Millard remained in Omaha while Willard returned to St. Louis and made arrangements to ship a stock of goods on the *Roanoke*. If this was the case, then it seems that Barrows and his daughter rebooked on the *Roanoke* at Omaha and continued up the Missouri on that boat, not on the *General Grant*, as the first version implies.

Barrows sold his interests and left Montana in 1867 and returned to his home in Davenport, Iowa, where he died of heart trouble on January 5, 1868.[60] Willard Barrows's wife, Ann Williams Barrows, died at Omaha in March 1887.[61]

Willard Barrow's son Benjamin led a very productive and fascinating life and was a much respected figure in Omaha society. He was born on December 30, 1847, on the family farm near Davenport, Iowa, and received his education at the Episcopal Griswald Academy. When Benjamin reached the age of seventeen, he accompanied his father and Joseph Millard to Montana, where he clerked in the Barrows & Millard Bank for two years before returning to Davenport to become a journalist for the *Davenport Democrat & Leader*. In 1872, he came to Omaha and became a partner in a newspaper before being nominated and elected to the Nebraska legislature. After his term, he returned to writing and editing for the *Omaha Daily Republican*, where his articles on state issues won him the admiration of U.S. senator Algernon S. Paddock and a commission as United States consul to Dublin on February 24, 1876. He served in Ireland for ten years, and there he met and married Lizzie Phelan, a daughter of a prominent barrister, in 1878. The Barrows had five children, three of whom died in infancy. In 1885, Benjamin and Lizzie came to Omaha with their daughter Hilda and son Willard. Lizzie died that year, and Benjamin went to work as chief of the advertising department in the Library Bureau of the Union Pacific Railroad, where he remained until he resigned on October 1, 1897, to do literary work for the National Republican Committee. In August 1901, he was appointed chief deputy in the office of the United States Surveyor of Customs, and in 1903 he was appointed to the office of surveyor. From 1901 to 1910, he

---

[60]Owing to his seventeen-page article ("History of Scott County, Iowa," *Annals of Iowa*, Vol. 1 (Des Moines: Iowa State Historical Society, 1863)), Willard Barrows was considered the historian of Scott County. However, the *Davenport Democrat & Leader*, June 26, 1921, carried an article titled "True History of Scott County—People Cities, Towns, and Institutions—A Monument to Our Predecessors, and an Example for Their Successors" by Aug. Peter Richter. Chapter 37, "Willard Barrows—Worthy Pioneer Citizen" is an excellent account of Barrows's life.

[61]Ibid.

was a surveyor of customs. Sometime in the late 1890s Barrows married Gertrude Carpenter Fitzpatrick by whom he had one son, Ronald C. Barrows. Benjamin Barrows died at Omaha on December 30, 1910, and was buried at Prospect Hill Cemetery.[62]

The Campbell Sisters—Anna and Fannie Campbell

Quite a bit has been documented concerning the lives of these two frontier sisters and Anna's siblings Gurdon and Helen. However, the story of the Campbell sisters and their husbands, Frank Dunbar and Elizur Thornburg, is strongly entwined with the lives of their parents and with the Gallaher family into which Helen married.

The father of the Campbell girls was Major James Blackstone Campbell, a merchant in furs, a pioneer builder of canals, a land speculator, and one of the early land owners in Chicago. Campbell was born in Maury County, Tennessee, on October 15, 1799. Very little is known about his parentage or the early years of his life. At age twenty-six, he lived in Vandalia, Illinois, and in 1831, he married Sarah Kain from Carlyle.[63] He and Sarah had four children: Gurdon, who became a successful trader and mercantile businessman in Gallatin, Montana; Helen, who married Montana state senator Judge James Gallaher; Anna (Anne, Annie) who married Montana rancher Frank Dunbar; and Fannie, a school teacher who married a former teacher and rancher, Elizur Thornburg of Logan.

The Illinois Census Index for 1830 listed James Campbell as a land owner in Tazwell County.[64] In the Tazwell County, Illinois Land Records Index for 1835, Campbell is recorded as having bought at least two parcels of land on May 27, 1835.[65] Campbell is again mentioned in Andreas's *History of Chicago* in 1839 as "Major James B. Campbell, real estate agent."[66]

Over a period of time, Campbell made loans on land to clients who defaulted, and he lost a good deal of money. In 1852, he moved his family

[62]"Death Comes to Ben H. Barrows, Omaha Pioneer," *Omaha World-Herald*, evening edition, December 30, 1910, 1.

[63]"Major James B. Campbell," *Headwaters Heritage History*, Diamond Jubilee ed. (Three Forks: Three Forks Area History Society, 1983), 54–55.

[64]*Illinois 1830 Census Index*, Ron Vern Jackson, Gary Ronald Teeples, David Schaefer-meyer, eds. (Bountiful: Accelerated Indexing Systems, Inc., Illinois, 1830).

[65]*Tazwell County Illinois Land Records Index*, Vol. 1, David C. Perkins, Comp. (Perkins: Tazwell County Genealogical Society, 1980), 1827–March 1838.

[66]A. T. Andreas, *History of Chicago from the Earliest Period to the Present Time, in Three Volumes*, Vol. 2, From 1857 until the Fire of 1871 (Chicago: The A. T. Andreas Company, Publishers, 1885), 568.

to St. Charles, Missouri, where he started another real estate business, and he and Sarah placed Anna and Fannie in the Seminary of the Sacred Heart convent school.[67] Although it remains unclear why, in 1862 James and Sarah Campbell and son Gurdon left for Montana Territory by bull train over the Bozeman Trail. Their companions on the trek were James Gallaher and his wife Helen Campbell Gallaher and their six-month-old daughter, family friend Samuel Weir, and a few others.[68] Driving a few of Campbell's prize short-horn cattle ahead of them, the party arrived at Bannack on July 20, 1863, and then proceeded on to the first/old Gallatin City on the north side of the Missouri River. The Campbells remained there until 1865, when they crossed the Gallatin River and built a home on the west bank of Rea Creek.[69]

When James and Sarah came west, they left daughters Anna and Fannie to attend convent school at St. Charles with the understanding the girls would join the family after completing their educations. Between June 1, 1862, and March 1865, Anna and Fannie boarded at the school. A surviving account record from the Seminary of the Sacred Heart dated September 1, 1864, shows that board and tuition from June 1, 1864, to vacation in 1865 was $200 for both girls. Extra fees were charged for "washing" (laundry), books and stationery, $30 for piano and guitar lessons, $95 for drawing and "Grecian Painting" lessons, and $19 for uniforms. The girls both took drawing lessons and one semester of "Grecian Painting." Anna took piano lessons, and Fannie took guitar, so both apparently were musically inclined.[70]

Major Campbell seems to have gotten off to a fast start after arriving at Gallatin City because in 1865 he was listed as a tax collector, and two years later he was licensed to operate a store that was stocked through a jobber and dealer in groceries and liquors in Helena and Fort Ellis named Robert H. Lemon. At some point after the business began, Campbell's son Gurdon operated the store. Campbell was a city booster and supporter who quickly became interested in promoting a Gallatin City Fair, which was first held there in 1866 on Major Campbell's property. James

[67]*Headwaters Heritage History*, 55.
[68]Ibid.
[69]Ibid.
[70]The copy of the account ledger sheet containing this information was transmitted to Jerome Petsche along with a few other useful notes in a letter from Sister Marie Louise Martinez, RSCJ National Archivist, National Archives, Society of the Sacred Heart— U.S.A., dated February 18, 1983. The ledger page and letter are in possession of the author. The archive is located at Villa Duchesne, 801 South Spode Road, St. Louis, Missouri.

FIGURE 6.
Mrs. Sarah Campbell with
daughters Fannie (*left*) and
Anna (*right*). The source of
this photograph is unknown.
It was given to the author by
Jerome Petsche's daughter,
Cathy Liberty, after his death
in 2008.

commissioned a race track and buildings for fair exhibits, and fairs were
held there annually for many years, contributing in large part to the social
and recreational affairs of area citizens. In November 1872, he bought four
shares of the Eastern Montana Agricultural, Mineral, and Mechanical
Association and boosted his support for fairs and exhibits in Montana.
In addition, in 1871 Sarah Campbell was running a boarding house in
the city.[71]

Major Campbell was a highly respected figure in Gallatin City, and
his wife Sarah was no less so. Daniel S. Tuttle, Episcopal bishop of
Montana, Idaho, and Utah, often stayed at the Campbell residence on his
trips through the territory. In Bishop Tuttle's reminiscences of December
1867, written in St. Louis on November 18, 1901, he said of Sarah Campbell: "Strength of character and sweetness of nature were wonderfully
blended in her. A Lady in every sense of the word, a Christian of holy
and humble devotion, a glad and generous minister of hospitality, with a
queenly dignity to her friends and all benighted wayfarers, she was withal
a motherly helper of unfailing kindness and wonderful efficiency to all
around her, far and near. Gentle of touch, sympathizing in soul, skilled
in nursing, almost expert in medicine and surgery, she was an angel of

[71]*Headwaters Heritage History*, 55.

mercy and succor to all. Her active, untiring and loving unselfishness and helpfulness caused her to be warmly and gratefully loved by all who knew or heard of her."[72]

After James Campbell passed away on January 3, 1873, Sarah journeyed to Chicago to recover her dower rights in land owned by the Campbell estate. Just how much was at stake is not known, but it was considerable, judging by an article that appeared in the *Chicago Tribune*: "Major Campbell's acquisitions of real estate were enormous. At one time he offered for sale in England a parcel of land which, it is calculated, would now be worth $20,000,000. Mrs. Campbell claims her dower rights in ten acres and 400 lots in Chicago. The land on which the Inter-Ocean building is situated is in the claim as well as the land on which the Northwestern Railroad Depot stands at Wells and Kinzie Streets."[73] Unfortunately, Sarah was never able to conclude her dower rights suit. In an unfinished letter dated March 5, 1875, to her daughter Fannie, she wrote: "It makes me so unhappy to know while you are young and ought to have advantages and enjoy life you are tied down to toiling. I do hope that this summer we will finish it so that we will have money coming by this fall."[74] Sarah Campbell passed away at the home of her sister in Galena, Illinois on March 13, 1875. At the time of her death, Fannie, Gurdon, and Anna (Mrs. Frank Dunbar) were living in Gallatin City. Helen Campbell Gallaher lived in Washington with her husband Judge James Gallaher.[75]

Anna Campbell was born on March 18, 1844, at Galena, Illinois, and she and her siblings were raised in the then-small village of Chicago before moving to St. Louis. After Anna arrived at Gallatin City, her life on the Montana frontier appears to have been fairly conventional. She was regarded by the family as a quiet intellectual, almost a recluse, at least for the first eighteen months, until she met a local Tobacco Root Mountain cattleman named Frank Dunbar and married him on February 27, 1867.

Frank Dunbar was born in Brecksville, Cuyahoga County, Ohio, on April 24, 1837, to John and Lucy Bliss Dunbar, who both were natives of Boston, Massachusetts. Dunbar's father was a pioneer stock raiser and farmer in the Cuyahoga Valley beginning in the 1830s. In 1856, John moved his family to Wisconsin for a few years and then returned to Ohio, where he and his wife both died. Frank was educated in public schools and

---

[72]"Major James B. Campbell," *Progressive Men of the State of Montana, Illustrated* (Chicago: A. W. Bowen & Co., 1902), 1097.

[73]*Headwaters Heritage History*, 55.

[74]Ibid.

[75]Ibid.

FIGURE 7. Anna (Annie) Campbell. Gift of Mrs. Mildred Prince, Dallas, Texas (1967), to Jerome Petsche. Permission to reproduce the photograph was granted to Jerome Petsche by the Missouri Historical Society. The photograph was given to the author by Jerome Petsche's daughter, Cathy Liberty, after his death in 2008.

made his home in the Cuyahoga Valley until 1855, when he went to Beloit, Wisconsin, and learned the plasterer's trade. After that, he moved to Montana County, Iowa, where he stayed until 1860, when he and his brother Thomas M. Dunbar traveled to Pike's Peak in search of gold. He was moderately successful mining gold until 1862, when he and Thomas outfitted for a trip to Montana. Arriving at Bannack City in August 1862, they stayed until November and then moved on to the confluence of the Madison and Gallatin Rivers, where they built the first log cabin at what would become Gallatin City, later Three Forks. Shortly thereafter, Frank Dunbar moved across the Gallatin River and began cattle ranching with his brother, but by the 1870s, Thomas Dunbar had moved California, dissolving the partnership. Thomas died at Los Angeles on May 12, 1913. Frank stayed on and eventually expanded the ranch to about 1,000 acres to accommodate as many as 500 prime short-horn cattle and a herd of sheep. Sometime in the 1880s, Frank and Anna purchased the Aiken Hotel in Gallatin City, but no further details about the business have been found.[76]

Frank Dunbar was a very much revered member of the community and served as county commissioner. Frank and Anna lived out their lives on the

[76]Ibid., 57–58.

Dunbar ranch and raised five children; Florence, Mary, Herbert, Frank, and Homer, who as adults also engaged in ranching and raising livestock. Frank was staunch supporter of the Republican Party, and Anna and Frank were active in the Episcopal church and community affairs. Frank Dunbar passed away on December 29, 1911. It is currently not known where Frank Dunbar died, but it is presumed to have been at Gallatin City.[77]

Fannie Campbell was the younger of the two sisters and the youngest of the Campbell children. She was born at Galena, Illinois, on November 4, 1846, making her eighteen years old when the *Bertrand* sank. "Charisma, charm, beauty. It was said that when Fannie walked into a room it was as though a light had been turned on. People responded to this most popular and marvelous personality, everyone would come to life."[78]

A year after Fannie arrived at Gallatin City, her father had her piano, which was manufactured by A. Steck & Son of New York, brought up the Missouri River to Fort Benton by steamboat and the hauled overland by wagon to their home.[79] This may have been the first piano in Montana Territory, and if so, it was hauled overland by the Diamond R Transportation Co.

The first school in Gallatin City opened in 1867, and sometime in 1869, Fannie was certified by C. F. Lovett, superintendent of instruction for Gallatin County, to teach "a common" school. Although her certification expired on May 30, 1870, it must have been renewed because by January 1872, a free school opened under the supervision of Miss Fannie Campbell. About $200 had been subscribed, which provided a salary of $50 a month. The Gallatin *Avant Courier* for March 11, 1872, said, "The select school, taught by Miss Fannie Campbell, is progressing finely, and is a credit to our town. We are proud of it, and well we may be, for it cannot be excelled."[80] The same newspaper carried an article titled "Gallatin City School," praising Miss Campbell and the school program commemorating the end of the school term. "The school at this place which has come under the management of Miss Fannie Campbell was closed yesterday in the presence of parents and friends of the children. The exercises on the occasion were very interesting." The article described the ceremonies and ended with: "Last, but by no means least, was the appearance of Judge Gallaher's little two year old son who, in the most approved style, recited 'The Instant Orator' and was awarded

[77]Ibid., 58.
[78]Ibid., 55.
[79]Ibid., 56.
[80]*Avant Courier*, March 11, 1872.

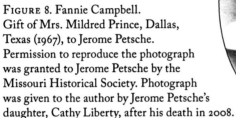

FIGURE 8. Fannie Campbell. Gift of Mrs. Mildred Prince, Dallas, Texas (1967), to Jerome Petsche. Permission to reproduce the photograph was granted to Jerome Petsche by the Missouri Historical Society. Photograph was given to the author by Jerome Petsche's daughter, Cathy Liberty, after his death in 2008.

by the enthusiastic applause of all the spectators. At the conclusion of the exercise the children and spectators partook of refreshments and then forthwith tripped the light fantastic."[81]

In 1873, Fannie filed on a homestead adjoining the Campbell homestead. When Major Campbell died on January 3, 1873, she took over the management of her father's property as well, and on May 18, 1874, she purchased the well-known Gallaher Ferry from her brother-in-law, James Gallaher.[82] That day in an article titled "Travelers Attention," the *Avant Courier* noted the new ownership: "The Gallaher Ferry near Gallatin City, has been put in excellent repair and the prices reduced. The roads leading to it are in excellent condition. It is said to be the most direct road to Helena and to possess many advantages over the other road."[83]

After Fannie's mother died near Chicago trying to settle her husband's estate, Fannie journeyed there in December 1876 to renew her mother's claims, but she met with many frustrations. It was two years, eight months, and fourteen days, according to her diary, before she returned to Gallatin City. While in the east, she made an exciting trip to Virginia. From her diary: "September 2, 1878—Returned from Virginia this afternoon. Spent four or five months with my dear aunt M and cousin Nannie. Remained in Washington City three days seeing sights, visited the White House, Treasury Department, Capital Art Gallery,

[81]*Avant Courier*, April 27, 1872.
[82]*Headwaters Heritage History*, 56.
[83]*Avant Courier*, May 8, 1874.

Smithsonian Institution, Agriculture Department and Patent Office all of which were exceedingly interesting to me. I should not omit my visit to Mt. Vernon. I came by the Ohio and Baltimore R. R. to Cincinnati and thence to Chicago by the Chicago Line."[84]

Fannie left Galena, Illinois, on August 28 for Dubuque, Iowa. To her dismay, no boat had arrived, and she had to spend two days there. In her diary, she wrote:

> August 30—left Dubuque this morning on steamer C. K. Peck, G. W. Davis, Captain. Sept. 1—Arrived St. Paul this evening after a very delightful trip of three days. The Captain's kindness I will never forget. (He escorted me to the train and after a conversation of fifteen or twenty minutes I bade him goodbye, probably forever, and was speeding over the prairies towards Bismark. Sept. 4—Boat left Bismark for Ft. Benton. Sept. 25—Reached Cow Island on the afternoon of this date and am very much horrified at hearing we are to go from this place by land to Benton. Oct. 1—Left Benton for Helena about 2:00 in the afternoon. Oct. 5—Started at 2 o'clock in the morning for Gallatin City. Reached my destination about 2 or 3 o'clock in the afternoon. My heart is full of gratitude to my Heavenly Father for permitting me to reach the end of my journey in safety. Mr. and Mrs. Akins and Susie kindly brought me over to Anna's in the light wagon.[85]

In 1890, Fannie purchased 160 acres from Samuel Seaman. Later she sold her landholdings and bought the Joe Wilson Ranch. In 1897, there was a serious fire in the outbuildings, including the large historic stable in which the first United States court in Montana was held.[86]

Although Fannie Campbell was single for most of her life, on October 30, 1910, she married a local rancher named Elizur Thornburg at St. James Episcopal Church in Bozeman. Elizur (or Edward) Thornburg was born at Mt. Hope, Ohio, on July 28, 1843. Fannie raised a few horses and loved to play the piano for her friends. She died June 24, 1919. Elizur continued living on the ranch, but on a trip to California to visit his nieces, Thornburg was hit by a train that severed both his legs at the Northern Pacific depot in Logan on March 25, 1921. He died at the scene and was interred alongside his wife Fannie in the Logan cemetery.[87]

The prominence of the Campbell family in Gallatin City probably was further enhanced when Helen Campbell married James Gallaher, Jr.,

---

[84]*Headwaters Heritage History*, 56.
[85]Ibid.
[86]Ibid.
[87]Ibid.

the third eldest son of James Gallaher, an eminent Presbyterian minister and one-time chaplin in Congress whose wife Lucinda Houston Gallaher was first cousin to the legendary Sam Houston of the Republic of Texas. Although there is a reference indicating that James Gallaher married Helen Campbell in or before 1863, they apparently were already married in the summer of 1863 when they accompanied the Campbell family to Montana and established themselves at Three Forks. Gallaher was born in Rogersville, Tennessee, in 1825, and was thirty-eight years old when he traveled across the Plains to Montana. He settled at Three Forks, where he and Samuel Weir built and operated a river ferry. It was the only ferry across the Madison and Jefferson Rivers. Following that, Gallaher attempted to build a bridge across the river above the ferry, but the entire structure washed away in a flood. Having no insurance on the structure, James suffered a heavy financial loss. Gallaher tried his hand at lots of things, including raising livestock, and during his time at Three Forks, he became the first probate judge in Gallatin County and later served in the first Montana legislature in Virginia City.[88]

During this period, it was common for several Missouri River steamboats to travel together for mutual assistance with mechanical failures, to help one another lighten loads to grasshopper over sandbars, and to defend themselves against Indian attacks. Such was the case with the *St. Johns*, which left St. Louis accompanied by the *Julia* on the same day. On April 3, the *St. Johns* passed the *Julia* and the *General Grant* and met the *A. J. Majors* coming down the river with news of the demise of the *Bertrand*. Another boat going up the river, but farther down, was the *Effie Deans*.

The *St. Johns* and the *General Grant* took turns passing one another on the river as each laid up for wooding or became stuck on sandbars. On April 9, the *St. Johns* tied up at the site of the *Bertrand* wreck, and Anna and Fannie Campbell came down to the site, surprised to see William Gallaher there.[89] The *St. Johns* continued up the river that afternoon,

---

[88] Ibid., 60.

[89] William H. Gallaher, *Ho! For the Gold Mines of Montana—Up the Missouri River in 1865. The Journal of William H. Gallaher, Parts I and II*, Vol. 57, Nos. 1 and 2, Part 1 (Columbia: The State Historical Society of Missouri, 1963), 163. According to William M. Lytle, the *St. Johns* was a 300-ton sternwheeler built at Wheeling, West Virginia in 1864 as a passenger packet for use between Wheeling and Cincinnati (William M. Lytle and Forrest R. Holdcamper, *Merchant Steam Vessels of the United States, 1817–1868* (Staten Island: Steamship Historical Society of America, University of Baltimore Press, 1975), 168). It had recently been purchased, and its new owners sought to use it in the Upper Missouri trade, believing that with its light draft, speed, and good capacity it could run between St. Louis and Fort Benton faster than any boat then in use on the river. Captain J. R. Sousley was its master on this maiden voyage up the Missouri River.

leaving the Campbell sisters to board the *General Grant* and continue their trip. Two days later on April 11, the two boats tied up together and a dance was held on the *General Grant*, attended by the Campbell sisters, "both in high spirits."[90] Thereafter, the boats swapped places on the river and assisted each other as necessary. When the boats tied up at Sioux City on April 20, William escorted the Campbell girls on a walk around town.[91]

Early in May, the *Effie Deans* caught up with the *St. Johns* and the *General Grant*, and the three boats pretty much remained together for the remainder of the trip up the river. According to Gallaher, on May 9, passengers from the *General Grant* came over to the *St. Johns* and everyone had a big dance followed by a "wine, oyster & sardine supper." "Anna and Fannie danced every set."[92] On June 15, the *St. Johns* reached the Marias River but could go no farther up the Missouri and had to unload its cargo.[93]

The light draft *Deer Lodge* was operating on the Upper Missouri between Fort Benton and several points of impasse during the 1865 season and took on part of the *General Grant*'s cargo and a number of passengers at the mouth of the Marias River, including the Campbell sisters. On June 16, while the *Deer Lodge* laid to at the Marias, it was met by Major James Campbell, who had come overland by wagon to rendezvous with his daughters. Campbell left his wagon to Gallaher and Houston to bring to Fort Benton and joined his daughters on the *Deer Lodge*.[94] By June 17, Gallaher had secured his belongings and freight from the *St. Johns* and set out for Virginia City and Last Chance Gulch, stopping at Fort Benton to return the wagon to Major Campbell. When Campbell arrived at Fort Benton, G. P. Dorriss and Mr. Atchison caught up with the party, and they and the Campbells, Gallaher, and Houston went together to Virginia City. At Virginia City, Gallaher and Adrian sold some of their goods—coffee at $.65 a pound, tea at $2.30, apples at $10 per bushel, and sugar at $.50 a pound—and headed on to Helena.[95] On June 24, Houston elected to go on to Gallatin City. Gallaher eventually staked a gold claim near Gallatin City but was unsuccessful as a miner. In 1870, he returned to St. Charles, Missouri, where subsequently he married Florida McElhinney. William Gallaher died in Minneapolis, Minnesota, in June 1874.[96]

---

[90] Ibid., 163.
[91] Ibid., 164.
[92] Ibid., 167.
[93] Ibid., 173.
[94] William H. Gallaher, *Ho! For the Gold Mines of Montana*, Part 2, 267.
[95] Ibid.
[96] Ibid., 271.

In 1875 James Gallaher sold his river ferry to Fannie Campbell and took his family to Waitsberg in Washington Territory. Samuel Weir stayed behind and continued to operate the ferry for Fannie Campbell. James and Helen Campbell had nine children: James, Preston, Fred, Frank, Thomas, Nellie, Cornelia, and Fanny. James Gallaher died on November 6 or 7, 1891.[97]

The last of the Campbell family profiled is Gurdon Campbell, the elder brother of the three Campbell sisters. Gurdon H. Campbell was born on November 29, 1835, in Chicago. As a young man, he worked in the Chicago post office until 1863, when he accompanied his parents and his sister Helen across the plains to Montana. In 1864, Gurdon and his father opened a mercantile in Gallatin City, and in 1865, he became a deputy county tax collector. He was a supporter of the Eastern Montana Agricultural and Mechanical Association that sponsored the popular Gallatin County Fairs and horse races. In December 1871, he raffled his horse "Gaiger" to raise money for the fair. In January 1871, the store became overstocked and Gurdon moved to Bozeman to take advantage of the silver mining boom there. The *Bozeman Courier* of January 31, 1878, noted, "G. H. Campbell, of Gallatin City, having an overstock of merchandise on hand, has removed it to Bozeman where it will be opened out in the building lately occupied by C. B. Fawcett. C. L. Clark will have charge of the Bozeman store."[98]

Gurdon Campbell passed away at the La Clede Hotel in Bozeman on April 16, 1878, at the age of forty-three. He was interred alongside his father at Hossafeld Hills overlooking the original 160-acre Campbell tract.[99]

The Walton Family

The Walton family history is long and complex, but the portion that relates to the steamboat *Bertrand* began during the Civil War, when Moses Edward Walton went to Montana Territory in 1864, followed by his wife Mary Elizabeth Walton and their five children in 1865. Mrs. Walton and the children were passengers on the *Bertrand* when it sank at De Soto in Nebraska Territory on April 1, 1865. Although John Edward Walton was a little more than eight years old when the incident

[97]Ibid., 273.

[98]"In Memory of Judge Gallaher," *Avant Courier*, November 7, 1891. See also "Judge James Gallaher and Helen Campbell Gallaher," *Headwaters Heritage History*, Diamond Jubilee ed. (Three Forks: Three Forks Area Historical Society, 1983), 60.

[99]*Headwaters Heritage History*, 56–57.

occurred, many years later he wrote one of the three firsthand accounts of the demise of the *Bertrand*. The events that brought the Waltons to Montana compose a truly intriguing frontier story.

Moses Edward Walton was born on June 10, 1824, at Nashville, Tennessee, to Joshua S. Walton of Virginia and Latitia Decatur Walton of North Carolina. Not much is known about Josiah Walton except that he operated a water-powered grist mill in 1835 at Gravois Mills, an unincorporated village on Lake of the Ozarks forty-one miles from Versailles, Missouri. In his youth, Moses was educated in common schools in Nashville, and as a young man, he moved to Cass County in western Missouri, where he farmed and raised livestock. On December 4, 1849, he married Mary Elizabeth Gates near Versailles in Morgan County, by whom he sired eight children, five in Cass County, Missouri, and three more in Montana.[100]

Moses enlisted in the Missouri State Guard, Army of the West, during the Civil War and served under Major General Sterling Price for three years. While Moses was away from his farm on military duty, a company of Kansas Jayhawkers came to his home. His son, John Edward, wrote a graphic account of the incident in his personal notes, "A Trip Up The Missouri—Memories as a Child" that he wrote in about 1939:

> In 1863, early one morning a company of Kansas Jayhawkers came by and asked for father [Moses]. Mother told them that he was in the army and wasn't home. He had been home on a furlough the day before, but had left early that morning. They went on to a neighbor's and he told them he had seen father the day before, so they came back and put a guard around the house. Then they went upstairs and cut a hole in the plaster with an axe and shoveled fire from the fireplace in the space between the walls. In a few minutes the whole house was in flames. The guard wouldn't let mother take anything out, so we lost everything. It was a damp December and we had to sit by the fire of the burning house all night to keep warm. The next day my uncle Smith came and took us to his place. We had been there about three months when the same band of Kansas Jayhawkers came and shot down my uncle. He had been over to see his father who was on his deathbed. A brother saw the band coming and gave warning. This brother ran to the north and got in the timber, so he ran through a corn field. The K. J.s tore down the fence and rode him down and shot him. His wife saw what was happening and [ran] screaming to where he lay. She was only a short distance away when they shot the last time. The next day uncle's father died, so mother and my

---

[100]Ibid., 57.

aunt Amanda had to dig the graves and bury the two men there with no men around.

These Jayhawkers were not the regular Northern army soldiers, but a body of men called the "Home Guard." They wore the Northern uniform but they were just out to kill and steal, using the war as an excuse. After they killed my uncle, we had to move to Versailia [Versailles], Missouri. After my father had served his three years, he came home to us, but they wanted to draft him, and he was convinced any further fighting was hopeless, so he set out west to what was called Idaho Territory in the Louisiana Purchase. Montana was formed from some of this territory. When the war was about over, mother borrowed some money on the farmland to buy tickets on the riverboat Bertrand. She bought tickets for herself and for her family to go to where father was. It took six hundred twenty five dollars to get us tickets up the Missouri River to Fort Benton, Montana.[101]

Mary Elizabeth Gates Walton must have been an incredibly strong woman. She was born on June 24, 1832 in Kentucky to William Gates and Sarah Chisholm (Chism) Gates. At age thirty-two, she was the mother of five children, all born in Cass County, Missouri. John Edward Walton was the third child. Sometime after 1866, Moses Walton moved from Helena to Trinity, where he took up mining and later engaged in farming and livestock raising. He died at Trinity in Lewis and Clark County on March 29, 1898. Mary Gates Walton died on January 3, 1906, at Los Angeles, California.[102]

Of the Walton family, the most information was found about the third oldest child, John Edward Walton. John was born on January 16, 1857, in Cass County, Missouri. John was reared in the Trinity Gulch gold strike country north of Helena on Prickly Pear Creek, where he worked a claim with his father. In 1876, at age nineteen, he went down the Missouri to Bismarck and then to Deadwood, where he worked in the mines before going to Spearfish, South Dakota, to help erect a stockade to protect settlers

[101]Most of the genealogical information about the Walton family can be found in David Crawford's Walton surnames list and narratives in "Crawford and Other Relatives," at www.crawfordclan.org. Other details concerning occupations, places of residence, etc. were extracted from the files of the late Jerome E. Petsche that are now in possession of the author. A biography of John Edward Walton appears in George W. Kingsbury, George Martin Smith, ed., *History of Dakota Territory—South Dakota Its History and Its People, Illustrated*, Vol. 5 (Chicago: S. J. Clarke Publishing Company, 1915), 546.

[102]John Edward Walton, "Up the Missouri—Memories as a Child," unpublished manuscript, 1939. The manuscript is in the possession of the author. It was given originally to Jerome Petsche by Mrs. Arthur Pederson of Scribner, Nebraska.

against the marauding Sioux Indians. He and several other ranchers and farmers in the Deadwood-Spearfish area finally attacked the Sioux and repelled them from the area for a while. Near Spearfish, he established a farm and married Mary Louisa Roberts, an English woman, on December 24, 1879. Their children, ten in all, were Robert Edgar, Letitia Emma, Lee Elmo, Nettie Anna, John Edward, Jr., Louise Hanna, Clyde Virgil, Amy Olive, Hugh Earnest, and Gladys Irene. John Walton eventually ended up in Pomona, California, where he died on December 6, 1947.[103]

Walton's account of the sinking of the *Bertrand* does not vary from that of Willard Barrows and begins after his father came home after three years of military service under Confederate General Sterling Price in Missouri. Walton wrote:

> After father had served his three years, he came home to us, but they wanted to draft him and he was convinced any further fighting was hopeless, so he set out west to what was called Idaho Territory in the Louisiana Purchase. Montana was later formed from some of this territory. When the war was about over, Mother borrowed some money on the farmland to buy tickets on the river steamer [*Bertrand*] for herself and the family to go to where father was. It took six hundred twenty-five dollars to get us tickets up the Missouri River to Fort Benton.
>
> Things were going along fine for some time when all of a sudden we felt a jar, and found out that the boat had struck a snag and punched a hole in the bottom. Soon the boat began to sink. There was great excitement and confusion, I climbed to the top deck right away, but the river was so shallow that the boat struck bottom before much of it was under water. When it hit it rolled part way over in its side and almost threw me overboard. We were all taken off the boat without a mishap and taken to a small town [De Soto] to await another boat [*General Grant*].[104]

Joseph Talbert Walton

Joseph "Joe" Walton, who was not quite four years old at the time the *Bertrand* sank, was born on May 4, 1861, in Index, Cass County, Missouri. Although he too followed in his father's footsteps, he later became an overland freighter. Not much is remarkable about him other than he settled in the Judith Basin near Hobson, where he served as justice of the peace for several years. He married Alice E. Riggs on October 7,

---

[103]"Crawford and Other Relatives."
[104]"Crawford and Other Relatives."

1886, and the couple had three children, Ethel, Etta, and Fred. He died on January 12, 1943, at Lewiston, Montana.[105]

Letitia Amanda Walton

Latitia "Tish" Walton, like her brother Joe, was born in Index, Cass County, Missouri, on December 5, 1858. Late in life, she married William Thomas Norris at Helena on June 23, 1882. After that, she left the territory with her husband to farm near Asotin, Washington. The Norris's children were Hattie, Lucy, Frances Eugenia, May Ellen, Leta Alice, and Elery. Although the information is unclear, she is believed to have died on February 21, 1929, at Watertown, Codington County, South Dakota, and was buried there.[106]

Martha Elizabeth Walton

Martha was a product of Independence, Cass County, Missouri. She was born there on June 23, 1854, and was a little more than ten years old when the *Bertrand* sank. She married a placer miner and freighter named George Booker on December 25, 1872, and thereafter resided in Helena. Their children were Ethel, Clinton, and Lester. Martha Elizabeth Walton Norris on died April 15, 1940, in Los Angeles, California.[107]

Mary Elizabeth Gates Walton

Mary Elizabeth Walton, mother of the five Walton children traveling up the Missouri, was born on June 24, 1832, in Kentucky to William Gates and Mary Chisholm (Chism) Gates. She married Moses Edward Walton on December 4, 1849. After Moses left Confederate military service and established himself in Montana, Mary and the children boarded the steamer *Bertrand* at Versailles, Missouri, and proceeded up the river to join her husband. Mary was quite literally forced to make the trip inasmuch as Jay hawkers had burned the Walton farm to the ground in December 1863, forcing her to live for a time with relatives at Versailles. There she borrowed money on the farm and booked passage for herself and the children on the *Bertrand*. Once in Montana, Mary bore Moses

[105]Walton, "Up the Missouri River—Memories as a Child."
[106]"Crawford and Other Relatives."
[107]Ibid.

three more children: Alice Mae, Robert Lee, and Ella Viola. She died at Los Angeles, California, on January 3, 1906.[108]

Virginia Annette Walton

Virginia was thirteen years old when she accompanied her mother up the Missouri River. She was born on September 19, 1851, in Independence, Cass County, Missouri. Known as "Nettie," Virginia Walton was sickly as a child. She married a Helena schoolteacher named Ferd R. Cooper on November 14, 1872. They had no children and established a small ranch at Trinity Gulch, near Bozeman, where she died on December 20, 1874.[109]

Nicholas J. Bielenberg

Nicholas Beilenberg was a German immigrant who was born in Holstein, Germany, on May 18, 1847, to Claus and Margaret Cruse Beilenberg. Claus Beilenberg was an industrious, well-educated man who engaged in farming near Davenport, Iowa, but also established a butcher shop in the city, where he became a well-respected businessman and town supporter. Nicholas learned the butcher's trade there and worked briefly at the trade in Chicago before he learned of the gold strikes in Montana and decided to go west to seek his fortune. Nicholas packed his butcher tools and took a riverboat from Davenport to St. Louis, where he stayed a few days. He then booked passage on the steamboat *Bertrand* for Montana. When the *Bertrand* sank, he continued up the Missouri on the *General Grant* with the intention of going to Helena. He eventually arrived at Fort Benton on June 18, 1865, but had only $.35 in his pocket and could not pay the cost of transporting his tools. Fortunately, Nicholas was befriended by the captain of the *General Grant*, who released his tools and ordered the steward to provide him with supplies enough to reach his destination. Upon arriving in Helena, he learned of a butcher business for sale by Henry Edgar, one of the discoverers of gold in Alder Gulch. Nicholas summoned his brothers from the east, and they partnered in their new butcher business at Blackfoot, Montana.[110]

Bielenberg worked in the business at Blackfoot until 1870, when he started his own business in Helena and worked there for two years before

---

[108]Ibid.
[109]Ibid.
[110]Ibid.

locating at Deer Lodge. At Deer Lodge, he engaged in stock raising and in buying cattle to sell in the east. He drove his cattle to Cheyenne, Wyoming, and then shipped them by rail to Chicago. In 1877, he established a meat business with a cold storage plant in Butte, Montana, under the name Butte Butchering Co. The business was immensely successful and brought Beilenberg considerable fame and notoriety. In 1884, he and his half-brother, Conrad Kohrs, established a large cattle business at the Grant-Kohrs ranch, but Nicholas soon branched out with another partner named Joseph Toomey to raise more than 130,000 head of sheep in various parts of Montana. They also bought livestock in the Pacific Northwest and in North Dakota to supply eastern markets.[111]

Nicholas Beilenberg eventually went on to become very active in territorial and state politics as a leader of the Progressive Party, and was a delegate to the convention that nominated Theodore Roosevelt for president in August 1912. Nicholas married Annie Bogk of Oshkosh, Wisconsin, at Deer Lodge on March 4, 1872. The Beilenbergs had five children: Alma Margaret, Augusta, Anne Marie, and Charles. It currently is not known when Nicholas Beilenberg died, and it is presumed that he died at his home in Deer Lodge.[112]

George Pool Dorriss
See Chapter V.

James D. Lucas
James Lucas was born to riverboat Captain James H. Lucas in 1837, probably in St. Louis. He was accompanying John T. Murphy to Helena with a stock of goods to open a mercantile when the *Bertrand* sank. The eighty-one-year-old Lucas described the event in a letter to newspaper columnist Captain G. B. Merrick of Madison, Wisconsin, on February 23, 1918. Merrick wrote columns for the *New York Times* and the *Saturday Evening Post* about the old steamboat days on the Mississippi and Missouri Rivers, and he published Lucas's letter in *The Saturday Evening Post*, on March 2, 1918. It is the third written account of the sinking of the *Bertrand*, and does not vary from the accounts of Willard Barrows

---

[111]Helen F. Sanders, "Nicholas J. Beilenberg," *History of Montana*, Vol. 2 (Chicago and New York: Lewis Publishing Co., 1913), 960–61.
[112]Ibid.

and John Edward Walton.[113] After the *Bertrand* sank, he made his way to Montana, but stayed there only two years before returning to St. Louis, where he went into the real estate business.[114]

John T. Murphy
See Chapter V.

John W. Noye
It is believed that John Noye was a passenger on the *Bertrand* and not a crewman, even though he roomed with First Engineer Albert Rowe and carpenter John Burns at the Herndon House hotel in Omaha the day after the boat sank. He listed his address as Colorado rather than St. Louis like the other crewmen.[115]

John Thornton
John Thornton registered at the Herndon House on April 2, 1865.[116] In all probability, he was a salesman for the dry goods dealer and distributor Bast & Pollock of St. Louis. St. Louis city directories from the mid-1860s list a John Thornton as a salesman for this firm. Inasmuch as a substantial amount of clothing recovered from the *Bertrand* cargo was associated with the name Bast & Pollock, Thornton may have been taking the merchandise to Montana.[117]

William McCoy Wheatley
Annalies Corbin's treatise on the material culture associated with *Bertrand* passengers says there is no evidence that the barrel (FSC-234, Catalogue No. 3949) containing cobbler's tools belonged to William Wheatley, but

[113]Ibid.

[114]This article has a long segmented caption: Captain G. B. Merrick, "The Old Boats—Additional Information from Men Who Know—Valuable Contributions to River History, Supplementary to Captain Merrick's Narratives—Communications Invited to this Column—Addenda—Addenda," *Saturday Evening Post*, March 2, 1918, 6.

[115]Jerome E. Petsche recovered the Lucas letter and other bits of information about James Lucas from the Merrick Collection at the State Historical Society of Wisconsin at Madison, Wisconsin. The article is in possession of the author.

[116]*Herndon House Register*, April 2, 1865.

[117]Ibid.

the possibility cannot be overlooked. In all likelihood, William Wheatley, who was a cobbler by trade, took his tools and supplies with him on the *Bertrand* in case his new sawmill venture in Montana failed.[118]

William Wheatley was born in 1827, and in his youth, he learned the cobbler's trade from his father in Northumberland, Pennsylvania. He worked in the trade through the 1840s. Sometime in the early 1850s, he went to Georgia, where he worked at variety of jobs before relocating to Gravois Mills, Missouri, where he took up farming. He courted Mildred Maria Humes on her father's plantation and married her in a double ceremony with Mildred's brother Joseph in 1858. William apparently did some cobbling for family and friends while he farmed in Missouri. In 1860, Wheatley returned to Pennsylvania to rent and work in his father's shoe shop, and stayed there through most of the Civil War. In 1865, he started a new business venture to cut limber for the Montana mining camps. William did not act alone. He partnered with his brother-in-law, Joseph "Jose" Humes, and a man named Wilson to buy and transport a sawmill to a site at Confederate Gulch in Montana Territory.[119]

On March 16, 1865, Joseph Humes booked passage on the *Deer Lodge* to Fort Benton, reaching there May 30. His purpose was to scout a location for the sawmill. William left his pregnant wife and four-year-old son John at St. Louis, and he and Wilson loaded the sawmill machinery on the *Bertrand*. On March 19, the day after the *Bertrand* left port, Mildred gave birth to their daughter Mary Eliza. When the *Bertrand* sank at De Soto on April 1, William and Wilson waited there for a salvage boat in hopes that it could recover their mill. Accordingly, on April 7, Wheatley wrote to John G. Copeland of the Montana and Idaho Transportation Co. expressing his predicament at having no insurance. On April 13, Copeland wrote back:

Wm. M. Wheatley, Esq.
De Soto Washington Co. D. T.

Dear Sir
  Yours of 7th at hand I answered you & dispatch to Can. J. A. Horbach of Omaha—Capt. N. J. Eaton agent of Board of Underwriters is now

---

[118]Corbin, *The Material Culture of Steamboat Passengers*, 77–87. Corbin provides a complete detailed list of all the tools and leather pieces found in the barrel.

[119]Most of what is known about William McCoy Wheatley comes from the online Wheatley Family History Project, Peter Binkley, "Historical Outline" and Chapter 6, "William's Montana Trip (1865–66)," www.wallanbinkley.com/wheatley/-Canada, last modified July 14, 1999.

at wreck and any arrangements you make with him about Salvage will be all right. The Machinery was not insured as I did not understand it to be your instruction to me to insure it. If you can get Mill and all the Machinery out so it will be of value and you can run it I will take you and Wilson and machinery all through on another boat, but would like to know about it if to go as soon as possible so as to provide for it.

Yours truly
John G. Copeland[120]

The salvers recovered the mill, and Wilson went ahead on an unidentified boat, leaving William to accompany the mill on the steamboat *Sam Gaty*. William did not reach Fort Union until June 26. It is not entirely clear, but it appears that at Fort Berthold, the *Sam Gaty* cargo was transferred to the *General Grant*, and it proceeded up the Missouri to the Milk River, where it discharged some of its cargo to lighten its load before going on to Cow Island. On July 7, a courier was dispatched from Cow Island to Fort Benton to advise that wagons should be brought to move the cargo overland. On July 19, Wheatley loaded his mill on a wagon or wagons and traveled overland to Fort Benton, reaching there at the end of the month.[121]

Ten days later, leaving his mill at Fort Benton, Wheatley joined a wagon train bound for Helena, hoping to find Joseph and Wilson. Arriving at Helena on August 14, he waited for the mill to come from Fort Benton. When it did not arrive, he backtracked to find it and returned with it to Helena in September, too late to put it into operation before winter. At this point, William learned that his Missouri farm was about to be repossessed. He and Joseph sold the mill and rushed back to St. Louis to see to the litigation.[122] William and Mildred farmed in Missouri for eight years after the Civil War and then selling out in 1873 and going to Pennsylvania when William's father was dying. In Pennsylvania, William joined the Altoona Iron Co. as a cashier and worked his way up to superintendent and treasurer. William prospered, and in 1883, he and a partner bought the Portage Iron Works at Duncansville. In 1889 or 1890, William sold out and moved his family to Post Falls, Idaho, and then to Spokane, Washington, where they began ranching. William died there in 1909, and Mildred followed eight years later.[123]

---

[120]Ibid.
[121]Ibid.
[122]Ibid.
[123]Ibid.

Yi-Shing

According to Jerome Petsche, there may have been a Chinese girl on board the *Bertrand* named Yi-Shing, but research has not confirmed this.[124] There is Chinese writing in brushed gold on a broken case of personal items from the *Bertrand* and transliteration of two characters refer to a girl named Yi-Shing. Unfortunately, no evidence has proven the box was directly connected to this person.

---

[124]Petsche, *The Steamboat Bertrand*, 125.

FIGURE 9. The steamboat *Bertrand* during excavation.

V

Consignees

BY DEFINITION, A "CONSIGNEE" IS SOMEONE TO WHOM SOME-thing is shipped. Because cargo manifests for the steamboat *Bertrand* have not been found, it is difficult to tell in some cases precisely to whom items in the cargo were being shipped. Fortunately, a good many clues and names were recovered from stenciling on shipping crates and barrels. Some of the consignees so identified are noteworthy because of their vision and success in business in St. Louis and in the mining communities of Montana. Indeed, the histories of Virginia City, Deer Lodge, Helena, and Hell Gate could not be told without reference to these men. When the cargo was removed from the holds, seven consignees were recorded:

> Vivian & Simpson, Virginia City, M. T., or, V. & S. Virginia City, M. T.
> Stuart & Co., Deer Lodge, M. T.
> G. P. Dorris, Virginia City, M. T.
> J. Murphy, Ft. Benton, M. T.
> Worden & Co., Hell Gate, M. T., or, Worden, Hell Gate, M. T.
> J. J. Roe & Co.
> M. Kingman & Co., Virginia City, M. T.

JAMES M. VIVION (AKA JAMES M. VIVIAN)

The first of these is James M. Vivian. From the historical perspective, it is interesting that his correct name is James M. Vivion and that the consignment case stencils from the *Bertrand* consistently appear as Vivian & Simpson. This thirty-one-year-old business partner of Robert

Simpson must have been accompanying a shipment of goods bound for their Virginia City business when the *Bertrand* sank. The *Bertrand* contained a large amount of cargo consigned to Vivian & Simpson, including sugar and syrup, canned goods, champagne, bitters, honey, fireplace tools, candles, matches, indigo, boots, coats, trousers, vests, sweaters, cigars, smoking pipes, tools, and sewing supplies.

James was born on April 29, 1833, in Missouri to James and Mary Vivion.[1] Little is known of his childhood, but as a young man, he was a gold miner in Colorado before going to Montana in 1863 hoping to find gold in the strike at Bannack City.[2] Immediately after the discovery of gold near Alder Gulch, James Vivion and Robert Simpson decided that gold was better acquired from miners' pockets than from the ground, and they started a mercantile in Virginia City. Apparently the loss of goods on the *Bertrand* did not deter Vivion and Simpson from going ahead with their new business venture. According to the *Montana Post*, in July 1865, Vivion & Simpson bought a building in Virginia City from George How.[3] A month later, the same newspaper indicated they had brought a stock of goods from the east to locate in the store bought from How.[4] By the 1880s, Vivion had left Montana and settled at Cripple Creek, Colorado. After that time, there is no record of his activities, and nothing has been found concerning Robert Simpson.

GRANVILLE STUART

Another well-known figure in Montana history is consignee Granville Stuart. Although there are multiple published references relating to his life, two of the best sources are *As Big as the West: Pioneer Life of Granville Stuart* by Clyde A. Milner II and Carroll A. O'Connor, and one written by Stuart in his own hand, *Forty Years on the Frontier as Seen in the Journals*

---

[1]James U. Sanders, ed., "James M. Vivion," *Society of Montana Pioneers: Constitution, Members, and Officers, with Portraits and Maps—Register*, Vol. 1 (Helena: Historical Society of Montana, 1899), 168.

[2]Michael A. Leeson, ed. *History of Montana, 1739–1885, A History of its Discovery and Settlement, Social and Commercial Progress, Mines and Miners, Agriculture and Stock Growing, Churches, Schools and Societies, Indians and Indian Wars, Vigilantes, Courts of Justice, Newspaper Press, Navigation, Railroads and Statistics, with Histories of Counties, Cities, Villages and Mining Camps; Also, Personal Reminiscences of Great Historic Value, Views Characteristic of the Territory in Our Own Times, and Portraits of Pioneers and Representative Men in the Professions and Trades. Illustrated* (Chicago: Warner, Beers & Company, 1885), 387.

[3]*Montana Post*, July 22, 1865.

[4]*Montana Post*, August 12, 1865.

and Remembrances of Granville Stuart, edited by Paul C. Phillips.[5] Granville
Stuart was born on August 27, 1834, in Clarksville, Virginia, to Robert
Stuart and Nancy Currence Hall Stuart. Three years later, the family
located in Illinois, but the difficult journey took more than a month. They
traveled by steamboat from Wheeling down the Ohio River, up the Mississippi River to Rock Island, and then by wagon to Princeton in Bureau
County, Illinois. At Princeton, Granville's father set about surveying land
for new settlers. Because the government had purchased Indian lands in
Iowa and opened them for settlement, the Stuarts took claim on land in
the new Iowa Territory in 1838 and crossed the Mississippi River, where
they built a one-room cabin and began farming.[6] In 1843, the Stuarts
moved again, this time to the Cedar River.[7] Robert Stuart seemed to have
some genetic propensity to seek his fortune in various places, and when
he heard rumors of gold being discovered in California in 1849, he made
the trip there, where he mined part of the time and hunted elk, deer, and
antelope to sell to prospectors.[8] He returned to Iowa in the winter of 1851.
Ascertaining that gold had been found, he moved his family in spring
wagons across the plains to Sacramento early in 1852.[9] After arriving in
California, he and his sons had some success as placer miners near Dog
Creek until their water supply dried up. They decided to move on and
again succeeded in finding some gold on the west branch of Little Butte
Creek near Butte Mills, and lesser amounts on Big Butte Creek.[10] By the
summer of 1853, Robert apparently had had enough of gold mining and
returned to Iowa.[11] By the spring of 1857, having varying degrees of success mining, James Granville, Rezin (aka Reese or Reece) Anderson, and
eleven others decided to travel overland back to Iowa to see relatives.[12]

They inadvertently got caught up in the Mormon War/Rebellion of
1857–1858. On their way east, they met a horse trader named Jake Meek
who was headed north to the Beaverhead Valley to winter his cattle and
horses, and not wishing to be involved in the Mormon conflict, the Stuarts

[5]Clyde A. Milner II and Carroll A. O'Connor, *As Big as the West: The Pioneer Life of
Granville Stuart* (New York: Oxford University Press, 2009); Paul C. Phillips, ed. *Forty
Years on the Frontier as seen in the Journals and Remembrances of Granville Stuart, Two Volumes
in One* (Glendale, Calif.: Arthur H. Clark, 1967).

[6]Phillips, *Forty Years on the Frontier*, Vol. 1, 23–25.

[7]Ibid., 28.

[8]Ibid., 37.

[9]Ibid., 39.

[10]Ibid., 57–76.

[11]Ibid., 78–79.

[12]Ibid., 105.

wintered in 1857–1858 with Meek on the Beaverhead River at the mouth of the Stinking Water.[13] Gold was never far out of the minds of the Stuart boys, for they had a condition known in those days as "a pocket full of rocks and quartz on the brain." On May 2, 1858, they accompanied Reese Anderson, Thomas Adams, and John Ross to the Beaverhead to prospect on Benetsee Creek in what was then part of Washington Territory.[14] Finding gold, they determined to stay, mark their claim, and mine their stake, but they needed mining tools and supplies to sustain the effort. Granville wanted to register the claim right away, fearing someone else would do so, but was convinced by the others to wait a few days. Starting from Benetsee Creek on June 16 with dried moose meat and twenty-five horses to sell, they reached Fort Bridger on June 28 and replenished their grocery supplies. They stayed at Fort Bridger about two weeks and then drove the horses to Camp Floyd and sold them, hoping to buy mining supplies with the proceeds. No supplies were available, but the men heard that trading with emigrants on the Oregon Trail was profitable, so they decided to try to increase their money supply before returning to mining. Reese Anderson and John Ross bought supplies and headed north into Flathead Indian country. (Ross drowned in the Bear River in June 1860.) In July 1858, James and Granville went to the Green River east of Fort Bridger and bartered with army supply trains and emigrants for tired, worn-out livestock that they rested and fed and then disposed of at a good price.[15]

The Stuart brothers flourished in the livestock trade on the Green River, and in 1860, they were rejoined by Reese Anderson. Having recouped their investment, and having an ample number of livestock, they departed for Benetsee Creek via the Beaverhead Valley to resume mining.[16] After spending a mild winter in the Rocky Mountains, they found themselves in the Deer Lodge Valley where they encountered Francis L. Worden and Captain C. P. Higgins who had brought a pack train up from Walla Walla in the fall of 1860.[17] With another stock of goods in hand by the spring of 1861, they had befriended and established good trade with the Nez Perce Indians, trading calico, red cloth, calico shirts, vermillion paint, beads, and combs for buffalo robes, dried buffalo meat and tongues, and miscellaneous furs.[18]

---

[13]Ibid., 119.
[14]Ibid., 136.
[15]Ibid., 141–49.
[16]Ibid., 153.
[17]Ibid., 157. See also Robert H. Fletcher, "The Day of the Cattlemen Dawned Early," *Montana The Magazine of Western History*, 2, no. 4 (1961): 22–26.
[18]Ibid., 158.

In the early and middle 1860s, it was becoming clear to the Stuart brothers and Reese Anderson that they had a far better chance of mining miners than mining gold. Wherever the brothers went, Granville would set up a small blacksmith shop and consistently earned more for his work than most miners did for theirs. Accordingly, on August 28, 1863, Granville Stuart and Reese Anderson open a small blacksmith shop in Virginia City and did a good business until March 1864, when they and their third partner Frank McConnell dissolved the business. They continued to prospect as a sideline, and as the gold strikes near Virginia City matured, so did the business acumen of the Stuart brothers. They realized that the dreams of unequipped miners could not be fulfilled without the goods the brothers were prepared to sell to them. In early June 1864, they formed a partnership with Frank Worden and opened a store at Deer Lodge. James managed it, and Granville managed the store in Virginia City and kept business accounts for his older brother as a salaried employee.[19] They offered groceries, wines, liquors, Queensware, hardware, clothing, blankets, boots and shoes, buffalo overshoes, saddles, whips, harness, and California mining tools including shovels, pick axes, and hardware for sluices.[20] Gold strikes around Virginia City caused the population to explode to 10,000, and in the fall and winter of 1864, the need for mining tools and groceries was reaching critical proportions, and was definitely outstripping the supply. Ironically, these were the very goods that the Stuart brothers had ordered from St. Louis and expected to be shipped on the steamboat *Bertrand* for the 1865 season. At some point after this, James Stuart took on another partner named Walter P. Dance. The Virginia City store was known as Dance & Stuart until they sold it in 1865 and merged with James and Frank Worden and Granville Stuart to become Dance, Stuart, & Co. in Deer Lodge in 1866.[21]

Because the life and times of Granville Stuart are some of the most engaging historical accounts of the history of Montana Territory, a few more anecdotes about him are appropriate. After a failed first marriage, Granville married a Shoshone woman named Aubony (Ellen) Tookanka on May 2, 1862, by whom he fathered nine or ten children. Aubony died in 1887 at Maiden, Montana.[22] As time went on, Granville came to know more than anyone about the geography, native people and their language and customs, and the history of early Montana. In 1864, he

---

[19]Phillips, *Forty Years on the Frontier,* Vol. 2, 16, 20.
[20]Milner and O'Connor, *As Big As the West,* 104.
[21]Ibid., 117–18.
[22]Phillips, *Forty Years on the Frontier,* Vol. 2, 26.

elsewhere. He was soon offered an opportunity in the mercantile business in Frankfort, in what was then southern Illinois. George stocked his business with goods bought on credit from St. Louis and Louisville. In 1831, George married Sarah Henderson in Shawneetown, Illinois (or Todd County, Kentucky). He stayed in his not-so-profitable business in Frankfort for about two more years, during which time he served as a general in the United States Army during the Black Hawk War of 1832.[28]

Then a fortuitous event occurred. On June 7, 1836, the United States government purchased 3,149 square miles of land from the Iowa and Sac and Fox Indians in the unorganized northwest portion of Missouri Territory and extinguished prior tribal rights that had been granted in perpetuity. Referred to as the "Platte Purchase," this acquisition had been proposed as early as 1835 by General William F. Switzler and Joseph Robidoux and gathered steam with support from Senator Thomas Hart Benton. After Missouri assented to the act of incorporation on March 28, 1837, President Van Buren proclaimed the land part of the state of Missouri and opened it for settlement. The tribes were paid $7,500 for their land, and they were to relocate to reservations west of Missouri River. The agreement, presided over by William Clark at Leavenworth, Kansas, said that five large houses would be built for each tribe and further provided fencing for 200 acres of land. A farmer, blacksmith, teacher, interpreter, agricultural implements, livestock, and other necessities were also to be provided. At the time of treaty, the western border of Missouri ran north and south through the mouth of the Kansas River (94 degrees 36 minutes west longitude), and the acquisition extended the newly created state of Missouri northwest to 95 degrees 46 minutes west longitude, making the largest state even larger.[29]

All of this comes back to George Dorriss, who preempted a valuable tract of land in the Platte Purchase and moved his family to Martinsville (Platte City), Platte County, Missouri, where he built a brick house and began cultivating successful business ventures. Active in public affairs, he eventually was elected to the Missouri General Assembly, once to the House and once to the Senate. With money in hand and with an expanding reputation, Dorriss engaged in real estate and owned thousands of acres, including a large plantation worked by slaves.[30]

When gold was discovered in California, Dorriss saw another promising business opportunity. He outfitted forty wagons with goods and went

[28] *Treaty with the Iowa, Etc. (September 17, 1836)* 7 Stat., 511. Proclamation, Feb. 15, 1837.
[29] Scharf, *History of St. Louis City and County*, 1862.
[30] Ibid.

to Sacramento, where he established a profitable mercantile operation. As things progressed, he was one of the first merchants to ship his goods to California by way of Cape Horn. When the gold rush ended, Dorriss returned to Missouri, where he stayed until the start of the Civil War, at which time he removed to St. Louis. In 1863, he started a mercantile business supplying mining equipment and tools and general merchandise in Helena, Montana, where he remained four years.[31] It was during this time, in 1865, that George Dorriss shipped a large quantity of mercury and other mining supplies to Fort Benton on the steamboat *Bertrand*.

When the gold rush in Montana declined, Dorriss returned to St. Louis, where he devoted most of his time to acquiring real estate. He eventually owned seven of nine stores in Davis Row (the other two stores in Davis Row were owned by his daughter and son and were valued at $22,000 each) on Olive Street Road, and considerable real estate throughout the city and county. During this time he purchased fifty acres on Olive Street Road and built the imposing Dorriss mansion for his family and landscaped it at a cost $2,000 an acre. General George Poole Dorriss fell ill in August 1882, and although he sought relief in the healing waters at Eureka Springs, Arkansas, he died in St. Louis on November 29, 1882, and was buried at Bellefontaine Cemetery. At the time of his death, three of his five children born between 1864 and 1875) and seven grandchildren survived him.[32] Several details about the life of George Dorriss have not been completely researched, including the time and place of death of his wife Sarah.

JOHN T. MURPHY

A substantial part of the *Bertrand*'s cargo, including groceries, clothing, bitters, and mining tools, was destined for Murphy & Neal Co. of Fort Benton, but the loss of the *Bertrand* was only a minor setback. Murphy already had a thriving business at Virginia City, and he ordered more goods from St. Louis and shipped them to Fort Benton on the steamers *Roanoke* and *Benton*. Those on the *Benton* were transported overland from Fort Benton to Helena for the new business there.

Research yielded quite a bit of information about John T. Murphy. He was born to William S. and Amelia Tyler Murphy, both of Pennsylvania, on February 26, 1842, on a farm in Platte County, Missouri. It is not known whether the Murphy and Dorriss families knew each other (both

[31]Ibid.
[32]Ibid.

were from Platte County), but the possibility is likely. John was one of two children and helped his father on the farm. He attended private school until age seventeen, when he left for the California gold fields in 1859. He first made his way to Denver, where for a year and half he clerked in a store before moving to Nevada City, Colorado (Nevadaville), where he opened his own store. He ran the business for a year and half before selling out and going into the wagon transportation business. Having made enough money to enter into a new venture, in 1864 Murphy went to Virginia City, Montana, with a wagon train of merchandise and sold the entire stock in quick order right off the wagons at Alder Gulch. He then floated down the Missouri River to Nebraska City on a flatboat, where he ordered goods to be transported overland to Helena in the spring of 1865. He proceeded down the river to St. Louis, where he ordered additional goods to be shipped by steamboat to Fort Benton for delivery to Helena in the spring of 1865. Presumably these goods were on the steamboat *Bertrand* when it sank. Goods reordered from St. Louis and transported on the *Benton* and the goods shipped overland must have arrived at Helena in good time because Murphy opened a new store there on July 1, 1865, with partners named Tutt and Neel under the name Murphy, Neel, & Co.[33] Although Murphy was successful and ran the Helena business until 1890, he branched out and opened stores in other places and expanded into the freighting business at Fort Benton to move supplies and equipment to Montana mining camps. According to the National Register of Historic places for Cascade County, Montana, in 1882, he partnered with Edgar Maclay to open two hardware stores in Helena and Fort Benton under the name Murphy-Maclay Hardware Co. Two years later, they opened another store in Great Falls that operated from 1886 into the 1960s. Their stores sold everything from flour and teas to window glass, hardware, and blasting powder.

It seems that John Murphy was one of those rare individuals who could touch anything and turn it to gold. He branched out into real estate, banking, and Florida citrus farming, but had marked success in stock raising. On October 14, 1911, he partnered with R. P. Heron, A. L. Smith, and John H. Tucker to form the Powder River Land & Cattle Co. with ranch operations on 24,153 acres in Custer and Carter counties and other pasturage in South Dakota on which they raised herds varying in size from 2,300 to 13,000 head of stock. The company incorporated the

---

[33]A. W. Bowen & Co., *Progressive Men of the State of Montana, Illustrated* (Chicago: A. W. Bowen & Co., 1902), 104.

famous Seventy-Nine Ranch with its "79" brand between the Yellowstone and Mussel Shell rivers as an open-range operation that later became a fenced ranch where both cattle and sheep were raised. Through profitable and troubled times, the company finally gave up and leased certain areas for oil and gas exploration in 1938. In 1943, the company sold all of its remaining assets to John McNierney of New Mexico.[34]

Murphy knew well where the money was, and he was one of the first organizers of the Helena National Bank in 1890. In 1891, he organized the Montana Savings Bank. His mining interests included in the Poorman, the Jay Gould, the Rumley and the Silver Bell mines. John T. Murphy died at Helena on May 23, 1914. He led a long and exhausting career. His first wife Elizabeth Morton Murphy died in 1897, and his son in 1904. A few months after the death of his wife Elizabeth, he married Clara Cobb of Providence, Rhode Island, but the time and place of her death are not known at present.[35]

FRANCIS (FRANK) LYMAN WORDEN

One of the most successful consignees and Montana businessmen was Francis (Frank) Lyman Worden. Worden was born at Marlborough, Vermont, on October 15, 1830, and was the oldest of eight children born to Rufus Worden and Susan Powers Worden. At age fourteen, he went to Troy, New York, to learn bookkeeping and merchandising, but by 1852, he was ready to start his own business. Borrowing $300 from his cousin Ellis K. Powers, he traveled from New York on the clipper *Harriet Hoxie* to California, where he first worked as sailor on the steamship *Oregon* that ran between San Francisco and Panama City, Panama. Following that he had several jobs, including clerking at the Occidental Hotel and working at the Gordon Co. in San Francisco. Subsequently, he tried his hand at trading in machinery and general merchandise at Port Orford, Oregon, before returning to California. The lure of gold must have had a magnetic effect on Worden because in 1856 he was back in the Coleville District of Oregon searching for his fortune.[36] Hostilities between white miners

[34]All material relating to the Powder River Land and Cattle Company can be found in Collection MC83 of the Montana Historical Archives under the title "Powder River Land and Cattle Company Records 1911–1944 (inclusive)," Helena, Montana.

[35]"John T. Murphy Papers 1849–1973," Manuscript Collection 84, Montana Historical Society Archives, Helena, Montana.

[36]Walter F. Sanders, "Francis Lyman Worden," *Contributions to the Historical Society of Montana; with its Transactions, Act of Incorporation, Constitution, Ordinances, Officers and Members,* 2: 363.

FIGURE 11. Francis Lyman Worden.
From *Contributions to the Historical Society of Montana, with its Transactions, Act of Incorporation, Constitution, Ordinances,* Vol. 2 (Helena, Mont.: State Publishing Company, State Printers and Binders, 1896), 12.

and the Yakima Indians continued to grow in the Coleville gold fields and Worden joined the Oregon Volunteers ("Stevens Guards" First Regiment Washington Territory Mounted Volunteers, Army of the United States) under Washington Territorial Governor Isaac Ingalls Stevens in a campaign to put down the Indian unrest along the Columbia River.[37]

Frank was an ambitious young man and moved up quickly to the Quartermaster Corps of the Office of Indian Affairs (sometimes referred to as the "Indian Service"). There he met and formed a partnership with Lieutenant A. H. Robie, who had merchandising interests in the Dalles region in Oregon after he bought out the mercantile business of Wooden & Isaacs in Walla Walla in 1860. He and Robie realized there was good money to had trading with the Indians. On February 1, 1858, at Walla Walla, they obtained a one-year permit for trading under the name Worden & Co. By October 1, Worden's reputation had grown sufficiently for him to be named postmaster at Walla Walla.[38]

Construction of the Mullan Road between Fort Benton and Walla Walla in 1859–1860 foretold the opportunity for trade with emigrants traveling west. Accordingly, Worden and an acquaintance, Captain Christopher P. Higgins, were quick to take advantage by setting up a business in Walla Walla and then traveling to the gold country at Hell Gate in August, 1860, with a few cattle and seventy-five horses loaded with goods for a mercantile.[39] Higgins had come to the Missoula Valley in the

---

[37]Albert J. Partoll, "Frank L. Warden, Pioneer Merchant, 1830–1887," *Pacific Northwest Quarterly* 40, no. 3 (1949): 190.

[38]Ibid.

[39]Ibid., 191.

mid-1850s as a wagon master for Gov. Isaac Stevens's survey party in the Bitterroot and Missoula valleys in 1853–1854. Later, Higgins thought the Missoula Valley would become a major trading center after the advance of railroads into the territory, and he secured a permit to open a store. Shortly afterward, he partnered with Frank Worden to open a store in Missoula clerked by Frank Woody. As the business struggled for lack of merchandise, on March 1, 1861, Worden traveled from Fort Benton to St. Louis, arriving on April 23, where he bought $9,000 worth of goods, only to see them lost when the steamboat *Chippewa* caught fire and exploded on the Missouri River at the mouth of the Poplar River near Fort Union, June 23 on the trip to Fort Benton. The goods were insured, but Worden decided to go to Portland, Oregon, secure a loan, and stock his business in Hell Gate with 20,000 pounds of goods valued at $7,000 rather than risk his business with steamboat transportation on the Missouri River.[40] Nothing more is known about the fate of the store in Missoula.

As more gold discoveries were made in the area, travel along the Mullan Road increased to the point that Worden and Higgins opened another store at Gold Creek, about 60 miles east of Hell Gate on June 29, 1862. Run by their clerk James Stuart (elder brother of Granville Stuart), the store did a brisk business with miners and emigrants on a cash basis, mostly in gold, which they banked at Hell Gate. The business continued to prosper, and in early June 1864, Worden and Higgins entered into partnership with James Stuart and Walter B. Dance as Dance, Stuart, & Co., with stores in Deer Lodge and Virginia City.[41]

Frank Worden soon became a very powerful political figure in Hell Gate, and in January 1864, when Idaho Territory was established, "Councilman" Worden nearly had the town named after him as "Wordensville." Worden strenuously objected, and the town retained the name Hell Gate as the county seat of Missoula County.[42] During the winter of 1864–1865, Worden and Higgins set about a large business venture involving construction of a combination sawmill and gristmill at the future site of Missoula. In the fall of 1865, the mill went into operation, powered by water from Rattlesnake Creek. The grist mill contained two sets of 3 1/2 foot burrs that had been shipped from St. Louis as part of their $30,000 investment. Operated by partner and millwright David Pattee, it turned out flour as well as lumber to meet the ravenously growing needs of the

[40]Ibid.
[41]Ibid.
[42]Ibid., 193.

community. The Missoula Mills were some of the first in the region, being preceded only by the mills at St. Mary's Mission at Stevensville, Montana, in the 1840s and mills at St. Ignatius Mission in the Flathead Valley in the 1850s. Very soon thereafter, Worden and Higgins moved their store from "Hell's Gate Village" closer to the mills, thus becoming the first permanent residents and founders of Missoula Mills, which eventually became known as Missoula.[43] On November 29, 1866, Frank Worden married fourteen-year-old Lucretia Miller at Frenchtown in western Montana, by whom he had seven children. Lucretia was the daughter of Henry W. Miller, who with his wife, Carolina Bitner Miller, and two daughters came to Frenchtown in 1862 from Somerset County, Pennsylvania.[44]

The Worden and Higgins businesses continued to grow, and in 1872, they changed their name to Worden & Co. The following year, on April 5, 1873, they joined company with S. T. Hauser, Hiram Knowles, and J. D. Welsh and founded the National Bank of Missoula with capital stock of $50,000. Higgins was president of the bank, which was located in the new brick store of Worden & Co.[45] All was going well, but they were not without competition. Soon another store was opened by Richard Eddy, Edward Bonner, and David Welsh, known as Bonner & Welsh. This firm was so successful that it took a new partner in 1876 named Andrew Hammond, a salesman from New Brunswick, Canada, and the company became Eddy, Hammond, & Co. A year later, Eddy, Hammond, & Co. opened a new store that eventually evolved into the Missoula Mercantile Co. in 1885 as one of the most powerful business entities in western Montana.

Although Frank Worden was the patron saint of Hell Gate, the original name of the community was derived from geographic features named by early French Canadian trappers. The large round valley at the mouth of the canyon was called "Hell's Gate Ronde," and the river flowing into it through the nearby canyon the "Hell Gate River." By 1883, Worden turned his interest to laying out streets and developing city water works in the town. Francis Lyman Worden died there on February 5, 1887.[46]

Francis Worden and his father-in-law, Henry W. Miller, are prominently mentioned in an 1867 *Harper's New Monthly Magazine* with regard to their farms and the establishment of Missoula Mills:

Mr. Spencer of Tennessee also rejoices in an excellent farm; and so does Mr. Miller, of Pennsylvania; and so do some fifty gentlemen of French

[43]Ibid., 194.
[44]Ibid., 195.
[45]Ibid.
[46]Ibid., 196.

FIGURE 12. Captain John J. Roe.
From L. U. Reavis, *St. Louis:*
the Future Great City of the World.
Biographical Edition (St. Louis: Gray,
Baker & Co., 1875), 160.

extraction, from whom the settlement is named, who have from twenty to one hundred acres under the choicest and ripest cultivation. There is, moreover, a fine saw-mill here, the property of Messrs. Campbell and Van Dorn; another in the immediate neighborhood belonging to Mr. Simms; and a third down at Missoula Mills, which turns out flour as well as lumber, owned by Messrs. Worden and Higgins, which cost $30,000, and the machinery which came all the way from St. Louis.

And here . . . at this very stately mill, the National Flag flying proudly and prosperously from it, with sixteen bushels of wheat flying from it every hour into the finest and snowiest dust, miles of lumber sliding out of it every month, and one of the handsomest stores close by, under the same proprietorship, doing a brisk and hearty business all the year round.[47]

CAPTAIN JOHN J. ROE AND CAPTAIN JOHN G. COPELIN

Ink stenciling on a few of the crates and boxes recovered from the steamboat *Bertrand* indicate that J. J. Roe had goods on the boat trans-shipped from the East Coast. That having been said, it is known that Roe was a commission merchant and did business with the houses of J. Eager & Co. of New York (probably with Patterson, Eager, & Co. of Boston) and D. W. C. Sanford of New Orleans. He had warehouse and merchandising interests in St. Louis and Fort Benton and was part owner in the Montana and Idaho Transportation Co. that owned the steamboat *Bertrand.* More about John J. Roe is found in the next chapter.

[47]Thomas Francis Meagher, "A Ride Through Montana," *Harper's New Monthly Magazine* 35, no. 209 (October): 583–84.

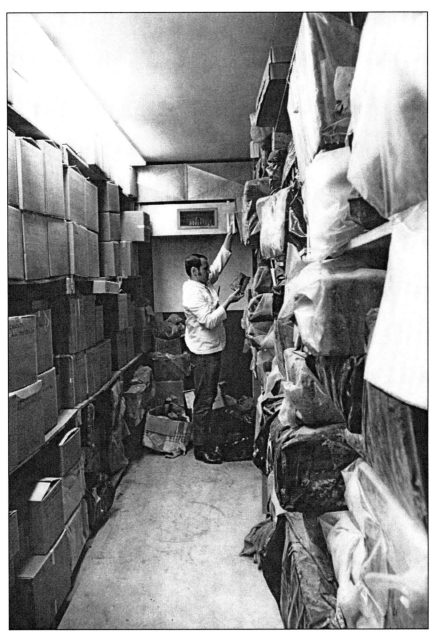

FIGURE 13. Supervisory Laboratory Technician Russell Rocheford
deciding what to tackle next.

VI

The Cargo

THE *BERTRAND*'S CARGO IS A TIME CAPSULE CONTAINING A wealth of mid-nineteenth-century Americana. It provides a glimpse of a former time and tells us much about commerce and the industrial nature of the country in 1865. Some items had only recently been invented and patented, while others had been in existence for some time, but both reveal the extent of American inventive genius and the extraordinary individuals who not only moved the nation through a rapid period of industrialization but also, by virtue of their success in business, contributed to the growth and prosperity of the West and the nation as a whole.

The growth in U.S. technology between 1800 and 1880 was truly astounding when one considers that it transformed the economy of the nation from a largely cottage industry prior to the Revolutionary War to an industrial giant by 1880. What took place in the industrialization of America was unlike anything that had happened before. In Europe, particularly in Britain, components of goods were manufactured one piece at a time in homes (cottages) or shops and then assembled into their final form in the last step in the chain of production in another place or shop; hence, the term "cottage industry." In post–Revolutionary War America, the development of industries capitalized on abundant river power to operate factories in which raw materials were taken in the back door and finished goods came out the front door to be wholesaled, consigned, and shipped to market. Nearly all manufacturing processes came to be managed under one roof. As industrialization shifted from water power to steam power, more inventions focused on industrial efficiency, and the output of American goods grew exponentially. Increased efficiency and productivity rapidly transformed villages and towns into major cities and commercial hubs. When gold was discovered in California in 1848, the first flush of easterners rushed out there hoping to make their fortunes. Transportation across the continent from towns on the upper Mississippi and upper Missouri Rivers was limited mostly to wagons, and only a few transportation companies offered passage around Cape Horn to San Francisco from the eastern seaboard. The age of steamboating on the Upper Missouri had not begun, and it would be several more years before gold strikes in Montana and Idaho would usher in another rush to the west, giving impetus to eastern businesses and entrepreneurs to provide safe, relatively fast, cheap transportation to Montana Territory and the opportunity to profit by supplying the needs of miners and settlers in their burgeoning new communities. Steamboat transportation on the Upper Missouri to Fort Benton grew rapidly in response, and by 1865, large numbers of steamboats were seen at the wharfs in St. Louis, being loaded with tools, mining supplies, groceries, dry goods, farm machinery, and building materials for transport to the Montana frontier. It is fortuitous in one respect that steamboat *Bertrand* did not reach her destination at Fort Benton, because its cargo represents a time capsule of trade and commerce in 1865 that was frozen in time and from which we have learned so much.

Although there is a good deal more to be learned about the *Bertrand*'s cargo and about the manufacturers and technologies represented, what follows is, for lack of a better term, a catalogue of the artifacts annotated to indicate what is known about them and the people who made them. It is not complete, but represents a starting point for future researchers to pursue. For ease of comparison with Jerome Petsche's characterization of the cargo, the itemization that follows is organized into the main categories of materials he established, namely: (1) foodstuffs, liquor, and patent medicines; (2) textiles, wearing apparel, and sewing supplies; (3) household goods; (4) mining supplies; (5) agricultural supplies; (6) hardware, tools, and building supplies; and (8) miscellaneous.[1] To this list has been added (7) powder and munitions.

Fifty percent of the cargo was badly crushed and had to be removed from its containers/cases during excavation. Up to 40 percent of the case stenciling was illegible. It is not known how many items were so badly deteriorated that they were not saved for further study, but field notes and accession records indicate there were some.

[1]Petsche, *The Steamboat* Bertrand, 48–49.

FOODSTUFFS, LIQUOR, AND PATENT MEDICINES

Although only a few of these items could be traced to manufacturers, there is a wide variety of food products in the cargo, including:

almonds	mackerel
allspice	meat (dried, salted, and pickled
butter	mutton, beef and pork)
candy	mustard (dried and bottled)
catsup	oysters
cherries (brandied and canned)	peaches (brandied and canned)
chowchow	peanuts
cod fish	pecans
cod liver oil	pepper
coffee	pepper sauce
flour	pickles (including pickled
ginger	vegetables)
gooseberries	pineapple
grain	prunes
grapes	saleratus (baking powder)
hazelnuts	sardines
honey	soda crackers
horseradish	spices
jelly and preserves	strawberries
lard	sugar
lemon extract	syrup
lemon sugar	tamarinds
lemon syrup	tomatoes
lemonade (concentrate)	"Worcestershire Sauce"
"London Club Sauce"	yeast

There are fewer varieties of liquor and patent medicines, although some like "Hostetter's Bitters" number in the hundreds of bottles. Liquor and patent medicines include ale, bitters, "Bourbon Whiskey Cocktail," "Brandy Cocktail," schnapps, wine, champagne, and possibly some gin.

Bottled Fruits and Vegetables

Cherries (Brandied)

There is one case of twelve aqua-colored, transparent bottles some of which contained brandied cherries and others that contained brandied sliced peaches. The bottles are tall and cylindrical, with slightly depressed

FIGURE 14. Brandied cherries bottle.
FIGURE 15. Jelly bottle.

bases bearing nub-like pontil scars. Blown in three-piece molds, they exhibit rounded shoulders, long necks, and large orifices finished with slanting collars. They are closed with corks and bear no label fragments. The bottles are 10 15/16 inches tall, 2 15/16 inches in diameter at the bases, and have outside neck diameters of 1 7/16 inches. There is no description of the crate in which they were packed.

Jellies

There are at least four twenty-four-bottle cases of assorted jelly bottles with label fragments, and thirty-two additional bottles that are morphologically the same but bear no identification as to their contents. Bottles from the four cases indicate they contained a variety of jellies, including apple, current, quince, raspberry, and strawberry. The variety of jelly is printed on a four-color paper label with the words "PREPARED / NUMSEN, CARROLL & CO / BALTIMORE" in red ink.

These half-pint wide-mouth bottles are 5 inches tall and have cylindrical bodies, slightly flared necks, and thin rolled collars. The bases are dished and have pontil scars. They are 1 13/16 inches in diameter at the base, and the outside diameters of the necks are 1 1/2 inches. The shipping cases are marked "2 DOZ 1/2 PINTS / ASSORTED / JELLY." The consignee was "VIVIAN & SIMPSON / VIRGINIA CITY, M.T. / ST. LOUIS."

FIGURE 16. Brandied peaches and foil seal. Bottled by W. K. Lewis Bros.
FIGURE 17. Pickled vegetables bottle.

Peaches (Brandied)

Records indicate there is one twelve-bottle case of brandied peaches in
the cargo. The free-blown bottles containing about one quart of fruit
have rounded basal edges and high kick-ups. The cylindrical bodies taper
to wide mouths with rounded flaring lips. Each is closed or stoppered
with a large cork that is covered with a stamped foil seal reading, "W. K.
LEWIS & BROTHERS / BOSTON / PRESERVES / PICKLES /
SEAL'D MEATS &c." Tri-colored paper labels from the bottles bear
similar lettering (see Figure 15).

Pickles and Honey

There are twenty-five lots of pickles and white clover honey packed in
aqua-colored cathedral bottles of various sizes. These are packed twenty-
four bottles to the case, and the cases are stenciled thus:

GERKINS FROM GITHENS, REXAMER & CO., DELAWARE
MARKET, DELAWARE RIVER PICKLE & PRESERVE WORKS
ASSORTED PICKLES from GITHENS, REXAMER & CO.
DELAWARE MARKET, DELAWARE RIVER PICKLE &
PRESERVE WORKS.

The somewhat ornate bottles are of the Gothic cathedral style with arch-shaped side panels.[2] Blown in two-piece molds, the bottles were made in 10-, 14-, and 20-ounce sizes. The bases are flat except for dish-shaped depressions at the centers. Sixteen bottles have bases exhibiting a raised "C" and an upside-down and backwards "R." In all probability, the latter were made by Curling, Ringwalt & Co., in Pittsburgh, Pennsylvania, before 1863.

Nine twenty-four-bottle cases of white clover honey are part of this lot. All are of the ten-ounce size and are classified as subtype 9d in Switzer's *Bertrand* bottle book.[3] They were closed/stoppered with corks and coal tar and bore lettered foil seals, none of which survived in any condition to provide information. Black-on-white labels on some of the side panels read:

WHITE / CLOVER / HONEY – ALDRICH / & / YERKES /
N___/____.

Box stenciling indicates the honey was consigned to "VIVIAN & SIMPSON / VIRGINIA CITY, M.T." and reads:

2 DOZ. NET / WHITE CLOVER HONEY / FROM / ALDRICH &
YERKES, PHILADELPHIA

There are fifty whole bottles and fragments of yet another bottle subtype (9f) containing white clover honey. Some had lettered foil seals reading:

W. K. LEWIS & BROTHERS / PRESERVES / PICKLES /
SEAL'd MEATS &c / BOSTON[4]

Case marks read:

TWO DOZEN PINTS / HONEY / FROM / W. K. LEWIS &
BROTHERS, BOSTON / STUART & Co. / DEER LODGE, M.T.
1 DOZEN PINTS / HONEY / FROM / W. K. LEWIS &
BROTHERS / BOSTON / WORDEN & CO. / HELL GATE

[2]Switzer, *The* Bertrand *Bottles*, 54–55.
[3]Ibid.
[4]Ibid., 56.

FIGURE 18. Honey and pickle bottles.

Tamarinds

Consigned to "Worden and Co., Hell Gate," the tamarinds are packed in twelve pint (7 3/16 inches tall) bottles to the case. One case was recovered with contents intact. The bottles are of the Gothic pickle style and are similar to others in the cargo except in capacity and the lack of raised columns flanking the cathedral panels. They also exhibit a cross motif at the top of the panel arch. The bottles were closed/stoppered with corks and coal tar and bore lettered foil seals reading:

W. K. LEWIS & BROTHERS / PRESERVES / PICKLES / SEAL'D MEATS / &c. / BOSTON.

Manufacturers stenciling reads:

ONE DOZ. PINTS TAMARINDS FROM W. K. LEWIS & BROS., BOSTON

Not much is known of the early history of W. K. Lewis & Brothers. William K. Lewis was in partnership with Charles Haskell in the pickle business as early as 1837–1838 at 56 Broad Street, Boston. This relationship must have changed because by 1846, William Lewis was in another partnership with one or more of his brothers at the same address. The company of W. K. Lewis & Brothers apparently began in 1849, and by 1853, it was well established in Boston, specializing in packing pickles. From 1856 through 1858, the company was owned by W. K. (William) Lewis, Charles P. Lewis, Edwin J. Lewis, and George F. Lewis. In 1854, fire damaged the factory, but the firm recovered, and by 1861, it had a large government contract for $30,000; within three years, it had become a large business in Boston and had increased its product line to include tamarinds, honey, lobster, and other canned foods.

In ill health, Charles P. Lewis retired on October 16, 1865, and by November, A. C. Comey was added as partner and manager. On September 1, 1866, Horace H. Lewis joined the firm, and nine years later, W. K. Lewis withdrew from the company. George F. Lewis died on November 2, 1883, at which time it was rumored that the worth of the company had increased to $250,000.[5]

Bottled Sauces and Oils

Catsup

Of the four lots of bottled catsup in the cargo, three were directly identified as coming from Underwood & Co. Records indicate there were at least five cases, each containing either twelve or twenty-four bottles. Only sixty bottles survived, none with legible labels. The first case was marked:

[R] & CO. / UNDERWOOD & CO. / TOMATOE / KETSUP /
67 BROAD STREET / ST. LOUIS, MO.

The tall aqua-colored transparent glass bottles were made in two-piece hinged molds. The twenty-two whole bottles each contain twenty-three ounces of catsup and are stoppered with tapered corks.

The second two cases are marked:

WM. UNDERWOOD & CO. / ST. LOUIS / N.T. CO."; "1 DOZ /
TOMATO KETCHUP / WILLIAM UNDERWOOD & CO. / 67
BROAD ST. BOSTON.

The consignee was "J. MURPHY." The two-piece mold-blown bottles exhibited eight evenly spaced plain facets on their sides and were sealed with tapered corks. There are twenty whole bottles remaining from the two cases, each bottle containing about 22 ounces of catsup.

The third lot, consisting of two cases, had only twenty-two complete bottles of catsup. These aqua-colored plain clear glass bottles are

---

[5]The brief history of W. K. Lewis & Brothers was found with the help of Robert W. Lovett of the Baker Library, Harvard University Graduate School of Business Administration. In correspondence with the author dated September 13, 1974, Lovette relates that he found records of the firm in the Boston Dun & Bradstreet volumes. Volume 71, page 150, summarizes the business up to 1864. Notes of Charles Lewis's health and the addition of Horace H. Lewis to the firm are contained on page 20HH. Volume 75, page 294, states that the company packed lobsters, notes the death of George F. Lewis, and the worth of the firm in 1883. Correspondence is in the possession of the author.

FIGURE 19. Underwood & Co. "Tomatoe Ketsup" bottle.

somewhat smaller than the others, and hold about 9 1/2 ounces. Case stenciling indicates that this catsup was bottled in New York, but the product manufacturer is unknown.

A good deal is known about William James Underwood. In the early 1800s, he apprenticed in pickling and preserving in London and came to New Orleans in 1817. Not finding the city a good place to start a cannery, he walked all the way to Boston in 1821, where he established a cannery. There he produced bottled fruits and berries for export to South America and the Orient. For a time, Americans did not like canned and bottled foods, and those who did limited themselves to canned foods from Europe even though they were more expensive than domestic products.[6]

By 1828, Underwood was canning milk for export to South America. In the 1830s, he added pie fruits to his line, and in a few years when Americans got over the misconception that tomatoes were poisonous, Underwood imported tomato plants from England and raised them for canning. Each can contained the "substance" of two dozen tomatoes cooked by slow heat to evaporate the watery particles after the seeds and skins were strained out. Underwood's genius and knack for marketing made for a successful company that is still doing business in the United States and abroad.[7]

Numerous wholesalers listed in the Underwood records did business in St. Louis, but only Charles S. Kintzing is identified as a wholesaler in the *Bertrand* cargo. Charles S. Kintzing did business from 54 N. Levee

[6]Biographical information about William Underwood and the history of the William Underwood Company was derived primarily from a series of letters between the author and George C. Seybolt, president of the Wm. Underwood Co., Watertown, Massachusetts, and P. W. Bishop, curator, Division of Manufacturing, Smithsonian Institution, Washington, D.C., between June 17, 1971, and September 9, 1974. This was supplemented with fragments of information from other sources, some of which was published in Switzer, *The* Bertrand *Bottles*, 78. Correspondence is in possession of the author.

[7]Correspondence with P. W. Bishop, and Switzer, *The* Bertrand *Bottles*, 78.

at the corner of Vine in St. Louis between 1865 and 1866 and at 700–702 N. 2nd between 1867 and 1868. As a matter of interest, most of the others are listed below:

S. M. Chartney & Co.	Scott Perkins
W. L. Ewing & Co.	Spaunhorst and Hackman
McKay & Foot	Longly & Co.
Dameron White & Co.	Thomas Morrison
Moody Michel & Co.	Dawson & Keech
E. A. January & Co.	Francis Lepere
Lepere & Richards	O'Neil & Co.
J. F. Lauman & Co.	Cabot & Sinter
W. O. Gilson	John L. Conroy & Brothers
Strode Rubey	Henry Meier
H. Gilhause	John Shields
M. Lamoreux	Foot, Miles & Co.
W. J. Alkire	E. A. Biggers
Jos. Hamil	Mitchell & Fellow
D. Nicholson	J. R. Windover & Co.
McElhany & Fellow	

According to P. W. Bishop, Curator, Division of Manufacturing, National Museum of American History, Smithsonian Institution, most of the glass bottles purchased by Underwood came from the Ellenville Glass Co.[8] Cans were made on the premises, the tinplate being purchased from Boston suppliers and/or importers. Founded by a group of stockholders, some of whom were connected with the Willington Glass Co., the Ellenville Glass Co. began operations in 1836 in Ulster County, New York. By 1865, the firm's assets were $368,000 in materials and finished products.[9] The next year, 1866, the company changed ownership, and its name changed to Ellenville Glass Works. Some *Bertrand* bottles are marked Ellenville Glass Works, so the new molds had to have been in use by 1864 or else the changes in company ownership took place two years earlier than previously believed.[10]

The fourth lot is actually a mixed lot of eighteen crates of morphologically similar bottles except that some are embossed "WESTERN SPICE MILLS" and others are embossed "ST. LOUIS SPICE

---

[8]P. W. Bishop, curator, Division of Manufacturing, Smithsonian Institution, Washington, D.C., correspondence dated December 14, 1971. In possession of the author.

[9]Toulouse, *Bottle Makers and Their Marks* (New York: Thomas Nelson, Inc., 1971), 79.

[10]Ibid.

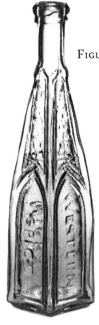

FIGURE 20. Western Spice Mills tomato catsup bottle.

MILLS." Both are morphologically classed as pepper sauce bottles, but the former held tomato catsup.

There are three dozen of the former, and one dozen bottles were shipped to the crate. The pale greenish glass square bodied bottles stand 8 3/4 inches to 8 7/8 inches tall, and the letter paneled bodies taper from the shoulders to long cylindrical necks that terminate with two rounded, tooled collars. Three of the four sides of the bottles are embossed vertically with one word each inside a gothic style window: WESTERN / SPICE / MILLS. The fourth side is plain and probably bore a paper label. The bases are flat, with dish-shaped depressions, and the bases are 1 7/8 inches square with beveled edges.

Case stencils reveal the bottles contained catsup and read:

_____OTHIC / _____B_____
THIS SIDE UP WITH CARE
WESTERN / ____E MILLS / TOMATO / CATSUP /
ST. LOUIS, MO. / ___ * ___ / ONE DOZEN
ONE DOZEN / WESTERN / SPICE MILLS / TOMATOE /
CATSUP / ST. LOUIS, MO.
GLASS / THIS SIDE UP WITH CARE / GOTHIC / _____ /
Ft. BENTON

The remaining seventy-nine bottles held pepper sauce.

Horseradish

There are sixty-five whole horseradish bottles and enough fragments to indicate there may have been three cases of two dozen bottles each. Blown in two-piece molds, these stubby seven ounce bottles have cylindrical bodies, short cylindrical necks with "blow over finishes," and are stoppered with corks. The bases of these aqua-colored transparent bottles are flat and measure 2 1/8 inches in diameter. They stand 4 7/8

FIGURE 21. St. Louis Spice Mills pepper sauce bottle.
FIGURE 22. Superior Bird Pepper Sauce bottle.

inches tall and have outside neck diameters of 1 5/16 inches. Shipping cases are marked:

2 DOZ. / HORSE _____ ";
"_____ / HORSERADISH /
_____ /
2603 SIXTH STREET /
CIN., O.

Pepper Sauce
The seventy-nine bottles from the lot embossed "ST. LOUIS SPICE MILLS" contained pepper sauce. They are about the same height, but the bases are slightly smaller at 1 1/8 inches square.

The crates are stenciled:

WARRANTED EXTRA / PEPPER SAUCE / FOR FAMILY USE
_____ / Ft. BENTON
WARRANTED EXTRA / PEPPER SAUCE / FOR FAMILY USE
_____ / Ft. Benton / THIS SIDE UP WITH CARE

Several other cases of gothic paneled pepper sauce bottles were found in the *Bertrand* hold. They were packed twenty-four bottles to a case, and the contents all appeared to be red pepper sauces. Judging from the case stencils, there was only one manufacturer, even though the cases show some minor differences:

SUPERIOR / RED BIRD / PEPPER / SAUCE / NEW YORK /
TO: J. MURPHY / Ft. BENTON / VIA C. S. K., ST. LOUIS, MO.
B_____ / PEPPER / SAUCE / NEW YORK STUART & CO. /
DEER LODGE

SUPERIOR / BIRD / PEPPER / SAUCE / NEW YORK
J. MURPHY / FT. BENTON, M.T. / VIA C. S. K . / ST. LOUIS, MO.

The Superior Red Bird Pepper Sauce bottles are represented by ninety-five whole bottles and one broken specimen. They are small, 6 1/2-ounce aqua-colored glass blown-in-mold bottles with hexagonal bodies and shoulders, exhibiting six inset gothic cathedral panels or windows on the sides. The shoulders bear smaller, plain, five-sided panels/windows. Each shoulder panel has a five-sided window with a tri-lobbed depressed element at the center. Above each shoulder window is single floral motif. The bottles are 8 3/4 inches tall, the necks terminate in rounded tooled collars with beveled rims, and the bases of the bottles are slightly dished. It is probable that these artifacts were wholesaled by C. S. K. (Charles S. Kintzing) of St. Louis.

Although William Underwood apparently did not pack these bottles, the Wm. Underwood Co.'s records for the cost of bottling pints of pepper sauce in 1865 were:

5 Doz Fluted Pts.	.62 1/2	3.13
4 Galls Pepper Sauce	.80c	3.20
3 1/2 Galls Vinegar	.45c	1.57
5 Hours Girl Labor	.7	.35
1/2 Hours Man "		.13
5% Breakage & Washing		.27
Corks labels _____	.20c	1.00
5 Boxes	.16	.80
		10.45
Add the 15%		1.56
		12.01
1 Doz Packed cost $2.40		
Stamps	12	2.52
1 Doz Packed cost $1.87 March 11[11]		

[11]After I corresponded with V. A. Fulmer, Wm. Underwood Company on August 22, 1974, he sent me copies of microfilm records of the Underwood business for the period of the 1860s. The first set of records for William Underwood & Company, "Records of Packs and Costs of Various Items 1855–1866," were copied from a brown leather account book and contain numerous pages regarding the cost of packing various food products. Page 116 for 1866 lists the costs for bottling pepper sauce. The second set of records were copied from a black leather account book dated 1867–1888 and contain many more details about the costs of preserving vegetables, pickles, sauces, meats, etc. In addition, there are extra sheets dating from 1896 showing receipts for can making costs and instructions for packing clam chowder written by R. B. Burnham, Jr., 1909–1910.

FIGURE 23. Parker Bros. London Club Sauce bottle.
FIGURE 24. Olive oil bottle.

Parker Brothers London Club Sauce

There were perhaps eight dozen six-ounce Parker Bros. London Club Sauce bottles in the *Bertrand* cargo, of which seventy-six whole bottles and fragments of others survive in the collection. The bottles are of pale aqua glass and were blown in two-piece molds. They have cylindrical bodies, long tapering necks, and rounded shoulders. The necks are finished with rounded, tooled, ring-type collars with slightly flared extensions at the bases of the collars. They are embossed vertically on one side to read "PARKER BROS.," and the shoulders are embossed horizontally with "LONDON CLUB SAUCE." They are stoppered with corks and stand 7 1/8 inches tall. Basal diameters are 2 inches, and the outside diameters of the necks are 1 3/8 inches.

The crates bear wood-burned labels reading:

LONDON CLUB SAUCE / A. J. PARKER / N. Y. /
SOLE AGENT FOR THE / U. S.
1 DOZ. / PARKER BROS. / LONDON CLUB SAUCE / J.
PARKER / N. Y. / AGENT FOR THE / U.S.
ST. LOUIS, MO. / SPAULDINGS / _____ / EXPRESS /
PMLM _____ C / _____ B _____ O _____

Olive Oil

French olive oil was shipped in slender 8-ounce bottles with cylindrical bodies that taper to a smaller diameter from the shoulders to the bases, which have deep kick-ups. The necks terminate in flat-lipped collars.

The bottles were shipped twenty-four to a case and were marked:

POSSELFIL HUIL D'OLIVE,
MARSEILLE, SURFINE.

Mustard

FIGURE 25. Mustard bottles.

There are forty-five whole barrel-shaped clear glass French mustard bottles and fragments in the collection. These bottles are unusual not only because of their shape, but also because they represent an imported product at a time when American-made mustards were available. Blown in two-piece molds, the small bottles have four bands at the tops and bottoms, and the bases are slightly dished. They are stoppered with corks covered with lettered foil seals reading "___IN_____ERLE BORDELAISE EUR BOUSCAT / CHOCOLATERIE BORDELAISE MOUTARDE DE BOR-DEAUX." The bottles measure 4 1/2 inches tall, 2 1/4 inches in diameter at the base, and 1 3/4 inches in outside diameter at the lip.

Mustard has a long history as a condiment going back at least to Roman times, when the ground seed was combined with young wine must to form a paste called *mustum ardens* or "burning must." By the tenth century, mustard was being produced all over Europe, and by 1634, mustard was deemed so important in France that only the men from Dijon were allowed to make it. In 1729, an English woman named Clements from Durham reduced mustard seeds to an easy-to-use powder that became widely distributed. By 1814, Jeremiah Coleman of Norwich blended milled black and yellow mustard seeds with wheat flour and began marketing the powder all over the world as "Coleman's Mustard." By 1876, Robert Timothy French began preparing American white mustard seed with turmeric as a mild paste, and "French's Prepared Mustard" soon became very popular.

Worcestershire Sauce

FIGURE 26. E. F. Dixie Worcester Sauce bottle and stopper.

Glass stoppers in these bottles bore raised glass lettering reading, "LEA & PERRINS." The bottles are plain aqua-colored glass with cylindrical bodies, and were packed one dozen to the case, which was marked:

WORCESTERSHIRE SAUCE FROM
E. F. DIXIE, N. Y.

There are thirty-three whole bottles and a few fragments. They are embossed vertically on the sides "E. F. DIXIE" and "WORCESTER SAUCE" horizontally on the shoulders. The bottles were blown in two-piece molds and are 8 1/2 inches tall, with a capacity of about 12 1/3 ounces. Basal depressions are moderately deep and bear rough scars. They are finished with triple-ring collars bearing flat lips. The interiors of the necks are tapered to accommodate three-piece mold blown stoppers.

Lea & Perrins Worcestershire Sauce is named after two English chemists, John Lea and William Perrins, who were employed by Lord Marcus Sandys, ex-governor of Bengal. Lord Sandys brought the sauce recipe back from India and ordered Lea and Perrins to brew up a large batch of the sauce. A few weeks after they did so, Sandys returned to pick up the sauce and found it tasted "filthy and was nothing like how it should be," and left in disgust.[12]

A few months later, the chemists rediscovered the brew at the back of their store and sampled it again. The nasty-tasting anchovy liquor had fermented and matured into a spicy condiment. After purchasing the recipe from Lord Sandys, they launched the best known sauce in England in 1838. Originally called "worcester sauce," it was mispronounced worldwide as "worcestershire sauce." In the United Kingdom,

[12]"Welcome to Worcester—Worcester Sauce," http://www.birminghamuk.com/worcester_sauce.htm.

Worcestershire is pronounced "woost-ur-shire," and worcestershire sauce is referred to as "Worcester Sauce," pronounced "woos-tah."[13]

Research concerning Lea & Perrins Worcestershire Sauce indicates that it was introduced to the United States from Worcester, England, after 1838, probably in the early 1840s. It was imported by John Duncan's Sons, New York, until 1877 when the Duncans bought the rights to produce the sauce in their own plant in New York. According to Mr. Ransom H. Duncan, Technical Director of Lea & Perrins, Inc., the sauce bottles found on the steamboat *Bertrand* may be an early patent infringement. The bottles are embossed vertically on their sides "E. F. DIXIE CO." and exhibit three-piece mold-blown tapered glass stoppers with cork sleeves embossed "LEA & PERRINS." In any event, the bottles probably were not produced in England, because imported bottles were embossed on the bases "A B C Co." prior to 1880 and "J/D/S" after 1880. The bottles bore orange-on-black paper front labels and black-on-white back labels that were over-wrapped with parchment paper, tied at the neck with red string, and sealed with red sealing wax bearing the words "LEA & PERRINS WORCESTERSHIRE SAUCE."[14]

Candy

Although candy was not a major item in frontier stores until after the Civil War, simple stick candies were available for some time in eastern cities like Philadelphia, where by 1816, twenty confectioners were making and selling simple candies. Fancy confections such as bonbons, candied fruits, pralines, and hard sugar plums were imported. By 1850, candy sales in the United States were estimated at only $3 million, but by 1864, they had grown to $5.5 million. Demand grew during the Civil War, and by 1870, the American candy industry grossed about $16 million annually.[15]

Records vary as to how many cases of candy were recovered from the *Bertrand*, but it is estimated there were between eighteen and twenty-seven cases, indicating that western miners had a sweet tooth now and then. "EXTRASTICK" and "LONGSTICK CANDY," some identified as possibly horehound, was packed in 24 and 50-pound cases. One lot of assorted candy may have been shipped in a barrel. Cases were variously marked:

[13]Ibid.

[14]Switzer, *The* Bertrand *Bottles*, 79.

[15]Lawrence A. Johnson, *Over The Counter and on the Shelf—Country Storekeeping in America 1620–1920* (New York: Bonanza Books, 1961), 98–99.

NEW MAPLE SUGAR CANDY / WESTERN CANDY
FACTORY / NETT 20
S. H. BAILEY / WHOLESALE CONFECTIONERS / ST.
LOUIS / Horehound
FANCY CANDY FROM S.H. BAILEY / WHOLESALE
CONFECTIONERS / ST. LOUIS
50 LBS. LONGSTICK CANDY FROM S.H. BAILEY /
WHOLESALE CONFECTIONERS / ST. LOUIS [side]
U. S. S. (THIS SIDE UP) / VIRGINIA CITY (WITH CARE) /
MONTANA (top)

Note: This box had a tin liner and measured 20 inches by 12 inches by 10 inches.

F. WALTER / WHOLESALE CONFECTIONER / CORNER
MURTLE & 3RD St. / St. Louis / EXTRASTICK CANDY / Net 24
lbs.
50 LBS / EXTRA / ASSORTED CANDY / S. H. BAILEY / 71
THIRD ST. / ST. LOUIS [end] FULL WITH / KEEP DRY [side]
THIS SIDE UP / WITH CARE / V & S / VIRGINIA CITY / MT
[side]
ASSORTED CANDY / FRANK BUNKER / ST. LOUIS [box
fragments]
VIVIAN & SIMPSON / VIRGINIA CITY MT. / . . . ROS / 29
LBS.
MIXED / CANDY [may have been a barrel]

Samuel Bailey is listed in an 1860 St. Louis City directory as "Samuel H. Bailey, Manufacturer of Confectionary, 74 N. 3d, r, 120 Olive."[16] Another directory in 1863 listed Samuel Bailey as "S. H. BAILEY (Samuel H.) Confectioners Wholesale, 74 N. 3rd St.," but no other information is available on the firm other than the fact that it was listed at the same address one year later.[17] The Campbell & Richardson directory for 1863 also shows "'F. WALTER' as "FREDERICK WALTER, candy mfg., 3rd & Myrtle."[18]

The candy was destined for three consignees, Stuart and Co., Deer Lodge; Vivian and Simpson, Virginia City; and, G. P. Dorris, Virginia City.

[16]R. V. Kennedy, *Kennedy's 1860 St. Louis City Directory: Including, Also, a Business Mirror, Appendix, Co-Partnership Directory, &c., &c.* (St. Louis: R. V. Kennedy & Co., 1860), dirctory surname, initial "B," www.rollanet.org/-bdoerr/1860CyDir/1860CD.htm

[17]Edwards, *St. Louis Directory 1864–1865* (St. Louis: Richard Edwards), 599.

[18]R. A. Campbell and Richardson, *Campbell & Richardson's St. Louis Business Directory 1863* (St. Louis, Mo.: R. A. Campbell Publishers, 1863).

FIGURE 27. Sugar of Lemons lemon oil vial and paper label fragment.

Sugar of Lemons (Lemonade)

There are indications that there were six cases of "Sugar of Lemons" cans from Boston in the cargo. The cans contained a powdered form of lemonade that was mixed with lemon oil and water to make five quarts, as indicated on paper label fragments. Each can contained the powder and one small 1/2 ounce vial of lemon oil. There are 131 whole vials and numerous fragments of others. Field information on the cases is lacking.

The lemon oil vials were blown in two-piece molds and finished with patent lips at the orifices. They are 2 1/8 inches tall, with cylindrical bodies, flat bases, and conical necks. The bases of these colorless vials are 7/8 inches in diameter, and the necks are 5/8 inches in outside diameter.

Canned Fruits

The evolution of the tinned can, although sporadic, was uniquely American. Until the 1860s, cans were mostly handmade. Sheets of tinned iron were cut to size and rolled to the required shape, with the edges overlapped and soldered. Disks cut for the ends had the edges turned down so that the disks fit into the bodies to which they were soldered. The top disk usually had a circular aperture that was closed with a soldered patch after the contents of the cans had been cooked.

Tinned cans in America appear to have followed two lines of development: one with lapped seams, and one with locked seams and double seams. The first mechanization in production of the lapped-seam can began in 1847 with the invention of the drop-press to form flanges on the end disks. Slightly later, presses were invented to cut out the end disks and filler holes and flange them. At the end of the Civil War, machines were patented that completely automated production of lapped-seam cans.

Locked-seam cans seem to have developed more slowly, but appeared earlier than lapped-seam cans. Joseph Rhodes of Wakefield, England, is said to have invented the first machines to form locked seams about 1824. By 1870, these machines were in common use on both continents, the only addition being the recommended use of "caoutchouc" (natural or "India rubber") in the recesses of the tops and bottoms of cans containing liquids. The final step toward "open-top" cans came after 1896–1897, when the Ams patent was granted for applying a rubber composition to can ends to make perfect joints. Experiments with lacquer and enamel coatings on the insides of cans to prevent oxidizing of the tin and iron by fruit and vegetable acids began in France sometime in 1868. Perhaps the most significant figure in the development of canned foods was Nicholas Francois Appert, a Paris confectioner, brewer, distiller, and wholesale caterer, and his son Raymond Chevallier Appert, both of whom used autoclaves for sterilization and cooking between 1809 and 1855. Appert is credited with winning a prize of 12,000 francs from the French government for developing the first successful method of preserving foods so that decomposition would be reduced and the characteristics of fresh food were retained. Appert developed the process between 1804 and 1809, and his efforts were published in 1810.

Using Appert's method, an Englishman named Peter Durand obtained a patent in 1810 to preserve perishable foods in sterilized glass, tin, and other materials. The method did not come into common use until after 1820, when tin containers that were less susceptible to leakage were made. In this country, the "canning" industry was started by Ezra Daggett and Thomas Kinsett in New York in 1819 when they began packing oysters. After that, most packers packed seafood as their primary products. Fruits, vegetables, and preserves were incidental items.

Kinsett was a prominent figure in the New England canning industry and is sometimes credited with producing the first canned products with wide distribution in the country. By 1844, Kinsett was canning oysters on a large scale in Baltimore. Demand for canned foods increased gradually after 1844 up to the Civil War, when large volumes of preserved foods were necessary to feed troops. After the war, soldiers returning home demanded more of these new products, and the industry became a major economic engine on the eastern seaboard. During the 1850s and 1860s, Massachusetts canners hired tinsmiths to make cans for between one and four cents each. By 1857, inflation began to appear in the cost of making one pound soup cans:

1 Box 1c coke tinplate 675 bodies	$10.25
1/2 Box 1c Charcoal tinplate	8.50
24 lbs. Solder @ .33	7.92
7 Hours labor press work girl	.50
Tinsmith labor per hundred	4.05
One can costs 5 1/2 cents	$36.47[19]

Cherries

There is evidence of at least one case of canned cherries. These may have been wholesaled by "N. SCHAEFFER & CO. / ST. LOUIS, MO." Unfortunately, the metal cans in which cherries were processed badly deteriorated. Laboratory records show they were packed two dozen cans per case, and they were consigned to J. Murphy at Fort Benton.

Gooseberries

Packed in two pound cans at two dozen to the case, these too were badly deteriorated. One case and six cans survived. When some of cans were opened, the berries were green and sweet smelling, but once exposed to air, they turned black. The consignee was Stuart and Co., Deer Lodge, and other case stenciling reads "GOOSEBERRIES, WM. H. THOMAS / OYSTERS & FRUITS, BALIMORE." The cans appear to have been painted blue, and according to the laboratory notes, they measure 4 3/8 inches tall by 3 5/8 inches in diameter. The surviving case measures 16 1/2 inches by 12 3/4 inches by 10 5/8 inches. Field information indicates the consignee was Stuart & Co., Deer Lodge.

[19]William Underwood & Company, "Records of Packs and Costs of Various Items 1855–1866," 68.

Peaches

There were eighteen cases of canned peaches, packed in lots of twenty-four two-pound cans to the case. The cans were badly deteriorated, but the case stenciling identified three producers:

2 DOZ. 2 LB. CANS Fresh Peaches from BRINKLEY & REEVES, BALTIMORE
Wm. UNDERWOOD & CO., ST. LOUIS
JOHN L. SILVER & BROS. Oysters & Fruits, BALTIMORE, MD.
Nos. 13 & 15 Water St.

Consignees were Stuart and Co., Deer Lodge; J. Murphy, Ft. Benton; and M. Kingman, Virginia City.

Inasmuch as there were several cases provided by different packers, the case lots will be described below:

Case No. 1

This case measures 18 3/4 inches by 11 inches by 4 3/4 inches and fifteen cans from the contents survived. Stenciling that remains reads:

to / STUART & CO. / DEER LODGE [lid]
DOZ 2 LB. CANS / FRESH / PEACHES / FROM /
UNDERWOOD & CO.

The cans measure 4 7/8 inches tall by 4 3/16 inches in diameter. Field information is:

WM UNDERWOOD & CO / PEACHES / ST. LOUIS / N T. Co.

Case No. 2

The information for this lot is somewhat consistent, and the stenciling seems to match the field information. Field information reads: "24 cans, 3 lb. cans of Peaches / To: J. MURPHY / NUMSEN, CARROLL / & CO. / BALTIMORE MD," and continues, "FRESH / PEACHES / ... NU MSEN CAR ... OLL / & CO. / 18 Light / ... T. / BALTIMORE." The case measured 13 1/4 inches by 8 3/4 inches, and was stenciled:

2 DOZ. 3 LB. ... N ... / FRESH / PEACHES / NUMSEN,
CARR ... / & CO. / ... IGHT ...

Cases Nos. 3–5
There is no complete description of these cases, but they were similar to those described above.

Pie Fruits
Two dozen No. 10 size cans were packed to a case. Case stencils indicate only one producer:

2 DOZ CANS FRESH PIE FRUIT FROM RHODES &
WILLIAMS,
FRUITS & PICKLE WAREHOUSE, 107 So. WATER ST.
PHILADELPHIA.

The consignees were Stuart and Co., Deer Lodge; J. Murphy, Ft. Benton; and Worden and Co., Hell Gate. The cans were badly deteriorated, and no discernible labels were evident.

Pineapple
Pineapple was a prized commodity on the frontier. The *Bertrand* carried several cases of pineapple packed two dozen cans to the case. Containers were badly corroded, but the case stencils indicate they were:

FROM ALDRICH & YERKES, PHILADELPHIA 2 doz. 2 lb.
CANS FRESH PINEAPPLE

At least some of the fruit was consigned to J. Murphy, Ft. Benton.

Strawberries
There were nine cases of strawberries. Each case contained two dozen 2-pound cans, and there were two identifiable canners:

NUMSEN, CARROLL & CO., 18 Light St., BALTIMORE
2 doz. cans FRESH STRWBERRIES FROM FITHIAN &
POGUE, BRIDGETON, N. J.

Tomatoes
Several cases of canned tomatoes packed two dozen 2-pound cans to the case were recovered. Manufacturers stenciling reads:

2 DOZ CANS FRESH TOMATOES FROM BRINKLEY & REEVES, BALTIMORE.

Consignees were listed as Stuart & Co., Deer Lodge, and M. Kingman and Co., Virginia.

According to the William Underwood & Co.'s "Records of Packs and Costs of Various Items 1855–1866," the cost of fresh tomatoes in quart cans as of August 30, 1865 was:

85 Bushels Tomatoes @ 30	25.50
20 Girls peeling @ 50 cts day	10.00
9 Girls filling @ 66 2/3 " "	6.00
Labor of four men	7.00
Labor of soldering of	7.50
Fills 1700 cans cost per can 3 3/10 cts	56.00
2 doz 2 lb. cans @ 8 1/6 cts per can	1.96
Cost of tomatoes as above at 3 3/10 per can	.79
Cost of box including cans & gov't tax	.28
Cost of labels	.12
Labor cleaning, labeling etc.	.05
	3.20
Add 15%	.48
	3.68

1 doz tomatoes cost $1.84
The actual yield of tomatoes was 106 cans per
5 bushels the above figured at 100 cans
For 5 bushels[20]

Coffee

Essence of Coffee

There is one case of ninety-six cans of essence of coffee in the cargo. The cans were packed on their sides in three or four rows of eighteen cans each. The cans are 2 3/4 inches tall and 2 1/4 inches in diameter. Remains of yellowish-brown paper labels completely covered the sides of the cans. These read:

GEORGE HUMMEL'S / IMPROVED PREMIUM / ESSENCE OF

---

[20]William Underwood & Company "Records of Packs and Costs of Various Items 1855–1866," August 30, 1865, 130.

COFFEE / Manufactured by P. C. Thomson, / No. 248 North Third St., Philada. / _____ / One package of this Essence will go as far as four pounds of coffee, and coffee made by it will preserve perfectly the real taste of coffee, and will have a more delicate and fine flavor, a finer color, and will be much more wholesome than pure coffee; it will be clear without requiring anything to clarify it. _____ / $5,000 Reward will be given if any Essence of Coffee is as pure as this.

At each side of the label is a vertical certificate with a decorative border bearing the lettering "5000" in large type. Opposite the label side of the can are two vertical panels giving directions for use, one in English and the other in German. The directions are fragmentary, but a few words of the English text can be read:

> DIRECTIONS. / To make half a gallon of . . . middl . . . / strong coffee, take one tablespoonful / ground coffee . . . / of this F . . . and boil the coffee as . . . / . . . more or less quantity of coffee . . . / . . . st be made after this proportion . . . / for very strong coffee, takesome . . . / of this Essence.

(Note: Some of the German text was badly transcribed in the laboratory and is not included here). The shipping crate measures 15 1/8 inches by 12 3/8 inches by 8 1/4 inches.

Coarse-Ground Coffee

One 25-pound box of coarse-ground coffee was recovered that measured 17 5/8 inches by 17 5/8 inches by 12 inches. The case apparently was filled with one pound square packages packed four deep and five across. The reverse label impression inside the lid reads:

> ONE POUND / COMBINATION / COFFEE / ADABTIO / AND / GEORO

The coffee was consigned to Worden and Co.

Java Coffee

Thirty-five cans (no cases survived) of Java Coffee survived from the wreckage. These are tall cylindrical cans with overlapping lids that are painted blue, green, gold, or red with a black-bordered oval and lettering reading:

JAVA COFFEE / GEO. R. DIXON & Co. / COFFEEE SPICE & MUSTARD / MILLS / SYCAMORE BET 1ˢᵗ & 7ᵗʰ & s Sts. / CINCINNATI, O.

The lids may also have been decorated, but nothing of this survived. Field information indicates there was 32 pounds of coffee packed in 32-ounce tins, packed two dozen cans per case. Case markings indicate the consignee was G. P. Doris, Virginia City.

Dried Fruits

Currants

Stems and skins are all that remain of two 25-pound boxes of currents. The one surviving box measures 10 3/4 inches by 10 3/4 inches by 10 3/16 inches and was made of 3/4 inch pine. Black stenciling reads:

CURRENTS / PIMENTO / . . .

In all probability these are not currents, but allspice, as indicated by the term "pimento." However, in the muddy context of cargo removal and identification, this was a small error.

Nuts

As indicated earlier, there was evidence of almonds and pecans in barrels, chestnuts and hazelnuts in boxes, and peanuts in burlap bags and boxes. Only one packer was identified: ADOLFO PRIES & CO., NEW YORK PEANUTS. The consignees were G. P. Dorris, Virginia City; Vivian and Simpson, Virginia City; and Worden and Co., Hell Gate.

Almonds

Field records and other notes indicate that most, if not all, of the almonds were shipped in barrels, and there may have been as many as four barrels. These were consigned to G. P. Dorris, Virginia City, and Vivian and Simpson, Virginia City. Field information indicates only samples of the nuts were saved. Three barrels and one box/crate are noted in field notes:

Almonds & Barrel:
Vivian & Simpson / Virginia City / MT.

Barrel of almonds. Burned into barrel stave WORD . . . / HELL GATE
Barrel of almonds (on hull):—now discarded
Box Broken / FORT BENTON (no other label)

Hazelnuts

Only the field notes for three lots of hazelnuts remain:

Hazelnuts ca. 20,016:
. . . By . . . (on barrel end)
VIVIAN & SIMPSON / VIRGINIA / CITY, MT. (on barrel end)
Hazelnuts (ca. 100 lbs.) and barrel:
SR . . . O / ST. LOUIS MO. / . . . RE . . . RS / . . . . P.O

Peanuts

Field notes list seven boxes and three bags of peanuts, all of which were discarded except for two small lots of nuts. Pieces of two boxes saved are described:

LAYERS [end]
Adolfo P . . . & Co. / . . . nge [end]
L / . . . inse [side]
Adolfo Pries & Co / . . . alaga [lid]

Two large cans are catalogued as nuts, but no other information was found regarding the contents, other than field notes which shed no light on the origin of the peanuts.

Pecans

Two barrels and one crate are indicated in the field information. Container markings are:

Items lost, Pecans in a barrel / FROM / Grant & . . . [end]
Barrel Pecans – sample reboxed
Seeds, cloves, pecans / G. P. Doris
33 lbs. / Sundries

Flour and Baking Supplies

Flour

An undetermined number of broken 50-pound flour barrels were taken from the *Bertrand*'s hold. From the lettered fragments, it was determined that the flour originated at Clarksville, Missouri:

CALUMET MILL / E. B. CARROLL & CO. / 196 / CHOICE /
XXX /
FLOUR / CLARKSVILLE, MO.
TO: M. KINGMAN & Co. / VIRGINIA CITY / FLOUR

"Choice XXX Flour" was milled by E. B. Carroll & Co. at Calumet Mill in Clarksville, Missouri, and was consigned to M. Kingman and Co., Virginia City.

Located in Calumet Township, Pike County, Missouri, the Calumet Mill actually had its beginnings in 1856 as the Imperial Mill Co., founded by E. B. Carroll, B. P. Clifford, and John O. Roberts. Apparently their holding was short-lived, and they sold out to G. W. Wells & Co. The mill was in operation in 1857 and was run by Wells & Co. until 1862, when it was repurchased by E. B. Carroll & Co., in whose ownership it remained until 1876. It appears that the mill operated as the Calumet Mill between 1857 and 1876. By 1876, E. B. Carroll retired from the firm and its name was changed to Clifford, Roberts & Co. Business was successfully conducted until 1880 when Capt. Clifford died.[21]

At St. Louis, receipts for flour during the period of 1864–1865 show that flour production increased from 815,144 barrels to 1,161,038 barrels between 1864 and 1865, or a difference of 315,894 barrels. In August 1865, "Choice Family" brands sold as high as $13 per hundred pounds and remained at this price through the end of the year. By December, the stock on hand in St. Louis was about 80,000 barrels.[22] Thus, while there was an abundance of flour on the market, insufficient quantities were being shipped to the frontier to meet the growing demand. Shortages drove frontier prices beyond acceptable limits.

---

[21]*Missouri, an Encyclopedia of Useful Information and a Compendium of Actual Facts, It Contains a Condensed History of the State of Missouri and Its Chief City—St. Louis, The Constitution of the United States and of Missouri and an Abstract of the Laws Of Missouri; A Reliable History of Pike County: Its Legal, Political, Official, and War History; a Sketch of the Bench and Law; the Medical Fraternity; the Old Ladies of Pike County; Schools; Churches; the Press; Biographical Sketches, Incidents, Etc. Etc.—Illustrated,* Vol. 20 (Des Moines: Mills & Company, 1883), 534–35.

[22]Morgan, *Annual Statement of the Trade and Commerce of St. Louis for the Year 1865,* 19–20.

Black Pepper

It is uncertain how many black pepper bottles that were recovered, and none of the author's notes indicate how many bottles were packed per case. They are of the mustard or horseradish type and are about 6 3/4 inches tall, with eight sides, sloping shoulders, and slightly tapered necks finished with asymmetrical rolled collars. They are pale aqua colored glass and were blown in two-piece molds exhibiting flat bases. The bottles held about 8 1/4 ounces of ground black pepper and were stoppered with corks. Originally they bore two-sided black and white paper labels with an eagle and a vertically stripped union shield. The case labeling reads:

ALLEN MILLS / BLACK PEPPER / NEW YORK / B. S. GRANT & C) / WHOLESALE / GROCER / NO. 5317 _____ / ST. LOUIS, MO.

Baking Powder (Saleratus)

Two lots of glass bottles (twenty-four bottles) of B. T. Babbit's Pure Saleratus, shipped from Washington Street in New York, were taken from the *Bertrand*'s cargo hold. These were consigned to J. Murphy/ Ft. Benton.

The *New York City Directory* for the years 1864–1865 lists this manufacturer as "Babbit, Benj. T., Saleratus, potash and soap. 64-5-6-7-8, 70-2-4 Washington – office 70 & 72 h 49 W. 34th."[23]

As a young man in Utica, New York, Benjamin T. Babbit was employed as a wheelwright. He was intensely interested in science and thought of himself as an inventor. During his early days, he patented a fire engine, and during the Civil War he patented an ordinance projector and a mold for casting gun barrels.

Establishing a factory in Oneida County, New York, in 1843, he turned out potash, saleratus, and baking powder in addition to soap and soap powder. Saleratus was a leavening agent for baking and was made by injecting pearl ash into the fumes of fermenting molasses.

Babbitt was among the first soap manufacturers to put soap in a wrapper and sell it as "bar soap." Prior to 1851, soap was sold in bulk loaves to grocers, who cut and weighed slices in the same manner as they sold cheese. Owing to the fact that people did not take readily to packaged

---

[23]The New York City Directory information is contained in personal correspondence with James. J. Heslin, Director, The New York Historical Society, dated June 2, 1971. The correspondence is in possession of the author.

soap, Babbit packaged his goods in wrappers that had trade-in value for premiums, and demand for his product quickly rose.[24] Notwithstanding this imaginative idea, he packaged saleratus in one-pound paper containers and wholesaled them sixty to a case. He also put potash in tin cans with directions for use on the labels. Babbitt's marketing efforts were also unusual for the time because he placed colorful advertisements on theater curtains. In more recent times, the B. T. Babbit Co. is perhaps better known as the maker of BAB-O scouring powder.[25]

Yeast Powder

FIGURE 28. Preston & Merrill's Infallible Yeast cans.

Not much can be said of the several lots of yeast powder. The powder was packed 200 cans to a barrel. Barrels were marked:

INFALLIBLE YEAST POWDER

The small cans have overlapping lids and full paper labels highlighting "Preston & Merrills INFALLIBLE YEAST POWDER" on the fronts. This was a "Trade Mark Patented Apr. 29, -63," as indicated by vertical printed panels on the sides of the cans. The labels also bear the admonition not to buy the product if the paper seal over the cover was defective. These were consigned to Stuart and Co., Deer Lodge, and G. P. Dorris, Virginia City.

---

[24]Johnson, *Over the Counter and on the Shelf*, 101–102.
[25]Ibid.

Cream of Tartar

The remains of three cases that once contained cream of tartar were found in the cargo. In one case, the contents appear to show that the one-quarter-pound packages inside were paper-wrapped. One of the other two cases seems to have contained tins of this ingredient. The cases measure 12 1/2 inches by 11 1/2 inches by 7 1/4 inches, and 22 1/4 inches by 16 inches by 15 1/2 inches, respectively, and both are bound by split stick bands, perhaps painted black. The case bearing paper-wrapped cream tartar reads:

PURE GROUND / CREAM TARTAR / 20 LBS / 1/4 POUND PAPERS

Consignees for these cases were:

WORDEN & Co. / HELL GATE
VIVIAN & SIMPSON / VIRGINIA CITY, M.T.

Butter

There were perhaps as many as five kegs of butter in the cargo, one of which was stenciled "BERTRAND STORES." This keg is approximately 50 pounds in size, is banded with half-round withes of wood, and is said to have had the words "C. Puppy" wood burned in one end. The side is stenciled:

BUTTER / DOREMUS, N.Y.

Field notes also indicate that one barrel 20 inches tall and 12 inches in diameter was marked "Beech Wood / BERTRAND STORES / 100# / BUTTER," but the staves could not be located after excavation.

Lard

Viewed from today's perspective, it is difficult to imagine why so much lard was being shipped to the frontier. Evidence shows there may have been fifteen to seventeen cans of lard weighing 25 to 30 pounds each in the cargo. The tall rectangular metal cans have square tops and bottoms. No other information on lard cans is available save for the author's notes:

Rectangular vertical sides; square base & top. Edge of flat top extends slightly beyond body on all 4 sides and its raw edge is folded under. Top has one seam across middle, interrupted by a circular piece soldered at center. Base has one seam across middle, running transverse to seam on top and edge of base is turned up around body with raw edges folded under. Each side has vertical seam along midline and each side has one long edge bent around a corner of body with raw edge folded under. The folded edge of base and corners of body each form a raised band on exterior while seams along midlines of all pieces are flat on exterior & form bands on the interior.

Fresh Fruits

Grapes

Both field and laboratory information is sketchy, but indicates there may have been as many as four cases of white grapes. The one surviving box measures 20 1/2 inches by 10 inches by 9 1/2 inches and apparently is marked on the ends:

ANTONIO DECAMPOS
MALAGA

The side was marked:

SARIAS

Two other boxes apparently were marked on the ends:

BLANCA / LAYERS . . . / LAYERS

Field notes indicate the grapes were wholesaled by:

ADOLPH PRIES & CO. / KHILINGA (?)

Meat, Fish, and Oysters

Meat

There was some dried/salted beef packed in small barrels and several kegs containing beef and pork bones. Petsche noted some meat and tallow with no evidence of containers.[26] One lot of meat examined by the Armed Forces Institute of Pathology (Orthopedic and Soft Tissues Branch) was identified as mutton.[27]

---

[26]Petsche, *The Steamboat* Bertrand, 55.

[27]G. Migaki, DVM, Chief, Comparative Pathology Branch, American Registry of Pathology, Armed Forces Institute of Pathology, Washington, D.C., correspondence dated June 22, 1972. In possession of the author.

John J. Roe, who was part owner of the *Bertrand* and owner of a pork-packing house in St. Louis, ran this ad in the *Daily Missouri Democrat* in 1865:

CHOICE SUGAR CURED HAMS,
BREAKFAST BACON
DRIED BEEF
CLEAR SIDES
BACON SHOULDERS,
EXTRA MESS BEEF,
Mess Pork & Prime Mess Pork,
For Sale By
John J. Roe & CO.
At Pork House, Convent Street, between Second and Third[28]

Inasmuch as Roe's address in the advertisement is the same as his pork-packing house, it is not unrealistic to assume that some of the meat in barrels recovered from the *Bertrand* originated from this source.

The following article concerning the packing plant appeared in the *St. Louis Post-Dispatch*, on August 23, 1954:

Packing Plant Of The Civil War Era Being Torn Down
A building nearly 100 years old, used as a meat processing plant during the Civil War, is being razed by the American Wrecking Co. for the Viking freight Co. and the Second Convent Corp. The property will be used for future Viking expansion.

Dr. William Swekowsky, St. Louis dentist whose hobby is the study of old buildings, traced the history of the building at Third and Convent streets, which was the John J. Roe Pork Packing House and which changed hands several times.

With a tremendous volume of business during the Civil War era, it was the largest meat packing house in St. Louis, Swekowsky said, and was bordered by the original "Pigsfoot Alley" when pig's feet were thrown away instead of sold.

In those days, the hobbyist recalled, when there was no refrigeration, butchers would take orders door to door, and kill an animal only when they had it sold in advance.[29]

[28]*Daily Missouri Democrat* (St. Louis), 1865.
[29]*St. Louis Post-Dispatch*, August 23, 1954.

Sardines

Among the canned goods from the cargo are flat, tinned steel cans bearing embossed brass labels reading "CHAIGNEAU FILS / BREVETE [SARDINES a L'HUILE] S. D. G. / Sarles D'OLONNE 9LIEU DE PECHE." The morphology of the cans is nearly identical to modern sardine cans. The crate stencil reads:

DOITES 100 1/4 PLUMETTE ET HOSTIN BREVETES / SARDINES A L'HUILE / ETEL Par. Auray MORBIHAN.

According to Alan Revel, Agricultural Attaché, Ambassade de France aux Etats-Unis, Services de l'Expansion Economique in Washington, D.C., his inquiry with the Chambre Syndical Nationale des Industries de La Conserve indicates that the firm of Chaigneau & Fils specialized in Bordeaux wines during the 1860s. Revel states that it was common at the end of the nineteenth century for negotiators and shippers of Bordeaux, France, and other large harbors to deal in canned products bearing their names on sheet copper plates welded to the white metal cans. Shipments of wines to the United States frequently contained other food products.[30] Sardines were first packed at Nantes, France, in 1834, and by 1860, there was a good market for them in the United States. Efforts to establish sardine canning in this country did not begin until 1871 using young menhaden. It was not until 1877 that Julius Wolff successfully canned sardines at Eastport, Maine. Therefore, it is not surprising that the canned sardines in the *Bertrand*'s cargo were French imports.

Codfish

Two cases of codfish were recovered. The flesh had disintegrated, but the arrangement of the bones indicates the fishes were packed whole, neatly laid one on top of one another. The wooden cases, which measured 25 3/4 inches by 16 3/4 inches by 10 7/8 inches, are marked:

(100 LBS) / LARGE / BAY FUNDY / COD FISH / (. . . NO. . .) &
Co. / FISH DEALERS / BOSTON
100 LBS / LARGE / BAY FUNDY / COD FISH / F. SNOW &
CO. / FISH DEALERS

---

[30]Alan Revel, Agricultural Attaché, Ambassade de France aux Etats-Unis, Services de l'Expansion Economique in Washington, D.C., correspondence dated July 18, 1972. In possession of the author.

It is likely that both the codfish and mackerel shipped on the *Bertrand* were of the salted variety that was readily available from saltries in Boston. Salting fish was a large industry there, having become established well before the Revolutionary War. As a matter of history, the British tried desperately for many years to prevent American fish salters from fishing in the waters off the East Coast, causing open conflicts with the crown and serving as a contributing factor to war. After the war, in about 1783, American fishermen secured favorable fishing rights by treaty, and the United States' fish-curing industry prospered, nearly eliminating the salt cod markets in southern Europe and the Mediterranean controlled by the British and the Scandinavians.

Codfish and mackerel must have been in great demand during the 1860s, especially on the western frontier. *The Missouri Republican* for March 16, 1865, carried this notation:

[BY MAIL]
FIRST IN BOSTON ON THE 10TH
The market for codfish is steady and firm, with a good demand for export, and stocks reduced and in few hands. Sales of Grand Bank at $8.50 @ 9, and Bay Fundy $9.50 @ 10 for large; small $8 @ 8.50 per qtl. Hake are scarce, and selling at $5.50 loose, and $6.25 @ 6.40 packed. Mackrel $6.25 @ 6.50 packed. Pollack $5 @ 5.50 per qtl. Mackrel are very firm with a good demand. . . .[31]

Mackerel

Records show that there were four kegs of mackerel in the cargo. The kegs measure approximately 9 to 10 inches tall and 11 1/4 to 12 9/16 inches in diameter, each with a 7/8 inch bung hole and plug. Field information is more complete than laboratory records as it pertains to the source of the fish. Field notes read:

Small barrel of mackerel:
G. O. Parker / DEP. INS. / No. 1 / MACKEREL / BOSTON. / VIRGINIA CITY

Keg marks on three kegs read:

G. O. PARKER / DEP. INS. / No. 1 / MACKEREL / BOSTON MASS.

[31]*The Missouri Republican*, March 16, 1865.

No. 2 / MACKEREL / D DU . . . / 186 . . . / DEP . . .
. . . OZ – ON – SS / ST. . . . on . . . / N.T. C
. . . oston MASS / No.1 / MACKEREL / D / . . . / R & CO. /
St. Louis.

One has to wonder if "R & CO." might not be attributed to a business owned by John J. Roe.

Oysters

Tinned oysters seem to have been a popular commodity judging by the numbers of cans recorded in field and laboratory notes. There appear to have been at least sixteen cases of oysters, all but three of which were packed by Numsen & Carroll, Baltimore, MD. Two cases apparently were packed by A. Field, Baltimore, Maryland, and the remaining case was packed by "W. A. WENTZ & CO.," also of Baltimore.

Case No. 1

All that remains of this case is the field excavation information indicating it was marked:

W. A. WENTZ & CO. / FRESH COVE OYSTER / BALTI-
MORE, Md.

Case No. 2

The case measures 23 1/2 inches by 15 3/4 inches by 5 3/8 inches and bears two case markings:

2 dozen–2 lb. cans / CHESAPEAKE OYSTERS / B. FORT
BENTON / NUMSEN and CARROLL / 18 STREET /
BALTIMORE
. . . Benton [lid]

The surviving cans measure 4 5/8 inches tall by 3 1/2 inches in diameter and bear dark blue paper labels with white highlights and black-edged gold lettering reading:

SALABURY / LAKE . . . OYS . . .

Case No. 3

Field information indicates that when it was recovered, it contained "2 doz. of 2 oz. cans of Oysters. To: Stuart and Co., Deer Lodge – LEWIS & BRO. / BOSTON." The case measures 15 5/8 inches by 11 7/8 inches by 10 7/16 inches, and the surviving stencil reads:

S . . . U . . . RT & CO . / . . . ER LODG . . . / . . . / . . . DOZ . . .
Can . . . ers / . . . L . . . W . . . S & BRO

Apparently this case of oysters was packed by W. K. Lewis Brothers at 93 Broad Street, Boston. This firm was formed in 1845 by George F., Charles P., and E. J. Lewis and was known primarily for wholesaling and retailing pickles. The business lasted until 1880.[32]

Cases Nos. 4 and 5

All cans from these two cases are missing and were probably discarded at some point. Field information reads:

Boxes of Oysters – Numsen, Carroll / & CO. / 18 LIGHT ST. / BALTIMORE / 2 DOZ. 2 LB. CANS SPICED / OYSTERS

The cases both measure 19 3/8 inches by 13 inches by 8 7/16 inches, and the remaining stencils read:

. . . S / . . . S . . . O . . . / . . . TE . . .
. . . DOZ. 2 lb. Can . . . / SPICED / OYST . . . / . . . / . . . / 18
LIG . . . / BALTIMORE

Case No. 6

Four cans are all that remain of the contents of this case, and there are no surviving case stencils. The case measures 23 5/8 inches by 15 3/4 inches by 5 9/16 inches, and the cans measure 4 5/8 inches tall and 3 5/8 inches in diameter. Laboratory notes about the label fragments are quoted below:

> Labels: Cans were first partially painted a deep blue-green on lid, base and about 1/2 inch onto body at both ends. All once had paper labels fitting on a plain, unpainted body. 2 cans still have paper. Labels were bordered by a thin black line, space and then 1/8 inch wide black line

---

[32]Daniel M. Lohnes, Acting Librarian, The Society for the Preservation of New England Antiquities, Boston, correspondence dated May 25, 1972. In possession of the author.

inside which "A. FIELD" in white letters repeats. At both ends of label were vertically printed directions and/or content description: "f re- / . . . ppers, / . . . in . . . / . . . han . . . / . . . to Oysters . . . / . . . or any others / . . . in . . . the . . . "Right side beginning with a pointing hand illustration "The . . " in between the 2 sections was horizontally printed the name of the product and an illustration of some type: "STEAMED / FRESH COVE OYSTERS." Because the can label was not stabilized during processing this deteriorated to ". . . ERS" and a black portion of illustration. The unprocessed can reads "STEAM . . . / . . . T . . . H C . . . "with a black, arching illustration portion.

Cases 7-15

Of the ten cases shown in the field notes, only seven were catalogued, and there are no surviving cans. Field notes read:

(24) cans / A. FIELD / STEAMED OYSTER PACK(s) /
09(?) W. LOMBARD ST. / BALTIMORE, MD. / TO VIVIAN
and
SIMPSON.
OYSTERS
(1) Stuart & Co. / DEER LODGE
(2) ( ) A. FIELD
STEAMED OYSTER PACKS
209 W. LOMBARD
(NEW YORK)

The cases vary slightly in size, but appear to have been 24 inches by 16 inches by 5 7/8 inches. Surviving case marks are fragmentary and incomprehensible. It is interesting that at least one case was marked with a Diamond R stencil, indicating that it belonged to, or was destined for, John Roe's Diamond "R" Transportation Co.

Liquor

Whiskey

Ironically, the excavation and salvage permit granted to Jessie Purcell and Sam Corbino for recovery of the *Bertrand* artifacts would, in part, have allowed them to recover a percentage of the value of all whiskey "in oaken casks." No whiskey in oaken casks was found; only two twelve-bottle cases of "BOURBON / WHISKEY / COCKTAIL" consigned to Worden &

Co. of Hell Gate were recovered. In all probability, these cases originated with Calvin A. Richards, a wholesaler of cigars and liquor in Boston.

According to a *New York Times* article for February 16, 1892, Richards had died of heart failure the previous day. He was a prominent businessman for more than thirty years, having started as a merchant at 91 Washington Street. At some point after the sinking of the *Bertrand*, he relinquished his interest in this business and concentrated his investments on "South End" real estate, which made him an extremely wealthy man. He was a common councilman in the city from 1858 to 1861 and served on the Aldermanic Board in 1862. In 1877, he became president of the Metropolitan Street Railway Co., where he served until all the railroads in the city were consolidated.[33]

The bottles in this lot are twenty-five ounces in capacity and are 11 to 11 15/16 inches tall, with necks measuring 1 inch in outside diameter and 3 1/8 inches in basal diameter. Another case of "whiskey" bottles of the same morphology was consigned to G. P. Dorris of Virginia City, but the contents could not be identified generically as whiskey. These bottles are about 11 inches tall with 1 inch diameter necks and 2 13/16 inch diameter bases. The capacity is 21 1/2 ounces, leading to the belief that the contents were not the same as those of the first group of whiskey cocktail bottles. There are three distinctly different neck finishes represented in the two groups of bottles, each produced by a different glass house. Based on basal embossing, the bottle manufacturers are Willington Glass Works (marked WILLINGTON GLASS WORKS; the "N" in "Willington" and the "Ss" in "glass" are backwards); Ellenville Glass Works (marked ELLENVILLE GLASS WORKS), and McCully & Co. (marked W. McCULLY & Co. / PITTSBURGH PA).

The Willington Glass Co. of West Willington, Connecticut, was a well-known glass house during this period. Willington Glass Co. was organized in 1815 by Frederick Rose, Roderick Rose, Stephen Brigham, Jr., Elisha Brigham, Spafford Brigham, John Turner, Ebinezer Root, and Abiel Johnson, Jr. Not much is known of the company after that except that it probably changed management and ownership. During the period between 1815 and 1830, others associated with the company were R. B. Chamberlin, Elisha Johnson, and Dea Turner. About 1830, Gilbert Turner & Co. apparently acquired some interest in the Willington Glass Works and operated it until April 19, 1847, when it was sold to another concern

---

[33] *The New York Times*, February 16, 1892.

and continued under that management until 1872–1873, when it closed. Gilbert Turner & Co. owned glass works at Coventry, Connecticut, and several of its principals were Harvey Merrick, Elisha Carpenter, William Still, William Shaffer, Frank Shaffer, and James McFarlane.

It was a successful company and several of the partners became closely associated with other Connecticut glass houses and with the Ellenville Glass Co. in New York. By 1849–1850, the company had expanded its facilities and was planning to open three more glass production works. At its height, Willington Glass employed a dozen glass blowers and produced whiskey flasks, demijohns, cathedral pickle bottles, whiskey bottles, ink wells, medicine bottles, rolling pins, and glass telephone insulators. Like so many other businesses of the period, the glass works was severely affected by the bank panic of 1857 and struggled through two depressions and the Civil War before failing in 1872–1873.[34]

The Ellenville Glass Works was established in 1836 by a group of men who were stockholders in the Willington Glass Works and the Coventry Glass Works in Connecticut. Situated on a canal between the Delaware and Hudson Rivers in Ulster County, New York, in 1865 the Ellenville Glass Co.'s assets totaled $368,000 in materials and glass inventory. According to the McKearins, ownership of company changed in 1866 and it was renamed the Ellenville Glass Works.31 Inasmuch as the *Bertrand*'s whiskey bottles are embossed Ellenville Glass Works, the company must have put this mold into production in 1864–1865. The company changed hands in 1879 and became known as the Ellenville Glass Factory.[35] The history of William McCully & Co. is discussed further in the section on window glass.

Ale

These bottles are classified in seven subtypes in Type I of Class I in the *Bertrand*'s bottles book as being problematical as to their contents. About them, I wrote:

> Twelve imported wheel-thrown containers and 21 amber glass bottles remain a mystery. Two of the latter are embossed indicating they may

[34]An extensive account of the Willington Glass Company is found in Henry Hall White, "The Willington Glass Company," *Antiques Magazine* 40, no. 2 (1941): 99–100. See also George S. and Helen McKearin, *American Glass* (New York: Crown Publishers, Inc., 1971), 209.

[35]McKearin and McKearin, *American Glass*, 162, 181.

FIGURE 29. Ale (ginger beer) bottles.

have contained ale, but the remainder are plain and closely resemble modern beer bottles in shape. However, inasmuch as the brewing industry did not begin to pasteurize beer until 1873, it is unlikely the amber glass bottles contained the product. Unpasteurized beer has a very short shelf life and could not be exposed to alternating heat and cold, prolonged standing at room temperature, nor could it be shipped long distances. Ale, with its higher alcohol and undecomposed sugar content did not go stale or spoil quickly, and seems to have been a common beverage on the western frontier. No bottles recovered could definitely be identified as having contained beer or stout.[36]

Other researchers have examined these bottles, and some believe the contents may have been ginger beer. While there has been no decision either way as to the contents, the bottles are morphologically "ale" bottles and should be classified thus.

The shoulders and necks of the wheel-thrown bottles exhibit a pale to dark yellow ochre glaze, while the bodies are cream-colored and slightly glazed with clear glaze. Individual bottles are stamped on the bases with the letters J, O, W, S, L, H, D, M, C, or B.

Another twelve bottles of Amsterdam Ale were recovered from the cargo. The bottles are 10 1/2 inches tall, wheel-thrown, brown, unglazed stoneware, with a thick curved handle high up on the shoulder. Classified as Type 2 of Class I, these are closed with corks covered with imprinted seals reading "WYNAND FOCKINK / AMSTERDAM" around the

[36]Switzer, The Bertrand Bottles, 9.

FIGURE 30. Wynan Fockink
Amsterdam gin bottles.

FIGURE 31. Cooper & Conger
St. Louis Ale Brewery bottle.

borders. At the center of the seal is a nine-petal flower. Just below the shoulder, opposite the handle is an impressed oval seal of a lion wearing a crown, surrounded by abstract foliage. The lion is surrounded by the word "AMSTERDAMSCHE." Just above the basal ridge the bottles are imprinted with the word "AMSTERDAM."

Although the *Bertrand*'s bottles book says that these were "Amsterdam Ale," I have concluded that they probably contained gin or "Genever/Juniver," a strong malt liquor flavored with juniper berries. Ale had too short a shelf life to be imported to the United States.

The book also contains a description of six subtypes of amber glass bottles of Class I. Similar to brandy bottles in style, these were made in three-piece molds, and the cork stoppers are held in place with wire bails. They are 8 to 8 9/16 inches tall, and two of the subtypes had high basal kick-ups.

Type 4 of Class I in the Bertrand bottles book's classification includes brown glass ale bottles blown in two-piece molds with collar-and-ring brandy finishes and bulbous necks. Embossed letters on the bodies of the bottles read: "COOPER & CONGER / ST. LOUIS / ALE BREW-ERY." Unfortunately, nothing has been found about this company, and it is not known whether Cooper & Conger was one of the small breweries in St. Louis that was bought by Anheuser Busch or the Falstaff Brewing Co. during this period.

Schnapps

There was at least one case of two dozen pints of Udolpho Wolfe's Aromatic Schnapps in the cargo. The yellow-green colored bottles are 8 inches tall and 2 3/8 inches by 1 7/8 inches at the bases and have oil finishes. Three of the four sides are embossed vertically: one side reads "UDOLPHOWOLFE'S"; the opposite side reads "AROMATIC / SCHNAPPS"; and the third reads "SCHIEDAM." According to the field information, they were consigned to Stuart & Co. of Deer Lodge.

Located near Rotterdam, Holland, the town of Schiedam is known to have produced schnapps, but the appearance of the term on the sides of American-made bottles probably reflects a proprietary name, and not the place of origin of the contents. Udolpho Wolfe's (or Wolfe's) Aromatic Schnapps or medicated gin was bottled in New York and New Orleans and was marketed from the 1840s into the twentieth century. It was touted as a "superlative cordial" as well as an anti-dyspeptic.

FIGURE 32. Udolphowolf's Aromatic Schnapps bottles.

Although it was later bottled in foreign countries in bottles of domestic and foreign manufacture, the *Bertrand* examples were most likely blown in the United States between 1855 and 1865. Udolpho Wolfe's Aromatic Schnapps was touted in a very interesting journal, the *Water-Cure Journal*, in 1852:

> Wolfe's Schiedam Aromatic Schnapps, manufactured by the Proprietor exclusively at his factory, at Schiedam, in Holland, by a process peculiar to his own factory. It is Flavored and medicated, not by common harsh berry, but by the choice botanical variety of the aromatic Italian juniper berry, whose more various extract is distilled and rectified with its spirituous solvent, and thus becomes a concentrated tincture, of exquisite flavor and aroma, altogether transcendent in its cordial and medical properties, to any Holland Co., heretofore known.[37]

The article goes on at great length about the curative properties of the elixir, saying that it could cure rheumatism, gout, and gravel.

---

[37]"Holland Gin as a Medicinal," *The Water-Cure Journal and Herald of Reform. Devoted to Physiology, Andropathy, and the Laws of Life* 16, no. 5 (1852): 117–18.

Medicinals and Chemicals

Chemical Bottles

There are only four mold-blown clear aqua-colored chemical bottles in the collection, each of which is stoppered with a clear octagonal-topped pressed glass stopper blown in a two-piece mold. The bottles have capacities of twenty-eight ounces and cylindrical bodies with rounded shoulders and slightly dished bases. The cylindrical necks are finished with 1/4 inch wide collars with flat lips. The lower part of the cylindrical stopper is ground. The chemical bottles measure 9 1/4 inches tall, 3 3/4 inches in diameter at the base, and have an outside neck diameter of 1 1/2 inches. Because they were consigned to a mining supply company, it has been suggested that these contained acid for assaying ore from the Montana mines. The chemical bottles were packed in a crate with straw tow. Crate stenciling reads:

CHALLENGE CHEM / _____ U _____KEL & CO. /
ST. LOUIS, MO. / GLASS SIDE UP / G. P. DORRIS

Cod Liver Oil

Field notes indicate there were three cases of cod liver oil, packed two dozen sealed tinned steel cylindrical pails per case, or two dozen rectangular tins per case. The pails measure 4 7/8 inches high and 4 3/4 inches in diameter and have overlapping lids and wire bails. The rectangular cans measure 13 1/2 inches by 9 1/4 inches and are made with a bung at the top corner and two wire handles soldered to the side seams.

Although the oil was probably not produced in St. Louis, the wholesaler was identified as:

PETER E. BLOW / WHOLESALE DRUGGIST / 66 & 65 N. MAIN
ST / ST. LOUIS, MO.

The consignee was G. P. Dorris of Virginia City.

Blow advertised in the St. Louis *Missouri Republican* in 1865 on March 16, 1865:

**PETER E. BLOW
IMPORTER AND WHOLESALE DEALER
IN
DRUGS, MEDICINES, PAINTS, OILS,
DYES, PERFUMERIES, WINDOW GLASS
AND GLASSWARE**

I TAKE GREAT PLEASURE IN INFORMING the public that my recent purchases are now arriving, and that on the resumption of trade I will be prepared to meet them with a large and complete stock, embracing every article in my line, which I will offer at prices corresponding with the recent decline. Merchants visiting St. Louis are invited to an examination of any stock and prices. Having ample cases I feel satisfied that all examining same will be pleased with my stock and prices.

PETER E. BLOW
No. 66 and 68 Main Street[38]

While information about the location Blow's business is sketchy, he may have changed his business address late in 1864 or early in 1865. In 1863, Peter Blow was listed in a St. Louis business directory as "PETER E. BLOW, wholesale drug dealer, 66 & 68 Main."[39] Blow is listed at the same address in 1864.[40]

The Blow family is known for its entrepreneurial activities. Manufacturer, legislator, and diplomat, Henry Tyler Blow was born July 15, 1817, in Southampton County, Virginia, and died in Saratoga, New York, on September 11, 1875. It is not known exactly when Blow and his brother came to St. Louis, but some information suggests it may have been about 1830. According to the *Encyclopedia of the History of St. Louis*, Henry Blow completed his education at St. Louis University, from which he graduated with distinction. Thereafter, he read law, but abandoned the legal profession and turned his attention to commercial pursuits. At the age of nineteen, he became a partner with his brother-in-law, Joseph Charless, in the sale of drugs, paints, and oils, and later in the manufacture of castor oil, linseed oil, and white lead. In 1844, Blow and Charless dissolved their partnership, and Henry Blow's brother Peter retained the manufacturing side of the business. This ultimately developed into the Collier White Lead & Oil Co., of which he was president for many years.

Later, Henry Blow and his brother Peter partnered with Ferdinand Kennett in a large lead mining and smelting works in Newton County, Missouri. Upon Kennett's death, the Blow brothers bought his interest in the mines from the estate. After the Civil War, they and others organized the Granby Mining & Smelting Co., which they operated successfully for many years.[41]

---

[38]*Missouri Republican*, March 6, 1865.

[39]Campbell and Richardson, *Campbell & Richardson's St. Louis Business Directory, 1863*, ibid.

[40]*St. Louis Directory, 1864*, 602.

[41]Hyde and Conrad, *Encyclopedia of the History of St. Louis, A Compendium of History and Biography for Ready Reference*, 183.

FIGURE 33. William Brown's Highly Concentrated
Essence of Ginger bottle.

Essence of Ginger

There are 133 "French oval" clear glass medicine
bottles and numerous fragments. Most of the
five-ounce bottles bear fragments of labels which,
when reconstructed, read: "WM. BROWN'S /
HIGHLY / CONCENTRATED / ESSENCE
/ OF / GINGER / Dosage – One to two tea-
spoonsful in glass / full of water. / PREPARED
BY / D. B. SMITH / 228 Saratoga St. / Between
PINE AND PEARL / New York." The New
York City directory for 1865 does not list anyone
named D. B. Smith, and one has to wonder if
there was an error in the field notes. However, at
this time, the most famous druggist in America
was Daniel B. Smith of Philadelphia, about whom more will be said later.

The essence of ginger bottles were blown in two-piece molds and are
5 1/16 inches tall and measure 1 5/16 inches by 2 1/8 inches at the base.
They have rounded shoulders and short 3/4 inch cylindrical necks finished with applied prescription collars with flat or gently rounded lips.
The bottles are clear aqua-colored glass and have flat bases. The bottles
were originally stoppered with corks and bore paper labels printed in
blue, white, green, yellow, and pink.

It is suspected that the essence of ginger was prepared by a succes-
sor company to Daniel B. Smith's original business. Smith was born in
Philadelphia on July 1, 1792. Late in 1808, he began studying chemistry in
John Griscom's school in Burlington, and after completing his education
at the school, Smith apprenticed in the store of John Biddle to learn the
drug business. By 1818, Daniel Smith had completed his apprenticeship and
was taken into partnership under the firm name of Biddle & Smith. The
following year, Smith withdrew and started his own store in Philadelphia.
In 1828, he took on a partner named William Hodgson, Jr., under the name
of Smith & Hodgson. Hodgson was an excellent and experienced druggist
who received his pharmaceutical training in the well-known British firm
of John Bell & Co. of London. At this time, the Smith and Hodgson

store was the only supplier of chemicals and chemical apparatus especially adapted for schools, most of which were imported from Europe.[42]

About 1820, the Apprentice's Library was founded, and Smith began incessant lobbying for the establishment of a college of pharmacy. In March 1821, an institution was founded for the instruction of druggists called The College of Apothecaries, and D. B. Smith was elected secretary of the board of trustees. The next year, the institution became the Philadelphia College of Pharmacy, and in the ensuing years it published many of Smith's studies in its *American Journal of Pharmacy*. D. B. Smith migrated through a succession of chairs in the college, becoming president in 1829, a position he held until he resigned in 1854. He became a revered figure in American pharmacy and held positions in the Franklin Institute and the Academy of Natural Sciences. In 1829, he was elected as a member of the American Philosophical Society. By 1834, he moved to the Haverford School, where he became the chair of moral philosophy, English literature, and chemistry. In 1846, he resigned and returned to Philadelphia, where he gave utmost attention to his drug business.

In 1844, Charles Bullock apprenticed with Smith & Hodgson, and three years later he graduated from the Philadelphia College of Pharmacy. Bullock later associated with Edmund A. Crenshaw, a fellow graduate and employee of Smith & Hodgson. By 1849, they succeeded the firm of Smith & Hodgson, and Bullock began moving about Europe acquiring information about chemicals and apparatus that enabled the firm to develop a large and pertinent stock of imported chemicals and chemical apparatus. The company was so successful that it had to expand its footprint in 1868. The business continued until Crenshaw died in 1894, followed by Bullock in 1900. In 1901, George D. Feidt purchased the firm from Charles Bullock's estate and renamed it the George D. Feidt Co., which operated at least until 1912. Daniel B. Smith died in Philadelphia in 1883 at the age of ninety-two.[43]

It is not known what divestments were made by Daniel Smith of his business interests in pharmaceutical goods after 1849, but it is suspected those labeled as having been prepared by D. B. Smith of New York are somehow connected to him. Because of his prowess in the pharmaceutical trade, Daniel B. Smith is sometimes referred to as the founder of American pharmacy.

---

[42]Dennis B. Worthen, "Daniel B. Smith 1792–1883: Patriarch of American Pharmacy," *Journal of the American Pharmacists Association* 48, no. 6 (2008): 808–10, 812.

[43]Worthen, "Daniel B. Smith 1792–1883," 812.

FIGURE 34. Burnett Boston prescription bottle.

Prescription Bottles

Twenty small clear glass, letter-paneled Joseph Burnett Co. prescription or extract bottles were recovered from the *Bertrand*. The contents, if any, are unknown. The bottles are rectangular with flat bases and have cylindrical necks finished with flat-lipped prescription collar finishes. They are 4 inches tall, and the bodies measure 1 9/16 inches by 15/16 inches. The smallest paneled side is lettered "BURNETT," and the opposing side is lettered "BOSTON."

The Joseph Burnett Co. is well documented in historic pharmaceutical and grocery literature. Joseph Burnett graduated from the Worcester School of Pharmacy and began his career as an apprentice to a Boston druggist named Theodore Metcalf in 1837. In 1845, he partnered with Metcalf to form Metcalf and Burnett Co., and shortly thereafter Metcalf retired, leaving Burnett in the business. By 1847, after receiving a request from a patron for a vanilla flavoring comparable to what she had bought in Paris, he went to New York and bought a pound of the best vanilla he could get at $3.50 a pound, extracted the "delicate" flavor, developed a vanilla extract for flavoring foods, and subsequently earned the reputation of providing only the purest quality products. Metcalf apparently stayed somewhat active in the business. Burnett married Josephine Cutter on June 20, 1848, and the family lived in Boston until the early 1900s.

Curiously, Burnett became somewhat famous in 1845 when his "purified" ether was used successfully in surgical procedures. That year, Dr. Benjamin Codman of Harvard Medical School purchased Burnett's entire stock of dental supplies and opened a business called the Dental Depot in Boston. By 1853, Codman had added surgical instruments and anatomical supplies to his inventory and established Benjamin S. Codman

& Co., which later became Codman & Schurtleff, Inc. This company eventually was absorbed by the now-famous Johnson & Johnson Co.

In 1855, Burnett sold half of his interest in the business at a profit. Realizing that if one extract was good business, more than one would be better, Burnett rented a larger factory in Boston and partnered with William G. Edmonds as Burnett & Co. By this time, he was producing extracts of lemon, vanilla, almond, rose, nutmeg, peach, celery, cinnamon, cloves, nectarine, ginger, and orange. The new partnership began producing other products such as wood violet perfume, cologne, coacoaine (for the hair), florimel (handkerchief perfume), kalliston (complexion enhancer), Jamaica ginger (for the stomach), Oriental tooth wash, cod liver oil, and Jonas Whitcomb's Asthma Remedy, among others.

Before Dr. Joseph Burnett died in 1894, another factory was built and commenced manufacturing a new line of food colorings that eventually were marketed in liquid and tablet form. Sometime between 1891 and 1900, an office was opened in Chicago, and there may have been another for agents in New York, but by this time, Burnett's products were known the world over. Sons Harry, Robert, and John T. Burnett continued the business and the quality policies of their father, building yet another large factory in 1920 to accommodate demand for their products.

By 1919, the Burnett Co. added spices to its product inventory, and between the 1920s and 1940s, it added mint jelly, marshmallow, flavored puddings, mixes for ice cream and sherbet, pie crust, and muffin mixes. Harry Burnett died in 1927, and George H. Burnett, son of Robert Burnett, succeeded him as company treasurer. John T. Burnett died two years later, and a family member, Henry P. Kidder became president of the Burnett Co. Both men served until about 1946, when the company was sold to American Home Foods, Inc., a subsidiary of American Home Products Corporation. The factory and land were sold, and the company apparently moved to a new Boston location, where it remained until 1961. At some point thereafter, the company was acquired by Doxee Food Corporation, which merged with Snow's Seafood Corporation, and which in turn was acquired by Castleberry's Food Co. in 1994. Ads for Burnett products persisted in magazines and newspapers after 1861, and it is likely that Burnett Co. products were made for some time after that date. It is not known exactly when Doxee Food Corporation began discontinuing production of some Burnett products, but the Burnett name was used until the 1960s.[44]

---

[44]One of the most complete biographies of Joseph Burnett and the history of his various

FIGURE 35. Drakes Plantation Bitters bottle and label.

Patent Medicines

Drake's Plantation Bitters

There are 109 nearly square, amber colored, cabin-shaped bottles of Drake's Plantation Bitters and a few fragments in the collection. The bottle morphology is quite unique:

> The front and reverse sides of the bottled have six relief logs above plain panels which accommodated paper labels. The tiered roof shoulder on the front side is embossed with letters on all three tiers as follows: top: "S T / DRAKES"; middle: "1860 / PLANTATION"; bottom: "X / BITTERS." The middle tier of the reverse side is embossed: "PATENTED / 1862." The two remaining sides are molded to represent logs, which cross at the corners of the bottles, and the tiered roof above is corrugated. The necks are cylindrical and terminate in slanting collar finishes. On each bottle the edge of the base is flat and the center of the base bears a plain dished depression. All these specimens were stoppered with corks.[45]

companies is found at "History of the Joseph Burnett Company," Southborough Historical Society, Southborough, Massachusetts, http://www.southboroughhistory.org/History/Burnette%, last modified March 29, 2010.

[45]Switzer, *The* Bertrand *Bottles*, 36–37.

Label fragments were found adhered to some of the bottles, and others appear to have been wrapped in newsprint bearing testimonials of the effectiveness of the product. The bottles are 9 7/8 inches tall, with 2 3/4 inch square bases and outside neck diameters of 1 1/16 inches. Case stencils indicate the consignees were Worden & Co. of Hell Gate, Montana, and Vivian & Simpson of Virginia City, Montana. The remainder of the stencils read:

DRAKE'S PLANTATION BITTERS / DEPOT NEW YORK,

Or

S T 1860 by / G / G T O & S / WITH CARE VIA SARNIA

The meaning of the inscription on the case stencils and also the raised letters on the bottles was explained by Col. P. H. Drake in one of his *Morning, Noon and Night Almanacs*:

> S. T. 1860. X., like the initials on the old Roman banners, has a meaning. It represents St. Croix – S. T. being the conventional equivalent of Saint, and 1-8-6-0 standing for the letters C-R-O-I, and so forming, with the concluding X, the word CROIX. Nothing can be more simple, or, it may be, more appropriate, St. Croix Rum is a stimulating basis of the Plantation Bitters, and it is, therefore in accordance with the fitness of things, that St. Croix should be the basis of their business shibboleth.

The history of this company remains elusive, and the only reliable biographical information about Col. P. H. Drake is found in *The Kentucky Encyclopedia*.[46] Daniel Drake was born near Bound Hook, New Jersey, to Isaac and Elizabeth (Shotwell) Drake on October 20, 1785. When he was three, the family moved to Mays Lick, Kentucky, and two years later, Daniel's father apprenticed him to Dr. William Goforth, a Cincinnati physician, where he remained until 1805 when he began studying medicine at the University of Pennsylvania. Sometime after 1806, he practiced medicine at Mays Lick for a year before he assumed the practice of Dr. Goforth. In 1810, Drake partnered with his brother Benjamin to open a general store and pharmacy in Cincinnati, but Daniel sold the store in 1815–1816 so he could complete his medical degree in Philadelphia.[47]

Another item concerning Drake's business appeared in an 1864 issue

---

[46]John E. Kleber, Thomas D. Clark, Lowell H. Harrison, James C. Klotter, ed., *The Encyclopedia of Kentucky* (Lexington: The University Press of Kentucky, 1992), 270.
[47]Ibid.

of *The Nebraska Republican*. The advertisement for Drake's Plantation Bitters reads:

> Plantation Bitters—which are now recommended by the highest medical authorities, and warranted to produce an immediate beneficial effect. They are exceedingly agreeable, perfectly pure, and must supersede all other tonics where a healthy, gentle stimulant is required. They purify, strengthen and invigorate. They create a healthy appetite. They are an antidote to change of water and diet. They overcome the effects of dissipation and late hours. They strengthen the system and enliven the mind. They prevent miasfatic and intermittent fevers. They purify the breath and acidity of the stomach. They cure Diarrehea, Cholers and Cholera Morbus. They Cure liver Complaint and Nervous headache. They make the weak strong and languoid brilliant and are in steamboats and country stores.
>
> P. H. DRAKE & CO.
> 203 BROADWAY, N.Y.[48]

Hostetter's Bitters

There are 191 twelve-bottle cases of Hostetter's bitters in the *Bertrand*'s cargo, and the bottles are of two distinct sizes and colors. A large number of bottles retained their contents, and the average alcohol content tested at 27%, which is higher than the original Hostetter formula. In addition, many bottles bore thick foil seals over the corks that were covered with proprietary revenue stamps, as well as fragments of paper labels. On one plain side was a dark blue and gold paper label, and on the opposing side was a black-on-white label depicting St. George slaying a dragon. The dark blue labels read:

HOSTETTER'S
CELEBRATED
STOMACH
BITTERS

One wine-glassful taken three times a Day before meals, will be swift and certain cure for Dyspepsia, Liver Complaint, and every species of indigestion—an unfailing remedy for Intermittent Fever, Fever and Ague, and all kinds of periodical flux, Colics, and Choleric maladies— a cure for costiveness—a mild and safe invigorant and corroborant for

---

[48]*Nebraska Republican*, April 18, 1864.

FIGURE 36. Large Dr. Hostetter's Stomach Bitters bottle and proprietary stamp.
FIGURE 37. Small Hostetter's Stomach Bitters bottle with label in fragments.

delicate females—a good, antibilious, alternative and tonic preparation for ordinary family purposes—a powerful recuperant after the frame has been reduced and altered by sickness—an excellent appetizer as well as a strengthener of the blood and other fluids desirable as a corrective and mild cathartic and an agreeable and wholesome stimulant. Persons in a debilitated state should commence by taking small doses and increase with their strength.

The smaller of the two types are 22-ounce amber bottles blown in two-piece molds that have slanting collar and neck finishes and are stoppered with corks. The dish-shaped depressions in the bases show the raised letters "L&W" and are attributed to the Pittsburgh Glass Works, operated by Lorenz and Wightman. Embossing on sides of the bottles reads "DR. J. HOSTETTER'S / STOMACH BITTERS."

The larger bitters bottles are either dark green or amber in color and are morphologically the similar to the smaller bottles, except that they have a capacity of 28 ounces. In a group of eight bottles recovered in a wooden crate, four were plain and four were embossed with the Hostetter lettering. The wooden case was marked:

HOSTETTER'S / STOMACH / BITTER / BAR STORES / BERTRAND

The remaining metal-strapped cases bore black stenciling indicating they were consigned to "VIVIAN & SIMPSON / VIRGINIA CITY, M. T." They read:

HOSTETTER & SMITH / SOLE / MANUFACTURERS / & / PROPRIETORS / PITTSBURGH, P. A.

Hostetter & Smith may have marketed large 27-twenty-seven ounce and 31-ounce black glass bottles of bitters in San Francisco as early as 1858 through the wholesale firm of Park & White. These large bottles apparently were sold in great numbers on the West Coast and in some other western outlets until early in 1865, when Hostetter & Smith advertised they were discontinuing the large bottles in favor of smaller 20-ounce bottles. Inasmuch as both large and small Hostetter's bottles were present in the *Bertrand*'s cargo, the transition must have been well underway by April 1865, when the steamboat sank. While there are dozens of variants and many colors of glass in Hostetters bottles, it is likely that the majority of the *Bertrand* specimens were produced by Wm. McCully & Co. of Pittsburgh, Pennsylvania, although a few can definitely be ascribed to the Pittsburgh Glass Works of Lorenz and Wightman.

Inside many cases were eight almanacs packed in sets of two, or twelve almanacs packed in four sets of three. On top of the almanacs in each of these cases was a printed broadside lettered in reddish brown ink and bearing a woodcut of St. George slaying a dragon at the center. The broadsides measure 18 by 24 1/2 inches.

The recessed bases of the Hostetter's bottles from the *Bertrand* bear a variety of lettering. As noted previously, some bottles were definitely produced by Lorenz and Wightman at the Pittsburgh Glass Works. Frederick Lorenz was born in Germany, and after immigrating to the United States, he went to work in Craig & O'Hara's Pittsburgh Glass Works. After O'Hara's death, Lorenz leased the plant and later bought it and the Treavor & Ensell plant. By 1824, his success prompted him to build the Sligo Glass Works and the Temperenceville Glass Works, the latter producing window glass. By 1841, Lorenz, who was already in a partnership with Thomas Wightman, entered into a loose partnership with William McCully and A. W. Buchanan. The four-way partnership consolidated under the firm name of McCully & Co., but dissolved as a partnership ten years later. Between 1851 and 1860, Lorenz and Wightman continued to operate the Pittsburgh Glass Works under the name Lorenz & Wightman, whereupon they leased the works to Albree & Co. until 1862 when Albree defaulted and gave up the lease. The new Lorenz and Wightman Co. that was formed after this date was owned and operated by Frederick's son, Moses Lorenz, Thomas Wightman, and W. K. Nimick, until Moses died in 1871 and the firm was dissolved. After 1871, the business was known as Thomas Wightman & Co.[49]

It should be noted that most of the other amber bitters bottles bear no basal lettering. Amber bottles of unknown contents with 4 percent alcohol in at least one case were marked "W McCULLY & CO / PITTS-BURGH PA" on the bases and "PATENTED" on the shoulders. In the 1860s and continuing into the 1880s, many of Hostetter's Bitters bottles were made by Wm. McCully & Co. of Pittsburgh, Pennsylvania. William McCully was born in 1800 in Ireland, and his parents immigrated to the area around Pittsburgh. In his early years, he apprenticed as a glass blower in Bakewell's Grant Street factory before moving to the employ of Frederick Lorenz at the Pittsburgh Glass Works to learn the art of blowing cylinder window glass. By 1829, McCully entered into partnership with Captain John Hay to establish the Union Flint Glass Works. In 1832, the company was grossing $18,000 a year. The factory was destroyed by fire and flood in that year and the partnership was dissolved, but McCully replaced the plant and appropriately renamed his business the Phoenix Glass Co. It eventually grew to be one of the largest glass manufacturers of its day.[50]

Later, McCully purchased two other glass works and established a partnership with A. W. Buchanan, Frederick Lorenz, and Thomas Wightman. He remained in partnership with them until 1851, with each partner owning and operating his own plants in a loose confederacy. When the partnership dissolved in 1851, McCully was left with the Phoenix, Sligo, and Williamsport glass works. Although McCully died in 1859, the company was continued under his name by his son John McCully. However, Mark Watson, and John M. King, who had come into the firm in 1852 and 1855, respectively, actually managed the company. McCully's son-in-law William Grace joined the firm sometime before 1860. The company made

[49]Switzer, *The* Bertrand *Bottles*, 72.
[50]Toulouse, *Bottle Makers and Their Marks*, 351–52.

bottles, flasks (1856–1866), and fruit jars, and all basal marks on bottles exhibiting "Co." are dated after 1841, probably between 1856 and 1866, and originated at the Phoenix Glass Co. Some early Hostetter's bottles may have been produced by Lorenz and Wightman.[51]

As for the bitters, Dr. Jacob Hostetter was a successful physician in Lancaster County, Pennsylvania, who dispensed a private remedy to his patients for the cure of colic, constipation, and other ailments. His son David grew up on the family farm and at sixteen took a job as a chore boy in a dry goods store, where he rose to the position of manager in the ensuing seven years. Soon thereafter, David Hostetter entered into partnership with another man and opened a dry goods store of his own. In 1849–1850, lured by the discovery of gold in California, young Hostetter sailed around Cape Horn to seek opportunity in the west. Not finding fortune in the gold fields, David entered the grocery business in San Francisco, and within a month his store was destroyed by fire. The aspiring entrepreneur took his talents for business and promotion and returned to Pennsylvania.

At home, his partner left him with a failing grocery business, so David went to work for some railroad builders installing the Pennsylvania Line's tracks around Horseshoe Bend. Dr. Hostetter retired from practice in 1853, giving son David the rights to manufacture and sell his private remedy. Armed with a $4,000 contribution from his boyhood friend and partner George W. Smith, Hostetter started the Hostetter and Smith Stomach Bitters Co. in Pittsburgh. In 1853, the first bottles of the "Celebrated Stomach Bitters" came on the market. Bottles used by the small plant that he rented for $175 a year were never embossed with Smith's name, owing in part to the fact that the name Hostetter was probably more acceptable among the German-American people of Pennsylvania.[52]

After the first year of traveling and promoting the business, David Hostetter married Rosetta, and, by 1857, the business had to move to larger quarters. By the 1860s, the Hostetter business was a nationwide advertiser with a trademark exhibiting a nude, helmeted St. George astride a rearing horse, slaying a dragon. Every bit of profit that did not go into manufacturing went into promoting the bitters. Hostetter's advertisements began to appear everywhere, including broadsides on

[51]Ibid., 77.

[52]Dr. Thomas Cushing, *A Genealogical and Biographical History of Allegheny County, Pennsylvania, Part II* (Chicago: A. Warner & Co., 1889), 160–61.

barns and mountain sides. There were hundreds of kinds of bitters on the market, and to compete, one had to be aggressive in marketing or the business would surely fail. The nostrum contained 47 percent alcohol bittered with a variety of herbs and spices:

Cinchona bark (Cinchona succirubra) . . . . 15.00 grains
Century plant (Erythraea centarium) . . . . 0.65 grains
Anise fruit (Pimpinella anisum) . . . . 0.65 grains
Serpentaria roots (Artistolocha serpentaria) . . . . . . 3.00 grains
Yerba Santa leaves (Eriodictyon californicum) . . . . 2.00 grains
Calamus rhizomes (Acorus calamus) . . . . 2.00 grains
Culver's Roots (Veronica virginica) . . . . 0.42 grains
Ginger rhizomes (Zingiber officionale) . . . . 1.00 grain
Nux vomica seed (Strychmos Nux vomica) . . . . 8.00 m.
Glycerine . . . . 5 %
Sugar not to exceed . . . . 20.00 grains
Saccharin . . . . 1/15 grain
Oil of Orange. . . . . 0.5 m.[53]

A poet in Hostetter's employ summed up the effectiveness of the nostrum in Hostetter's *United States Almanac* in 1867:

Dyspepsia's pangs, that rack and grind
The body, and depress the mind;
Agues, that, as they go and come,
Make life a constant martyrdom;
Colics and dysenteric pains,
'Neath which the strong man's vigor wains;
Bilious complaints—those tedious ills,
Ne'er conquered yet by drastic pills;
Dread Diarrhea, that cannot be
Cured by destructive Mercury;
Slow constitutional decay,
That brings death nearer, day by day;
Nervous prostration, mental gloom,
Heralds of madness or the tomb;
For these, though Mineral nostrums fail,
Means of relief at last we hail,
HOSTETTER'S BITTERS—medicine sure,
Not to *prevent*, alone, but *cure.*[54]

---

[53]Switzer, *The* Bertrand *Bottles*, 77.
[54]*Hostetter's United States Almanac*, 1867.

Marketing of the nostrum apparently worked, and even the Union Army began employing it by 1861. After all, who could object to the use of soothing "medicine"? The use of Hostetter's Bitters also seems to have infiltrated the South, where whiskey had become such a problem for the Confederate Army that some states prohibited the use of corn for distillation purposes. Confederate General Bragg apparently banned whiskey in his army, except as medicine, while Adjutant General Cooper prohibited its use in all southern armies. By 1866, the company was grossing $750,000 a year, and the Hostetter publishing division was turning out a "United States" almanac in English and eight foreign languages. The almanac was so eagerly sought that its arrival in many households took on the character of a literary event. Hostetter did not rely on bottles whimsically shaped as log cabins, pigs, drums, fish, globes, lighthouses, or Indian maidens, like so many of his competitors. He stuck to a plain, square bottle with high slopping shoulders and a stubby neck. The labels bearing helmeted the likeness of St. George were simple, but the contents of the bottles were complex, potent, and palatable, and sales were enormous. In 1859, Hostetter marketed 432,000 bottles of bitters, and three decades after David's death, the company had sales exceeding 930,000 bottles. With his newfound wealth, David Hostetter diversified his interests, helping establish a bank, playing a role in promoting railroads, financing the Smithfield Bridge across the Monongahela River, and eventually investing in the profitable but turbulent oil industry, in which he held a quarter interest through Pittsburgh's natural gas monopoly. David founded the Pittsburgh and Lake Erie Railroad and became its president, serving in that position until his death. George Smith, David's partner, died in 1884, and David succumbed at age 67 to kidney trouble four years later, a malady his bitters did not claim to cure.[55] David Hostetter left a fortune of $18,000,000, and a name worth millions more. Hostetter's son, David Herbert Hostetter, assumed control of the company in 1889 and ran it much as his father had.[56] The business continued to prosper, even in the face of continuing prohibition forces and stiff competitors like James Ayers's Cherry Pectoral.

It is not widely known that Dr. David Hostetter was deeply involved in the oil industry in western Pennsylvania in the 1870s. Hostetter, who operated his bitters business in Pittsburgh, invested heavily in oil production in Butler County, and by 1874 found considerable difficulty

---

[55]Harvey, "Chapter 9: St. George and the Dragon," *The Toadstool Millionaires.*
[56]"Dr. Hostetter's Millions," *The New York Times*, December 6, 1889.

transporting the crude to Pittsburgh. It appears that in the early 1870s, Standard Oil gained control over most of the oil producers in western Pennsylvania and set about destroying the remaining independent producers by controlling the only means of transporting oil to Pittsburg refineries. Standard Oil formed the Central Association and had contracts with the Central, Erie, and Pennsylvania Railroads, giving them rebates on the lowest rates paid by independent producers. In 1872, the independent oil producers pressed Congress to regulate interstate commerce and to investigate the virtual monopoly of the oil industry by Standard Oil. Independent oil interests in Pittsburgh were going out of business in rapid succession, and some twenty-five refineries there had been reduced to two or three in three and half years. Congress appointed the Wisdom Committee to consider the situation in 1874.

The independent oil men did not completely trust Congress in the matter and began to look for alternative routes to get their oil to refineries at a reasonable cost. Hostetter was one of the independents affected by the Standard Oil monopoly, and he conceived the idea of piping his oil to Pittsburgh, where he could connect with the Baltimore and Ohio Railroad, a line that was not in the Central Association oil pool. Unfortunately, eminent domain for pipelines had been granted in only eight counties in western Pennsylvania, and Allegheny County, where Pittsburgh was located, was not one them. Obviously, the Pennsylvania Railroad did not want Hostetter to connect with a competing rail line, but he succeeded in buying right-of-way through the county to a point on a streambed where it had to pass under a bridge on a branch of the Pennsylvania Railroad. Hostetter maintained he had bought the right to the land under the bridge and that the railroad only had the right to span the water course. David Hostetter put in his pipes, but the railroad sent a force of armed men who tore up the pipes and dug in to resist. The independent oil men stormed the spot and took control, but the railroad succeeded in having thirty of them arrested for causing a riot. At trial, the men were acquitted, but Hostetter still faced a long, ugly litigation over his use of the right-of-way for his pipeline. Not long after, he became disgusted and impatient and leased his Columbia Conduit Line to three independent oil men named B. D. Benson, David McKelvy, and Major Robert E. Hopkins, all of Titusville. These resourceful men built tank wagons into which oil from the pipeline was run, carted across the tracks on a public highway, turned into storage tanks, and again repiped and pumped to Pittsburgh. In a short while, they succeeded in cutting off some of the Standard Oil monopoly and were doing a good business. Undoubtedly, Hostetter profited from the lease.[57]

Kelly's Log Cabin Bitters

FIGURE 38. Kelly's Old Cabin Bitters bottle.

Kelly's Old Cabin Bitters bottles were mold-blown and shaped like log cabins with windows and doors on the front and back sides. Front and back bottle shoulders take the form of shingles and are embossed "KELLY'S / OLD CABIN / BITTERS." The sides are plain panels topped with five relief logs and once bore paper labels. Under the pitch of the roof on the side panels is embossed "PATENTED / 1863." The bottles are 9 1/8 inches tall, and the bases are 2 3/4 inches by 3 7/16 inches. The outside diameter of the cylindrical necks is 1 inch. All have slanting collar neck finishes.

As evidenced by top case stencils, there are two consignees and one wholesaler:

GLASS WEIGHT / THIS SIDE UP WITH CARE / G. P.
DORRIS / VIRGINIA CITY / MONTANA, TY
WORDEN & CO. / HELL GATE
FROM / H. A. RICHARDS (*Probably C. A. Richards*) / WASH-
INGTON / 57, / BOSTON / GIN COCKTAIL / WORDEN AND
CO. / HELL GATE

Case ends are stenciled in red "KELLY'S / OLD CABIN BITTERS / DEPOTS NEW YORK & ST. LOUIS," and the side is stenciled in red "OLD CABIN / 1863" within a sunburst pattern at the center.

[57]Ida M. Tarbell, "Chapter 6, Strengthening the Foundations," *The History of Standard Oil Company* (New York: McClure, Phillips, and Co., 1904), 172–73.

FIGURE 39. Kelly's
Old Cabin Bitters crate—
end and top view.

Kelly's Log Cabin
Bitters represent yet
another elusive business
history. Apparently
James B. Kelly was a
whiskey merchant in
New York who evaded
federal revenues on
alcohol by printing his
own proprietary rev-
enue stamps with his
portrait on them. He applied them to his products, leading consumers
to believe that the appropriate tax had been paid. This scheme lay at
the heart of the Great Whiskey Ring in which distillers evaded federal
excise taxes on distilled spirits. In May 1875, federal agents stormed
distilleries in St. Louis, Cincinnati, Milwaukee, and other cities, seized
illegal whiskey and financial records, and arrested 240 whiskey makers.[58]

Kelly was in partnership with John H. Garnhart, who had a wholesale
liquor business in St. Louis. Garnhart was an unscrupulous rectifier who
added ingredients to raw alcohol and sold it as whiskey. Although there
is little reference to it, Kelly apparently had a business in St. Louis and
collaborated with Garnhart to produce Kelly's Old Cabin Bitters. John
Garnhart was arrested by federal agents in the May 10, 1875, raid, and his
business was taken over by Adler, Furst, & Co. Shortly thereafter this
company's listing disappeared, and Kelly's Old Cabin Bitters did, too.[59]

The wholesaler, H. A. Richards of Boston, was probably Henry A.
Richards and/or his brother, Calvin A. Richards. Calvin was a prominent businessman who died suddenly on February 15, 1892, at age sixty.
According to the *Boston Evening Transcript* of that date, Richards began
his career making proprietary medicines and later opened a liquor store

---

[58]Jack Sullivan, "Ulysses S. Grant His Whiskey History," *Bottles and Extras* (Raymore,
Missouri: The Federation of Historical Bottle Collectors, 2007), 59–61.

[59]Switzer, *The* Bertrand *Bottles*, 75–76.

on Washington Street and Williams Court. He invested his profits in real estate, including the Metropolitan Hotel, and in 1874 was a member of the Board of Directors of the Metropolitan Street Railroad. He was a member of the Boston Common Council in 1858 and 1859, and in 1863 was a member of the Board of Aldermen. He was married and had one daughter. Calvin Richards's brother Henry may have been a partner or had his own wholesale liquor business. In any event, C. A. and/or H. A. Richards are undoubtedly responsible for some of the Kelly's Old Cabin Bitters on the *Bertrand*, judging from the Washington Street address on one of the shipping crates.[60]

C. S. Kintzing Bitters

There is one case of twelve 26-ounce, dark green, square bitters bottles, eleven of which are vertically embossed "C. S. KINTZING / ST. LOUIS." The twelfth is plain. These French square bottles are nearly black in color and have slanting collar finishes. Eleven of them measure 8 7/8 inches tall by 2 3/16 inches square at the base, and they have 1 inch outside diameter necks. The odd specimen is 9 inches tall with basal dimensions of 2 7/8 inches square. The contents are 25 percent alcohol, and they are assumed to be bitters.

Little is known about Charles S. Kintzing except that he was listed in the St. Louis Directory at various times as Charles S. Kintzing at 153 Green St., St. Louis, Missouri. He may have been a partner in the wholesale grocery firm of Halfenstein, Gore, & Co. of St. Louis, at which time his residence was on Olive Street and his business address was 20th & 21st Streets.

J. H. Schroeder's Bitters

There are eight square embossed bitters bottles of olive green glass, some with paper label fragments, and sixty-nine dark amber leg bottles of Schroeder's Bitters catalogued into the collection. The former are French square bottles with beveled corners and slanting collar finishes applied with lipping tools. The basal edges are flat, and the bases exhibit shallow dish-shaped depressions. Three sides are plain, and the fourth side is embossed "J. H. SCHROEDER / 28 WALL STREET /

---

[60]Ibid.

FIGURE 40. J. H. Schroeder's Spice Bitters "leg bottle" and stopper.

LOUISVILLE, KY." The bottles stand 9 15/16 inches tall, and the bases are 3 1/16 inches square. Outside neck diameters are 1 inch, and the bottles are sealed with corks covered with red sealing wax. At least two of the blank sides bore 3 by 5 inch black and white paper labels, the fragments of one reading "Schroeder's / STOMACH / BITTERS / J H Schroeders Sons / LOUIS-VILLE / KY." To whom these were consigned is unknown.

In the second group are 28-ounce dark amber bottles commonly known as "leg bottles" owing to their distinctive leg shape. Basal edges are rounded, and the bases have small dish-shaped depressions. They are finished with single ring wine finishes and stand 11 15/16 inches tall. One side is embossed on all but one bottle. Eleven nipple-shaped pewter and cork dispenser caps may have been associated with the bottles. Basal diameters are 3 inches, and the necks are 1 1/16 inches in outside diameter. The contents are 44 percent alcohol.

While the bottles are embossed on one side "SCHROEDER'S / SPICE / BITTERS," the shipping crates are stenciled, "2 & 2 J. H. SCHROEDER'S / COCK-TAIL / BITTERS / LOUISVILLE, KY." The bitters were consigned to J. J. Roe & CO / St. Louis / MO. Whether they were cocktail bitters or spice bitters we do not know, but suffice it to say that most patent medicines had very high alcohol content regardless of their curative claims.

Although information about this company is sparse, J. H. Schroeder was listed in the *Louisville City Directory and Business Mirror* for 1858–1859 as being at 28 Wall Street between Main and Water Streets. The listing reads:

J. H. Schroeder,
Dealers in Foreign and Domestic
WINES AND LIQUORS
Sparkling and Dry Catawba Wines
28 WALL STREET
LOUISVILLE, K.Y.

The firm was still located on Wall Street in 1864, but by the next year, the company was renamed J. H. Schroeder & Son and had moved to a new location on Main Street.[60]

Brandy

Sixteen whole brandy bottles survived the sinking of the *Bertrand*. These olive green bottles are 9 3/4 to 10 1/4 inches tall, 3 3/8 to 3 3/4 inches in diameter at the base, and have fluid capacities of about 28 ounces. Dark gray print within a rectangular border on the cork stems reads, "F. & G. HIBBERT / LONDON." Several have wire bails, and the mouths are covered with silver foil. The cases are marked:

12 QT. / BRANDY COCKTAIL / FROM: C. A. RICHARDS /
91 WASHINGTON ST. / BOSTON and GLASS / WITH CARE /
STUART & Co. / DEER LODGE.

Lacking any definitive information, one can only assume the contents were brandy. There is no additional information on F. & G. Hibbert. What is known about Calvin A. Richards is in the section on whisky cocktail.

Champagne

One variety of champagne recovered from the *Bertrand* originated at the in Rheims, France. The green glass bottles have typical champagne shapes, with thick walls and high basal kick-ups. Inasmuch as they are 9 1/4 to 9 3/4 inches tall and have capacities of only 12 1/2 ounces, they may be termed "splits." The bases are 3 inches in diameter, and the necks are 13/16 inches in diameter outside. Distinctive foil seals on the bottles are illustrated in the Bertrand bottles book.[61] Champagne bottles showing two types of closures). Piper Heidseick Champagne is still produced in

---

[61]Ibid., 24, 27.

FIGURE 41. Champagne bottles showing two types of closures.

this region of France and is exported worldwide as a premium champagne.

The history of this company is somewhat convoluted and difficult to follow. The champagne house of Heidseick was founded in Rheims in 1785 by Florens-Louis Heidseick. Florens-Louis died in 1834, and over the next twenty years, three nephews established their own champagne houses using the Heidseick name. Today, these unrelated companies are known as Piper-Heidseick, Heidseick et Cie Monopole, and Charles Heidseick. When Florens-Louis Heidseick died, one of his nephews, Christain Heidseick, continued the business and kept the Heidseick name. Among his three assistants was Henri-Guillaume Piper who was a great nephew of Florens-Louis, and Jacques-Charles Kunkelmann. When Christian died in 1837, his widow continued the business under the name Veuve Cie, but continued to sell "champagne" under the Heidseick name. Later, the company became Piper-Heidseick because the widow married Henri-Guillaume Piper. The company became H. Piper et Cie and then Piper-Heidseick. It was Henri who really expanded the business and ventured into the American market. When Henri died in 1870, his partner, Jacques-Charles Kunklemann, took control of the company and changed its name to Kunklemann et Cie. By 1877, he brought his son Ferdinand-Theodore, and Paul Delius into the business as partners. Jacques-Charles Kunklemann died in 1881, Paul Delius retired in 1892, and Ferdinand-Theodore Kunkelmann continued the business under the same name. Because the house had double patronage under Florens-Louis Heidseick and Henri-Guillaume Piper, it was renamed Piper-Heideseick.

Apparently, in 1851, Charles-Camille Heidseick, the son of Charles-Henri Heidseick and nephew of Florens-Louis Heidseick, started the House of Charles Heidseick. He began marketing the Heidseick product in the United States but experienced many major business difficulties along the way. He was well known in American business circles as "Champagne Charlie." Charles-Camille Heidseick was succeeded by his son Charles-Eugene Heidseick in 1871 and then by his grandson, great-grandson, and great-great-grandson in succession.[62]

Despite considerable effort, nothing has been found relating to company histories for the remaining champagnes from the cargo. Suffice it to say there were more than 200 bottles of champagne on the boat, most of which seems to have been imported from France. Further descriptions of the bottles, closures, and label fragments, as well as a classification can be found in the *Bertrand* bottle book. Figure 40 shows two unmarked champagne or sparkling wine bottles, each with a different type of closure.

Wine

Some of the wine found on the *Bertrand* may have been, and probably was, produced by the American Wine Co. The number and size of these bottles are not known. However, one case apparently was marked: AMERICAN WINE Co. / SPARKLING / CATAWBA / ST. LOUIS, MO., and was consigned to Vivian & Simpson in Virginia City, Montana.

The American Wine Co. was established in Chicago in 1859 and moved to St. Louis about 1860 because of the opportunities for grape growing and manufacturing wine. In St. Louis, it bought the winery and cellars of the Missouri Wine Co., which began making sparkling wine in 1856 under the partnership of William Glasgow, Jr., Amede Valle, Allen Glasby and plant superintendent William Disterick. When Disterick died in 1860, the company went out of business and the works were purchased by the American Wine Co. Utilizing Missouri grapes, the company expanded production of sparkling wine and also began to produce still wines and brandies. At its height, the American Wine Co. was producing 100,000 gallons of wine and 200,000–300,000 gallons of sparkling wine annually. Isaac Cook was president of the company, and Cook's Imperial Champagne, which gained great favor throughout the country, was named after him.[63]

---

[62]Ibid.

[63]*Second Annual Report of the Missouri Board of Agriculture, With An Abstract of Proceedings of the County Agricultural Societies, to the General Assembly of Missouri, for the Year 1866* (Jefferson City: Emory S. Foster, 1867), 505–506.

Dacus and Buel's 1878 *A Tour of St. Louis* reveals more of the history of this company:

The American Wine Co.

In the war waged by the great temperance crusaders against the use of alcoholic liquors, wine needs no defense. Nay, blessed syrup of the luscious grape, sweet nectar of the gods, the argument is in the beauty of the head and delightful influence of thy sovereignty. The mightiest and most sublime products of the pen inspired by thy melliforous grace and subtle invocation; by thy aid man's power has become unabridged, and cities have risen to empires under thy delectable enthusiasm. Delicious auxiliary of all pleasure; song creator, beauty's best adornment, thy defense is in the sweet perfection of thy invigorating effects.

Wine has, from the earliest record of antiquity, formed no small part of the world's commerce, and its use was general among all the orators, painters, novelists and historians are all descended from a wine-drinking people, while on the other hand the nomads of the South, the savages of the East, and the untutored warriors of the North lived in barbarism, without civilization, without happiness, and without wine.

The manufacture of this most delightful of all drinks is of a recent date in Missouri, the first distillation being about 1850. As early as 1853 the Missouri Wine Co. was manufacturing what was then considered a good quality wine, but as compared with Cook's Imperial of to-day was a very poor beverage. In 1859 the American Wine Co. was established in this city, and it is to that corporation the State is indebted for the development of one of its most important industries—the demonstration of the adaptability of the soil of the State for the production of the best vintage on the continent.

The American Wine Co. is an organization of large capital, with facilities for manufacturing more than five hundred thousand bottles annually, and their product finds ready sales, a larger part being consumed by New York, where Cook's Imperial has the best reputation of any wines sold in that market. At the Paris Exhibition of 1867 this company's champagne received honorable mention in competition with all for fine flavor. The American committee was so surprised at the excellence of Cook's wines that they confessed to a higher estimation of the possibilities and attainments of American wines. Shipments of Missouri wines are now frequently sent to Germany, where they are regarded with special favor by the best German judges, with a constantly increasing popularity.

The office of the American Wine Co. is at No. 119 Olive Street, but the cellars, where the immense product of the concern is stored, are on the corner of Cass and Garrison avenues. These cellars are three stories in depth, cover one block of ground, and employ sixty men. The capital in active use by the company is nearly two millions of dollars, the establishment being of the largest kind in this country.

To speak of the American Wine Co. without mentioning Isaac Cook, the President, would be like exalting wine that had lost its flavor. Mr. Cook was the organizer of the company, and has rewarded its active president ever since. Being a man thoroughly imbued with the importance of the interests he represents, and with a purpose to bring his wines to the very core of popularity, he has relied upon the purity of the vintage, and ever refused to use the slightest deleterious ingredient. He makes his wines in the glass, by the same process used in the champagne districts of Europe, and its great purity had made it preferable to European wines, even in the wine districts of France, Germany, Spain, and other countries. Cook's Imperial has a reputation co-extensive with the nation, and wherever drunk it sows seeds of preference, which bear fruit in great popularity and exclusive use.[64]

In addition to the American Wine Co.'s "Sparkling Catawba" wine, there are others. Notable among them are three large demijohns of red wine. Two of these specimens are of transparent, non-lead, aqua-colored glass, stoppered with corks. Discussions with wine chemists at Taylor Winery in Bath, New York, indicate the contents may have been imported from France. The bottles are free-blown, have pontil scars, and measure 18 inches tall. They have basal diameters of 7 1/2 inches and outside neck diameters of 1 5/8 inches.

The third demijohn was originally wicker-covered and was somewhat larger than the other two. It too was free-blown and bears a pontil scar. It measures 17 1/2 inches tall, is 7 5/8 inches in diameter at the base, and has an outside neck diameter of 1 9/16 inches.

TEXTILES, WEARING APPAREL, AND SEWING SUPPLIES
Textiles
Bandana Lengths (4)
Red Wool Netting (1)

[64]Joseph A. Dacus and James William Buel, *A Tour of St. Louis; or, The Inside Life of a Great City—1878* (St. Louis: Western Publishing Company, Jones & Griffin, 1878), 282–84.

Wearing Apparel

Textiles and clothing from the *Bertrand* are classified as either commercial merchandise or personal belongings of passengers. The cloth used to produce wearing apparel was most probably produced in the United States, since between 1859 and 1869, the American textile industry was producing between 66 and 75 percent of the cloth used in the country and no longer imported goods from Britain. However, luxury fabrics were still mostly imported. Textile manufacture in the United States followed the fluctuations of the rest of economy after the War of 1812 and did not expand until the 1840s. By 1842, there were textile mills in Ohio, Pennsylvania, and Illinois, and within five years, others were operating in Wisconsin. In the mid-1850s, more mills operated in Iowa, Oregon, and California. In 1869, only 25 percent of all textiles used in the country were imported, mostly from Germany and England, because the American industry was deficient in the production of mohairs, lustres, all-wool merinos, and cashmeres. In addition, even though there was fairly substantial ribbon production in Paterson, New Jersey, patterned ribbons for neckties were mostly imported.

By the middle of the 1800s, it was not uncommon for a single manufacturer's shop to transform crude wool fiber into finished textile, and many cotton mills had their own dye houses and print works. The mass production of men's wear, including work clothes, was also well established by this time, as was production of men's underwear. Although women's wear corresponded closely to the fashions established in the East, production took place mostly in the home. The hand-sewing process was facilitated by the distribution of commercially printed patterns by Ebenezer Butterick in 1863.[65]

Men's matched suits, consisting of a coat, waistcoat (vest), and trousers, came into production between 1850 and 1870, but changes in style during the middle and late nineteenth century were few. Basic colors were black, blue, brown, and gray, and over time, even the brighter waistcoats became muted, leaving the cravat as the only bit of color in men's attire. Often, a waistcoat was made of fabrics different from the rest of the suit, providing a little texture to the ensemble. Among the more popular fabrics were brocades, dotted velvets, paisleys, satins, cashmeres, tweeds, and embroidered fabrics.[66]

[65]Barbara Brenner, *Careers and Opportunities in Fashion* (New York: E. P. Dutton and Company, 1966), 18.

[66]Blanch Payne, *History of Costume* (New York: E. P. Dutton and Company, 1966), 464. See also Phyllis C. Willet Cunningham, *Handbook of English Costume in the Nineteenth Century* (London: Faber and Faber, 1966), 237.

Trousers were cut wide at the hip, with narrow ankles, and were long enough to touch the shoe/boot heel. Checks and plaids were used for everyday wear, while more formal attire was black, green and black mixtures, brown, steel gray, and grayish blue. According to Payne, during the 1860s, the overcoat underwent substantial change in design when the collar and cut were eased to make it resemble a sack coat. Frock coats, morning coats, cutaways, and a few other styles with seamed waists were also popular. The knee-length frock coat and the long frock great coat were the marks of respectability. These were cut in six pieces and could be either single- or double-breasted. Other types of coats were also in fashion, including box coats with belts or straps that were fitted with capes, the Inverness cape, and the Ulster with detachable cape.[67] Slickers of rubberized cloth came into use during this period and were in evidence on the *Bertrand*.

Shirts of plain white linen were for formal wear, while work shirts were made of cotton or linen in stripes or plaid patterns. Collars might be attached or not. Ties were either made-up bands of muslin or silk or simply a large square of cloth folded into a band.[68]

Fashions in women's clothing on the frontier during this period were largely a reflection of fashions in the East, which were, in turn, reflections of fashions in Europe. Apparently, two notable events influenced women's clothing between the 1850s and 1860s. First were the reintroduction of hooped petticoats in 1854 and the mass production of sewing machines in 1855. Owing to the high cost of sewing machines, most clothing on the frontier was either brought there from the East, ordered from mercantiles, or home-sewn and custom-made. Mass production of women's wear was only beginning in the 1860s. Women's styles were more susceptible to change than men's fashions during the period between 1830 and the 1860s. Between the 1830s and 1850s the typical women's dress was a bell-shaped silhouette that gave way to a cone shaped silhouette by the mid-1860s. In the late 1860s, the skirt became narrow from side to side, with a sharply jutting angle from the waist to the floor in the back. More fullness was added to the back by the late 1860s.[69]

Skirts in the 1850s might be double or triple and bear three to seven ruffles sewn to the already fashionably full base. When hoops were introduced in 1854, skirts covered the ankles and remained thus until at least 1863. *Peterson's Magazine* in 1861 carried an article endorsing

[67]Ibid.
[68]Ibid.
[69]*Peterson's Magazine* (November 1861), 384.

"Demorest's Prize Medal Hoop Skirts" as giving "a graceful flow to the outer garments." The article claimed that the poor design and manufacture of previous types of hoop skirts arose because they were designed by men.[70] By 1863, skirts were shortened by three inches to expose the ankle. and the lower edge might be looped to expose the petticoat. Bodices and skirts were often cut separately, with different bodices for day and evening wear, made of distinctly different cloths. If these garments were sewn together or the skirt and bodice were all one fabric, fit was achieved by shaping and goring the pieces. Goring refers to inserting tapered or triangular pieces of cloth into a skirt. By 1864–1865, it was more common to see skirts and bodices joined, and gored skirts became more popular. During the 1850s, bodices had front fastenings, and the front waistline dipped to a point. By the mid-1850s, women's sleeves were wide pagoda sleeves, but by the late 1860s, they had begun to narrow.[71]

After 1859, waistlines rose and were straight, and emphasis was shifting to the back of the dress. With increased attention on the foot and ankle, rich fabrics like satins were employed in the uppers of leather soled shoes, the edges of which might be fashioned into curves. Front lacing changed to side lacing, and colored shoes became more popular as well. Square-toed boots with elastic sides and peg-top heels became increasingly popular and were worn for casual dress along with stockings patterned with spots, stripes, and plaids.

Through the 1860s, traditional shawls were common. These were triangular or oval and made of cashmere, paisley, and printed and embroidered silks. Although Talma cloaks with circular capes of silk, velvet, or merino were worn, during the 1860s, fitted cloaks and burnooses with voluminous hooded mantles were perhaps more common.[72]

Women covered their heads with cotton caps edged with lace or with pointed-front fanchons, black hair nets, or spoon bonnets. Prior to 1832, when pin-making machines were invented, small handmade pins with decorative heads were used to secure lace caps, mobcaps, veils, and other things to heads and other attire. Handmade pins or "hair jewelry" were considered so valuable in some places that their theft was considered a hanging offense. The first simple hatpins were base metal skewers. Later these were replaced with silver shafts studded with semi-precious stones and pearls. In England, taxes were levied to pay for the Queen's pins, and the sale of handmade pins was limited to the first day of the New

[70]Ibid.

[71]Nancy Bradfield, *Costume in Detail* (Boston: Plays, Inc., 1968), 187–218.

[72]Ibid.

Year. Women saved for "Pin Day"; this may be the origin of the term "pin money."[73] The two long gold filigree-headed pins found among the personal possessions on the *Bertrand* are somewhat surprising because they are of a style more characteristic of the 1890s, when hats sat upon ridiculously high hair styles. Purses and gloves were universally mandatory during this period, especially shaggy bead purses with steel beads; fans, muffs, and parasols were optional.

Women's underwear made its appearance in the mid-nineteenth century, and women's "drawers" were made much like men's knee-length trousers with drop fronts. The legs might be joined or separate, and the length varied. Other accoutrements included corsets, hoops, crinolines, and petticoats. Therefore, it is safe to say that the wearing apparel on the *Bertrand* was fairly typical for the time in that it was mass produced and of prevailing fashion in style and color. After thorough literature reviews, including some work on the chemical differentiation of dye stuffs in anthropological specimens, several methods for determining dyestuffs in *Bertrand* textiles were utilized.[74] It is, however, beyond the scope of this work to describe the processes.

Bandanas
Bandanas were on bolts of printed cotton. There were two bolts of calico printed handkerchief stock in the cargo. When a handkerchief was sold it was cut from the bolt and not hemmed.

Billfolds (41)
Black Lace Net (1)
Buckles (54)
Coats (196)
Dresses (4)
Frock Coats (20)
Fur Wrap (1)
Gloves (8)

[73]Cunningham, *Handbook of English Costume in the Nineteenth Century*, 237.
[74]Ronald R. Switzer, "The Chemical Differentiation of Dyestuffs in Anthropological Specimens" (lecture, University of New Mexico, 1969). See also Catherine M. Schweiger, "Techniques for the Analysis of Dyes on Historic Textiles" (master's thesis, University of Nebraska, 1971).

Handkerchiefs (11)

Eleven squares of black silk cloth were found. These presumably were handkerchiefs or handkerchief stock and were accessioned as such.

Ice Skates (8)

Ladies' Capes (16)

FIGURE 42. Lady's knitted cape.

Triangular knitted ladies' capes with tasseled ties at the necks were of two colors of yarn, dark blue and pinkish violet. They are very typical of the time.

Leather Gloves

Field notes indicate there were eight pairs of leather gloves in the cargo sized for both adults and children. It is suspected that the smaller gloves were for ladies and not for children, but this cannot be confirmed.

Men's Hats (324)

Judging from the large number of hats recovered, they must have been in great demand on the Montana frontier. Although they were not particularly expensive to make, hats seem to have brought a premium price at retail. A reflection of the hat making industry comes from a January 3, 1862, *Article of Agreement* (partnership) between Joel Ruly and John H. Hoskinson of the City of DeSoto, Nebraska Territory, for the manufacture of hats:

Article of agreement made and entered into this 3rd day of January A.D. 1862 by ad between Joel Ruly of the City of DeSoto, County of Washington and Territory of Nebraska and John H. Hoskinson of the same place the above named parties to this article mutually agree with each other and by these presents do Enter into a co-partnership for the purpose of manufacturing Hats in the City of DeSoto County Washington & Territory of Nebraska and we the above named Joel Ruly and John H. Hoskinson do further agree and Bind ourselves by these presents to Each Share alike the expenses of furnishing the tools necessary to Manufacture Hats. And it is further agreed between us and that each one of us is to pay an equal proportion for the same but in the event that either one of the within named parties should furnish more stock than the other that the said party so furnishing shall be allowed to draw the amount of money so furnished out of the capital stock of the firm before any division shall be made & after the same shall be taken out by the respective party entitled to the same that the balance shall be then equally divided between the Parties to this instrument after first paying for the Making of Said Hats and we further agree by and between ourselves to each furnish and equal proportion all the material necessary to carry on a regular Hattery business Stock included and that in a good workmanlike manner out of the material so furnished and for such prices as is laid down in a Schedule or Bill of prices hereto attached marked A and in consideration for said Labor each of us the parties herein name viz Joel Ruly and John H. Hoskinson are to pay and equal proportion of said Labor which pay is to be taken out of the Hats so manufactured before any division Shall be made or any disposition made of it other than is heretofore expressed.

In Witness Whereof we have hereunto set our hand and Seal this 3rd day of January A.D. 1862

Joel Ruly   Seal
John H. Hoskinson   Seal

In Presence of
Charles D. Davis
P. W. Liscomb

Making Caster bodies each	50 cts
napping Caster bodies with beaver, otter or muskrat each	50 cts
making rabbit hats each	50 cts
napping wool bodies each	35 cts
making wool hat each	37 1/2 cts
Finishing caster hats each	37 1/2 cts
Finishing rabbit hats each	18 1/2 cts
Finishing wool Bodies napped each	12 1/2 cts

coloring each at napped	12 1/2 cts
blocking and washing out after coloring	5 cts
pulling and cutting coon skin	4 cts
pulling and cutting muskrat skin	3 cts
trimming cater hats each	12 1/2 cts
trimming wool bodies napped each	10 cts
trimming rabbit hats each	10 cts
trimming wool hats each	5 cts
scraping and cutting rabbit each	3 cts
making roram bodies	40 cts

The wool is to be carded equal by both parties pulling and cutting

Beaver skin each	25 cts
otter do.	25 cts
wolf do.	0 cts
Making smooth caster hat	75 cts[75]

Although making beaver fur hats involves multiple steps, the process is not terribly complicated. Carl P. Russell provides perhaps the best description of beaver hat making in his well-written book *Firearms, Traps, & Tools of the Mountain Men*:

> The first step in hat making was to shave both hair and wool from the skin. The bare skin was the sold to a maker of glue, and the wool and hair were separated by a blowing process. Only the wool found use in hat making. The soft, loose fur was applied in small quantities to a perforated copper revolving cone within which was a suction device that pulled the fur against the cone. A spray of hot water turned upon the cone, together with manipulation of the fur with the hands, started the felting process. Repeatedly fur was added, and the manipulation continued until the felt became tough in from the inside.
>
> Fine fur was then applied to the outside of the shaped hat. With the aid of hot water and careful handwork the outer surface was made to appear covered with a growth of fur.
>
> The final step in making the dress hat was to give it a high gloss and embellish it a band and lining. By means of a revolving block and the application of brushes, iron, sandpaper, and velvet, a finish as bright as that of silk was obtained. Because of its long velvety "pile" or fur, the "beaver" was characterized by an exquisite beauty that never distinguished the silk hat.[76]

[75]Addison E. Sheldon, ed., "First Hat Factory in Nebraska," *Nebraska History and Record of Pioneer Days* 4, no. 1 (1921): 214–15.

[76]Carl P. Russell, *Firearms, Traps, & Tools of the Mountain Men* (New York: Alfred A. Knopf, 1967), 6.

Mufflers (2)
Neck Scarves (2)

Rubberized Slickers (12) and Rubberized Slicker Leggings (12)

Although the maker of the rubberized slickers and leggings has not been identified, a historical note is in order. The Macintosh raincoat made with waterproof fabric was invented by the Scottish chemist and inventor Charles Macintosh. In 1823, while experimenting with masticated India rubber dissolved in coal-tar naphtha, Macintosh painted the sticky material on a piece of wool cloth and applied another layer of wool cloth on top to create a waterproof fabric. In 1837, Macintosh associated with Thomas Hancock, an Englishman who in 1821 patented elastic fastenings for gloves, suspenders, shoes, and stockings. Hancock made his fortune as the largest producer of rubber goods in the world, many of which were made with shredded India rubber that was masticated in machinery he invented in 1820 to use rubber scraps left over from other applications. Hancock's first masticator was a hollow wooden cylinder with teeth. Inside the cylinder was a studded wooden core that was rotated with a hand crank. In 1837, Hancock patented a steam-powered masticator that provided an ample supply of rubber for Macintosh's factory. Hancock's masticated rubber was also used for pneumatic cushions, mattresses, pillows, bellows, hose, tubing, solid tires, shoe soles, packing, and springs.

Apparently the fabric produced by Macintosh had its faults because it was easy to puncture when it was seamed and the natural oil in the wool caused the rubber cement to deteriorate. The fabric was very stiff in cold weather, and became sticky in hot weather. When vulcanized rubber was invented by Charles Goodyear in 1839, the new material could better withstand temperature changes and was used in Macintosh's fabrics.[77]

Shawls (4)

The shawls were knitted, but they are not distinctive.

[77]A recap of Charles Macintosh & Co. is found at: "Charles Macintosh and Co. The History of the Company," Bouncing Balls.com, http://www.bouncing-balls.com/serendipity/chasmacintosh.htm. Additional biographical information about Charles Macintosh can be found in O. E. Schoeffler and William Gale, *Esquire's Encyclopedia of 20th Century Men's Fashions* (New York: McGraw-Hill, 1973), 150, 156, 443.

FIGURE 43. Men's plaid shirt.
FIGURE 44. Knit stockings.
FIGURE 45. Men's trousers.

Shirts (60)

Men's shirts did not differ appreciably from those worn today, except that they were mostly plaids. They had narrow collars with a buttoned insert down the front and cuffs with buttons.

Socks/Knit Stockings

Laboratory notes indicate there are 156 pairs of plain and striped knit wool stockings in both adult and children's sizes in the cargo.

Shoelaces

Records indicate there were thirteen bundles of brass-tipped shoelaces in the cargo. Whether these were fabric or leather is not known.

Snoods (7)
Strap Guides (35)

Suit Coats (166)

Suit coats were shipped in pieces, presumably so they could be sewn together and tailored later.

Suspender Parts (93)

Sweaters

The remains of forty-five heavy rib-knit sweaters were recovered from the cargo. No other information about these items is forthcoming from laboratory or field notes.

Trousers (97)

Many of the trousers were rather sporty by today's standards. These plaid garments had flap pockets with buttons, buttons at the waist for attaching suspenders, and adjustable buckles at the back.

Underwear (Fragments)

Vests (24)

Wrist Warmer Cuff (1)

Boots and Shoes

According to Petsche, there were at least 700 pairs of boots and shoes in the *Bertrand*'s cargo, most of which were packed twelve or twenty-four pairs to a case.[78] The styles of these shoes and boots are a bit difficult to determine based on their appearance and the associated case stenciling. Figure 45 shows a popular square-toed style of the period called a "Congress" gaiter boot/shoe with an expandable top. Figure 46 shows a child's round-toed "Congress" or kipboot, and Figure 47 is a square-toed brogan-style "English Walking Shoe" with pegged sole and brass eyelets. Other styles include square-toed children's shoes with brass scuff plates and women's shoes with stacked heels, fabric tops, and brass eyelets. By far the largest numbers of boots were thigh-length hobnail miner's boots with heel caps.

Petsche lists the following manufacturers, quantities, wholesalers, and consignees:

Manufacturers and Quantities:

24 prs. IDAHO MINING BOOTS 1/2 D. Sole Oil Treed Fancy Nails

60 prs. DONELSON BOOTS FROM M. C. DIZER & CO. WEYMOUTH, MASS.

1 DOZ. PRS MENS SLAUGHTER BOOTS FROM W. S. BATCHELDER, HOLLISTON, MASS.

MENS IDAHO MINING BOOTS FROM LAFLIN, COBURN MASS

12 PRS. GENTS FINE CALF BOOTS 1/2 WELTED FROM ALDEN & HOWARD, RANDOLPH, MASS

12 PRS. OUR BEST BOYS KIP BOOTS, PATNA, FROM GEO. C. WALLS, BOSTON[79]

Wholesalers

J. R. LIONBERGER & CO. NO. 71 MAIN STREET, ST. LOUIS

12 PAIRS MEN"S HOBNAIL BOOTS FROM WILLIAM NORTH, 79 MAIN ST., ST. LOUIS

---

[78]Petsche, *The Steamboat* Bertrand, 60.

[79]Ibid., 60–62.

FIGURE 46. Square-toed "Congress" gaiter boots with expandable tops.

FIGURE 47. Boy's round-toed "Congress" or kip boot.

FIGURE 48. Square-toed brogan-style "English Walking Shoe" with pegged soles and brass eyelets.

24 PAIRS LADIES' BOOTS FROM WILLIAM E. NORTH, 79
MAIN ST., ST. LOUIS
FROM J. F. SCHIEFER SADDLERY AND LEATHER
WHOLESALE HOUSE, 90 MAIN ST., ST. LOUIS
12 PRS. FINE CALF DRESS BOOTS WELT FROM WILLIAM E.
NORTH, 79 Main ST., St. Louis

Consignees were Worden and Co., Hell Gate; Vivian & Simpson,
Virginia City; G. P. Dorris, Virginia City.

Other fragmentary information associated with boots in the cargo
implied that some were wholesaled by Nash, French, & Co., 40 Pearl
St., Boston, Massachusetts, or S.W. & E. Nash at the same address. The
former partnership consisted of William O. Nash and J. H. French. They
wholesaled boots and shoes from 122 Pearl Street, Boston.[80]

Erastus M. Nash of Abington, Massachusetts, was a member of the
firm Nash & Griffin of Boston, a well-known boot manufacturer. Nash
was a highly respected businessman who served two terms in the state
legislature. He took an active role in the Masonic Lodge, serving as
treasurer for more than thirty years for John Cutler Lodge, Abington
Council, Pilgrim Royal Arch Chapter, and Old Colony Commandery.
Nash died at the age of seventy.

According to Petsche, there were twelve pairs of fine calf gentlemen's
boots in the cargo that were retailed by Alden & Howard at 75 Pearl,
Boston.[81] Apparently, there were other partners in the business, one of
whom lived at Randolph, Massachusetts.

Twelve pairs of boy's kip boots were also recovered. These were attributed to George C. Walls, who was listed at 15 Pearl, House of Roxbury in
1865.[82] It is not known whether Walls was a retailer or wholesaler or both.

Petsche also notes that some of the boots came from lots marked
"BOOTS FROM S. WALKER & CO., BOSTON." These probably
came from Samuel Walker & Co. at 54 Elm, Boston. Walker, who lived
at Milford, and his partner G. H. Otis specialized in boots, shoes, and
leather on a wholesale and retail basis. Samuel Walker's wholesale business may have been conducted from 167 Pearl Street, Boston. During the
1850s, they were located at 40 Fulton Street and in the 1860s at 54 Elm
Street. By the late 1870s, they are no longer listed in Boston Directories.[83]

---

[80] *The Boston Directory, 1865*, 301.

[81] Petsche, *The Steamboat* Bertrand, 62. See also *Boston Directory, 1865*, 26.

[82] *Boston Directory, 1865*, 414.

[83] Daniel M. Lohnes, Acting Librarian, The Society for the Preservation of New England
Antiquities, Boston, Massachusetts, correspondence dated May 25, 1972. In the possession
of the author.

It is interesting to note that there was another wholesale shoe and boot dealer named Walker in Boston at this time. W. Walker Co. is listed in the 1865 *Boston Directory* as a wholesale enterprise: "Walker (William), Johnson (George W.) & Co. (V. Wood) boots and shoes, 87 Pearl Street, Boston."[84] This company has the same listing in the 1867 directory, but that same year, the *Massachusetts Business Directory* lists a W. H. H. Walker & Co. at 124 Pearl Street, likewise a wholesaler in boots and shoes.[85] Whether the Walkers were all related and doing business under various partnerships is conjectural, but I surmise that they were.

Miner's Boots

FIGURE 49. M. C. Dizer miner's boots with "diamond and leaf" pattern soles and steel heel caps.

Sixty pairs of miner's boots recovered from the *Bertrand* cargo are attributed to M. C. Dizer & Co. of East Weymouth, Massachusetts. Dizer was probably the largest producer of "Donelson" fancy nailed miner's boots during the 1860s. These were made on a single last, there being no right or left foot to worry about. They are 27 inches at the front and 22 inches at the back. These hip-length boots have soles studded with steel studs in floral patterns and were sometimes called "tackety boots." The heels have steel caps/cleats attached.

Marshall C. Dizer was born in Weymouth, September 23, 1822, and at twenty-two years of age, he began making shoes. Starting with capital of $35 in 1843, Dizer built a substantial business, and by 1894, he was said to be "the largest in the world for the class of goods he made."[86] He built a factory at 112 Pearl in Boston in 1861. Dizer's partners in the

---

[84]*Boston Directory, 1865*, 414.
[85]*Boston Massachusetts Business Directory, 1867*.
[86]William T. Davis, "Marshall Dizer," in *The Professional and Industrial History of Suffolk County, Massachusetts (1894)*, Vol. 3 (Boston: The Boston History Co., 1894), 354.

venture were his sons, Silas C. and Walter M. Dizer. The firm, which wholesaled Dizer products, was credited with paying "a hundred cents on the dollar" to its investors.[87]

Men's Slaughter Boots

A dozen pairs of slaughter boots in the cargo were wholesaled by W. S. Batchelder, Holliston, Mass., and considerable is known concerning this firm, located at 57 Hanover Street in Boston.[88]

William S. Batchelder was born in Hampton, New Hampshire, in 1800, the son of Odlin Batchelder. He and his brothers, William, John, and Benjamin moved with their family to Holliston, Massachusetts, early in their lives. Bachelder and his brothers were all interested in the manufacture of shoes and started out on a humble scale, buying only enough leather to make a few pairs of shoes, often with the help of their wives. When the shoes were made, they were sold and more leather was purchased. It paid off well because all three brothers became well-known manufacturers of boots and shoes by the mid-1800s.

William married Rhoda Whitney in 1821 and must have prospered rapidly because in 1833, he built a large Greek-revival mansion with several buildings nearby for his factory. He was known as a generous man, well-liked by his employees and fellow townspeople. He gave $500 to help outfit the Co. of Holliston that went to fight in the Civil War. He was the first president of the Holliston National Bank, and held the position until his death at seventy-six years of age.[89] W. S. Batchelder was a wholesale dealer in shoes, located at 57 Hanover Street between 1860 and 1875. By 1877, the firm was known as Batchelder and Lincoln.[90]

Apparently, some of the boots were wholesaled by "J. R. LION-BERGER & CO., NO. 71 MAIN STREET, ST. LOUIS." John R. Lionberger represents yet another entrepreneurial success story in the history of St. Louis. According to Hyde and Conrad, Lionberger was born in Luray, Virginia, on August 20, 1829, to Isaac and Mary Tutt Lionberger.[91] He was sent to college at Kemper Academy in Booneville, Missouri, and

---

[87]Ibid.

[88]*Boston Directory, 1865*, 43.

[89]Mrs. Frank A. Rees, Holliston Historical Society, correspondence dated September 25, 1974. In the possession of the author.

[90]Lohnes correspondence, 1972.

[91]Hyde and Conrad, *Encyclopedia of the History of St. Louis: A Compendium of History and Biography for Ready Reference*, 1291–92.

at sixteen years of age, he entered Missouri State University at Columbia, Missouri. Disliking classical studies, he turned his attention to the study of history in St. Louis. He was sent to college commercial activities and began a merchandising business in Boonville. In 1851, he married Margaret Clarkson of Columbia, Missouri, by whom he had four children: Marion, Isaac, Margaret, and Mary. By 1865, Lionberger had moved to St. Louis, where he established the wholesale boot and shoe house of Lionberger & Shields. Two years later, he purchased his partner's interest and operated the firm as sole proprietor. After a time, he admitted William Campbell Orr and others as partners and the firm became J. R. Lionberger & Co. and remained so until 1868 when Lionberger retired from the company.[92]

As a successful businessman, John Lionberger, like other St. Louis moguls, directed his energies to a variety of interests and especially to the development of transportation in St. Louis. He was a prime mover in the construction of the Eads Bridge and later, in company with other investors, saw to the completion of the North Missouri Railroad to Kansas City. For many years, he served as president of the St. Joseph and St. Louis Railroad Co.

Active in banking and finance, Lionberger helped organize the Southern Bank in 1857 and served as an officer until 1864, when the bank was reorganized under national banking laws and became the Third National Bank. Lionberger as the bank's president between 1867 and 1876. He was founder of the St. Louis Clearinghouse Association, a director of the Chamber of Commerce Association, and organizer of the St. Louis Safe Deposit Co. Not satisfied with these endeavors, Lionberger helped finance the Union Depot & Shipping Co. in 1881 and carefully watched the construction of a grain elevator with a capacity of 760,000 bushels. John Lionberger died in St. Louis, May 20, 1894.[93]

Other names associated with the manufacture and shipping of boots and shoes were the Boston firms of Clement, Colburn & Co. (plain boots), Laflin, Coburn, & Co. (hobnail boots), J. F. Schiefer & Co. (saddlery), C. H. Tilton (plain boots and lady's shoes/boots), and George C. Walls (boy's kip boots). While very little has been learned about these firms, Clement, Colburn, & Co. was a partnership between James H. Clement, George D. Colburn, James Erskine, and John B. Clement that did business in Boston at 135 Pearl Street in the 1860s.[94] This firm apparently later

[92]Ibid.
[93]Ibid.
[94]*Boston Directory, 1861*, 95, 99. *Boston Directory, 1869*, 144.

became Colburn, Fuller, & Co. Nothing is known of Laflin, Coburn, & Co., J. F. Scheifer & Co., or C. H. Tilton. Another name taken from leather goods was Alden & Howard of Randolph, Massachusetts. No references to any business run by these two gentlemen have been found, but there is ample information about various Aldens and Howards who were involved individually in the shoe industry. The *Massachusetts Business Directory* for 1856 lists several shoe manufacturers in Randolph under the names Hiram Alden, John Alden, Daniel Howard, John S. Howard, and Howard & French.[95] The 1860 directory complicates things, listing H. and H. C. Alden as shoe manufacturers, Daniel S. Howard as a Boston shoe wholesaler at 15 Shoe and Leather Exchange, and yet another Daniel Howard as a wholesaler at 85 Pearl Street in Boston. Whether any of these men became partners remains a mystery.

Yet another firm is shown in the records as F. H. & C., about which I have no information. William E. North of Saint Louis is also mentioned as being associated with men's Idaho mining boots, men's fancy nailed boots, men's gents boots, and men's "fire calf" boots. He was probably a wholesaler/distributor of these for Laflin, Coburn, & Co. of Boston.

It is interesting that some dress boots of unknown manufacture from the *Bertrand* were marked "McKay Stitched." A few things are known about Gordon McKay. He was born in Pittsfield, Massachusetts, and as a young man, he was educated as an engineer and worked on a railroad along the Erie Canal before he established a machine shop. In 1858, he bought a patent for a machine to stitch the uppers of shoes and boots to the soles from its inventor, Lyman Blake, for $8,000 in cash and a $62,000 share of future profits. With the help of the master mechanic and original inventor, McKay began perfecting it for his own patent. When the Civil War began, the Union Army needed thousands of pairs of sturdy boots that did not cost too much, and McKay was awarded a contract for 25,000 pairs of boots in 1862. Although he was not above capitalizing on being in the right place at the right time, McKay realized that the real money in boots and shoes was in boot and shoe machinery, and from 1862 to 1890, he and his partners patented forty sewing, nailing, tacking, lasting, and pegging machines for manufacturing shoes. Being a brilliant businessman, McKay sold his machines to shoe manufacturers who had to keep production records of shoes made with them and buy stamps redeemable for shares in McKay's company based on output production. This obviously monopolistic business practice earned McKay

[95] *Massachusetts Business Directory, 1856* (Boston, Mass.).

$500,000 a year on production of 120 million pairs of shoes, half the country's shoes in 1870.[96]

The flamboyant McKay first married in 1845, a marriage that lasted 22 years and ended in a nasty divorce when McKay published a thirty-page pamphlet about his wife's desertion and the meddling of his mother-in-law in his marriage. After that, Gordon McKay became a real Don Juan, marrying his housekeeper's daughter, twenty-one-year-old Minnie. When McKay was fifty-seven, he and his wife moved to Florence, Italy, where he built a palatial house, and where Minnie bore him two sons. By 1890, the marriage was over, with McKay accusing his wife of adultery with Arturo Fabricotti of Florence. After the divorce, Minnie married Count von Bruening of the German embassy. In his 1887 will, McKay left each son $500 a year until the age of twenty-one, declaring they were "her" sons, fathered by Fabricotti.[97]

Nonetheless, Gordon McKay's shoe machinery revolutionized the American shoemaking industry. He left $4,000,000 to Harvard University, principally because of his admiration for Harvard geologist Nathaniel Schaler, who enticed him to invest in a Montana gold mine that yielded about 10 percent of McKay's total wealth. McKay's last patent was for a mining dredge. He died at Providence, Rhode Island, on October 19, 1903.[98]

Sewing Supplies

Beads

Field notes indicate there were 4,604 round and tubular glass beads recovered. However, beads continued to appear in the back dirt of the excavation, indicating there probably were many more. The study and classification of the beads would be an interesting topic for some enterprising researcher.

Bolts of Cloth

Field notes indicate there were eleven bolts of cloth in the cargo, but lab notes do not indicate the nature of the fabrics on the bolts.

---

[96]Edward Tenner, "Gordon Mckay (1821–1903)," *Harvard Magazine* 103, no. 1 (2000): 37.

[97]"Death of Gordon Mckay," *The New York Times*, October 20, 1903.

[98]Ibid. More information about the Massachusetts boot and shoe industry can be found in Orra L. Stone, *History of Massachusetts Industries*, Vol. 1 (Boston and Chicago: S. J. Clarke Publishing Co.), 1143, and in "Randolf Early In The Shoe Industry," *Randolf Herald Souvenir Edition, Randolf Herald*, July 2, 1968.

Hooks and Eyes

Eight hundred and forty-two steel and brass hooks and eyes of modern form were recovered from the *Bertrand.*

Buttons

Among all the goods that appeared in frontier mercantiles, buttons of various kinds seem to have been extremely plentiful. Unfortunately for historians and historical archaeologists, descriptions of common buttons made before 1876 are rare. By this date, East Hampton, Massachusetts, and Waterbury, Connecticut, seem to have been the seats of the button industry, save for cottage industry mussel shell buttons produced along the Missouri River in Iowa and Missouri. It is known that in about, 1831 Joel and Josiah Hayden began manufacturing tin and japanned-tinned buttons in the Mill River Valley of Massachusetts. Their mill was destroyed by fire in 1832 and again by floods in 1874. They rebuilt the business after 1832 and subsequently made the first flexible metal-shanked lasting (prunella) buttons produced in the United States.[99] Apparently these replaced the sewn buttons being made in the same area by Samuel Williston, a storekeeper who also made wooden buttons. Williston is credited with inventing the machinery to make covered wooden buttons.

Hayden and Williston entered into a partnership and employed about 200 men and women to make buttons. They continued this venture until about 1848, when Williston moved the business to Easthampton, Massachusetts, where the firm produced about half of the world's supply of covered buttons.[100] Sometime around 1851, Williston left the firm and Hayden began making plumber's goods in partnership with A. D. Sanders in Hayden's button factory building. By 1876, new machinery had been invented in this country to make other kinds of buttons. Iron molds, or shells, made of tagging iron became quite common. One die machine could cut and press about 7,000 buttons an hour. At about this time, vegetable ivory buttons became popular, most of which were produced at Leeds, Massachusetts. India rubber buttons were also widely used.

[99]Sally C. Luscomb, *The Collector's Encyclopedia of Buttons* (New York: Bonanza Books, 1967), 95.

[100]Ibid., 222. See also "Williamsburg," *Massachusetts Historical Commission Reconnaissance Survey Report—Associated Regional Report: Connecticut Valley* (Boston, Massachusetts Historical Commission, 1982), Section 7: Federal Period (1775–1830), 7, and Section 8: Early Industrial Period (1830–1870), 9.

By 1870, there were 64 button factories in the United States employing about 2,000 workers whose aggregate salaries were $600,000 per year. The annual product produced was valued at about $2,000,000.

Pearl buttons were produced in great numbers along the Missouri and Mississippi Rivers, but the first descriptions of them do not appear in print until the first third of the nineteenth century. These were hand-made until about the middle of nineteenth century, when machines were invented to punch and drill buttons from fresh water mussel shells.

Bone Buttons

Accession records show there are 487 bone buttons of various shapes and sizes, but specific descriptions do not appear in the author's notes.

China Buttons

Among the several hundred cubic feet of textiles of various kinds were quantities of sewing notions and supplies. These included hundreds of thimbles, needles, straight pins, hooks and eyes, suspender guides and 13,000 buttons There are more than 100 different styles and types of buttons made of hard rubber, mother-of-pearl or mussel shell, glass, china, bone, wood, fabric, pressed fiber, tin, and brass. An extensive article about brass "Tally Ho's" or sporting buttons and hard rubber novelty buttons from the *Bertrand* appears in *Just Buttons* in 1972, and another article about small porcelain china buttons of several types from the cargo was published in the same journal in 1974.[101]

Approximately 34 percent of the buttons recovered from the *Bertrand* were small china varieties, which is not unusual considering that by the mid-nineteenth century, these represented the most popular kind of buttons on the frontier. In the *Bertrand* collection, there are 2,670 plain white china buttons, seventy-eight white piecrust china buttons, 1,264 calico printed china buttons of the four-hole sew-through type, and a lesser number of gaiter and ringer buttons. The plain white four-hole-sew-through china buttons range in size from 5/8 inch to 7/16 inch in diameter. The seven three-hole plain china buttons found measure 1/4 inch in diameter. The pie crust buttons measure 7/16 and 1/2

[101]Ronald R. Switzer, "Tally Ho's from the Steamboat *Bertrand*," *Just Buttons* 30, no. 4 (1972): 416–26; and "Small Chinas from the Steamboat *Bertrand*," *Just Buttons* 32, no. 5 (1975): 135–42.

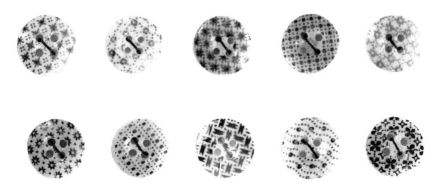

FIGURE 50. Various patterns of four-hole sew-through calico buttons.

inches. In addition, there are eighteen turquoise-colored four-hole buttons in the collection measuring 3/8 inches in diameter.

The china calico buttons have decorative patterns similar or identical to patterns on calico cotton fabric imported to Europe from India in the seventeenth century. Calico cloth was especially popular in frontier America during the 1800s, but the calico cloth recovered from the *Bertrand* was in the form of two bolts of handkerchief stock. A few calico buttons were found sewn to men's flannel underwear. Most of the designs were red, green, blue, and brown, and a few were black or yellow. The four-hole calico buttons measure 7/16 inches in diameter.

Until the 1840s, plain china or porcelain buttons were comparatively expensive because they were handmade. In 1840, English button maker Richard Prosser invented a molding press for dry china clay that enabled mass production of glazed china buttons. Not long thereafter, several factories were producing calico printed buttons, and the well-known Minton pottery works in Staffordshire, England, made calico chinas until about 1846. In addition, from the 1850s until the early twentieth century, Bapterosses of France was an extremely successful calico button maker.

Calico buttons were made by transfer printing the design onto greenware or bisque-fired buttons that were then clear-glazed and refired. Transfer printing of this kind was developed in England in the mid-eighteenth century and involved etching or engraving a copper plate to which mineral ink was applied. The plate was placed in a small printing press and the design was transferred to tissue paper. Sizings were used

FIGURE 51. Double and single band four-hole sew-through "Ringer" buttons.

in combination with the inks so that the designs readily transferred to the unfired/bisque-fired button stock.

Luscomb says that the first American examples of calico buttons were produced by Charles Cartledge and Herbert Fergerson at Cartledge & Co. of Greenpoint, Long Island, New York, in June 1848. Cartledge came to this country from Staffordshire, England, in 1832, and soon after established his company. Before the company closed in 1856–1857, it produced calico buttons in a hundred different patterns, most of which were sold for three cents a dozen on cards so merchants could cut the desired number of buttons off for the purchaser.[102] Little is known of other American producers that might be associated with the *Bertrand* examples.

All of the 345 gaiter buttons were found with or attached to textile materials. The majority of the gaiter buttons are white porcelain with brass or white metal shank plates and loop shanks. A few others are black or brown and dome-shaped or cone-shaped. A few are small white "aspirins" or flat pill-shaped gaiters.

The remaining small china buttons are typical ringer buttons made of white porcelain with one or more colored bands encircling the button faces. Within this group, the most common are white-bodied, saucer-shaped buttons with a single wide band of color around the border. The colors are blue, green, pink, and peach. They measure 7/16 inches in diameter.

---

[102]Luscomb, *The Collector's Encyclopedia of Buttons*, 31.

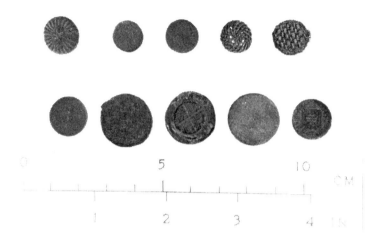

FIGURE 52. Various sizes and patterns of cloth and cloth-covered buttons.
FIGURE 53. Various patterns of small cloth-covered buttons.

Cloth and Covered Metal and Wooden Buttons

Records indicate there are fourteen cloth-covered metal buttons of various sizes, shapes, and colors, 399 cloth buttons, and seventy-eight cloth-covered wooden buttons. Laboratory notes indicate that most, if not all, of these are associated with items of clothing. The only descriptions come from a set of photographs and line drawings that illustrate fabric patterns on the button faces. Laboratory notes do not include descriptions of the other button types in the category listed above or of the other 416 miscellaneous buttons noted in the author's files. A study of the entire collection of *Bertrand* buttons would make an interesting investigative paper.

Shell Buttons

Accession records show there are 714 shell buttons of various sizes, shapes, and descriptions in the collection. While the author's notes contain no descriptions of these, two-hole, four-hole. and five-hole sew-through mussel shell buttons were very common during this period, so finding them on the *Bertrand* is not surprising. There are few references to mussel shell pearl button making until about 1855. when immigrant button makers from England and Germany introduced the trade to the United States. Most of the shells used in button manufacturing were imported from China until 1891, when a German immigrant named "John Beopple" (Johann F. Bopple) established a shell button factory at Muscatine, Iowa, where he produced pearl buttons from "Unio" mussel shells with a foot-powered machine he had invented.[103] Therefore, it is safe to say that the *Bertrand* examples probably did not come from this source. Their origin will remain a mystery.

Tally-Ho and Novelty Hard Rubber Buttons

There were four varieties of "Sanders" type brass sporting buttons in the cargo. Seventy- one of the largest sporting buttons apparently were made up in twelve button sets. Animals depicted on the stippled background button faces are hunting dogs, roe deer, horses, ponies, hares, wild boars, stags, and weasels. Measuring 1 5/32 inches in diameter, the brass under-blanks of all but one button are back-marked "EXTRA QUALITY—HAMMOND

---

[103]Ibid., 25. See also Jeffrey J. Kurtz, "The Old Pioneer: The Journey of John F. Boepple, Founder of the Fresh Water Pearl Button Industry" (Muscatine, Iowa: Pearl Button Museum, 2003), 3 pages.

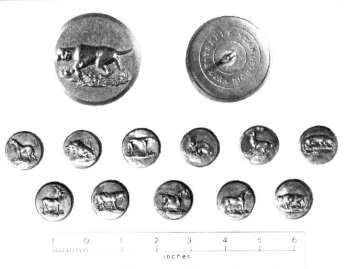

FIGURE 54. Large brass "Sporting Buttons."

TURNER & SONS" and bear a small crown above the center. A single button of this size with a hunting dog on the upper blank is stamped on the reverse "TREBLE STAND—EXTRA RICH." Three of the largest sizes of sporting buttons were affixed to five duster-like garments intended to be worn by men. Three buttons were sewn on the coat backs in a line perpendicular to the split of the coat tail. Six more buttons were sewn up the front for closing the garments.

The smallest brass sporting buttons were sewn in sets of four to waistbands of black plaid wool men's trousers and were spaced to accommodate suspenders. Ten pairs of such pants were recovered, but only four pairs had brass buttons. The pants had flap pockets buttoned with small brass or hard rubber buttons and were belted at the back with small brass buckles; none had cuffs. The covered fly of each pair bore three unusual, small hard rubber buttons.

The second type of brass sporting button seems to have been made up in six button sets; there are twenty-one buttons of this type in the collection. These buttons have convex faces with hunting scenes and animals on their faces, surrounded by a filigree pattern. The buttons measure 1 1/32 inches in diameter. The button under-blanks are stamped "HAMMOND TURNER & SONS." Both types had copper shanks braised into loops and inserted in a small hole in the centers of the under blanks.[104]

---

[104]Luscomb, *Collector's Encyclopedia of Buttons*, 127, 176.

FIGURE 55. Medium brass "Sporting Buttons."

Hammond Turner & Sons were button manufacturers in Birmingham, England, in the middle of the nineteenth century. The name has been found on Confederate uniform buttons and fine quality sporting buttons of the period.[105] Apparently, the company of Hammond, Turner, & Dickinson was founded in Birmingham in 1717 and operated under that name until about 1823, when it became Hammond Turner & Sons. The company made decorated, plain gilt, and especially fine sporting buttons. About 1850, the firm became Hammond Turner & Sons Ltd. and remained so until it quit operating about 1955.

The term "Sanders" type is well known to button collectors. B. Sanders and his son, B. Sanders, Jr., were both button manufacturers and inventors in Birmingham and are best known for inventing cloth-covered buttons with metal shanks and, in 1826, a canvas shank button.[106] By the mid-nineteenth century, the Sanders's method of crimping the upper button blank over the under-blank to form a complete button was applied to metal buttons by Hammond Turner & Sons.

A third type of brass sporting button is represented by forty-one buttons with concave faces and a raised leaf motif around the edge. Each bears a raised animal head on its face, and there appear to have been six buttons to a set. The animals represented are stags, foxes, horses, boars,

---

[105]Ibid., 47, 93–94. See also David F. Johnson, *Uniform Buttons: American Armed Forces 1784–1948—Descriptions and Values*, Vol. 1 (Watkins Glen, N.Y.: Century House, 1948), 209.
[106]Luscomb, *Collector's Encyclopedia of Buttons*, 17.

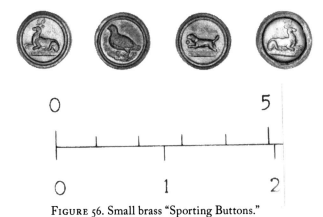

FIGURE 56. Small brass "Sporting Buttons."

wolves, and dogs. The buttons are about 1 inch in diameter and have a fiber core, and the under-blanks are made of tinned iron with a rivet type shank. The under-blanks are stamped "FEINE QUAL."

The remaining brass button type is 17/32 inches in diameter and was probably made up in sets of three or four. There are only three designs in the twenty-two buttons of this type, a dog, a stag, and a partridge. The slightly concave faces of the buttons have a raised rim around the circumference and a stippled background bearing a raised animal design. The fiber core buttons are backed with tinned iron under-blanks with rivet-type copper shanks. The under-blanks are stamped "Feine."

Brass, Tinned, and Japanned Metal Buttons

Exact quantities of other metal buttons are not listed in laboratory notes.

Hard Rubber Buttons

The small hard rubber buttons found on the flys of several pairs of men's trousers have grooved radiating bands around the edges, and the depressed faces have raised bulls jumping through the depressed centers. The loop-shank buttons have back marks reading "N. R. CO.—GOODYEAR'S PT." These buttons were manufactured by the Novelty Rubber Co., New Brunswick, New Jersey, probably under Goodyear's Patent Number 8075, which was dated May 6, 1851.[107] The buttons measure 19/32 inches diameter. There are sixteen such buttons in the collection.

---

[107]Ibid., 140.

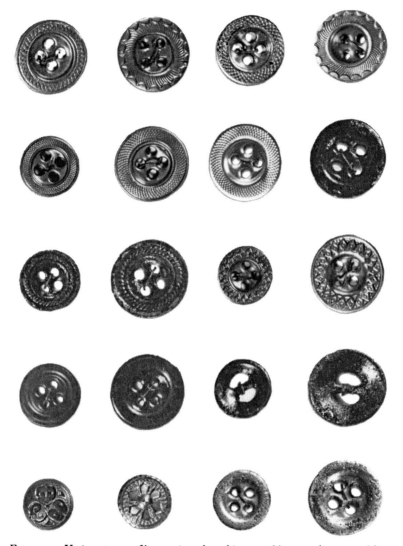

FIGURE 57. Various types of brass, tinned, and japanned buttons (not to scale).

A good deal is known about Charles Goodyear, but not so much is known about the Novelty Rubber Co. that used Goodyear's patent to produce hard rubber buttons. Charles Goodyear was born on December 29, 1800, at New Haven, Connecticut, the eldest son of Cynthia Bateman Goodyear and Amasa Goodyear, an inventor of farming implements and a hardware manufacturer. Amasa Goodyear may have been the first person in this country to manufacture pearl buttons in 1807. He also made metal buttons for the government during the War of 1812 and patented flexible steel tine hay and manure forks, from which he derived a considerable fortune. In his Connecticut factory, Amasa turned out a variety of hardware and other items, including spoons, scythes, and clocks. Charles Goodyear moved to Naugatuck, Connecticut, and as a boy of seven, he worked in his father's pearl button factory and on the family farm until 1816, when he apprenticed at the hardware manufacturing firm of Rogers & Brothers in Philadelphia.[108]

In 1821, young Goodyear returned home to partner with his father, but the business fell on hard times and was dissolved in 1830. During this tumultuous time, in 1824, Charles married Clarissa Beecher. The business recovered and grew rapidly, and the manufactory produced ample hardware stock for a store Charles opened in Philadelphia in 1826. In the spring of 1830, Charles became ill with dyspepsia, and along with the illness came the loss of business. Falling into debt by 1834, Goodyear was insolvent and was sent to debtor's prison in Philadelphia, where he explored a new interest in rubber.[109] His first experiments in prison involved a bench and marble slab, a few cents worth of gum rubber provided by a friend, and his mother's rolling pin. Until 1836, most of his early experiments were unsuccessful. That year, he found that an application of nitric acid produced a curing effect on rubber. Soon he found a new partner and leased an abandoned rubber factory on Staten Island, New York, only to see his fortunes dashed in the bank panic of 1837, leaving him again as an insolvent debtor. Nevertheless, Goodyear later partnered with the Roxbury India Rubber Co. to make rubberized mail bags, but these too were a failure. Although deep in debt, Goodyear kept things going by selling his patents for improvements in farm implements and other inventions. He also continued his early experiments with India rubber, and in 1839, he accidentally discovered the true process of vulcanizing rubber by

---

[108] Rev. Bradford K. Peirce, *Trials of an Inventor—Life and Discoveries of Charles Goodyear* (New York: Carlton & Porter, 1866), 18–27.

[109] Ibid., 18–46.

adding sulfur and heating it with steam under pressure for six hours at 270 degrees Fahrenheit. Unfortunately, no one believed that the process worked, and by this time, most of his friends had abandoned him. He lived on charity and moved his family five times in five years before taking out a patent (Patent No. 3,633) on the vulcanizing process on June 15, 1844. Unfortunately, an Englishman named Thomas Hancock used Goodyear's ideas and patented vulcanized rubber with an English patent one week before Goodyear received his American patent. The ensuing patent wars culminated in the infringement case of *Goodyear vs. Day* in 1852, in which Daniel Webster defended Goodyear against Rufus Choate; Goodyear was victorious. Goodyear then traveled to England and France, where he engaged with a French company to produce vulcanized rubber goods. The company failed, and he was arrested and jailed for debt in Paris. During the next few years, he invented rubberized cloth, and in the sixteen years before his death, Charles Goodyear took out sixty patents on rubber manufacture. Owing to high litigation costs and bad business decisions, he died a poor man in New York City on July 1, 1860, leaving his family a debt of $200,000. Others prospered from his inventions, but Goodyear was never a part of the company that eventually bore his name.[110]

Common hard rubber buttons are often found with mold marks reading "Goodyear" and "1849–1851." Obviously these dates refer to material patents and not to the date of the button's manufacture. The Novelty Rubber Co. (N.R. Co.) manufactured rubber buttons 1/4 to 1 3/4 inches in diameter between 1855 and 1870.

Needles

In the cargo are at least 142 common sewing needles. Although needles appear to be simple implements, during this period, most of the good steel needles used in this country were handmade in Redditch or Birmingham, England. It was said that a needle passed through about 120 separate operations before it was ready to sell. Steel wire was sorted, cleaned and straightened, and cut into lengths before being pointed by hand grinding. After the heads were flattened, the eyes were punched by hand or by machine, and the needles were filed and straightened before

---

[110]Charles Morris, "Charles Goodyear, the Prince of the Rubber Industry," *Heroes of Progress in America* (Philadelphia and London: J. B. Lippincott Co., 1919), 171–77. See also Holland Thompson, "The Story of Rubber," *The Age of Invention, A Chronicle of Mechanical Conquest*, Book 37 in the Chronicles of America Series (New Haven: Yale University Press, 1921).

being hardened in an oven and then tempered in a bath of water or oil. They were again straightened, scoured by machine, cleaned, winnowed, and sorted by size, after which they were blued and polished.

Apparently needle making was introduced to the Birmingham region by a German named Elias Crowse about 1541, early in the reign of Queen Elizabeth I, and the village of Redditch derived most of its employment and income from needle making thereafter.[111]

Ribbons

Notes indicate there are at least forty-five silk and velvet ribbons of various colors in the collection and twelve ribbon spools. Other information is lacking.

Straight Pins (2 1/2 Pounds)

Although these appear to be of the modern type, it is difficult to determine whether they were produced domestically or imported from Britain. Like needles, pins were the product of several manufacturing processes. At this time in history, pins were made mainly by machines. Metal wire, mostly brass, was pulled through holes in a draw block to reduce its diameter and then straightened by rewinding and pulling it between a series of pins on a straightening bench. Then it was cut into lengths that would make two pins each. A workman took a bundle of lengths and swiftly pointed the ends of the bundles on a grinding wheel. Then the wires were cut in to pieces for heading on a machine that pinched a small ball of metal at the end opposite the point and automatically tapped the ball to flatten it into a head. Pins were next immersed in a bath of cream of tartar and tin to give them a white metal appearance, dried, and "papered" for inspection. Birmingham and nearby village manufacturers made hundreds of millions of pins annually for export using this process.

Thimbles

Laboratory notes indicate there are 118 brass thimbles in the collection, none which bear manufacturer's marks. In all probability, these were wholesaled by Bast & Pollack at No. 150 Main St. in St. Louis.

---

[111]Benjamin Vincent, *Hayden's Dictionary of Dates and Universal Information Relating to All Ages and Nations* (New York: G. P. Putnam's Sons, 1906), 925.

Thread and Thread Spools

Laboratory notes indicate there are 770 skeins of two-ply black, pink, blue, and yellow cotton thread and twelve wooden thread spools.

HOUSEHOLD GOODS

Buckets and Tubs

Butter Churns

There are two types of butter churns in the *Bertrand*'s cargo, both of which were manufactured by "OLIVER AMES & SONS / SUCCESSORS TO / NORSE, MASON & CO. / BOSTON & WORCHESTER MASS."

Perhaps the most successful of the many personalities associated with goods in the cargo was Oliver Ames, Sr. and two of his sons, Oliver Ames, Jr., and Oakes Ames. Ames, Sr. was the youngest son of John Ames of West Bridgewater, Massachusetts. He was born on April 13, 1779, and received some education in Easton, Massachusetts. Additional legal studies took him to North Andover and the Franklin Academy, but Oliver abandoned his studies to apprentice in his father's factory. John Ames made shovels in West Bridgewater from 1777 until his death in 1805, at which time Oliver inherited his father's forge and land. Oliver apparently had moved to Easton in 1803 and started a business, so he ran two businesses after his father's death. On November 5, 1807, he and his wife Susannah Angier Ames had their third son, Oliver, Jr., in Plymouth, Massachusetts, and in that year, Oliver partnered with Asa Waters under the name Ames, Waters, & Co. to manufacture hoes. Late in that year, he moved to Plymouth and started a shovel-making plant under the name of Plymouth Iron Works. Oliver Ames moved back to Easton in 1814 and expanded his operation. In 1844, he turned the management of his company over to his sons, Oaks Ames and Oliver Ames, Jr., who managed the company as Oliver Ames & Sons between 1844 and 1901.[112]

The demand for shovels during the early part of the California gold

---

[112] *The National Cyclopedia of American Biography Being the History of the United States as Illustrated in the Lives of the Founders, Builders, and Defenders of the Republic, and of the Men and Women Who are Doing the Work and Moulding the Thought of the Present Time* (Brooklyn: James T. White & Company, The Scientific Press, Robert Drummond and Company, 1910), 201–202.

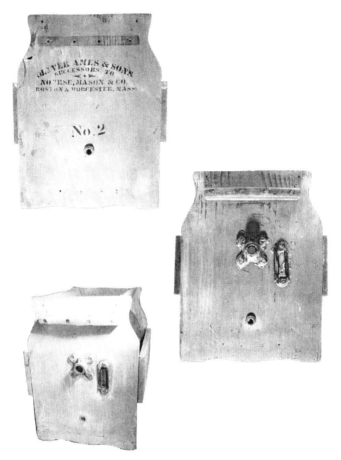

FIGURE 58. Oliver Ames & Sons butter churns.

rush far exceeded the supply, and, with a readily available source of cheap Irish immigrant labor, the Ames business expanded to huge proportions. From 1854 through the Civil War and continuing until 1871, the company also engaged in the manufacture of hinges, nails, butter churns, plows, mowing and threshing machines, and shoes.[113]

Beginning in 1852, when Oliver Ames was elected to the state senate, his genius surfaced. Although he was elected to the senate again in 1857, Ames directed most of his efforts to business, and with his brother Oakes built the Easton Branch Railroad in 1855. Owing to their

---

[113]*Boston Directory, 1865*, Vol. 1, 1, 28.

business knowledge and their success in politics, their fortune is said to have exceeded eight million dollars during the Civil War. Increasing their wealth through government contracts for shovels and swords, the Ames brothers turned over their management interests to their sons and focused on financing the transcontinental Union Pacific Railroad. Between 1866 and 1871, Oliver Ames served as acting president and president of the Union Pacific, and as a director until his death on March 9, 1877.[114]

In 1870, with more than half of its assets committed to investments, Oliver Ames and his nephew brought the company back to fiscal order, but not before Oakes Ames died in 1873. As the owner of the Easton and Bristol National Banks, Ames also served as a director for the Atlantic and Pacific, Kansas Pacific, Colorado Central, Old Colony, and other railroads. During his illustrious career, he donated land to churches, schools, and small colleges, and before his death left funds for libraries, schools, and road improvements. Today, Oliver Ames is commemorated in the business literature of Boston and by a sixty-foot high truncated stone pyramid at Sherman, Wyoming, the highest point on the continent reached by the Union Pacific. The captivating story of Ames's involvement in the transcontinental railroad is described in *Empire Express: Building the First Transcontinental Railroad*, by David Haward Bain, published in 1999.

An obituary for Oliver Ames appeared in a March 10, 1877, issue of a local newspaper:

THE HON. OLIVER AMES

The Hon. Oliver Ames. The Hon. Oliver Ames of North Easton died of pneumonia at his home yesterday forenoon, at the age of sixty-nine years. He was the last of the well-known family of Oliver Ames & Sons (father and five sons), shovel-makers in North Easton. He was early associated in business with his father, and showed good business capacities. He was much interested in railroads and was for many years one of the directors of the Old Colony and Newport Road. He was better known, however, by his connection with the Union Pacific. He was director for ten years. In 1866 he became president pro tem of the road, succeeding General Fremont, which place he held till March 12, 1868, when he became president. He held his position until March 8, 1871, when he declined a reelection. A few years since he presented to the Unitarian Society of north Easton, of which he was a member, a handsome edifice, which cost over $100,000,

---

[114] *The National Cyclopedia of American Biography*, 201–202.

and subscribed a large sum toward the erection of the new building of the Young Men's Christian Union on Boylston street. Mr. Ames leaves a wife and two children. His estate is worth several million dollars. He has long been a prominent and valued citizen, and will be missed both in his business and social relations. The funeral will take place at one P.M. on Monday.

Boston city directories show that Oliver Ames & Sons did business between 1860 and 1867 from the agricultural warehouse at Quincy Hall. Sometime before 1867, an affiliate company was formed known as the Ames Plow Co., but the principle Ames firm of Easton, Massachusetts, which merged with H. M. Meyers Shovel Co., T. Rowland's Sons, Wright Shovel Co., and Elwood Steel Plant in 1901 operates to this day as the Ames Shovel and Tool Co.

Candles and Soap

Among the interesting items in the cargo were twelve cases of soaps and forty cases of candles. Soap box stencils read:

N. SCHAEFER & CO	N. SCHAEFFER & CO.
OLEINE SOAP	PALM SOAP
ST. LOUIS, MO	SAINT LOUIS, MO.

In addition, there were several cases of candles packed 240 per crate in layers with alternating wicks and bases marked:

SOLAR SPERM CANDLES	N. SCHAEFER & CO.
N. SCHAEFFER & CO.	STAR CANDLES
ST. LOUIS, MO.	ST. LOUIS, MO.
40 Gs	40 Gs

The soaps and candles were undoubtedly products of the Schaeffer Manufacturing Co. of St. Louis. Nicholas Schaeffer was a young German-educated chemist who came to St. Louis in 1839 and established a soap-making company that later became Schaeffer Manufacturing Co. The original address for the business was 22nd and Washington Streets. In the beginning, soap products were manufactured for use in the St. Louis area, and later candles were made. This was the first specialty manufacturing company west of the Mississippi, but candles and soap eventually did not account for the majority of the company's sales. Red oils and axle grease became the principal products and were widely

FIGURE 59. N. Schaeffer & Co. Solar Sperm Candles crate.

used in both the riverboat trade and for the famed covered wagons that were the principal methods of transportation in this section of the country during this era. The company changed its name to Schaeffer Brothers and Powell, and in 1949, the company name reverted back to Schaeffer Manufacturing Co. Upon the death of Nicolas Schaeffer, his three sons took over operation of the business.

Nicholas Schaeffer was born in Marlem, Alsace, France, on December 4, 1814. His father was a shoemaker who died two years after his birth, leaving a widow and seven male children, of which Nicholas was the sixth. His father was well enough off that Nicholas received a basic education, but by the age of fourteen, he was engaged in candle and soap making in Strasburg. Saving his money for passage, Nicholas and his mother and brothers immigrated to America in 1832. When they arrived in Baltimore they purchased a horse and wagon and set out for Cincinnati, but were robbed of the horse at Hagerstown, Maryland. They sold the wagon for $7 and the harness for $5. Schaeffer's mother obtained a ride in a freight wagon, and her sons walked to Wheeling, West Virginia, where the family obtained passage on a steamboat to Cincinnati.[115]

Nearly destitute, Nicholas obtained work mixing mortar for a stone mason for seventy-five cents a day. He soon left to work in a tannery for $15 a month before finding work making soap and candles for $30 a month. With $250 in his pocket, he made his way to New Orleans and then to Vicksburg, where he found employment quarrying marble. This was not to his liking, so he found employment as a steward at the Old Mansion House hotel for $40 a month and found. Thereafter, he returned to Cincinnati,

---

[115]L. U. Reavis, *St. Louis: The Future City of the World, Illustrated, Biographical Edition*, 565–67.

where he, two of his brothers, and a fourth person purchased a flat boat and plied the Ohio River for a year delivering supplies. By 1836, as quarter owner in the flat boat, he was caught in the Bank Panic of 1837 and the business failed. He returned to Vicksburg to open a store selling general merchandise and liquor. This was short-lived, because Mississippi passed an anti-liquor bill that damaged his business, so he sold out. Returning to Cincinnati, he purchased the means to make candles and returned to Vicksburg but sold out his business there within six months and made his way to St. Louis in 1839. He started a candle works and soap-making business and was immediately successful, making a $4,000 profit. Unfortunately, business declined and Schaeffer was forced to move his manufactory several times, finally establishing it on Washington Avenue in St. Louis. Business over the next few years boomed, and gross sales exceeded $1 million. His goods were marketed and sold all over the country.[116]

Nicholas Schaeffer became one of the leading citizens of St. Louis, where he served on the city council and was president of the Pacific Insurance Co. and director in the St. Louis Fire and Marine Insurance Co. He also distinguished himself as president of the Illinois and St. Louis Railway Co. and served as a member of the Merchants Exchange. Schaeffer was married in 1843 and had six children, five of which survived.[117] Nicholas's oldest son, Jacob, became president of the company upon his father's death in 1880. Jacob Schaeffer died in 1917, and his son-in-law, William Shields, became company president until his oldest son Tom Shields assumed the position. After World War II, in 1947, the company more or less reinvented itself, and Tom's brother Gwynne Shields was put in charge of production. The company continues today.

As a side note, bar soap was branded by the company as "Boss" soap, and the candles were branded "Star" candles. Schaeffer Manufacturing Co. closed its soap and candle making operations in 1950 to concentrate on manufacturing lubricants. The production of lubricants earlier in company history was an outgrowth of the production of soap and candle animal fat by-products. One lubricant named Red Engine Oil was used by steamboats on the Missouri and Ohio Rivers. Schaeffer also made Black Beauty grease. By 1859, the company turned to manufacturing petroleum-based lubricating products.[118]

---

[116]Ibid.
[117]Ibid.
[118]Peter S. Adam, "Schaeffer Manufacturing Company, History," Schaeffer Oil, History of Schaeffer Oil—Lubricants, http://www.schaefferoil.com/company/ history.html.

Carpet Runners

There is one long wool carpet runner that is several yards long and that has chevron designs in black, brown, and maroon.

Clocks (70-plus)

According to *Bertrand* curator Leslie Perry Peterson, remnants of Seth Thomas mantel clocks and some examples of an early version of the Thomas lever clock were found in the cargo. Wholesaled by R. Campbell & Co., most of the clocks were destined for G. P. Dorriss of Virginia City.

Some of the mantel clocks had glass pendulum doors decorated with decalcomania. Between 1840 and 1863, William B. Fenn of Plymouth, Connecticut, was among the best known producers of stenciled clock case parts and reverse decorated glass tablets for clocks. Among his customers was the firm of Seth Thomas. However, it is not known whether the *Bertrand* specimens are attributable to Fenn.

If these clocks were produced by Seth Thomas, they are products of an incredibly interesting company. Seth Thomas was the fifth of seven children born to James Thomas and Martha Barnes Thomas, on August 19, 1785. His father, a Scottish immigrant to the United States, was a cooper at Wolcott, Connecticut, from whom young Seth learned carpentry skills sufficient to become an apprentice to Daniel Tuttle of Plymouth. Following his apprenticeship, Thomas worked as a carpenter building barns and houses. In 1800, he attempted to establish a clock-making business in Wolcott. Using seasoned mountain laurel for wooden clock wheels and spun flax clock weight cords, the young businessman produced enough clocks to be profitable.[119]

Sometime before 1807, he went to work for Eli Terry and Silas Hoadley, who were making clocks to wholesale. At the same time, he tried to purchase the mill property of Daniel Byington on the Mad River, but when he could not convince the town of Wolcott to build a road so he could market his wares, he went to Plymouth Hollow. By 1807, Seth Thomas had joined Eli Terry and Silas Hoadley as a partner in the firm of Terry, Thomas, & Hoadley, where he worked fitting clock parts together. Between 1807 and 1810, they made 4,000 "hang-up" or "wag-on-the-wall" clocks without cases.[120]

---

[119]Florence Goodman, "Seth Thomas" (dissertation, Thomaston Historical Society, Wolcott, Conn., April 10, 2000). See also Florence Goodman, "Seth Thomas, His Wolcott Years," Wolcott Historical Society *News*.

[120]Florence Goodman, "Seth Thomas" (dissertation).

In 1810, Thomas and Terry bought out Hoadley's interest and worked together until 1812, when Thomas sold his share of the company. In 1813, he bought Herman Clark's clock making business in Plymouth Hollow and began making thirty-hour wooden clocks with time and striking trains that had a greater number of wheels than other clocks. By 1817, he was making his own wooden shelf clocks. These cased pillar and scroll clocks were made until 1830, when bronze looking glass and other styles came on the market. In 1842, brass movement cased clocks became popular, and by 1845, wood movements were phased out. The Thomas mill produced clock parts, rolled brass, and brass wire, and operated successfully until 1853, when he established the Seth Thomas Clock Co. and purchased the rights to a shelf clock from Eli Terry. Thomas automated his factory and produced the very popular mantel clock for which the company is still famous. Wooden geared clocks were cheap to produce, and competition was keen because other clock makers at Waterbury, Winsted, and Bristol also made shelf clocks in large numbers and sold them all across the country.

From his first marriage to Philinda Tuttle in the early 1800s came a son, Seth Thomas, Jr., who later went into the clock business with his father. Seth Thomas apparently married twice, and from his second marriage came eight more children. Although Seth Thomas died in 1859, Seth Thomas, Jr., expanded the clock factory and developed it into a global business. Part of Plymouth Hollow was eventually renamed Thomaston in honor of Seth Thomas.[121] Thereafter, his less conservative son expanded the business and the number of clock patterns produced. By 1860, the famous Regulator clocks were introduced based on patents that Seth Thomas, Jr., purchased from the creditors of bankrupt clockmaker Silas B. Terry. Spring-driven clocks were introduced between 1855 and 1860, and perpetual calendar clocks were made between 1863 and 1917. Numerous other varieties followed.

One reason the Seth Thomas story is so engaging is because he was so inextricably associated with two other clock makers and inventors, Eli Terry and Silas Hoadley. These men had similar backgrounds and became the best-known clockmakers in the United States. Of these, the most is known about Eli Terry of East Windsor, Connecticut. Born on April 13, 1772, Terry was apprenticed to a master clockmaker at age fourteen, and by 1793, he owned his own clock shop in Plymouth, Connecticut. There he adapted waterpower to the clock wheel cutting equipment

---

[121]Ibid.

and hired men to mass produce wheels, cogs, and other parts for clock assemblies. About 1797, Terry invented clock works that registered the difference between mean and apparent time, but their cost was far too high and they never became popular.

In 1807, he partnered with Seth Thomas and Silas Hoadley to build 4,000 clocks for Connecticut businessmen Edward and Levi Porter, a project that required three years of labor. As time went on, Thomas and Hoadley bought out Terry's interest. Terry went on to invent a wooden shelf clock with interchangeable parts that had weights and pulleys suspended within the clock on either side of the face inside attractive wooden cases. Mass-produced interchangeable parts enabled Terry to build 12,000 clocks a year, which he paid peddlers to sell door-to-door in New England. From this venture, Thomas and Hoadley began to amass their fortunes. Terry retired from clock making in 1833 and died on February 24, 1852, at Terryville, having fathered eleven children in two marriages. His sons Eli Terry, Jr., and Silas Burnham Terry and his grandson, Eli Terry III were all involved in clock making and inventions relating to clocks through the latter part of the nineteenth century.[122]

The last of the three, Silas Hoadley, was born at Bethany, Connecticut, in 1786 and apprenticed in carpentry under his uncle Calvin Hoadley. After serving his apprenticeship, he became a partner with Seth Thomas and Eli Terry to make clocks at Greystone, which was then part of Plymouth. As his partners withdrew, Hoadley continued making clocks until 1849, when he closed his business. He died at Plymouth, Connecticut, on December 28, 1870.[123]

Coffee Grinders/Mills and Cases

There were forty-seven wood and tinned sheet metal coffee grinders/mills, of which only a few survived. These have V-shaped hoppers, the fronts of which bear oval embossed brass medallions reading "CHARLES PARKER'S / BEST / QUALITY / MERIDAN CONN." They are of a type usually found attached to a piece of wood screwed to the outside of a wagon box on a military or emigrant wagon. A similar grinder can be seen on a wagon displayed at Fort Larned National Historical Site at Fort Larned, Kansas.

---

[122]Walter A. Dyer, "The Clockmakers of Connecticut," *Early American Craftsmen* (New York: The Century Company, 1915), 108–18.
[123]Ibid., 122–23.

FIGURE 60. Charles Parker's coffee mill.
FIGURE 61. Large unmarked coffee mill.

In addition, there were two wooden cases in the cargo, each containing six box type, top-feed, hand crank coffee grinders/mills. The grinders are made with cast-metal hoppers, handles, and gears set on square wooden tennon-joined boxes with knobbed drawers in the fronts under the hoppers. Both have wooden bases. These are of two types, one larger than the other, with the smaller ones being more ornate in their casting and having stirrup-like handles attached to the tops of the dome-shaped hoppers on their left sides.

The knobbed grinder handles on this type are gracefully curved upward and away from the hoppers, leaving clearance for the stirrup handles. These also bear a raised kerf-like design on the flanges around the bases of the hoppers. The smaller coffee grinders bear fragments of paper labels attributing their manufacture to Charles Parker. The label fragments read "PARKER'S / 431 / [Co]ffee Mill / [PA]TENTED / [CHARLE]S PARKER Co. / [MERIDE]N / [CON]N." More information about Charles Parker can be found in the section about his Britannia spoons.

The larger grinders have wooden tops through which the grinding mills are attached by means of wing nuts. The open topped hoppers and gears are plain, and the curved grinder handles bear necked wooden knobs. The grinders bear no manufacturer's marks.

Cookware
Frying Pans
One case of forty-eight to fifty cast-iron frying pans was recovered. No other information is found in the author's notes, and the maker is unknown, although it is suspected they were made by Giles Filley.

Waffle Irons
There are two hinged cast-iron waffle irons in the cargo. One is round, and the other is rectangular. Both are marked "GILES FILLEY."

Born in Simsbury (Bloomfield), Connecticut, on February 15, 1815, to Oliver and Annis Filley, Giles F. Filley was reared on a farm and educated in part in local schools. He finished his studies at Wilbraham Academy in Wilbraham, Massachusetts. In 1834, Giles Filley moved to St. Louis and joined his brother, Oliver D. Filley, apprenticed in the tinner's trade, and eventually became a partner in the business, where he stayed until 1841.[124] In 1844, he married Maria M. Farrington at Hartford, Connecticut, by whom he had nine sons, six of whom survived to adulthood.[125] These were Frank D. Filley, Charles H. Filley, Robert E. Filley, Christopher G. Filley, and Victor G. Filley.

By 1841, he transferred his interest in this business to his brother Oliver and engaged successfully in the crockery trade, where he accumulated considerable wealth. In 1849 he sold the crockery business to Edward A. and Samuel R. Filley, his cousins, and started a new firm called the Excelsior Stove Works for the manufacture of stoves and "all the appurtenances thereto." It is likely that Filley began making cast-iron cookware shortly after formation of the company. He made a large variety of full size pots, kettles, spiders, and griddles and other products as well miniature stoves and toy-sized cookware marked "G. F. Filley."

Both the pottery and cast-iron cookware businesses were successful. Starting out small with twenty-five molders and twenty laborers in other

[124]William Hyde and Howard L. Conrad, *Encyclopedia of the History of St. Louis*, Vol. 2, 743.
[125]J. Thomas Scharf, *History of St. Louis City and County*, 601.

departments, the business grew rapidly, and by 1865, he employed 230 molders and 300 men in other departments. The works covered two city blocks and included a foundry and machine shops that produced cast-iron stove parts and tinner's supplies. In that year, the firm was incorporated as the Excelsior Manufacturing Co. Along the way, Giles Filley patented a number of cast-iron products and in 1851 invented the famous Charter Oak cooking stove. St. Louis Hollowware, which was larger and better finished, was also made by Excelsior. The firm name changed after Filley's retirement in 1895 to the Charter Oak Range and Iron Co.[126]

As a successful businessman, Giles Filley engaged in many civic and public works. He provided stone for the great Eads Bridge and was one of the builders of the Kansas Pacific Railroad. As one of the organizers of the "Free Soil" party in 1848, Filley became a prominent supporter of President Lincoln and used his "Union" newspaper to support the northern cause during the Civil War. It was Giles Filley who armed a 100-man company of his employees to assist General Lyon in the defense of the United States Arsenal at St. Louis. These were among the first volunteer troops equipped for the suppression of the secession movement. During the Civil War Filley served on a commission to assess fines against Southern sympathizers in St. Louis, a job that he very much disdained, but felt it was necessary to perform.[127]

Corkscrews

There is virtually no way to identify the maker of the twenty-three corkscrews with certainty. Corkscrews were not all that common in the United States until the 1860s, when straight cylindrical-necked wine bottles and straight corks became popular, making it possible to store wine bottles on their sides. The common corkscrew as we know it probably derived from a single helix spiral gun worm, which was a device for cleaning wads from musket barrels or for removing unspent charges or balls from the barrels. While the first patent for a helix-type bottle screw with a button at the top of the shaft was granted to Samuel Henshall in England in 1795, corkscrews were slow to mature as inventions until Rockwell Clough of New Jersey invented machinery in 1876 that could bend a single piece of wire into a complete corkscrew. At one end of the

[126]Hyde and Conrad, *Encyclopedia of the History of St. Louis*, 744.
[127]Scharf, *History of St. Louis City and County*, 601.

helix, the wire was twisted into a finger loop handle. One of the first T-handled corkscrew patents in the United States was granted to M. L. Byrn of New York, on March 27, 1860 (Patent No. 27,615).

Cutlery
Butcher Knives

FIGURE 62. Lamson Goodnow & Co. butcher knife.

In my "Butcher Knives as Historical Sources," I noted that, "Of all the knives in history, perhaps the least is known about butcher knives."[128] Three different types of butcher knives, represented by ninety-seven complete specimens and some fragments, were found in the cargo. Most numerous are two types of butcher knives produced by Lamson and Goodnow.

The first type is 10 5/8 inches long and has a two-piece checkered walnut handle secured with four rivets and a two-piece steel bolster held in place with a single rivet. The blade, which is "v" ground, has a clipped point and a rather long false edge. The tang runs the full length of the handle. The left side of the blade is stamped "LAMSON GOODNOW & CO. / PATENTED MARCH 6, 1860." Interestingly, the imprinted patent (No. 27,343) was issued to Francis Baschnagel of Beverly, Massachusetts, for an improved plastic compound used to make knife handles. None of the knives from the cargo have plastic handles, so why knife blades were stamped with this patent number is a mystery.

The second type of Lamson and Goodnow butcher knife is made of heavier steel and has a longer and broader blade. The blade is 11 1/4 inches

---

[128]Ronald R. Switzer, "Butcher Knives as Historical Sources," *The Museum of the Fur Trade Quarterly* 8, no. 1 (1972): 5.

long and has a short clipped point. The handle is plain hardwood, held in place with four brass rivets against a steel bolster. The "v" ground blade bears no false edge, and is stamped with the same markings as the previously described type.

By 1840, English blades began to be displaced by American-made knives produced by John Russell. In the shadow of his Green River knives were those made by Lamson and Goodnow, who between 1844 and the end of the fur trade in 1865 dominated the American cutlery market. Ebenezer G. Lamson and Nathaniel Lamson were the sons of Silas Lamson, who invented bent scythe snath handles. Ebenezer began manufacturing cutlery in 1842, and two years later, he became associated with Aabel F. Goodnow (and possibly Ebenezer Goodnow) in the firm of Lamson & Goodnow.[129] The firm expanded its cutlery line in 1844 to include the Bowie knife and other styles.

At the time, most quality cutlery was manufactured in England, and the Lanson & Goodnow shop was relatively small, employing only forty men. However, with the addition of machinery, they produced uniformly good quality cutlery exceeding the manufactory in Europe "in the excellence of the metal used, but especially in the practical utility of their patterns, and in the remarkable degree of the finish of their work." The Lamson & Goodnow factory began producing table cutlery, butcher and pocket knives, augers, and bits. Knife blades were forged by trip and drop hammers and by punching presses that insured uniformity of the blade shape. Once a blade was produced, the company name was pressed onto it. About 3,500 knife blades could be pressed by a single operator in a day. The company also invented and patented a process to secure knife handles to the blade that prevented the handles from becoming loose through use or exposure to hot water. One has to wonder if the patent number for plastic handles on the Bertrand examples reflects this patent. Knife handles were made from ivory, pearl, horn tips, cattle shin bones, cocoa wood, rosewood, ebony, or buffalo horn.

As the company's production grew, it manufactured about 500 different styles of cutlery and consumed enormous amounts of steel and handle materials:

> 200 tons of Steel
> 400 tons of Coal
> 100 tons of Grindstones

---

[129]Harold L. Peterson, *American Knives* (New York: Charles Scribner's Sons, 1958), 164.

FIGURE 63. J. Sanger butcher knives.

10 tons of Emory
5 tons of Sheet Brass and Brass Wire
18,000 pounds of Ivory
150 tons of Ebony
300 tons of Rosewood
300 tons of Cocoa wood
300,000 pieces of Shin Bones

Over a period of years. the company works were owned and incorporated as Lamson & Goodnow Manufacturing Co., with E. G. Lamson as president, A. F. Goodnow as treasurer, and J. W. Gardner as agent. At its peak, the company employed 500 workmen and produced $600,000 of cutlery annually. The company became so prosperous that by 1860, it was the largest producer of cutlery in America.[130]

In 1858, E. G. Lamson purchased an armory at Windsor, Vermont, where the first rifles were made by machinery to use the minie ball or its equivalent, surpassing the quality of rifles made in England. In cooperation with E. G. Lamson, this firm was named E. G. Lamson & Co., and by 1861, the company was making 50,000 Springfield rifled muskets a year for the government. Soon they began making machinery for manufacturing guns and pistols, and by about 1862 they were making breech-loading rifles incorporating ammunition magazines that could be fired about twenty times per minute. By 1863, E. G. Lamson & Co. employed about 400 men in its armory and machine shop.

The last type of butcher knife recovered is 10 inches long and has a stubby pointed blade that is "v" ground. The plain hardwood handle has no bolster and is attached by three equally spaced brass rivets. The

[130]Ibid. See also J. Leander Bishop, *A History of American Manufactures from 1608 to 1860: Exhibiting the Origin and Growth of the Principal Mechanic Arts and Manufactures, from the Earliest Colonial Period to the Adoption of the Constitution: and Comprising Annals of the Industry of the United States in Machinery, Manufactures and Useful Arts, with a Notice of the Important Inventions, Tariffs, and the Results of Each Decennial Census* (Philadelphia: Edward Young & Co., 1864), 688–91.

blades are stamped "J. Sanger / Cast Steel." I know nothing about this manufacturer.

Pocket Knives (61)

Accession records indicate there are sixty-one pocket knives of various kinds in the cargo. Only a little has been found regarding the companies that produced them, but in the case of one variety, a few surprises were encountered. Some are hallmarked, indicating they were of British manufacture:

[Base of blade]
WILLIAM
FRIEDRICHS
CELEBRATED
CUTLERY
[Left side of blade]
SENATORS KNIFE
[Opposite base of blade]
N̲o̲ 6
NORFOLK
STREET
Sheffield
[Base of blade]
RUBENS
FRIEDRICHS
& C̲o̲
PATENTED

Another style:

[Left side of blade]
CONGRESS KNIFE

There are nine knives with mother-of-pearl handles and tortoise shell handles. These are 3 3/8 inches long closed and 6 5/8 inches long when open. They are 1/2 inch wide and 3/8 inches thick and have four blades and nickel silver threaded bolsters. The oblong casements have two thumbnail depressions for lifting the blades. Each has a small oblong German silver shield inlaid on the top handle. The four blades are spear, pen, coping, and manicure. Inset into the bolster of the spear blade ends of the knives are small glass lenses 9/32 of an inch in length and

FIGURE 64. William Friedrichs and Ruben Friedrichs
three-blade pocket knives.

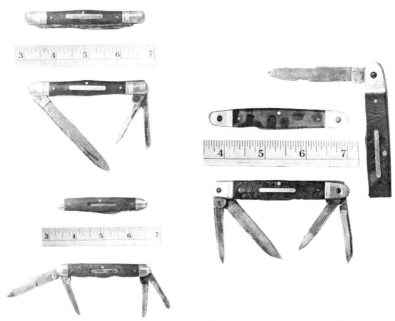

Figure 65. Joseph Rogers and Sons "Stanhope Lens" pocket knife (*right*)
and two additional styles of three- and four-blade pocket knives.

1/8 inch in diameter. These knives are of the Senator Pen Pattern and
were manufactured by Joseph Rogers & Sons, Sheffield, England. This
was one of the most famous cutlery firms in the world during the nineteenth century, advertising itself as "Cutlers to Her Majesty" Queen
Victoria. Much to our surprise, long after the conservation work was
accomplished, Jeanne M. Harold, conservator for the *Bertrand* collection,
and Mark Zalesky, knife expert, discovered that the glass insets were
not glass insets at all, but rather rare Stanhope lenses with at least two
images from France inscribed "Made in LeMans."[131]

What on earth is a Stanhope lens? The lenses were invented by Lord
Charles Stanhope, Third Earl Stanhope of England. The lens itself is a
small glass rod with one polished convex end to allow high magnification
at a short focal length. Fixed to the opposite end is a small disc of glass
with its picture. When the convex end is held very close to the eye, one
can see the image contained in the lens. The picture only covers about
one third of the cross-sectional area. Lord Stanhope died in 1816, long

---

[131]Jeanne M. Harold, "Have You Checked Your Pocketknife Lately?" *Cultural Resource
Management* 19, no. 7: 15–17.

before the invention incorporated the use of microphotographs in novelty items like pocket knives, letter openers, and charms.

The evolution of microphotography began in 1839, when John Benjamin Dancer of Manchester, England, invented the process. In 1852, Dancer used a wet plate collodion process to produce a microphotograph on collodion film and mounted it on a glass microscope slide. Unfortunately, the slide could only be viewed through a microscope. Seven years later, Rene Prudent Dagron of France developed the process of combining the Stanhope lens with a microphotograph to produce a tiny magnifying unit. Dagron applied his 1859 patent to many cheap novelty items and in 1862 established a factory in Gex, France, to meet the growing demand for Stanhope lens novelties in Paris. Thereafter, he marketed them worldwide. By 1870, Dagron was using the Stanhope lenses to smuggle messages in small pocket knives and other trinkets out of Paris during the Franco-Prussian War.[132]

Unfortunately, *Bertrand* preservation technicians did not recognize these small glass inclusions in the pocket knives as Stanhope lenses and used acetone and other corrosive chemicals to preserve the knives, thereby destroying some of the earliest Canada balsam mounted Stanhope lens and photos ever recorded.

Scissors

There are twenty-four pairs of scissors of various sizes in the cargo. The largest of these are cast steel, measure approximately 9 1/4 inches long, and have offset handles of the type commonly found on modern sewing shears. The knuckle handle is long and ovate to accommodate the fingers, and the other is smaller and round to accommodate the thumb. The two blades are secured at the pivot with a slotted screw. Both types are stamped "WILLIAM FRIEDRICHS."

In the course of researching scissors testimony was found presented by George Wostenholm (Geo. Wostenholm & Sons) to the House Ways and Means Committee of Congress on February 18, 1909, in regard to raising tariffs on imported penknives and shears. Wostenholm represented twelve American penknife and shear manufacturers. He contended that American scissor manufacturers could not compete with British and German manufacturers owing to the considerably higher cost of labor in the United States and to the low importation tariffs on

---

[132]Nick Berman, "Stanhopes: The World in Miniature," *Knife World* (1990): 33–38.

British and German products. In addition, European shears were made of solid high quality cast steel, while American shears were steel laid upon a malleable-iron or a forged steel base. Furthermore, no solid steel scissors or shears under six inches were being made in the United States. Annual costs of production for domestic shears were over $3 million, while production costs of European shears were $1,100,000. That meant that imported German shears cost about $3.50 per dozen with a labor cost of 40 percent, compared to American shears at about $6 per dozen with a labor cost of 80 percent. While both retailed for about the same price, there was considerably more profit to be realized from quality steel imported products owing to cheaper production and low import tariffs. Wostenholm said that raising the tariffs on all classes of imported shears would increase revenue and protect American manufacturers and labor, and good commercial shears could be brought within reach of consumers. He also contended that raising tariffs would spur the development and production of quality cast steel shears in this country.[133]

This testimony is interesting in light of what will be said later about the production and import of British cast steel files and cutlery. Between 1840 and the early part of the 1900s, Americans generally preferred imported steel tools and cutlery because they were cheaper and they rightfully believed imported products were of higher quality. This, of course, held back the development of these items by American manufacturers. In 1909, there were only twelve manufacturers of steel scissors and shears in the United States. The last irony concerning these tariff hearings is that George Wostenholm & Sons obviously was connected to or was one and the same firm that made cast steel files in Europe, some of which were found in the *Bertrand*'s cargo. Judging from the testimony, the company must have had a factory in the United States by the turn of the century.

Table Knives

Only one type of table knife is represented. The blades of these knives are 9 1/8 inches long and have parallel sides and rounded tips. The choil of each knife is thick and quite pronounced, and the ricasso is oval in cross-section, standing somewhat above the plane of the blade on its flat sides. The choil is an unsharpened section of the blade that is often

---

[133] *Tariff Hearings before the Committee on Ways and Means of the House of Representatives,* 60th Congress, 2nd Session, 1908–1909, Vol. 8, Appendix (Washington, D.C.: United States Government Printing Office, 1909), 7943–46.

used as a way to choke up on the blade for close work. The index finger is placed in the choil, and this close proximity to the edge allows for greater control. In addition, the choil is just in front of where the blade itself becomes part of the handle. The tapered tang runs the length of the blade, and the two-piece bone handle is secured with two equally spaced copper rivets. The left side of the blade is stamped with a "V," a crown, and an "R," under which are the words "CAST STEEL."

Since these knives appear to be imported from England, they may have been supplied by the firm of "Pratt and Fox, Hardware and Cutlery Importers, 20 Cliff Street, New York," a name that appears more than once in the field notes.

Forks

There are sixty-two cast steel forks, exhibiting two rather long curved tines, curved shanks, and two-piece wooden handles riveted with two equally spaced copper rivets. The handles are broader at the bases than at the bases of the shanks and have beveled edges. The forks measure approximately 6 1/2 inches long. These are not remarkable in form and no maker's marks are present.

Spoons

During the early and middle 1800s, Meriden, Connecticut, became a very active center for the production of cutlery and silver tableware, including German silver, white metal, pewter, silver, Britannia, silver-plate, electroplate, and plated iron wares. During this time, Meriden and Waterford and the surrounding area had numerous manufactories producing cut nails, screws, pewter buttons, ivory combs, piano and melodeon ivory, ladies' corsets and hoop skirts, ladies' cloaks, shawls, flannels, balmoral skirts, and cassimeres, cutlery with handles made of pearl, ivory, vulcanized rubber, horn, coacoa, ebony, and rosewoods, tinware and japanned tinware, lamp trimmings, furniture casters, spokes and wheels, numerous varieties of buttons, piano stools, coffin trimmings, boring tools, presses and punches, elastic furniture and door fenders, teapot knobs, inkstands, pen racks, bill files, and weights, lumber, platform scales, paper, locks, and lamp chains. Although research has not yet verify it, this industrial center may have produced some of the articles in the *Bertrand*'s cargo.

There are fifty-seven German silver teaspoons and six silver-plated tablespoons in the cargo. The teaspoons are back-marked "G. I. MIX," and the tablespoons are back-marked "C. PARKER." Although not captured in field notes, apparently one or more spoons in the *Bertrand*'s cargo are hallmarked "L. Boardman." One of these is on display at the Bertrand Museum and Laboratory at DeSoto National Wildlife Refuge.

Luther Boardman was born on December 26, 1812, in Stepney township, Fairfield, Connecticut, to Jason Boardman and Lydia Deming Boardman. At the age of sixteen, he came to Meriden, where he learned the art of making pewter and Britannia hollowware from Ashbill Griswald. In 1829, he was indentured by his father, Jason Boardman, as an apprentice to Griswald and was known to be making pewter ware either in Griswald's shop or at another location and turning it over to Griswald, who operated his business as Griswald & Couch. Boardman was to receive $25 a year and have all his expenses except clothing covered until he reached the age of twenty-one, at which time he was to be released and given $25 worth of goods. Apparently, about this time, Couch & Frary began in business. It is not certain just when Griswald left the business, but it was probably in December 1833. Boardman must have continued to work for Couch & Frary, because on October 18, 1838, he married Ann Frary, daughter of James A. Frary.[134]

Boardman was something of an inventor, and on October 7, 1842, he was issued Patent Number 2,802 for "Improvement in the Manner of Forming Molds for Casting Spoons, &c." Luther Boardman was issued another patent (Patent Number 2,794) on October 1, 1867, for a "Design for a Spoon-Handle." He continued refining his spoon patterns, and on June 28, 1870, he and his son Norman S. Boardman were issued Patent

---

[134]E. P. Hogan at the Historical Library of the International Silver Company, Meriden, Connecticut, correspondence dated July 14, 1971. Mr. Hogan sent the author thirteen pages of biographical information about Luther Boardman and Garry I. Mix, spoon makers in East Haddam, Meriden, and Yalesville. Two of the Boardman pages are captioned, "No. 4 *Connecticut Manufacturers* 8/25/39—B4 Luther Boardman, East Haddam," and "No. 4 *Connecticut Manufacturers* 3/27/41—B4 Luther Boardman," and two pages are captioned, "No. 7 *Connecticut Manufacturers* 3/15/39—Luther Boardman & Son, East Haddam—No. 1," and "No. 8 *Connecticut Manufacturers* 3/15/39—Luther Boardman & Son, East Haddam—No. 2." The Garry I. Mix papers are captioned, "No. 57 *Connecticut Manufacturers* 8/25/39—M 8—Garry I Mix, Yalesville, No. 63 *Connecticut Manufacturers* 3/15/39—Garry I. Mix & Co., Yalesville No. 1," and "No. 64 *Connecticut Manufacturers* 3/15/39—Garry I. Mix & Co., Yalesville—No. 2." In addition, there is a separate sheet titled "The Mix Family, Yalesville," and another titled, "G. I. Mix & Co. Yalesville" that contains an account by a long-time bookkeeper and employee of the Mix company, Edwin S. May, about the company after it failed in 1903. Finally, the pages include a copy of a newspaper obituary from the *Meriden Journal* 1890 of Captain William Mix, brother of Garry Mix. In the possession of the author.

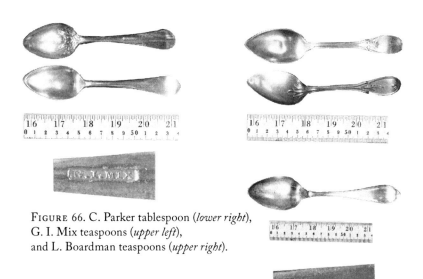

FIGURE 66. C. Parker tablespoon (*lower right*),
G. I. Mix teaspoons (*upper left*),
and L. Boardman teaspoons (*upper right*).

Number 104,822 for an "Improvement in Spoon-Molds." In February 1869, a "Walters" pricelist indicated Boardman's plain nickel silver table-spoons were selling for $42.20 per gross or $55.20 per gross for figured spoons. Plain teaspoons sold for $21 per gross, and figured spoons for $25.32 per gross. He also sold dessert spoons, table forks, medium forks, dessert forks, and forks for oysters, pie, beef, and pickles; solid handle and hollow handle dinner knives, butter knives, nut and pickle picks, salt and mustard spoons, sugar shovels, various kinds of ladles, plain and perforated napkin rings, and ice cream knives. The last entry for Board-man was in the 1880 census of East Haddam, where he was listed as a silver manufacturer. He and his son Norman were very active in local and state affairs and were known throughout the state for their "liberal works of practical benevolence." Luther Boardman died on March 29, 1887, in East Haddam. Lydia Boardman died sometime that same year. Norman Boardman died a few years later, but the business was continued by Luther Boardman's grandson Eugene Boardman at least until 1909.[135]

[135]E. P. Hogan correspondence, July 14, 1971, Luther Boardman pages, Ibid. See also *American Silversmiths*, "Luther Boardman," An Ancestry.Com Community (2005), http://freepages.genealogy.rootsweb.ancestry.com/-silversmiths/makers/silversmiths/120661.htm. Accessed March 16, 2009.

Quite a bit is known of Garry Ives Mix and G. I. Mix & Co. Mix was born about 1819 in Wallingford, Connecticut, to John Mix and Olive Ivers Mix. On December 7, 1842, he married Almira White, by whom he had one daughter, Francis A. Mix. Between 1845 and 1854, Mix was a pewterer in Wallingford, but moved his business to Yalesville, where he worked between 1854 and 1861. On October 27, 1857, he was issued Patent Number 18,513 for "Making Iron Spoons" (the patent was reissued on August 18, 1871, as Patent Number 4,506). Sometime in 1861, he moved back to Wallingford, where he made tinned iron spoons and hollowware until 1880. On February 26, 1861, he was issued Patent Number 31,555 for "Improvement in Manufacture of Spoons." Mix seems to have kept experimenting with spoon manufacture, and on October 9, 1866, he was granted another patent (Patent Number 58,665) for "Improvement in the Manufacture of Spoons." In 1868, Gary Mix was elected to the state senate from the Sixth District of Connecticut. The 1880 census for Wallingford, Connecticut, shows Mix as a manufacturer of spoons. Gary Ives Mix died on August 13, 1892, at New Haven, Connecticut.[136]

G. I. Mix & Co. continued as a business well after Mix's death. On January 12, 1903, G. I. Mix & Co. failed, and W. H. Squire was appointed trustee. On May 28, 1903, the old Mix factory was purchased from the trustee by Mrs. Cecelia I. Yale for $22,000. Yale was to form a joint stock company and run it independently. She hired her prospective son-in-law Charles L. O. Elynn as manager, but he soon left the company, and it was managed until 1907 by Philip Rinehart and Charles Peck, respectively, until sometime in 1907 when they were replaced by Arthur Benton until 1910. Sometime in 1912, the two main buildings burned. By World War I, Rinehart, who had remained with the firm, began experimenting with making spoon dies in the three remaining buildings. Sometime afterward the factory became idle. In 1939 or 1940, Backus Co. of Wallingford bought the plant and made fireworks and flares there, some for the government, until after World War II. Nothing more has been found about the G. I. Mix business after the last date mentioned.[137]

Of great interest are the tablespoons produced by Charles Parker. Born on January 2, 1809, in Cheshire, Connecticut, Parker completed several apprenticeships during his youth making pewter buttons and coffee mills. At the age of twenty, he made coffee mills on contract for Patrick Lewis

---

[136]E. P. Hogan correspondence. Garry I Mix pages. Ibid. See also, *American Silversmiths*, "Garry Ives Mix," An Ancestry.Com Community (2005), http://freepages.genealogy.rootsweb.ancestry.com/~silversmiths/makers/ silversmiths/120661.htm.

[137]E. P. Hogan correspondence. Account of Edwin S. May, G. I. Mix & Co., Yalesville.

and Elias Holt in Meriden, Connecticut, and shortly thereafter acquired a half interest in a spoon shop. In 1831, he sold his interest in coffee mill manufacturing to Lewis and purchased his partner's holdings in the spoon shop. In 1832, he purchased an acre of land and built his first factory to manufacture coffee mills and waffle irons. The manufactory was located in a two-story building that was 25 by 40 feet in size and used horses to power the machinery. That year, he patented one of his best-known inventions, the top-feeding hand cranked coffee mill.[138]

By 1833, Parker's successful business gave him opportunity to enter into partnership with his brother Edmund and Herman White under the firm name Parker and White. The business lagged during the depression of 1837, but by 1842, it had paid off its indebtedness. Edmund retired in 1843, and Herman White left the firm the following year, but Parker persisted in modernizing the business, adding an eighty-horsepower Corliss steam engine and renaming the factory the Union Works. That year, he began plating Britannia and German silver spoons, many of which were made in dies manufactured by Garry I. Mix of Yalesville, Connecticut.[139] Eventually, the Parker business occupied sixteen buildings and manufactured iron spoons, ladles and forks, scales and hinges, machinery and guns, Britannia spoons, and German silver spoons and forks. In addition, Parker had four other operating factories making coffee mills, screws, spectacles, eyeglasses, tobacco boxes, vises, butt hinges, lanterns, match safes, faucets, iron bench screws, scissors and shears, cranks and rollers, barn door hangers and rollers, gate and plain hinges, gridirons, bed keys, wagon jacks, scrapers, pulleys, lamp hooks, window springs, thumb latches, hammers, gimlets, call and hand bells, and other items. In all, the company employed about 500 workers.

---

[138]E. P. Hogan at the Historical Library of the International Silver Company, Meriden, Connecticut, correspondence dated June 24, 1971. In the possession of the author. Hogan sent to the author five pages of biographical information about Charles Parker and Charles Parker Co. The first page is captioned, "No. 69 Connecticut Manufacturers—Additions 8/25/39, P.2 Charles Parker, Meriden, Connecticut." "The second page is captioned, No.70 Connecticut Manufacturers—Additions 8/25/39, P. 2 Charles Parker, Meriden, Connecticut." The third page is captioned, "No. 72 Connecticut Manufacturers—3/15/39, Charles Parker Co., Meriden, No. 1." The fourth page is captioned, "From New Haven County Commemorative Record, 1902 J. H. Beers & Co., Chicago—Page 16—Charles Parker." The fifth page is captioned, "From New Haven County Commemorative Record, 1902 J. H. Beers & Co., Chicago—Page 1051—Charles Parker Co." This citation is from the fourth page. See also Ronald R. Switzer, "Charles Parker's Britannia on the Steamboat Bertrand." Museum of the Fur Trade Quarterly 7, no. 4 (1971): 6–10.

[139]E. P. Hogan correspondence, June 24, 1971, fourth page.

By 1855, Charles Parker branched out to acquire the Bennett Jerolds spoon factory in Meriden and moved the equipment to Yalesville. In 1847, the Rogers brothers began making electroplated silver spoons in Hartford, and in 1862, the Meriden Britannia Co. bought Rogers Brothers Silver. About 1898, the Meriden Britannia Co. was purchased by the International Silver Co. In 1871, Parker began making silver-plated spoons for Cephas B. Rogers and his brother and put their names on them. Even though the spoons were supposed to be marketed by Rogers's representatives, Parker also marketed the spoons, which were stamped "C. Rogers & Bros." Apparently this led to a lawsuit by Meriden Britannia Co. in which Parker was ordered to discontinue marking his spoons and selling them under the name of Rogers & Bros. Thereafter, he produced silver-plated spoons with his own name on them.[140] It is assumed that the spoons in the *Bertrand*'s cargo were produced by the factory in Yalesville and not in Meriden, but this is still uncertain. Nothing is known of the St. Louis wholesaler who shipped the spoons or of the consignee that was to receive them in Montana.

Other highlights in the Charles Parker story include the fact that in 1842 he began making vises. Stelle and Harrison in their *Gunsmith Manual* (1883) recommended Parker's vise as the "best vise for general use." After 1844, the Parker business expanded and diversified, and by 1862, Parker catalogues listed several hundred items, including corn and coffee mills, German silver tableware, vises, hinges, door knockers, locks, and waffle irons. A new and unusual item produced in 1862 by "Parker, Snow, Brooks, Co." under contract with the Reading Railroad was the Springfield rifle. The next year, Parker and his associates were making America's first repeating rifles.[141]

Meriden was a small village during the Parker years, and as late as 1866 had a population of only 7,426. It was not incorporated as a city until 1867. It had two banks, five churches, an academy, and several fairly large manufactories, with a few smaller ones scattered throughout the surrounding township. As the popularity and demand for its products grew, so did this small manufacturing hamlet. According to *Lippincott's Gazetteer of the World*, by 1893, the population tripled and business was booming.

It is known as the silver city, and is one of the most enterprising of New England's cities. The capital invested in manufacturing is over $10,000,000, the annual product therefrom exceeding $25,000,000. The manufactures

---

[140] E. P. Hogan correspondence, June 24, 1971, third page.
[141] William B. Edwards, *Civil War Guns*, 54.

include electro-plated and solid silver-ware, brass and bronze goods, lamps, Chandeliers, clocks, tinware, cutlery, steel, steel pens, malleable iron goods, firearms, organs, cut-glass, woolen goods, saddlery, harness and leather goods, power and stamping presses, coffee-mills, etc. The Meriden Britannia Co. employs nearly 1,600 hands and have an annual output of over $3,000,000. Meriden contains the state reform school, 3 national banks, 2 savings banks, 18 churches, high and grade schools, 1 weekly and 3 daily newspaper offices, and gas and electric works. The streets are lighted by arc lights. . . . Pop. of the township in 1890, 25,423: of the city, 22,652.[142]

In 1863, Charles Parker established the American Screw Co., and by 1870, he owned another machine and gun works, a Britannia and German silver works, and an iron spoon works in Meriden. Given the diverse nature of the products that Parker produced, it is not unreasonable to assume some of the hardware from the *Bertrand* was produced by his company in addition to that produced/sold by the Shapleigh hardware firm.

It is not surprising that Parker's manufacturing business prospered and supplied many of the products needed by westerners. As the Civil War approached, Parker branched out into gun making. Under the name Parker, Snow, & Co., he produced 15,000 Springfield pattern carbines for the Union Army, and in the waning months of the war, he produced a few thousand patented breech repeating carbines under the name Meriden Manufacturing Co. These guns never saw action in the war and were sold to the Kentucky militia. These are known today as Tripplett and Scott carbines.[143]

Several other members of the Parker family in addition to Edmund Parker were business partners at various times. Under the name "Parker Brothers," he and his sons began making their famous double-barreled breach-loading shotguns between 1866 and 1868, and continued making them until 1934. These famous post–Civil War guns had self-locking barrels and rebounding hammers and used central fired, coned, metallic cartridges capped with ordinary percussion caps. They weighed between 7 1/4 and 7 3/4 pounds and sold for $45 to $250 dollars, according to advertisements in *The American Sportsman* in 1874. At some point, Edmond Parker and his son Wilber acquired *The American Sportsman* magazine and Wilber became the editor. In 1934, Remington Arms Co. acquired

[142]Joshua Ballinger Lippincott, ed., *Lippincott's Gazetteer of the World. A Complete Pronouncing Gazetteer or Geographical Directory of the World* (Philadelphia: J. B. Lippincott Company, 1893), 1809.

[143]Louis C. Parker III, Law Offices of Heyman and Sizemore, Atlanta, Georgia, correspondence dated September 29, 1971. In possession of the author.

the rights to make Parker shotguns, and in 1938 moved the factory to Ilion, New York. About 1,600 Parker shotguns were later made by Remington Arms Co. at Ilion before production stopped in 1942.[144]

Feather Dusters (3)

Fireplace Shovels

The cargo yielded thirteen small, square-bladed shovels with rod-like handles, some of which bore decorative brass handle ends. There are no manufacturer's marks on these artifacts.

Fireplace Tongs

In addition to the fireplace shovels, there are thirteen narrow-armed fireplace tongs. The joints are of decorative brass, and the gripping plates are at the ends of the arms are nearly circular in shape. There are no maker's marks.

Flatirons

Field notes indicate there are at least two small flatirons in the collection. They are embossed under the handles "G. MARSHALL / 7." Nothing is known about this company at present.

Glassware

Ale Glasses

An unconfirmed number of honeycomb pattern ale glasses were recovered. These may have been manufactured by McKee and Brothers (J. and F. McKee), Pittsburgh.

Bar Lip Decanters

Nothing is known about these artifacts save for the photographs depicting one decanter with a stopper and one without a stopper.

---

[144]"An Account of the Past and Present Activities of the Charles Parker Company and the Bradley and Hubbard Division," (n.d.). This commemorative booklet was provided to the author by E. P. Hogan of the Historical Library, International Silver Company, June 24, 1971.

FIGURE 67. Bar lip decanters and cruet.

Bar lip decanters seem to have been invented in America for storing and serving small quantities of liquor or bitters. In the decade of the 1830s, mold-blown and engraved bar lip decanters became common for decanting liquor from barrels into more manageable glass decanters that were then stored behind the bar. The size, shape, and design/engraving frequently denoted the contents for barkeepers, since most liquors look alike. Although some decanters were produced in Europe, these were meant for export to America and were not produced for European use. American bar lip decanters remained popular between 1830 and 1875. The O'Hara glass works and McKee & Brothers were especially known for producing flint glass bar lip decanters and bar tumblers, and one of the bar tumblers illustrated in this text appears to be a Huber pattern used by several companies, including the Northeast Glass Co. After 1850, pressed glass decanters became more common than blown glass articles.

Candy Dishes

Two clear glass shallow oval dishes were found. They have chains of glass balls decorating the rims, and the bodies are decorated with a diamond pattern. The maker is unknown.

Castor Sets and Cruets

One type of glass cruet recovered from the cargo was manufactured by "A. & D. H. CHAMBERS GLASS MANUFACTURERS / No. 117 WATER St. / PITTSBURGH" and was wholesaled by "R. B. S. & CO. / St. Louis." There are thirteen whole clear glass condiment bottles of various patterns, eight clear glass stoppers of various shapes, two silver-plated castor/cruet stands, and two complete caster/cruet stands and bottles with stoppers in the collection. More than likely these are pattern mold wares.

The firm of A. & D. H. Chambers began as Chambers, Agnew, & Co. on Brownsville Avenue outside the city limits of Pittsburgh in 1842. John Agnew apprenticed to William McCully in 1833 at the age of fourteen, and then worked for the Chambers brothers. Producing vials, bottles, and window glass, the business became John Agnew & Co. in 1854 when Alexander Chambers withdrew. Thereafter, the company specialized in the production of flint glassware and druggist's green glass.[145]

One year after Chambers entered into partnership with Agnew, he and his brother David H. Chambers established a small glass house in Pittsburgh to produce window glass and green and black vials and bottles. In addition, Alexander and David Chambers were the first in America to make large panes of cylinder window glass. In 1852, two years before Alexander Chambers left Chambers, Agnew, & Co., A. & D. H. Chambers built a new factory that they called the Pittsburgh Glass Works. David Chambers died in 1862 and Alexander twelve years later. After Alexander Chambers's death, John Chambers and Henry B. Patton operated the factory.[146] During the Civil War, the Pittsburgh Glass Works produced the new and eventually famous "Union" flasks. Later, in the 1870s and 1880s, the firm made beer bottles and wax-sealer fruit jars in addition to other glass products.

Another type of flint glass cruet is tentatively identified as the Ashburton pattern, manufactured by McKee Brothers of Pittsburgh, Pennsylvania. Produced as goblets, compotes, sugars, creamers, wines, and decanters, this pattern was one of the first for general use. Other possible makers of this type of cruet were the New England Glass Co. of East Cambridge, Massachusetts, Ovington Brothers of Brooklyn, Long Island, and Bakewell Co. of Pittsburgh, Pennsylvania. Both the New England Glass Co. and Bakewell Co. produced flint glass in this pattern.

---

[145]McKearin and McKearin, *American Glass*, 604.
[146]Toulouse, *Bottle Makers and Their Marks*, 37–38.

A little is known about the McKee brothers. When it was founded in 1834 by Samuel and James McKee, the name of the plant in the Birmingham area of Pittsburgh was not recorded. In 1836, it became S. McKee & Co. when Samuel's brother Thomas McKee joined the company. Soon after its founding, the company was running three furnaces to produce window glass, an art in which Samuel McKee was especially proficient. By 1840, the brothers built a second factory nearby for making flint glass bottles.[147]

Mention is made of the McKee brothers, J. & F. McKee, because they produced large amounts of barware during this period. James and Frederick McKee established their flint glass factory about 1850 in Pittsburgh (east Birmingham), Pennsylvania, under the name J. & F. McKee. According to the McKearins, in 1853, the company became McKee Brothers. In 1854–1855, they advertised molded and plain flint and fancy colored tableware, but also made barware, druggist's furniture, jars, and lamp chimneys. By 1860, James and Thomas had died, and sometime after 1863, Thomas's sons, who were well-trained glassmakers, established a glass factory that they named "McKee Bros." In 1865, S. McKee & Co. was still operating four furnaces to manufacture window glass and bottles.[148] If the *Bertrand's* cruets were produced by the McKees, they were marketed under the firm name McKee Brothers because the business did not become "McKee & Brothers" until after Steward McKee was taken into the business in 1865.

One reason for believing these cruets could have been produced by the New England Glass Co. of Boston, Massachusetts, is that they are made of flint glass. Even though many glass companies moved away from manufacturing lead-based glass after 1874 when William Leighton developed a successful soda-lime glass, New England Glass Co. believed the new glass was inferior and refused to use it, continuing instead to manufacture pressed flint glass products. Ashburton pattern products were commonly produced by the New England Glass Co. between the 1840s and the 1870s, at least until 1872, when William Libby pushed its production more toward elaborately cut and engraved glass. The New England Glass Co. reached the pinnacle of its success during the "Brilliant Cut Glass" period of the 1870s, vindicating its decision to stay with lead flint glass. However, increased competition and widespread use of cheaper soda-lime glass eventually drove the company out of business in 1877. It was sold to William Libby in 1878.

[147]Ibid., 476–77.
[148]McKearin and McKearin, *American Glass*, 607.

Chamber Lamps with Handles

There are two types of squat clear glass chamber lamps represented. These were blown in molds and have single applied open loop handles. The smaller plain ones strongly resemble the early "Sparking" lamps in form. They are fitted with brass burners with thumb wheel wick advancers. The clear glass shades are held in place with friction screws. The lamps are about 1 3/4 inches tall and about 3 1/4 inches in diameter at the base. The bases have a radiating spoke pattern. They were designed to be used as bedchamber lights in place of loop-handled tin and porcelain candleholders. The manufacturer of these lamps is unknown.

The larger chamber lamps are more ornate. The loop handles are heavier and squarish in cross-section. The lamp bodies are squat and globular and bear a drapery-like design below the shoulders over equally spaced sets of vertical flutes. The bases are turned out and indented and bear a radiating spoke design on the bottoms. The burners have friction thumb screws to advance the wicks, and the clear glass shades are held in place with friction screws. The manufacturer of these lamps is not known.

Covered Compotes and Footed Dishes

FIGURE 68. Covered compote and footed dishes.

There is one complete, footed dish with a matching lid made of clear faceted pressed glass. It has been categorized as a compote because the bowl is somewhat larger deeper than the bowl of those above.

It is difficult to tell how much glassware was broken and discarded, but there are seven round, footed, clear, pressed glass dishes in the collection, some of which have, or are associated with, corresponding lids. These are variously referred to in glass literature as sweetmeat dishes. The manufacturers are unknown.

Goblets

The cargo contained forty-one or more footed, clear, pressed glass goblets of two distinctly different shapes, the maker of which is unknown. One type is globular with a thick lip and a raised tulip pattern around the body, while the other is tall, slender, and thin lipped, somewhat resembling a poussé café glass.

Half Pint Huber Tumblers

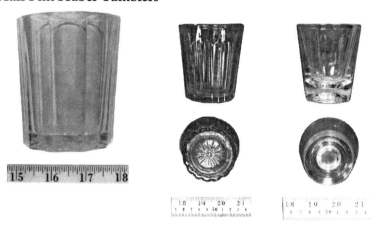

FIGURE 69. Huber tumblers and a shot glass.

This type of tumbler with simple panels or flutes was manufactured by the King Glass Co., Bakewell Co., and McKee Brothers (J. and F. McKee) of Pittsburgh, New England Glass Co., and possibly by others. The pattern was produced in a variety of forms, including goblets, compotes, and sugars. There are thirty-seven of these in the collection. They measure 3 15/16 to 4 1/8 inches tall, 3 inches in diameter at the lip, and 2 1/8 inches in diameter at the base and have a capacity of about 9

244 THE STEAMBOAT BERTRAND AND AMERICAN FRONTIER COMMERCE

ounces. They were wholesaled by Garnes & Co. of St. Louis and were destined for Hell Gate, Montana.

There is not much information about the King Glass Co. This Pittsburgh manufacturer was in business from 1851 to 1906, when it became part of the U.S. Glass Co. along with eighteen other glass producers. If the colored "stretch" glass lamp bases for peg lamps found on the *Bertrand* were not made by the Boston Sandwich Glass Co., it is likely they were made by this company.

Half-Pint Prism Tumblers

These probably were manufactured by King Glass Co., Pittsburgh, Pennsylvania.

Lamp Chimneys/Flues

There are at least twenty hand-blown clear glass oil lamp chimneys of two sizes in the collection, some of which have frosted bodies and clear top flues. There is no way to estimate the number of broken flues, but glass fragments indicate there were more than the number indicated in records. The manufacturer is unknown.

The larger of these, a total of 14 flues, are 9 5/8 inches tall with a maximum diameter at the shoulder of 3 3/8 to 3 1/2 inches. They are 1 5/16 inches to 1 1/2 inches in diameter at the base.

The six smaller flues are 6 3/16 inches tall and 2 1/4 inches in diameter at the shoulder. The bases measure 1 11/16 inches in diameter. Field notes indicate the shipping case was marked:

GLASSEX / 1/2 Doz. No. 14 1/2 / Deer Lodge, Montana

Lamp Fonts

When research was done on peg-base lamp fonts found in the *Bertrand*'s cargo, it became obvious that the pressed glass fonts for freestanding lamps and most of the other components were unusual and were not represented in reference works or in museums. The font patterns have not been identified or associated with any particular glass works. (Perhaps one reason is that the fonts may have been produced under a relatively new patent (Patent No. 34345), granted February 11, 1862, to J. S. Atterbury, T. B. Atterbury, and James Reddick of Pittsburgh, Pennsylvania,

FIGURE 70. Peg-base lamp fonts.
FIGURE 71. Square, colored glass peg bases for lamps.

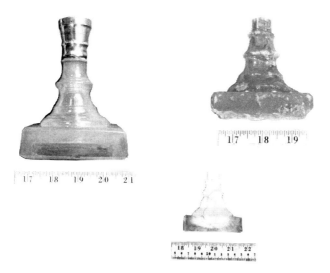

for the manufacture of an improved hollowware with open illuminated surface relief work.[149]

If this is so, the eight different fonts represented were produced at the White House Works, in the Birmingham area of Pittsburgh. This business was established in 1859 as Hale, Atterbury, & Co. By 1862,

---

[149]This patent is listed by the Carnegie Library of Pittsburgh in "Pittsburgh Patentees 1790–1879," copyright November 2009.

James Reddick was apparently in the business, and, in that same year, Patent N. 34345 was issued. The White House Works specialized in blown and pressed flint glassware and became well-known producers of lamps between 1867 and 1876. In 1867, the firm name was changed to Atterbury & Co. by its principals, James S. and Thomas B. Atterbury. The business was still operating in 1886.[150]

In addition, there were a few square, colored opaque -glass, peg bases. These measure approximately 4 inches by 4 inches, and they are about 3 3/4 inches tall. Several colors are represented including black, sky blue, white, and yellowish alabaster. While their maker is not known with certainty, the Sandwich Glass Works in Boston produced this kind of lamp base.

Hanging Parlor Lamps and Lamp Brackets
There are seventeen pear-shaped twisted brass frames and five opaque white opaque flower-shaped glass smoke bells. The associated clear glass fonts are of two patterns. None of these artifacts have been identified as to origin, but the Atterbury Co. was known for its glass smoke bells.

Freestanding Lamps/Glass Fonts

FIGURE 72. Freestanding glass font.

Records indicate there were several freestanding clear-glass fonts in the cargo. The bodies exhibit domed shoulders and have a distinct raised band around the circumference at the mid-point. The bases are footed and bear a raised scalloped design. They are approximately 5 inches tall. The maker is unknown.

---

[150]McKearin and McKearin, *American Glass*, 609–10.

Mugs

Only one mug was found. It is milk white glass with "Remember Me" in gold script within a floral motif on one side. The maker is unknown. This may have come from personal effects.

Salt Cellars

There are only three square, plain, clear glass salt cellars. There are no distinctive markings, and the maker is unknown.

Shot Glasses

There are 166 cylindrical, clear glass, shot glasses in the collection, about which nothing is known. It can be speculated that glasses such as these were in high demand in frontier saloons.

Grease Pails (24)

Griddles

Two round flat cast-iron griddles with loop-shaped handles and slightly raised bases were recovered. The maker is unknown, but the griddles could possibly be attributed to Giles Filley or Charles Parker Co.

Indigo Cases

These two small rectangular wooden cases may or may not have contained indigo. Research indicates they could have contained wash bluing, but there is no way to confirm this. Indigo and bluing are fugitive under most conditions.

Lamp Burners

Several brass lamp burners have thumb wheels bearing the words "HOLMES BOOTH & HAYDENS PAT JAN 14 1860—E. F. JONES PAT JAN 11th 1859." They are of a type known as coronet burners in which the ornate tabbed circular gallery receives the flared base of the chimney, which is locked in place by a friction screws. These parts were manufactured at the Holmes, Booth, & Haydens Co. in Waterbury, Connecticut, under a partnership between Hiram W. Hayden and his brothers, Henry H. and James A. Hayden, Israel Holmes, and John C. Booth. This firm was incorporated on February 2, 1853, with Israel Holmes in charge of the rolling mill. Hiram Hayden was in charge of manufacturing, and Henry Hayden ran the marketing part of the company.[151]

Although very little is known about John Booth, Israel Holmes, and Hiram Hayden they all were consummate inventors and entrepreneurs. Holmes, Booth, & Haydens Co. was assigned fifty-six lighting fixture patents between January 24, 1860, and January 30, 1894. Holmes began his career in 1820 with Leavenworth, Hayden, & Scovill and was in charge of the company store in Waterbury. Although Israel Holmes stayed with the company, which became J. M. L. & W. H. Scovill on April 4, 1827, he partnered with seven other men about 1825 to form the firm Holmes and Hotchkiss to manufacture sheet metal and wire. The company became Brown & Elton in 1838 and continued until 1856 when it was dissolved and half the business was purchased by Holmes, Booth & Haydens. In 1830, Holmes left J. M. L. & W. H. Scovill and formed the partnership of Holmes & Hotchkiss. Holmes left the business in 1869 to form Holmes, Booth, and Atwood, which later became Plume & Atwood. Israel Holmes died in 1874.[152]

Hiram Hayden was a well-known inventor who developed more than thirty lamp and lighting patents, in addition to holding patents for a breech-loading rifle, breech-loading canon, magazine rifle, buttons, medals, and a machine to make solid metal tubing. He invented a process to make a brass kettle from a single sheet of brass in 1851 and sold the patent to The Waterbury Brass Co. the following year. Hayden is perhaps best known for his work developing the daguerreotype photographic process that produced the first photographs on paper in 1851.

Several brass lamp burners have thumb screws marked "CORNELIUS & BAKER / PHILA / PATENTED / DEC. 9 1862." According to Russell, silver platter and patent lamp manufacturer Christian Cornelius was doing business in Philadelphia as early as 1825. By 1839,

[151]Daniel Edminster, "A Brief Historical Profile of the Holmes, Booth & Haydens Company," The Lampworks, Hurleyville, New York, 2004, http://www.thelampworks .com/lw_companies_hb&h.htm.

[152]Daniel Edminster, "A Brief Historical Profile of the Holmes, Booth & Haydens Company." See also William Gilbert Lathrop, *The Brass Industry in Connecticut: A Study of the Origin and the Development of the Brass Industry in the Naugatuck Valley and its Subsequent Extension over the Nation* (New Haven, Conn.: The Price, Lee & Adkins Co., 1909).

his business was known as "Cornelius Co., Lamps (C. Cornelius and R. Cornelius)." Between 1845 and 1853, they added another partner, Isaac Baker, to become Cornelius, Baker, & Co. In 1856, the firm was composed of Robert Cornelius, Robert Cornelius, Jr., and Isaac F. Baker and was listed as Cornelius & Baker until 1870 when it became Cornelius & Sons. During this period, William C. Baker and John C. Cornelius became members of the firm. By 1887, the company was known as Cornelius & Hetherington and from 1888 through 1891 it was known as Cornelius & Rowland when George L. Rowland was a partner.[153]

Cornelius & Baker was widely known for its award-winning products such as solar lamps and later as a major producer of chandeliers, gas lamp fittings, and gold-plated brass statuettes. It is not surprising that some of the brass lamp burners from the *Bertrand* bear this company's name.

Matches

Packed forty-eight boxes to a case, each box of 500 matches was wrapped in brown paper bearing a black-on-white paper label and a tax stamp. There were thirty-three cases of matches in the cargo stenciled: "TELEGRAPH MATCHES, A. EICHELE, ST. LOUIS." The cases were consigned to Stuart Co., Deer Lodge; Vivian and Simpson, Virginia City; Worden Co., Hell Gate; and, G. P. Dorris, Virginia City. They were manufactured as "SUPERIOR TELEGRAPH MATCHES by AUG. EICHELE, ST. LOUIS."

August Eichele was in partnership with James Brunaugh, and their factory was located at 2011 Columbus in St. Louis, according to the *St. Louis Directory* for 1864.[154] Nothing further was learned about the company and only a little about August Eichele. He apparently produced Superior Telegraph Matches in St. Louis from 1865 to 1881. He produced 10,715,000 black-and-white stamps on old paper featuring a portrait of himself between June 1865 and mid-February 1869. Presumably these were placed on his matchboxes or on the paper wrappers. He also was foreman of Eichele & Co. of St. Louis. It is suspected that August Eichele was in some way associated with Thomas Allen Co., but the connection has not been proven.

Only a little information has been found about James Brunaugh. He

[153]Loris S. Russell, *A Heritage of Light, Lamps and Lighting in the Early Canadian Home* (Toronto: University of Toronto Press, 1968), 127–28.

[154]*St. Louis Directory, 1864*, 295.

FIGURE 73. August Eichele matchbox label, tax stamp, and inside lid
of match crate showing wrapper transfer from matchboxes.

was born in Clermont County, Ohio, on November 17, 1832, to William
and Elizabeth Young Brunaugh. After education in country schools, he
ended up working in a bank in Mt. Pleasant, Iowa, and later operated a
string of warehouses for the Chicago, Burlington, & Quincy Railroad
when the line was completed through Iowa from Burlington. In May 1861,
he enlisted in the Sixth Iowa Volunteer Infantry and was appointed regi-
mental quartermaster, but resigned from the Army in poor health before
the close of the Civil War. He married Sarah E. Brazelton in 1855, by
whom he sired three children, William, Samuel, and James F. Brunuagh.
Sometime in 1865, he engaged in the manufacture of matches in partnership with August Eichele in St. Louis and continued in the business
until 1881, when the Diamond Match Co. purchased the factories in St.
Louis and other locations. After the sale, Brunaugh became the manager
of Diamond Match Co. with an office at 1800 S. 2nd Street in St. Louis.
His brief obituary was published in the *New York Times* on April 29, 1920:

Brunaugh, James F. Wednesday, April 28, at his residence, 318 West 84th Interment at St. Louis. Omit Flowers. Philadelphia and Omaha papers please copy.[155]

Brass Matchboxes

There are thirty small brass matchboxes with jointed sliding tops. None of these are marked.

Starch

An undetermined number of cases of starch were shipped on the *Bertrand*. Accession information indicates that the starch was manufactured by Andrew Erkenbrecher at A. Erkenbrecher's St. Bernard Starch Works in Cincinnati, Ohio. Andrew Erkenbrecher was the son of a weaver named Henry Erkenbrecher, who was born at Heilgersdorf, Germany, on July 4, 1821.

He was schooled in his village, and at age fifteen, he immigrated with his father, mother Catherine, and his sister to New York. Thereafter, they moved to Cincinnati, where he and his father entered the employ of a spice merchant named Carl Reemelin. After a short employment, the Erkenbrechers entered the employ of a confectioner named John Meyers. Later, Andrew worked as a laborer on the farm of Colonel Gano near Carthage. By age twenty-two, Andrew had saved enough money to start a grain mill, which he later combined with a starch factory. As his business prospered, he enlarged his starch factory and built another at Morrow, Ohio, which burned down in 1860. The uninsured Erkenbrecher was nearly ruined financially, but recovered sufficiently to build another starch factory on a canal near St. Bernard.[156] Among the improvements that helped his business grow was the invention of a new starch-making apparatus, patented on August 6, 1867 (Patent No. 67, 515). Soon his products achieved national and international recognition, including "Two Medals of Progress, The Highest Premiums At Vienna, 1873, For Process of Manufacture and Quality of Goods Against 149 Competitors From All Parts Of The World." Other recognition came

---

[155]James F. Brunaugh," *New York Times*, April 29, 1920, 13. See also John William Leonard, ed., *The Book of St. Louisans: A Biographical Dictionary of Leading Living Men of the City of St. Louis* (St. Louis: The St. Louis Republic, 1906), 88.

[156]Charles Frederick Goss, *Cincinnati, The Queen City, 1788–1912*, Vol. 3 (Chicago and Cincinnati: S. J. Clarke Publishing Company, 1912), 75–76.

at the Bremen and Philadelphia Expositions. On July 3, 1873, Cincinnati Bell Telephone was incorporated to provide direct communication between the city's homes and businesses, and in 1874, Andrew Erkenbrecher became the company's first president.

Erkenbrecher had a son and a daughter with his first wife Amanda Meyers, and a second son, Cornelius, by his second wife. Cornelius was associated in his father's business. In 1877, Andrew Erkenbrecher's health began to decline, and on January 4, 1885, he died in Cincinnati at the age of sixty-three. He was a well-regarded philanthropist in Cincinnati and is credited with establishing the Cincinnati Zoo and protecting the grounds from insect pests by importing insect-eating birds from Europe.[157]

Stoneware/Ironstone China

Leslie A. Peterson has written a very informative and detailed examination of the ironstone from the *Bertrand*'s cargo in *Ironstone Treasures Aboard The Steamboat Bertrand*, published in 1999.[158] As Peterson points out, among the white ironstone manufacturers represented in the *Bertrand*'s cargo is "James Edwards" and "James Edwards & Son," of Dale Hall, in the Staffordshire district of England. Although ironstone was first patented in 1813 by Charles James Mason of Staffordshire as "English porcelain," and marketed as Mason's Ironstone China, between 1813 and 1827, other potters experimented with Mason's patent, decorating the ironstone with transfer patterns or brush stroke designs. These are called by such names as opaque porcelain, English porcelain, stone china, and semi-porcelain. These were too fussy for the likes of practical American "colonials," who wanted plain, durable china. By 1852, James Edwards was marketing the first white ironstone to America, and during the 1850s and 1860s large quantities of "thrashers' ware" were being sold in American agricultural communities. Forms were generally dinner plates and tea and chamber sets. The Edwards Dale Hall Pottery Works at Burslem, Staffordshire, was begun in 1852 under the name James Edwards and was one of the first to mass produce durable white ironstone ware. It later became James Edwards & Son(s).[159] The factory was in business until 1882 and was succeeded by Knapper & Blackhurst.

---

[157]Ibid.

[158]Leslie A. Peterson, *Ironstone Treasures Aboard the Steamboat* Bertrand (Chesterfield, Missouri, The White Ironstone China Association, 1999).

[159]Lllewellynn Frederick William Jewitt, *The Ceramic Art of Great Britain from pre-historic times down to the Present Day Being a History of the Ancient and Modern Pottery and Porcelain*

The *Bertrand*'s examples include pitchers, bowls, bowls with lids, cas- seroles with lids, elongate dishes or celeries, footed dishes, oval and deep bowls, platters, dessert plates, luncheon or salad plates, dinner plates, cups and saucers, ladles, candlesticks, and chamber pots. There are no complete sets of any one design, although as Peterson points out, the designs of some pieces are sympathetic to one another. At least three manufacturers are represented, two of which have been identified. In addition to wares produced by James Edwards, the second largest num- ber of pieces were hallmarked simply "IRONSTONE CHINA / J. F.," referring to Jacob Furnival Co., and some items such as pitchers are backmarked "MAYER & ELLIOT / BERLIN (probably BURSLEM misspelled or miscatalogued) IRONSTONE."

Pieces attributed to Jacob Furnival & Co. came from the Colbridge area of Staffordshire. The company was in business between 1845 and 1870. It is known that Jacob and Thomas Furnival established a pottery in Han- ley, Stoke-on-Trent, in the Staffordshire District about 1843 to produce earthenware and ironstone. The Furnivals must have had a parting of the ways because Thomas is listed in directories of the time as Thomas Furnival & Co. at the same location between 1844 and 1846, while Jacob Furnival & Co. is listed at Cobridge, Stoke-on-Trent, between 1845 and 1870. Thomas is again listed as Thomas Furnival & Sons at Cobridge between 1871 and 1890. The only other listing is for Furnivals (Ltd.) between 1895 and 1968 at Cobridge. If these pieces were not produced by the Furnivals, they may have been made by J. F. Wetherbee, but this seems unlikely in view of the fact that the J. F. backmark matches that used by Jacob Furnival during this period.

Of the pieces marked "MAYER & ELLIOT," it is known that Thomas, John, and Joshua Mayer began making pottery at the Furlong and Dale Hall Works in 1843. They produced large earthen tableware known as the "chef-d'oeuvre of the potter's art" after having exhibited at three British exhibitions and receiving a medal in the 1851 show. From 1855 to 1858, the firm was known as Mayer Bros. & Elliot and from 1858 to 1861 as Mayer & Elliot. From 1862 to 1869, the company was known as Liddle, Elliot, & Son. Therefore, the *Bertrand* examples must have been made between 1858 and 1861, exported to the United States, and wholesaled after 1861 before ending up in the *Bertrand* cargo in 1865.

White ironstone must have been the "melmac" of the frontier, because fragments and whole vessels turn up frequently in historic

---

Works of the Kingdom and of their Productions of Every Class, Vol. 2 (London: Virtue and Co., Limited, 1878), 267–69.

FIGURE 74. Various designs of ironstone china.

archaeological contexts across the West. Accession and laboratory records indicate the following numbers of these artifacts:

Ironstone baker bowls	16	Ironstone saucers	10
Ironstone sugar bowls	2	Ironstone platters	20
Ironstone soup bowls	18	Ironstone coffee cups	12
Ironstone dishes	5	Ironstone butter dishes	1
Ironstone ladles	1	Ironstone pitchers	5
Ironstone plates	70	Ironstone sauce boats	1
Ironstone tureens	1	Ironstone creamers	1

Ironstone perforated disks	1	Clay/ceramic mixing bowls (decorated with blue lines, wheel-thrown)	1
Ironstone chamber pots	11	Ironstone wash pitchers	2
Clay/ceramic basins	4	Ironstone candlesticks (with finger rings)	4

Tin and Copperware

There are six vertical walled tin colanders, seven kettles with copper bottoms and long cylindrical spouts, two square tin cake pans, twenty-one round tin basins, five tall slightly conical cylindrical coffee pots with lids and snub spouts, three pie tins, ninety-seven tin coffee cups with strap handles, one tin salt shaker, one flat oval lacquered tin serving tray, and two large oval copper laundry boilers in the collection.

The manufacture of tin and copper cookware and other items began fairly early in St. Louis, where, by 1816, tinsmith Tom Dowling had started a shop at the back of Robideaux's store. In 1817, Reuben Neal started a tin shop on Church Street, and by 1820–1821, a large shop was opened by Neal & Liggett on South Main Street.[160] By 1833, Oliver D. and Giles F. Filley entered the business and became so successful that St. Louis became the source for copper and tinware for nearly all of Illinois, Missouri, and the lower Mississippi region. Large stocks were sent yearly to Santa Fe, New Mexico, and to Chihuahua, Mexico. By 1890, there were 122 tinworks in St. Louis employing 1,166 people, paying out $643,236 in wages, and turning out product valued at $2,369,540.[161]

Last in this category are nine tin-plated candle molds and several square tin-plated candle lanterns. The candle molds have small pedestal bases and cup-like loop handles attached to reverse pedestals at the tops. They are nearly 4 1/2 inches square and about 10 1/2 inches tall and are made to turn out four candles. These bear no maker's marks. The tin candle lanterns are square-bodied with wire cross braces on the exterior of three sides and a vertical wire strap handle on the fourth side. The round cupola-style tops are vented with punched holes and bear strap-loop hangers/handles.

---

[160]John A. Paxton, *St. Louis Directory and Registry* (St. Louis: John A. Paxton, 1821), under alphabetical heading "N."

[161]Hyde and Conrad, *Encyclopedia of the History of St. Louis—A Compendium of History and Biography for Ready Reference*, Vol. 1 (New York, Louisville, and St. Louis: The Southern History Company, 1899), 485.

It is not known who specifically produced the copper and tinware on the *Bertrand*, but it would not be unlikely to assume that Giles Filley may have manufactured some of items since the cargo also contained a waffle iron made by his firm.

Wall Bracket Lamp Hardware and Lamps

The cargo included twelve floral motif cast-iron wall-mount lamp brackets that were made to hold glass fonts. Notes indicate there were six fonts complete with burners for these wall brackets.

Washboards

In the collection are twenty-two zinc-ribbed washboards. No manufacturer could be identified for any of them.

MINING SUPPLIES

Mortars and Pestles

Cargo contents included two large footed black iron mortars and accompanying pestles. The mortars are approximately twelve inches tall and ten inches in diameter at the lips. The pestles are approximately twelve inches long and are tapered, terminating in a bulbous end on one end and a round flat-bottomed crusher on the opposing end. These are of a common type for the period, and it is surmised they were for crushing ore for assaying. They are too large and of the wrong material for use in preparing medicines.

Mercury

Perhaps the single most valuable material removed from the cargo hold was mercury, which was commonly used to amalgam gold from ore during this period. The origin of the metal found is still unknown, as is the total amount of mercury the *Bertrand* carried. Presumably the salvage boat tending to the wreck enlarged the forward hold and used a diving bell to secure a good portion of the mercury before being called away to the *Cora*, a sister boat owned by the Montana and Idaho Transportation Co. that sank nearby a few days after the *Bertrand*. The steamer *Bertrand* is rumored to have carried as much as 35,000 pounds of mercury, valued today at more than a quarter million dollars

In all, nine wrought iron carboys containing approximately 830 pounds of mercury were taken from the hold during excavation. The carboys appear to have been hand-wrought, or perhaps made with a trip hammer, the tops and bottoms of which are hand-fitted and welded to the cylinders. The tops bear threaded orifices fitted with iron plugs that protrude above the bosses at various heights. The ends of the plugs are flattened and perforated with a single hole at the top. The plugs measure approximately 3/4 inches in diameter and exhibit 10–12 threads per inch. The empty weight of the carboys varies between 13 and 16 pounds 2 ounces, but exterior stamped weights are 13.3 pounds to 16.6 pounds with six of the carboys in the 13-plus pound range. The gross weight when full of mercury averaged 90.5 pounds, with the lesser weight being 89.5 pounds and the larger being 92.5 pounds. The cylinders range in height from 12 7/8 inches to 13 1/8 inches, and the diameters range from 5 inches to 4 3/4 inches. There are several miscellaneous stamp marks on seven of the carboys, none of which shed any light on the makers of the cylinders or on the origin of the contents. At least one, and perhaps all of the cylinders, was consigned to G. P. Dorris, Virginia City.

AGRICULTURAL SUPPLIES

Cowbells

Although not exactly agricultural supplies, six large copper cowbells with strap handles are in the collection. If they were found in a contemporary context, they would not stand out as different from those made today.

Plows and Parts

The *Bertrand* cargo yielded three large plows with 21- and 22-inch bottoms made by Toby, Anderson, & Co. of Peoria, Illinois. It also carried walking plow handles, and parts for twenty to twenty-seven smaller plows with 9- to 13-inch bottoms, some of which were made by Tyrone and by Jas. Wood & Co. Most of the plow beams were made by John Deere. Although nothing is known of the plowshare and moldboard companies, John Deere was a well-known producer of sod plows in the 1860s.

The biographical and company history relating to John Deere was extracted from the very comprehensive John Deere Co. website and its component chapters on history and timeline.[162] Born in Rutland, Vermont, on February 7, 1804, to Sarah Yates Deere and William Rinold Deere, a tailor, who ran away to England in 1808, John Deere was educated in a public school and then left home in 1821 to serve an apprenticeship in blacksmithing at Middlebury, Vermont, under Captain Benjamin Lawrence. By 1825, he was an accomplished journeyman blacksmith in Colchester Falls, Vermont, making highly polished forks and shovels that were very much in demand and that supported his business until the general economic downturn of 1837. Deere began courting a lady of fine upbringing from Middlebury named Demarius Lamb (1805–1865) while he was an apprentice, and married her at her parent's home in Granville on January 28, 1827.

In 1828, John and Demarius had their first child, Francis Albert Deere, and in 1829, John Deere purchased land and started a blacksmith shop in Leicester at the crossroads of major stage lines. Twice in close succession his shops burned down, forcing Deere to sell his property and leaving him deeply in debt. In 1830, Deere's second child, Jeannette, was born, and between 1830 and 1834, he moved the family four times in search of employment. In 1833, he moved to Hancock and bought some land, but fell on hard times again and had to mortgage the property. In 1834, the third child, Francis Alma, was born to the Deere family, and Demarius was soon pregnant with the fourth child. In debt, demoralized, and in danger of losing his land, John Deere sold his blacksmith shop to his father-in-law and left his family for the prairie of Illinois at Grand Detour on the Rock River in search employment. He arrived there in the fall of 1836 and built a forge. On that site in 1837, Deere built a twenty-six by thirty-one foot shop on rented land and began construction on a wood frame house. At Grand Detour, he quickly learned that the rich Midwestern soil clung stubbornly to the cast-iron plows in use at the time. He became convinced that highly polished and properly shaped moldboards and shares would scour themselves as they turned furrows.[163]

---

[162]A full description of the history of Deere & Company is found in Wayne G. Broehler, Jr., *John Deere's Company, A History of Deere & Company and its Times* (Garden City: Doubleday & Company, Inc., 1984). See also "John Deere—Our Company," John Deere, http://www.deere.com/wps/dcom/en_US/corporate/our_ company/about_us/history/history.page?%0A%09%09%09; http://www.deere.com/wps/dcom/en_US/corporate/our_company/about_us/history/timeline/timeline.page?%0A%09%09 %09; and http://www.deere.com/wps/dcom/en_US/corporate/our_company/about_us/history/past_leaders/past_leaders.page?%0A%09%09%09. Copyright 1996–2005 Deere & Company.

[163]"John Deere—Our Company."

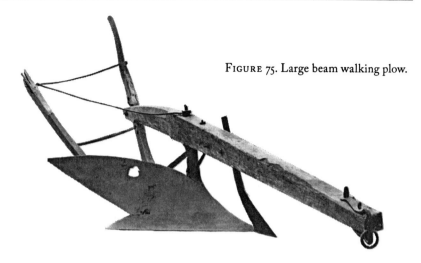

FIGURE 75. Large beam walking plow.

In 1837, using steel from a saw blade he acquired from Leonard Andrus's pounds, Deere hand-shaped and tested his first self-scouring plow. Unlike other blacksmiths of the day, John Deere made plows ahead of orders and took them to the country and sold them; he did not custom-make each order as it came in. In 1841, he patented his first grain drill, and by 1843, he was in partnership with Leonard Andrus in the blacksmithing business. He soon accepted another partner named John Gould. Deere suffered with the problems of importing steel from Britain at $330 per ton. In 1843, he entered into partnership with John Gould and Robert Tate and moved the business to Moline, Illinois, to take advantage of the abundant coal, water power, and better transportation. The new building was completed on August 31, 1848, and the factory produced 700 plows by the end of the year.[164]

Sometime in 1844, Deere began making plowshares with improved steel produced by Lyon Sharb & Co. of St. Louis, but continued making moldboards from wrought iron until 1846, when he was able to have cast steel shipped from Jones and Quigg Steel Works of Pittsburgh to Moline, Illinois where Deere opened a factory to take advantage of water power on the Mississippi River. By 1847, John Deere was producing 1,000 plows a year at his three-story blacksmith shop, and his strong business ethics and high product standards won him even more satisfied customers in ensuing years. By 1849, he employed sixteen workers and

[164]Ibid.

built 2,136 plows. The company became Deere, Tate, and Gould in 1850 and began handling the Seymour grain drill. In 1852, Deere bought out his partners, and for the next sixteen years, the company was known variously as John Deere, John Deere & Co., Deere & Co., and Moline Plow Manufactory. In 1853, his only surviving son, Charles, joined the firm as a bookkeeper. As things prospered, Deere paid most employees 58 cents to $1.50 per day, and good piece workers could earn as much as $18 a week. In 1857, his ingenuity rose again with the invention of an "Improved Clipper" plow with a rolling coulter to cut vegetation with a clean slice. The business suffered a downturn during the national business panic of 1857–1858, but Deere teamed up with Joseph Fawkes, developer of a steam-powered plow.[165]

By 1863, the company added another non-plow implement when it began producing the Hawkeye riding cultivator under a patent arrangement with inventor Robert W. Furnace. In 1864, wheels were added to the plow to create a single-bottom sulky. Deere also patented "A New and Useful Improvement in Molds for Casting Steel Plows and other Articles." By 1867, the company had added two moldboards on a frame to make a two-bottom gang that could plow about five and one-half acres per day. On August 15, 1868, the business was incorporated as Deere Co. and, after reorganization in 1869, John Deere's son Charles took over the business and ran it for forty-nine years. During the next two decades, the company prospered, making walking and wheeled plows, cultivators, harrows, seed drills, planters, wagons and buggies. Deere's success enabled him to engage in other civic and business opportunities, including the organization of the First National Bank of Moline, of which he became president in 1866. In 1873, he was elected mayor of Moline. The company weathered the recession and panic of 1873–1876 and continued to grow. By 1911, the company had acquired six other competing implement makers and became a full-line farm equipment manufacturer. The company has prospered ever since as a nationally and internationally known tractor and agricultural implement producer.[166]

Sadly, Deere's wife of thirty-eight years, Demarius, died in 1865, but in 1866 John Deere married Lucenia Lamb (1809–1888), Demarius's younger sister. John Deere, the famous inventor and entrepreneur, died on May 17, 1886, at the age of 82 in Moline, Illinois. Lucenia Deere died two years later.[167]

---

[165]Ibid.
[166]Ibid.
[167]Ibid.

Pitchforks/Hay Forks

There are fifty-three round-tine pitchforks/hay forks, about which there is no information. These forks may have been produced by David J. Millard's Paris Furnace Co. at Paris, New York.

Scythe Blades

FIGURE 76. Detail of David Millard scythe markings.

Although there are sixty-nine large scythe blades recorded in the accession record, the only recorded scythe blade (Cat. No. 269-887) was produced by David J. Millard's scythe works at Paris, New York, on the Sauquoit River. This is a typical curved scythe blade with a tang at one end for mounting on a long two-handed handle. It measures 39 1/4 inches long by 1 3/4 inches wide, and one face is grooved or rilled. The grooved face bears two stamped inscriptions, one near handle tang reading "2 & 3" and the other at the base of the blade reading "D. J. Millard/ Silver Steel." The opposite face bears remnants of a paper label reading "[S]TEEL BACK SY __[ES] / Manufactured [by] [Pa]ris Furnace Co. / [DA]VID [J.] M[IL]LAR[D]." It should be noted that most of the very hard tempered silver steel at this time was shipped in bar form from England.

Documents of the time lauded the Millard Scythe and Hoe Works for producing agricultural implements that "were the best made in the whole country."[168] The superintendent of the works was Cornelious J. Knickerbocker of Utica, New York. David J. Millard apparently had

[168]Daniel E. Wager, ed., "The Town of Paris," *Our County and Its People, A Descriptive Work on Oneida County, New York* (Boston: The Boston History Company, Publishers, 1896), 495, 497. See also Freeman Hunt, ed., *Merchants Magazine and Commercial Review* 18, no. 1: 562.

agents selling his products throughout the west. The growth of Paris between 1830 and 1845 is largely attributed to the Paris Furnace Co., Empire Woolen Mills, and the Millard Scythe and Hoe Works. David Millard was the town supervisor of Clayville and Paris and a close friend of Senator Henry Clay. In addition to the production of scythes and hay forks, Millard also had the capability to manufacture sabers. In December 1861, Millard contracted with the U.S. Ordinance Department to make 10,000 M1860 light cavalry sabers for the Union Army, all of which are dated 1862.[169] Millard also owned a sawmill at Clayville. He died on February 11, 1871, at the age of seventy-five. After his death, the shops were taken over by Benjamin F. Avery of Louisville, Kentucky.

Scythe Handles

Records indicate there are three wooden handles in the cargo, but there is no information regarding the manufacturer. One has to wonder about the disproportionate ratio of scythe blades to handles in the cargo?

Spading Forks

Records indicate there were fifty-one forks with four rectangular tines. No other information is found in laboratory notes.

HARDWARE, TOOLS, AND BUILDING SUPPLIES

Hardware

Hardware items were packed in mixed lots in wooden crates weighing from 200 to 550 pounds, or in large wooden steel-banded barrels. A mixed lot case might include a dozen axe heads, several dozen door locks, lock plates and knobs, keys, wood screws, files, hinges, and hoe blades. One box weighing 552 pounds contained parts for a circular saw, whet stones, cork screws, turnbuckles, and two feather dusters. At least one of the crates was marked:

No 1

FROM

F. Shapleigh & CO.

---

[169]D. J. Millard sabers are rare, but can be found offered for sale by antique military arms dealers throughout the United States.

DEALERS
HARDWARE
&
CUTLERY
ST. LOUIS

The story of Augustus Frederick Shapleigh is truly remarkable. He was born in Portsmouth, New Hampshire, in 1810, the son of Captain Richard Shapleigh, who died in a shipwreck in 1813, and Mrs. Abner Blaisdell Shapleigh of Portsmouth. At age fourteen, he sought employment for which his pay was $50 a year, less room and board. A year later, he shipped on a sailing vessel and spent three years at sea before his lonely mother persuaded him to come home. At age nineteen, Shapleigh accepted a clerkship with a wholesale hardware company in Philadelphia known as Rogers Brothers Co. that had begun business in 1819. After thirteen years, he became a junior partner in the firm. In 1838, he married Elizabeth A. Umstead of Philadelphia by whom he had eight children. Rogers Brothers Co. had the foresight to establish a foothold in the west by establishing a branch house in St. Louis in 1843 with young Augustus as the point man.[170] He set up business at 414 Main Street, between Locust and Vine, ideally located near the river and thus convenient to customers and shipping. Within a year, the total value of stock and fixtures had grown to $23,529.55 and included the essentials for pioneer life in the west. Among the items sold were axes, saws, hatchets, nails, hinges, locks, shoemakers', tanners', and carpenters' tools, some harness equipment, firearms and ammunition (mostly powder and ball), bear and animal traps, cutlery, razors, pocket knives, hunting knives, limited table and silverware, and a few extremely crude shovels and spades, farming implements such as scythes and grain cradles, violins, harmonicas, and Jew's harps.[171]

In 1848, operating as Rogers, Shapleigh, Co., the firm annexed adjoining buildings. Ben Bogy, their first salesman, traveled with a handmade price book and samples he carried in saddle bags. Bogy worked for Shapleigh for fifty-two years. In 1847, when Rogers died, Thomas D. Day came into the company and reorganized it into Shapleigh, Day & Co. By 1850, the gold rush in California had provided even more profitability for the

[170]Hyde and Conrad, *Encyclopedia of the History of St. Louis*, Vol. 4, 2047–48.
[171]"Shapleigh Hardware Company," Shapleigh Family Association, http://shapleigho .tripod.com/shapleighfamilyassociation/id13.html. See also *One Hundred Years of Growth, Shapleigh Hardware Company, St. Louis 1843–1943*.

company, and the prosperous population of St. Louis rose to 77,860. Two years later, the first steam railroad came to St. Louis. In 1854, the citizens had subscribed $6,400,000 to construct the Missouri Pacific Railroad.

In 1853 Shapleigh, Day, Co. published the first hardware catalogue west of the Mississippi, and in 1854, the company adopted its famous Diamond Edge trademark and the slogan "Diamond Edge is a Quality Pledge." Diamond Edge tools were the first line of edge tools in the United States to be covered by a jobbers' trademark. Thomas Day retired from the company in 1863 and the name was changed to A. F. Shapleigh & Co. Shapleigh's sons Alfred Lee and Richard W. Shapleigh accepted the challenge of moving the company forward, and the business prospered under various names and partners such as Shapleigh and Cantwell Hardware Co. in 1880, A. F. Shapleigh Hardware Co. in 1886, and Norwell-Shapleigh Hardware Co. in 1901, until it closed in the early 1960s. A. F. Shapleigh died in February 1902.[172]

Butt Hinges (900)

Some of the butt hinges from the cargo are stamped by the New England Butt Co. in Providence, Rhode Island. This company was established by N. A. Fenner in 1842 to manufacture cast-iron butt hinges and industrial machinery. The main building of three was designed and constructed by Spencer R. Reed in 1865. By 1880 cheaper stamped metal butt hinges replaced cast-iron butts, so like so many other companies that changed their product lines when one was no longer profitable, the company turned to the manufacture of braiding machinery. By 1901, the New England Butt Co. employed 200 workers in the manufacture of braiding machines for silk, worsted, and cotton braid. It also made braiding machines for telephone, electric light, and crinoline wire. It continues to make braiding and cabling machines at this site and at the site of the former Providence Steam Engine Co. under the auspices of Wanskuck Corporation, a company that previously ran a woolen mill.[173]

---

[172]"Shapleigh Hardware Company," 2002, ibid.

[173]"New England Butt Company," The On-line Industrial Sites and Commercial Buildings Survey in a partnership between the Providence Preservation Society and the Providence Plan, http://local.provplan.org/pps/detail.asp?UID=NEBC. See also Jane Lancaster, "Scientifically Managing New England Butt," *Making Time—Lillian Moller Gilbreth—A Life Beyond* Cheaper by the Dozen (Lebanon, N.H.: Northeastern University Press, 2004), 133–42.

Cabinet Locks

These are typical simple, rectangular, small brass cabinet locks. None of these are marked as to manufacturer.

Chain Bolt Door Locks

There is only one simple black cast-iron chain bolt, similar to those found in homes today. There are no manufacturer's marks.

Curtain Rods, Curtain Rod Finials, and Curtain Rings

There are at least three wooden rods with finials and as many as four brass curtain rings in the collection.

Cup Hooks

There are thirty-one black metal cup hooks. There is no other information about these artifacts.

Door Knobs (151)

The accession record shows that 151 white or swirled brown ceramic door knobs with black lacquered shanks were in the cargo along with three black lacquered metal knob plates.

Door Lock Sets, Keys, Keyhole Covers, and Latch Receiver Plates

Recovered from the cargo were 104 square, black lacquered metal door locks, sixty of which had keys. In addition, there are ten complete door lock mechanisms with keys, knobs and receiver plates, sixty sliding plate metal keyhole covers, black lacquered and brass trimmed tongue receiver plates, and thirty-one metal door keys of various types and sizes. There also are a number of door lock parts.

The most interesting locks and lock parts in this group are perpendicular action "rim locks" for doors manufactured by Carpenter & Tildesley. Patented in 1830 as Patent No. 5880 by James Carpenter and inventor John Young, these iron-cased locks usually have brass knobs, although none were found in the *Bertrand*'s cargo. They have a distinctive lever-type striker that rides up a diagonal incline on the keeper and drops into the

FIGURE 77. Carpenter & Tildseley rim lock.

latched position instead of withdrawing into the case as modern door locks do. Because they were made to be screwed to the face of a door, they were rather blocky and imposing, but they were easy to manufacture, cheap to export to the United States, and much in demand from the British hardware export trade.[174] This invention soon led to the invention of modern mortise locks. The plain faced, keyed rim locks from the *Bertrand* bear a brass medallion with the Carpenter & Tildesley trademark and patent number and the brass-rimmed receivers are stamped "CARPENTER PATENTEE."

James Carpenter was born in 1775 and came to Willenhall, England, early in his life. By 1795, he had become an iron worker in Willenhall and began inventing a variety of things, including a new type of currycomb for horses in 1815. In 1830, he partnered with Wolverhampton inventor John Young to invent and patent a new type of perpendicular latch bolt and lock for doors (Patent No. 5880). Later, the partners agreed to divide the patent into rim lock use and mortise lock use, whereupon Carpenter went on to manufacture "Carpenters lift up locks," which he named "Number 60" locks. Young acquired the right to make mortise locks. As the business grew, James Carpenter built the large Sommerford Works lock factory at New Road. When he died in 1844, his son John Carpenter inherited the business. He partnered with his brother-in-law James Tildesley, and the company name changed from Carpenter & Co.

[174]James L. Garvin, *A Building History of Northern New England* (Lebanon, N.H.: University Press of New England, 2001), 83–84.

to Carpenter & Tildesley in 1845. The firm made locks, currycombs, steel horse scrapers, singing lamps, trunk clips, and other items.[175]

In 1852, the partnership was dissolved and Carpenter became the sole owner of Carpenter & Tildesley. He patented an improved rim lock called the "J25" and began exporting locks to Australia. John Carpenter died in 1857. James Carpenter died in 1876, and the company passed to his sons James C. and Clement Carpenter, who continued the business. Although James became an invalid in 1904 and died in 1907, the business continued until 1919, when Clement Carpenter died at age ninety-five. Other Willenhall companies continued making the Carpenter patent No. 60 locks.

Drawer Handle Plates and Drawer Pulls

Curiously, there are seventy-two diamond-shaped brass plates made to accommodate drawer handles. They have lead gussets for screws, but there are no handles associated with the plates. None of these are hallmarked. There are also twenty-four brass drawer handles suspended from daisy-tasseled attachments for the through-holes on drawers or drawer handle plates. None of these are hallmarked.

Nails

While only one unmarked nail keg was recorded in the cargo of the *Bertrand*, thousands of square-shanked cut nails were found during the excavations. When the steamboat left the Dunlevy and Co. shipyard in Wheeling, West Virginia, in November 1864 for St. Louis, it presumably was loaded with 6,000 kegs of nails and other metal goods. The *Bertrand* also stopped at Cincinnati, where it loaded 200 cases of bitters and wines. Jerome Petsche and the author were convinced that the nails were products of the Belmont Nail Co. works in Wheeling because it was the most important nail-making works in the Ohio Valley at the time.

Operating two blast furnaces, one in the city proper, the Belmont works was the second largest factory in Wheeling and part owner in the Wheeling Steel Co., which provided it with steel for rolling into nail plate. Belmont Nail Co. had its origin in 1849, when E. M. Norton

---

[175] Jim Evans, "Carpenter and Tildesley, Summerford Works, Willenhall," *A Gazetteer of Lock and Keys Makers* (2002), http://www.localhistory.scit.wlv.ac.uk/Museum/locks/gazetteer/gazc.htm.

joined with William Bailey, S. H. Woodward, Henry Wallace, C. B. Doty, Holstin Harden, F. D. Norton, William Hay, Hugh McGivern, and John Wright to form the partnership of Norton, Bailey, & Co. They elected F. D. Norton president, appointed William Bailey plant manager, bought two acres for $1,600, and built a mill containing eighteen nail machines. Adding improved equipment and a new partner, Henry Moore, the company nearly put the nearby Virginia Mill out of business. About 1851 Baily, Woodward, and others sold their interest in the Belmont works to Henry Moore and started another plant called the LaBelle. The Belmont Co. became associated with Joseph Bell in 1853, and the name was changed to Norton, Acheson, & Co. The business prospered, and by 1860, it had eighty nail machines.[176]

In 1863, the partnership expired, and the mill property was sold to Henry McCullough of Pittsburg at public auction for $127,000. Thereafter, the company was reorganized as McCullough, Acheson, & Co. with M. B. Cox as a new partner. Not long after, that the company was again reorganized as Lahr & Co., which merged into the title of Belmont Iron Works with Henry Moore as president. In 1865, the firm name was changed to Belmont Nail Works Co. and operated as such until June 13, 1879. In 1872, the company incurred a bond debt of $200,000 to build a new blast furnace costing $163,000. Work commenced on construction, but was halted by the taking of $180,000 in profits by the shareholders and by the bank panic of 1873. By 1874, the work was finished, and the company had 110 nail machines in operation. Unfortunately, even though it was the largest factory in Wheeling and the third largest nail manufacturer in the United States, mill work was severely affected, and by 1878, operations were suspended. In June 1879, the company was sold at a trustee's sale for $150,000 to Samuel Laughlin, who represented the bond holders. After new additions were made to its coal privileges, a new syndicate was formed with A. Wilson Kelly as president, Joseph D. DuBois as secretary, and Nicholas Riester as the company's manager. Soon thereafter, the factory was rebuilt and enlarged and had 152 nail machines in operation with a capacity of 350,000 kegs of nails and spikes annually.[177]

---

[176]"The Bellmont Nail Works," *Wheeling Intelligencer*, September 14, 1886.

[177]Ibid. Perhaps the best description of the manufacture of cast, cut, and wrought nails is found in: Benjamin Park, ed., *Appleton's Cyclopedia of Applied Mechanics: A Dictionary of Mechanical Engineering and the Mechanical Arts*, Vol. 2 (New York: D. Appleton and Company, 1881). In addition, see T. Scott Kreilick, "The Ubiquitous Nail: An Annotated Bibliography" (Oreland, Pa.: T. Scott Kreilick, March 1999), a good source for information on nail production.

Glass Panes

Sixty glass panes from the cargo measure 12 to 12 1/16 inches by 10 inches and are 3/16 inch to 1/8 inch thick. All have a slight bluish-green cast. Field information indicates these were manufactured by William McCully & Co. of Pittsburgh. Case stencils read, "W. McCully & Co. / Pittsburgh / W / Glass / . . . ET / 10 by 12." W. McCully & Co. was making glass long after William's death in 1859, so finding McCully glass products on the *Bertrand* is not surprising.

William McCully was born in Ireland, but the date of his birth and the date when he immigrated with his family to America are not known. As a young man, McCully became an apprentice glass blower at Bakewell's Grant Street factory in Pittsburgh. He later worked for Frederick Lorenz at the Pittsburgh Glass Works, where he became proficient in blowing cylinder window glass. In 1829, he partnered with Captain John Hay to build the Union Flint Glass Works, which was destroyed by fire and flood in 1832. Although the partnership dissolved, McCully built another plant late in 1832, calling it the Phoenix Glass Co. By 1840–1841, McCully had acquired two additional plants in the Williamsport area of Pittsburgh.[178]

Two years later, McCully partnered with A. W. Buchanan, Frederick Lorenz, and Thomas Wightman. Lorenz was the principle owner of the Pittsburgh Glass Works, the Temperanceville Glass Works, and Sligo Glass Works. This loose partnership apparently dissolved in 1851 with ownership reverting to the original owners, except that Lorenz sold the Sligo Glass Works to McCully & Co. William McCullly's son John McCully continued the business after his father's death in 1859. Several other partners were added to the company both before and after William's death.[179]

Mirrors and Frames (21)

Padlocks and Keys

In the cargo are nine heavy, metal, heart-shaped padlocks, but only five keys. None of the locks are hallmarked.

---

[178]Dr. Thomas Cushing, ed., *A Genealogical and Biographical History of Allegheny County, Pennsylvania* (Boston, Retitled and Reprinted for Clearfield Publishing Co. By Genealogical Publishing Co., Inc., 1975, 1993, 2007), 224.
[179]Ibid.

Spring Bolts

There are six cast-iron sliding tongue spring bolts. The bolts were held closed by springs. There are no manufacturer's marks.

Stove Parts

It was not known how many miscellaneous stove parts are represented in the collection immediately after excavation, but there are a number of burners, burner parts, legs, and grills, none of which can be identified with a manufacturer.

Strap Hinges, Triangular (4)

T-hinges

These sixty-nine hinges have unequal wings, with one wing being elongated and tapered. They are not distinctive, and no manufacturer has been identified.

Wall Hooks/Coat Hooks

The cargo yielded seventy-two two-pronged wall hooks. These have six-sided base plates. No information is noted about the manufacturer.

White Lead (14 kegs)

White lead mixed with linseed oil comprised a large portion of the white house paint available at this time in history, and it was no surprise to find fourteen kegs of white lead among the building supplies on the steamer *Bertrand*. The kegs were marked as having come from the Collier White Lead and Oil Co. of St. Louis.

George Collier was born on March 17, 1796, on a farmstead in Worcester County, Maryland, to Peter and Catherine Collier. Besides being a farmer, Collier's father was engaged in the Atlantic coasting trade until he died in 1810, leaving the family fairly well off. George's mother sent him and his brother John to Mr. Wylie's Academy in Philadelphia where they became educated in mercantile pursuits. By 1816, John Collier had moved to St. Charles, Missouri, where he opened a mercantile, followed soon thereafter by a branch house in St. Louis. About 1818, George Collier joined his brother and worked in the business before becoming a partner in the general mercantile business of supplying retail and wholesale goods to companies that traded in St. Louis.[180]

In 1821 when John Collier died, George elected to continue the business for several years before entering into partnership with his friend Peter Powell under the name Collier & Powell. By 1830, having amassed a fortune, George Collier withdrew from the business, and realizing that the future prosperity of St. Louis relied on the river trade, he engaged in building steamboats. He selected men with river experience and sent them to Pittsburgh to make boat building contracts and superintend the construction, in return for which Collier gave them an interest. Owing to Collier's maxim to hold no property that brought no return, he held ownership in most of the steamboats only long enough to establish their "character" in the trade and then sold them to realize the highest value. At any one time, Collier was said to have had eight or ten steamboats plying the upper Missouri River. This was an extremely profitable time to be in business in St. Louis, since there could be as many as 200 steamboats at any one time loading and unloading products at St. Louis wharfs.[181]

George Collier was a man of great vision, and he often turned his attention to other interests such as the lead/galena mines near Galena, Illinois, and the mines farther south in Missouri. Collier became engaged in the purchase and shipment of lead, much of which was shipped to Philadelphia through the business house of Thomas Fassit for the production of white lead. As Collier purchased more mines, more lead was shipped to France and other parts of Europe, making St. Louis one of most important centers for the lead industry. Using his own steamboats, Collier also shipped lead to New Orleans along with other products like flour, in which he had considerable investment at St. Louis. When sold, the profits derived in New Orleans were invested in heavy groceries, sugar, coffee, salt, and molasses for shipment on the return trip to St. Louis.[182]

Collier became involved in the banking and exchange business in 1835–1836 with William G. Pettus, the husband Collier's first wife's sister. The firm of Collier & Pettus dissolved in 1840, and Collier formed a new partnership in 1842 with his brother-in-law William M. Morrison as commission merchants and dealers in lead. As Collier's health began

---

[180]J. Thomas Scharf, *History of St. Louis City and County*, Vol. 2, 1254.

[181]Ibid., Vol. 2, 1255.

[182]Ibid.

to deteriorate, he began a slow withdrawal from business and sold his interests in steamboats. By 1847, he retired from the firm Collier & Morrison. Collier was also a member of the first board of directors of the Missouri Pacific Railroad.

Between 1837 and 1850, the manufacture of white lead and of oil from castor beans became well established in St. Louis. Among the more prominent businesses in this commodity was Charless and Blow, which pioneered in its establishment there (Peter Blow's business record is described in some detail elsewhere in the section about pharmaceutical bottles). In 1850, the factory operated by Charless and Blow burned to the ground, but it was reestablished and incorporated the next year with the help of a principle stock holder, George Collier. The firm became the Collier White Lead and Oil Co. and was actively managed by Henry T. Blow.[183]

In 1851, Collier was a heavy subscriber in support of the Mercantile Library Hall Association that promoted the construction of a large building at the corner of Fifth and Locust Streets to house all manner of records associated with the Missouri River trade. The library is still in existence, and some of the records reported herein were located with help from this institution. Collier died July 18, 1852, at the age of fifty-six, having been twice married. His first wife, Francoise E. Morrison, died January 1, 1826, leaving him with a daughter and infant son. In 1838, he married Miss Sarah A. Bell, by whom he had five sons and one daughter; five of the sons survived at 1898 and all had successful careers in politics and law.[184]

The Collier White Lead and Oil Co. factory was erected in 1865 on North Second Street at Cass Avenue at a cost of $200,000 and produced white lead, litharge, red lead, linseed oil, castor oil, and cotton seed oil. The factory had eighteen stacks and five thousand pots holding forty thousand pounds of metal. The company employed eighty-five men at an annual cost of $60,000.[185]

Wrought Iron Strap Hinges, Heavy Duty (1)

---

[183]Ibid., 1256.

[184]Ibid., 1257.

[185]Ibid. See also, Joseph A. Dacus, James William Buel, *A Tour of St. Louis: Or, The Inside Life of a Great City* (St. Louis: Western Publishing Company, Jones and Griffin, 1878), 242–47.

Tools

FIGURE 78. Blacksmith's tools, including cross-peen sledge hammers, hot chisel, and hardy chisel.

There is a variety of carpenter's and blacksmith's tools from the *Bertrand*'s hold. Whether some of these tools were parts of a ship's carpenter's tool kit or those of a company blacksmith or others is unknown. Among the blacksmithing tools are a very large wood and leather bellows, sledgehammers, cross-peen sledgehammers, a long handled hot chisel, anvils, and a hardy chisel for an anvil. None of these tools except the sledgehammers bear maker's marks. Nothing is known about the bellows.

Auger Handles and Bits

Axes

Accession records indicate there were 113 axe heads not associated with identifiable shipping crates. These were presumably packed in five cases of one dozen axe heads each. In addition, there are 207 axe handles.

Axes recovered from the cargo are stamped "DOUGLAS AXE MFG. CO." and were made in East Douglas, Massachusetts. Axes were made in East Douglas as early as 1798 by Joseph and Oliver Hunt. Oliver Hunt and his sons Warren and Otis eventually took over the business. When Warren Hunt was about eighteen years of age, he assumed control of the firm and greatly expanded its facilities and production methods. About 1832, Alexander Scudder became a partner, but sold out to Hunt within three years. In 1834–1835, Douglas Axe Manufacturing Co. was formed. By 1865, it was capitalized at $400,000 and employed 300 workers who produced more than one half million edge tools valued at $580,000. Growth of the company in the 1860s was largely the result of government contracts during the Civil War. By 1870, the company had grown from two small buildings to six located along the Mumford River. The Douglas Axe Manufacturing Co. continued producing axes until 1897.[186] Apparently some of the earlier Douglas axes were hallmarked "W. HUNT" or "WHUNT & CO.," and "CAST STEEL WARRANTED." Detailed information about this firm is difficult to find in any single source.

Backsaw

Accession records show that are 125 hand and circular saw blades of several varieties in the cargo. The author has information on only a few of these. One backsaw recovered from the *Bertrand* is no different morphologically than modern backsaws. It measures 17 1/2 inches long, including the handle, and the blade is 14 inches long, 1/16 inch thick, and 4 3/8 inches wide, including a 5/16 inch top edge stiffener. Three handle screws are set in a triangular pattern with 1 1/2 inches between the centers. No manufacturer's marks are present.

Bucksaws

Although there were forty-four buck saw frames and turnbuckles recovered, notes refer only to one buck saw blade. This saw is 30 inches long and 2 1/8 inches wide, with one 1/4 inch diameter hole in each end, drilled 1 1/8 inches down from the top edge and 1/4 inch from the ends. The saw is marked "HENRY DISSTON / PHILA. / CAST STEEL / WARRANTED." More will be said of Henry Disston later.

Buttress or Crankshaft Chisel

One crankshaft chisel or buttress was found measuring 18 inches long overall, including the handle. The steel shaft is 1/2 inch in diameter,

---

[186]William Andrew Emerson, "Chapter 18," *History of the Town of Douglas, (Massachusetts,) from the Earliest Period to the Close of 1878* (Boston: Frank R. Bird, 1879), 268–74. See also Sean Svadilfari, "Douglas Axe Manufacturing Company," http://www.flickr.com/photos/22280677@N07/3310985772/in/set-72157608426967282/.

and the blade is spade-shaped, being 2 inches wide at the base and 2 1/2 inches wide at the bit. The handle has a knob-like pommel 2 1/2 inches in diameter with a bulbous body measuring 2 7/16 inches in diameter at the mid-point and 1 1/4 inch in diameter at the brass mounting ferrule. The top side of the blade is stamped "HAMMOND / PHILADA / STEEL."

Not much is known about this company other than Hammond ran an edged tool factory in Philadelphia with his son. He had government contracts during the Civil War for 5,000 axes and 5,000 hatchets, and also made tomahawks and a small number of sabers. His swords are rather crude in appearance, and the blades apparently were handmade and bore no U.S. stamp or inspection marks. Philadelphia directories show that Hammond was making edged tools in 1864 and C. Hammond & Son were making edged tools as late as 1876.[187]

Carpenter's Square

What remains of a nicely made square is the brass mounted rosewood base; the blade is missing. The rectangular piece measures 6 1/2 inches long, 1 7/8 inches wide, and 11/16 inch thick. The blade end has a 1/16 inch slot and bears fancy brass cheek plates held in place with brass escutcheon pins. The bottom edge of the base is fitted with a brass plate held in place by five small flat-headed brass screws. This piece bears no maker's marks.

Chisels and Gouges

Only the blade survived of the 1/4 inch socket chisel from the *Bertrand*. The blade is 7 5/16 inches long and the socket is 5/8 inch in diameter, tapering to 5/16 inch at the top of the shoulder. The blade is approximately 1/4 inch thick from the shoulder to the bevel. This piece bears no manufacturer's marks.

The next size socket chisel represented has a 5/8 inch wide blade with a 3/4 inch diameter socket; it is approximately 5 inches long. The socket is 7/16 inch in diameter at the top of the shoulder. Only a fragment of the handle remains, and there are no manufacturer's marks stamped on the blade.

[187]Mike McWatters, "Manufacturers of Regulation Model Enlisted Swords During the Civil War—American Manufacturers," http://www.angelfire.com/wa/swordcollector/ marks/page1.html. See also Bruce S. Bazelon and William F. McGuinn, *Directory of American Military Goods Dealers & Makers 1785–1915* (Woonsocket: Andrew Mowbray Publishers, Inc., 1999), 111.

There are two wooden-handled 3/4-inch blade socket chisels. These chisels measure 14 1/2 inches long overall. The blade has a 1/2 inch shoulder between the base of the socket and blade. It is 3/8 inch thick at mid-point and 1/4 inch thick near the tip. The blade is 11/16 inch wide at mid-point, tapering to 3/4 inch wide at the cutting end. The bulbous, dark colored wood handle measures 1 1/4 inches in diameter at the base and 1 1/16 inches at the top of blade socket. There are no manufacturer's marks on either example.

Other chisels found include two 1-inch socket gouges measuring 15 3/4 inches long overall. The sockets are 1 1/16 inches in diameter, tapering to 3/4 inch at the top of the blade shoulder. The blades are nearly half-round, measuring 1 inch wide, 1/2 inch thick at the shoulder, and tapering to 3/8 inch at mid-point and 1/16 inch at the bevel. The handles have 1/2 inch-wide metal bands on the palm ends, about halfway down from the ends. The handles measure 1 3/16 inches in diameter at the mid-point. Both are stamped "P. MERRILL & CO. / CAST STEEL."

One wooden-handled 1 1/2 inch socket chisel is represented, measuring 16 1/4 inches long overall. The blade has a beveled shoulder at the base of the socket, and the blade is 3/8 inch thick at the base of the shoulder, tapering to 1/4 inches at mid-point and 1/8 inch near the tip. The blade is 1 1/2 inches wide from the base of shoulder to the tip. The bulbous handle is 1 3/16 inches in diameter at mid-point and 1 1/8 inches in diameter at the socket and bears a 9/16 inch knob at the top or palm end. The chisel bears no manufacturer's marks.

There are three 2-inch socket firmer chisels measuring 17 3/8 inches long, overall. These are of the same design as the 1 1/2 inch chisel described above, the only differences being in some dimensions. The blade sockets are 1 1/8 inches in diameter and taper to 7/8 inch at the top of the blade shoulders, which are 1 3/4 inches. The blades are 2 inches wide and measure 7/16 inch thick at the tops of the shoulders, tapering to 1/4 inch in thickness at the mid-points and 1/16 inch at the edge bevels. The handles have a 5/8 inch knob at the palm end and are 1 3/8 inches in diameter at the mid-point. All three chisels are stamped "MERRILL / CAST STEEL."

P. Merrill, or Pliny Merrill, was born in Shelburne Massachusetts, in 1800 and learned his trade from his brother Pardon Hayes Merrill (1788–1879), who was said to be an excellent ironworker who made agricultural edge tools, including hoes of his own patent in Hinsdale, New Hampshire, around 1820. Merrill was an industrious young man, and he and Pardon built a canal in the center of Hinsdale in 1828. In 1832, he built a shop, and in 1840, he was manufacturing drawknives, chisels, and gouges at his edge tool business on Canal Street using water power from the Ashuelot River. His earliest known tool stamp was on 20-inch long draw knives and read "P. MERRILL / CAST STEEL / HINSDALE, N. H." However, for a number of years beginning in 1848, he dropped the Hinsdale designation and stamped his tools "P. MERRILL & CO." About this time, his nephew, George S. Wilder (1828–1900), began working with him. By 1858, Wilder was a partner in the firm. Merrill sold the business to Wilder in 1866 and died in 1869, leaving an estate valued at $13,000, of which $2,152 went to his nephew George S. Wilder.[188]

Sometime between 1866 and 1869, the firm began marking its tools with the imprint "MERRILL & WILDER," although the old imprint apparently continued for some time. Wilder apparently took a new partner in 1866 when the firm became Wilder & Thompson, but the union only lasted until 1868. There are no known tools stamped "Wilder and Thompson." By 1870, Wilder had partnered with his brother-in-law, Richard Henry Hopkins (1831–1877), but the partnership died in 1872–1873 and there are no known tools bearing the stamp of this company. In ensuing years, after 1873, Wilder incorporated as G. S. Wilder Cast Steel and marked his tools with this name until 1883, when he sold the firm to C. E. Jennings, principal owner of a large hardware firm in New Haven, Connecticut. By 1885, the firm was known as Jennings & Griffin, and Gorge Wilder became manager of the Jennings Edge Tool Works in Hinsdale, where he served until 1891. Enjoying the firm's previous reputation, Jennings chose to continue stamping tools "MERRILL & WILDER."[189]

George Wilder was also a New Hampshire state representative from 1869 to 1970, and his son, Herbert W. Wilder (1864–1915), became a famous cartoonist for *Harper's Weekly*. Wilder died insolvent in the mid-1900s, and his estate inventory on July 1, 1900, showed he had thirty-six dozen small chisels, fifteen dozen firmer chisels, and a milling machine and equipment totaling $86.[190]

[188]Roger Smith, "Notes on New England Tool Makers, I: Edge Tool Makers, Hinsdale, N.H., 1840–1900, P. Merrill 1840–1858," Mid-West Tool Collectors Association (2001), http://www.mwtca.org/the-gristmill/sample-articles/96-notes-on-new-england-edge-tool.
[189]Ibid.
[190]Ibid.

Claw Hammers

There is one standard-size claw hammer and six smaller claw hammers, which may be farrier's hammers. One of these, which may be a farrier's hammer, measures 11 3/4 inches long overall, including the handle. The hammer head is 4 1/16 inches long, head to claw, and has an octagonal tapered nose 9/16 inch square and a 1 inch long by 5 /16 inch oval eye. The handle tapers from 1 5/16 inches at the eye to 13/16 inch at mid-point to 1 inch in diameter at the grip. The head stamped on one side "DIA-MOND / PHILADA / CAST STEEL."

The second hammer measures 13 1/4 inches long overall and has a slightly longer head at 5 inches. The faceted neck of the strike is 1 inch square with facets of about 3/8 inch each. The eye is a 1 1/4 inch long oval with 9/16 inch diameter ends. The handle is 1 1/4 inches in diameter at the head, tapering to 1 inch and widening to 1 3/8 inches in diameter at the grip. The grip end is slightly tear-drop shaped. The hammer is stamped "C. HAMMOND / PHILADA / 2."

Crosscut Saws

Only the handle and a small piece of very rusty blade are all that survived of one saw. The top edge of the handle measures 8 1/4 inches long overall and 5 3/8 inches across the ears at the back of the handle. The finger hole is 3 9/16 inches long, 1 1/2 inches wide at the top, and 2 inches wide at the bottom. The three blade mounting screws are 1/4 inch in diameter are flat on one side and have a 1/8 inch hole at the center, and a 1/16 inch wide slot across the face on the opposite side. The blade remnant measures 4 1/4 inches wide by 1/16 inch thick. A brass medallion mounted in the cheek of the handle pictures an eagle with outstretched wings clutching arrows and lightning bolts and is lettered "H. DISSTON / PHILDA." In all probability, this saw was produced before 1865 because in 1865, Hamilton Disston joined the company, and shortly thereafter the handle medallion was changed to read "Henry Disston & Son."

When carpenter's tools began to appear in the *Bertrand*'s cargo, it was no surprise to find Henry Disston saws of several varieties. Disston was fourth in the line of a succession of prominent saw makers in Philadelphia. Henry Disston was born at Tewkesbury, England, in 1821, the third child of Thomas and Ann Harrod Disston, and as a boy learned lacemaking from his father. Soon after coming to America, his father died, and subsequently Henry apprenticed in saw making to the firm of Lindley,

FIGURE 79. Henry Disston saws.

Johnson, & Whitcraft in Philadelphia, until the company went bankrupt and Henry was compensated for his work with tools and materials.
At twenty-two, he attained journeyman status in the trade and left his
employers to start an opposition factory at the corner of Second and Arch
Streets. With $350 capital and a borrowed wheelbarrow in which to haul
coal from the wharf, he produced $400 in saws from his own hand-built
furnace. Three years later, after a series of setbacks, he found himself no
wealthier[191] because the English controlled the tool and cutlery trade
during this period and imported tools were thought to be far superior to
American products. No one, it seemed, was interested in Disston's saws.

Disston married Amanda Bickley in 1844, survived his business losses,
borrowed $200, and outfitted the first steam-powered saw factory in the

---

[191]Erik Von Sneidern, "A Brief Rendering of the Disston and Sons History," Online
Reference of Disston Saws—Disston Centenntial 1840–1940, Distonian Institute, http://
www.distonianinstitute.com/100anniversary.html.

country. The factory building was professed to have been owned by a stranger, Mr. H., but the stranger only leased the premises. One night, the stranger was discovered attempting to steal Disston's goods and quickly disappeared, leaving the landlord and the sheriff to seize Henry Disston's property for back rent and any other deficiencies that might arise.[192]

Shortly thereafter, and still deeply in debt, Henry Disston saw his fortune hit still another low ebb when Mrs. Disston succumbed to a severe illness. Henry borrowed $5, produced and sold a few saws, and extricated himself from indebtedness. Soon his business was in good order, but his landlord doubled the rent, forcing Disston to move to a new location as a tenant under William H. Miles, a local machinist. When the boiler exploded and the shop burned down, Henry Disston bought a property sixty feet away from the Miles property, and within two weeks had his own factory in full operation. Owing to Henry's inventions, including the manufacture of the first crucible poured saw steel in America and his thorough knowledge of how to make tools and machinery to produce saws, he prospered and managed to survive the severe financial crisis of 1857.

Henry's first wife Amada died soon after giving birth to twins who also did not survive. In 1843, Henry Disston married Mary Stillman, by whom he had five sons. Two of his sons, Hamilton and Albert, were later associated with him in business as Henry Disston & Sons Saw Manufactory. In 1861, at the outbreak of the Civil War, Disston, a patriotic Northerner, began manufacturing swords, cavalry bits, guns, bullets, files, and other articles of war to fill government orders. He sent twenty-five men, including his son Hamilton, to the Union Army, paying their wages and holding their positions open during their absence. In 1862, Henry Disston established a rolling mill for making iron plate with which to build war ships.[193]

The Disston works was partially destroyed by fire in 1864, only to be back in operation under a sail cloth awning ten days after the conflagration. Buying more of the adjacent property and expanding the business, Disston nearly doubled his monthly production of $33,000 to $70,000 per month. Disston began to capture the foreign tool market and rapidly expanded his domestic trade. In 1871, Disston established agencies

---

[192]Ibid.
[193]Louis M. Iatarola, "The Life and Influences of Henry Disston," *Profiles in Tacony History*, Vol. 1 (Tacony: The Historical Society of Tacony, 1994), 2, http://members.aol .com/historictacony2/profile_disston.html.

in London and San Francisco and an agency and factory in Chicago. By 1875, the eight-acre Philadelphia factory employed 700 persons and produced $15 million in saws and other products annually.[194]

Dividers

One set of dividers on display at the Bertrand Museum on De Soto National Wildlife Refuge is hallmarked "C. Bemis." This stamp raises some questions, because Stephen Charles Bemis probably quit making tools under the name S. C. Bemis & Co. sometime after 1855. Whether this was an old tool or Bemis used his own name on tools after 1855 is not known. Stephen Charles Bemis started his business career at the age of fourteen as a clerk in a store owned by Joseph Pease in Chicopee, Massachusetts. In 1821, he became a partner in the company, and the name was changed to Pease & Bemis, but Pease soon sold his interest to Bemis. Stephen Bemis then partnered with Chester Chapin as Bemis and Chapin in 1825, but Chapin soon sold out to Bemis. In 1831, Bemis moved his business to Willimansett, Massachusetts, and partnered with Joseph Sheffield in the firm of Bemis & Sheffield. By 1828, Bemis and Sheffield were company officers and agents for the Willimansett Manufacturing Co. that made machine cards and small hardware. In 1835, Stephen Bemis took control of the company and began making tools under his own name, S. C. Bemis and S. C. Bemis Co.[195]

As early as 1838, Bemis was making saw sets, and sometime in 1847, he lost a patent infringement proceeding brought against him by Herrick Aiken for $2,000. The company moved to Springfield, Massachusetts, in 1844, where he partnered with Amos Call to form the Bemis & Call Co. Bemis and Call were married to two sisters named Julia and Ruhema Steele in 1828 and 1838, respectively, making Call his brother-in-law. Bemis's son William took over his father's side of the business in 1855, when the company was incorporated as Bemis and Call Hardware and Tool Co. with Call running the manufacturing department. During its existence, Bemis & Call were famous for the manufacture of combination

---

[194]Ibid., 3. See also Jacob S. Disston, Jr., *Henry Disston (1819–1878) Pioneer Industrialist Inventor and Good Citizen* (Princeton: Princeton University Press and Newcomb Publications, 1950). http://www.distonianinstitute.com/disstonbio.html. See also Charles Robinson, ed., *The Manufactories and Manufacturers of Pennsylvania of the Nineteenth Century* (Philadelphia: Galaxy Publishing Co., 1875), 119–22.

[195]Mark Conley, "The Saw Set Collector's Resource-Bemis and Call," 2010, http://members.acmenet.net-on12a/saw%20set%20website/wierdstuffbemis.htm.

and pipe wrenches, calipers, dividers, knives, saws, scales, and other tools. Stephen Bemis left the company and engaged with other business interests in Springfield, while Amos Call eventually became president of the company and remained so until he died in 1888. Bemis served as mayor of Springfield in 1861–1862, and Call served as alderman in 1861, 1867, and 1868.[196]

Draw Knives

Three draw knives are represented in the *Bertrand* tools. The cutting edges of the blades measure 8 inches, 18 inches, and 19 inches in length. All three have typical bulbous hardwood handles with brass ferrules. The blade of the smallest knife is 13 3/4 inches long overall, with an 8-inch cutting bevel measuring 1 1/4 inch wide. The steel is 1/2 inch wide at the ears. The bulbous handles are 4 1/4 inches tall and 1 1/4 inches in diameter and are mounted with 1/2-inch diameter brass ferrules. The piece bears no manufacturer's mark.

The blade of the second knife is 16 3/4 inches long, overall, with a 10-inch cutting bevel measuring 1 1/4 inches wide. The steel is 1/2 inch wide at the ears. The bulbous handles are 4 7/8 inches tall and 1 5/8 inches in diameter, and are mounted with 1/2-inch diameter brass ferrules. There are no manufacturer's marks.

The third knife blade is 19 inches long overall, with a 15-inch long cutting bevel measuring 1 3/4 inches wide. The steel is 5/16 wide at the ears. The bulbous handles are 4 1/2 inches tall and 1 3/4 inches in diameter and are mounted with 1/2-inch diameter brass ferrules. The blade is stamped "BEATTY / CAST STEEL."

The "Original Wm. Beatty & Son's Edged Tools" were made by John B. Black, a company that apparently started operating in 1806 in Chester, Pennsylvania. Among the more unusual edged tools Black produced were Beatty Brady tobacco spears.

Files

Thanks to the fine descriptive work by Laboratory Technician Kermit E. Hanson, a good deal is known about these tools.[197]

---

[196]Ibid.

[197]Kermit E. Hanson, "Files From the Steamboat *Bertrand*," *Museum of the Fur Trade Quarterly* 9, no. 4 (1973): 7–11.

Before describing the types of files found on the *Bertrand* and identifying their makers, it is best to spend some time on the file terminology Hanson provided. The length of a file is measured from the heel to the point, exclusive of the tang. The term "kind" refers to the shape or style. In the case of the *Bertrand*, files shapes range from quadrangular to round and triangular, with variations. Files are further distinguished by whether they are tapered (in width, thickness, or both) or blunt, having a consistent sectional size. The term "cut" refers to the character of the cutting surfaces (single cut or double cut) and to the coarseness of the teeth (coarse, bastard, second cut, and smooth cut). A summary of types, quantities, and lengths of files from the *Bertrand* follows:

> Mill and flat files with straight edges—95
> 4 1/2, 6, 8, 9, 14 inches long
> Mill files with one curved edge—77
> 10, 14, 16 inches long
> Round files—60
> 6, 8, 10 inches long
> Half-round files—108
> 4,5,6,8,9,12, 14 inches long
> Triangular files—177
> 3, 3 1/2, 4, 4 1/2, 5,6 inches long
> Horse Rasps—28
> 13, 14 inches long

Nearly all the files are tapered in width, and about two-thirds of the files are single cut.[198]

Before 1880, files were used for more purposes than they are today. A practical hacksaw did not come into common use until about 1880, and high-speed grinding wheels had not yet been invented. A small selection of files could be used for sharpening, cutting, and making repairs. The manufacture of files in America, like most saws, knives, and cutlery, lagged behind those imported from Britain because English files were thought to be much superior. Tradesmen generally relied on British brands they knew rather than on domestic brands that did not have established reputations. Most of the files from the *Bertrand* were manufactured by firms in Sheffield, England, where superior crucible steel had been made for perhaps a hundred years and the cutler's guild produced quality workmanship in hand-cut files. The cutting surface of

[198]Ibid., 7.

hand-cut files was made by chiseling the appropriate tooth pattern with a small, short, hard metal chisel or punch and a sledge weighing several pounds. Each craftsman concentrated on a particular kind and pattern. This process was best described by Walter White in 1858 in *A Month in Yorkshire*[199] and in an article by an unknown author titled "Making Files in Sheffield, Early 1840's" that includes excerpts from "A Day at the Fitzalan Steel and File Works, Sheffield."[200]

American file cutting machines were experimented with between 1845 and 1864, and improved file-cutting machinery was patented in 1845 by Solomon Whipple of Rhode Island. In 1847, Richard Walker of New Hampshire patented a file-cutting assembly consisting of fifty file-cutting machines powered by a fifty horsepower engine. Each machine could produce six or eight common files per hour. However, the first really successful American machine dates from 1864, when William T. Nicholson put one into production. Like the hand-cut files, most cast steel from which early machine-cut files were made was imported because American production of cast steel was just getting underway in the 1860s.

More than half of the files were made by William Butcher, and they probably were made in Sheffield, England. William Butcher was born in 1791 in Sheffield, where he and his brother Samuel apprenticed in cutlery making to their father until he died in 1806. In 1819, William and Samuel opened their own business, and by 1822, they were making small numbers of edge tools from their own crucible steel. As the American demand for Sheffield tools grew in the 1830s, Samuel became the company's New York agent, supplying hoes, chisels, saws, hammers, and complete tool chests to the American trade, and especially crucible steel cutting irons to New England plane makers. In 1835, they purchased another tool and steel works in Sheffield. By 1845, they had opened a tool and steel works in Philadelphia on the Don River.[201] With support from importer Philip Justice and banker Edward Clark, Butcher was in immediate competition with Pencoyd Iron Works and Henry Disston's crucible steel plant in the Northern Liberties section of Philadelphia. Between the 1850s and 1860s, the Butchers began making Bowie knives and also became the chief exporters of files to America. The demand for Butcher hand-cut files outstripped production until the Butchers

[199] Walter White, *A Month in Yorkshire* (London: Chapman and Hall, 1858), 303–307.
[200] "Making Files in Sheffield, Early 1840's, *Penny Magazine Supplement*, 13: 121–28.
[201] "Steel City Founders, William Butcher 1791–1870," 2003, http://www.tilthamer.com/bio/butch.html.

installed a file cutting machine at their Sheffield plant. Unfortunately, machine-cut files lagged behind the hand-cut files in quality, and the equipment was abandoned.[202]

During the 1860s, William Butcher worked with the Pennsylvania Steel Co. and in 1865 he helped install Bessemer converters to produce bulk steel. While in Philadelphia, William began to set up his own steel works, which opened in 1867 under his name. His crucible steel production methods and English workman could not compete with plants using the newest open hearth process and automated machinery, and the company was taken over by its American shareholders in 1871. Undaunted, William Butcher moved his English crew to Lewistown, Pennsylvania, where they continued to produce crucible steel for tools. Samuel Butcher died in Sheffield in 1869, and William died the next year at their family home.[203]

All of the Butcher files are stamped with "CAST STEEL" or "IMPE-RIAL CAST STEEL" and the name "W BUTHCHER." Some are stamped at the butt above the tang "W. BUTCHER," underneath which is a small encircled "B" followed by an arrow and a Formee cross.

G. B. Hubbel & Co., another British file company represented, also made the horse rasps found on the *Bertrand*. Flat single-cut bastard files made by Joseph Wolstenholm are also of British manufacture. Other British files are represented by William Goodlad and N. Spencer. Although the Wilson, Hawksworth, Ellison, and Co. files on the *Bertrand* were made in England, the company apparently had agents in the United States because it is listed in McElroy's Philadelphia Directory at 31 Commerce Street as early as 1855.[204] Files made by L. A. Taylor were produced by Taylor Brothers of Philadelphia starting in 1860. A little can be said of the remaining names, especially Moss & Gambles. Less is known of Dr. Roebucks and Joseph Roebuck & Son Warranted Cast Steel.

Although the Sheffield directory shows several cutlers and file makers between 1830 and 1857, including the master cutler George Wolstenholm, who captured much of the cutlery and spring cutlery market

---

[202]Ibid.

[203]Ibid.

[204]Edward C. and John Biddle, *Mcelroy's Philadelphia Directory for 1855: Containing the Names of the Inhabitants, their Occupations, Places of Business, and Dwelling Houses: A Business Directory, a List of the Streets, Lanes, Alleys, the Banks, &c., &c., Also the Names of Housekeepers and Persons in Business in Bridesburg, Frankford, Germantown, Manayunk, P.A., &c., &c.,* 8th ed. (Philadelphia: Edward C. and John Biddle, 1855), 605.

FIGURE 80. Stamped manufacturer's marks on files—Joseph Wostenholm and W. Butcher.

in America after about 1837, there appears to be a Wolstenholm lineage in Sheffield, but just how George Wolstenholm and Joseph Wostenholm are connected is not known. George Wolstenholm and his son George, Jr., descended from master cutler Henry Wolstenholm, who probably invented the spring knife (pocket knife) and later the Barlow folding knife. George Wostenholm was born in Sheffield, England, on January 31, 1800. Henry Wostenholm (son of George Wostenholm) had a son named George (1755–1833), and his son George, Jr., was apprenticed to his father at the Rockingham Works. At the age of twenty-four, he became an assistant to the Cutler's Co. He was brought into the company as George Wostenholm & Son and advertised as producing table knives, forks, pen, pocket, and sportsman's knives, and general dealers in cutlery. By 1826, George was made a freeman of the Cutler's Co. and given his own trademarks. In the 1830s, George and his father partnered with William Stenton, who opened markets in America for surplus stock. In 1835, Wostenholm and other Sheffield cutlers controlled the cutlery market in America, and by the time of the Civil War, they still controlled 90 percent of the market.[205] It is speculated that George Wostenholm fathered a son named Joseph, but there is no record of this thus far. Nevertheless, he and his son also became engaged in the cutlery trade. Joseph Wolstenholm and his son were file makers during

[205]"Steel City Founders, George Wostenholm 1800–1876," 2.

this period and exported their wares to America until about 1905, when the company of Joseph Wostenholm & Son, Ltd. was dissolved. Joseph Wolstenhom & Son were famous for producing quality razors and farrier's knives. George Wostenholm died on August 18, 1876, having been married three times. It is recorded that he had no children, but from where did Joseph trace his heritage?

Of Moss & Gambles, a little is known. The cementation furnaces used by Joshua Moss Oater were probably built in 1828 at Bower Springs, New York, by Thomas Turton, and were acquired by Moss & Gamble in 1860 and operated until 1911. Directories for New York from 1841 to 1852 show Joshua Moss Oater as a "steel manufacturer," and in 1856, he is listed as "Moss, Joshua & Gamble Brothers, merchants and manufacturers of steel, files, saws, tools, &c., Franklin Works, Russell Street; and New York and Boston." The address given was Thomas Turton's earlier address, so Moss must have been operating the Franklin Works and must have taken over an out-site at the Bower Springs address around 1853.[206] Therefore, Moss & Gamble must have been producing files in New York during the time the *Bertrand*'s cargo was bought and enlisted.

Nothing has yet been found concerning British makers William Goodlad and N. Spencer, Wilson, Hawkworth, Ellison, & Co., or of files made by L. A. Taylor of Taylor Brothers of Philadelphia starting in 1860. Nor is there anything known at this time of Dr. Roebuck and Joseph Roebuck & Son Warranted Cast Steel. The William Goodlad files are impressed across the heel on one side with "IMPERIAL / CAST STEEL" and along the tang on the other side with "WM GOODLAD." The rat-tailed round files attributed to William Goodlad are impressed on one side of the tang with "CAST STEEL," on another with "Wm GO[O]DLAD," and on the third side with "IMP[ER]IAL / CAST STEEL." Goodlad may have been associated with William Butcher because in Eileen Woodhead's study of trademarks on base-metal tableware, there is a silver spoon hallmark stamped "Wm Goodlad" with an anchor motif, beneath which appears "W. Butcher Warranted Cast Steel."[207] These files may date from the period in which Butcher was working with Pennsylvania Steel Co. in Philadelphia between 1865 and 1867.

One of the Taylor triangular files is stamped along one side of the

[206]Derek Bayliss, "Bower Springs Furnaces in 1858," *The Cutting Edge*, no. 8, http://www.topforge.co.uk/Magazines/Bower%202.html.

[207]Eileen Woodhead, *Trademarks on Base-Metal Tableware*, Studies in Archaeology, Architecture and History (Ottawa, Ont.: National Historic Sites, Park Service, Environment Canada, 1991), 42.

tang "L. A. TAYL[OR] / PHILA, XCLR," and one another side of the tang is stamped with "[C]AST STEEL / [WAR]RANTED."

The Spencer single-cut files are impressed with "N SPENCER / SHEFFIELD" on one side of tang and "27 / BEST CAST STEEL / DOUBLE REFINED" on the other.

The Roebuck examples are stamped "JOSEPH ROEBUCK & SON / WARRANTED CAST STEEL."

Froe

One cast-steel froe is represented. It measures 13 inches long and the blade is 2 1/2 inches wide at the bit and 2 inches wide at the eye. The eye is 2 1/8 inches in diameter at the bottom and 1 15/16 inches in diameter at the top. The steel is 1/2 inch thick, and the blade has a 1/2-inch bevel at the bit end. There are no maker's marks.

Gimlets

At least one large gimlet and thirty-three small gimlets were recovered. The purposeful use of the large gimlet-like tool is unknown. The half-round cone-shaped blade is 8 1/4 inches long from the bottom of the T-shaped handle to the threaded tip and is 3/8 inch in diameter at the top of the sharpened edge. The shank between the handle and the top of the cutter is 3/16 inch in diameter. The tapered point is threaded 1/2 inch up from the tip. The turned hardwood T-handle is slightly more than 6 1/8 inches long and has bulbous ends 1 9/16 inches in diameter at their widest point. This piece has no manufacturer's marks. There is no information on the smaller gimlets.

Grinding Stones

There are two large circular grinding stones and the associated assemblies for hand grinding wheels as well as five additional large circular silica-rich limestone grinding stones. None of these bear manufacturer's marks.

Keyhole Saw

This saw measures 17 3/4 inches long overall, and the exposed portion of the blade measures 13 5/8 inches long on the top edge. The base of the saw blade is 1 inch wide, and the blade is 5/8 inch wide at the midpoint, 3/16 inch wide at the tip, and 1/16 inch thick. The pistol-grip handle with bifurcated base measures 4 1/2 inches tall, 1 7/16 inches wide at the grip, and 7/8 inch thick. There are two slotted steel mounting screws in flat-sided brass sleeves securing the blade.

Measuring Tape

FIGURE 81. Measuring tape.

One or possibly two brass-bound fifty-foot measuring tapes were found among the *Bertrand* tools. The one for which information is available has a japanned-steel case and measures 3 11/32 inches in diameter and 5/8 inch wide. It has a folding brass winder, like modern tapes, is bound in brass, and is marked "50 Ft." No maker's marks are present.

Adjustable/Monkey Wrenches
Eleven monkey wrenches were found in the cargo measuring about 13 inches long each. No identifying marks are seen on these artifacts.

Open-End Wrenches
There are four S-shaped open end wrenches, none of which bear manufacturer's marks.

Picks

Apparently there was at least one case containing twenty-four pick heads in the cargo, but accession records indicate there were seventy-one additional pick heads and 131 pick handles in the cargo.

One pick head for which there is good information is 23 inches in length, with the top of the socket measuring 2 3/8 inches wide. The eye measures 2 7/8 inches long by 1 3/4 inches wide. On one arm of the pick near the socket is stamped "S[I]MMONS & CO. / COHOES-N.Y. / CAST STEEL." This pick was not made by E. C. Simmons & Co. because Simmons was a wholesale hardware dealer that marketed all kinds of tools, but was not a manufacturer of tools. The company did have a controlling interest in the Walden Knife Co. in the 1890s and was bought out by A. F. Shapleigh Hardware Co. in 1940. Simmons had a long list of trademarks on tools produced by companies.

Edward Campbell Simmons was born in 1839 and moved with his father to St. Louis in 1846. At the age of seventeen, he began working in the wholesale hardware business at Child, Pratt, & Co., and in 1859 he began working in the firm of Wilson, Levering, & Walters as a clerk. Eventually Simmons gained a foothold in the company, and it evolved into E. C. Simmons & Co. He developed the company into an extensive corporation with divisions in Wichita, Sioux City, Ogden, Toledo, New York, Minneapolis, and St. Louis. The company's tool manufacturing plants were in the northeast, in New York, New Hampshire, and other states, and its pocket knife company in New York was the largest in the United States. Simmons owned controlling interests in many companies, producing everything from food grinders, lard presses, knife sharpeners, and grist mills to waffle irons, coffee grinders, apple peelers, china, silverware, stoves, sewing machines, and parlor stoves. Other products produced by Simmons-owned companies included fishing equipment, razors, strops, honing stones, tobacco cutters, pocket knives, locks and watch fobs. In 1908, the Simmons hardware catalogue had over 5,000 pages. Although Simmons retired in 1898, he remained active in the business. He was responsible for the development and success for the "Keen Kutter" tool line. His relationship with A. F. Shapleigh & Co. is detailed in the section of this chapter dedicated to hardware.[208]

---

[208]An account of E. C. Simmons & Co. is found in Elaine and Jerry Heuring, "Brief History of The Simmons Hardware Company," The Winchester *Keen Kutter* Diamond Edge Chronicles, The Hardware Kollectors Klub, http://www.thckk.org/history/simmons-hdwe.pdf.

Planes

Laboratory notes indicate there are nineteen wood-body rabbiting planes. One rabbit plane recovered from the cargo was hallmarked, indicating it was produced by the Arrowmammett Works of Middletown, Connecticut. The Arrowmammett Works was owned and operated by Baldwin Tool Co. The company has a long history, starting with Enos Baldwin, who was born in Cavendish, Vermont, in 1783, where he received his first training. By 1807, he was known as a toolmaker in Albany, New York. Eventually, he made his way to New York City and opened a shop in lower Manhattan under the name E. Baldwin, where his sons Austin and Eldridge worked with him in the business until 1829 when Enos died at the age of forty-five. Austin Baldwin was born on June 11, 1807, in Albany, New York, and died on May 28, 1866. The brothers partnered under the name A. E. Baldwin in 1830, and the partnership lasted until 1841, when Austin left the firm and opened The Baldwin Tool Co. on the Arrowmammet River (now the Coginchaug River). The company later became the Arrowmammet Works and produced planes and other edge tools. Austin continued in business until about 1860, when he sold his interest to Globe Manufacturing Co. Eldridge Baldwin continued in the tool making business using the "E. Baldwin" imprint until 1850 and probably continued making plane blades for the Globe Manufacturing Co. Interestingly, some of the plane blades used in Baldwin products are stamped with the hallmark "W. Butcher Cast Steel." Planes produced by the Baldwin Tool Co. until 1859 may have had seven different trademarks. In all probability, the plane from the *Bertrand* was either part of the ship's tools, or was someone's personal property and had been acquired prior to 1859.[209]

Scales

Four scales from the *Bertrand* were manufactured by E. T. Fairbanks Co. of St. Johnsbury, Vermont. All four are calibrated to avoirdupois weight based on the sixteen ounce pound. The counterweights, or poises, of the two smallest scales were drilled by the manufacturer to adjust their exact weight.

The largest scale is a portable platform scale on wheels constructed of cast-iron. It has a hardboard platform and a brass beam calibrated in five

---

[209]Mark Thompson, "Baldwin History," The Society for the Preservation and Study of American Wooden Planes, http://www.woodenplane.org/Bald-History.htm.

pound increments. Marked as a No. 10 1/2 size scale, it has a capacity of 900 pounds and sold for $48 in 1872. The four slotted cast-iron poises with the scale are stamped with graduated increments of 100 to 400 hundred and weigh .996 pounds to 4.42 pounds. The japanned iron base exhibits cast marks reading "FAIRBANKS' PATENT. No 10 1/2," and the beam stabilizer is marked "PATENTED FEB. 11 1862," and the beam itself is marked "FAIRBANKS / PATENT" on one side and "125073" on the bottom. The end of the beam is stamped "PATENTED APR 9 1850."

The third scale is of the uneven balance type, sometimes referred to as a "Union" or "family" scale. This cast-iron, brass beam scale was meant for use on store counters and was equipped with a large brass scoop pan. It has a one pound beam eight and three slotted cast-iron poises with graduated cast marks of "10-80," "10-80," and "5-40" weighing .74 pounds. to 1.81 pounds. The poises have drilled backs, apparently to adjust their weights, and the brass beam is calibrated in pounds one the upper side of the face and in ounces on the lower. A one pound counterweight is suspended from the end of the beam by a hooked rod. Cast letters on the base, which is also scrolled with red and gold lacquer reads: "E. T. FAIRBANKS $ CO. / ST. JOHNSBURY VT. / PATENTED JULY 24, 1855." The scale was capable of weighing 1/2 ounce to 240 pounds.

The two smallest scales are equal-arm counter scales with capacities of 1/2 ounce to 10 pounds and are equipped tinned metal scoop pans and graduated sets of seven cast-iron poises. The nested poises have been drilled to adjust their weights and have cast marks of 1, 4, and 8 on them. The poises are of graduated weights from .06 pounds to 4 pounds, 1 1/2 ounces.

Thaddeus and Erastus Fairbanks represent yet another fascinating story of invention and success. Their father, Major Joseph P. Fairbanks, came to the Sleeper River in Vermont from Brimfield, Massachusetts, in 1815, where he paid $300 for some land and the rights to some falls on the river. He and his two sons used water power to establish a grist mill and a sawmill, and soon after that the Fairbanks scale factory.

At nineteen years old, Thaddeus began making wagons, and by 1823, he had established a small iron foundry. In 1824, his older brother Erastus joined him, and the two began making wagons, plows, and stoves. Two years later, in April 1826, Thaddeus patented a new plow. Over the next four years, the brothers produced gear wheels and fluting machines to make rollers for hemp dressing machines. Securing a patent for a hemp dressing machine, Thaddeus took up the management of the St. Johnsbury Hemp Co., which eventually failed. Undaunted, he soon applied for a patent for a weighing platform supported on an A-shaped lever, the apex of which was connected to calibrated steelyard or beam with a strong metal rod. He improved the design by adding two short levers to the long ones and established support points at all four corners of the platform, making the pit-mounted platform scale much more stable. Bringing a large weight on the platform into equilibrium with a smaller weight by means of levers made it possible to accurately and quickly weigh large loads of hemp. This one invention, with a few improvements, allowed the company to grow to world-wide proportions between 1835 and 1861. In the 1830s, Thaddeus sold manufacturing rights to H. Poole & Sons in England to capture the growing international market, and by 1846 he began selling scales in China.[210]

By 1860, the company was selling scales in the Caribbean, South America, and Russia. A few years after 1835, Thaddeus developed the portable platform scale and several unequal arm scales and balance scales. His brother Joseph joined the firm of E. T. Fairbanks Co., and by 1843, the business grossed $50,000, a figure that doubled every three years thereafter.

For thirty-five years, Thaddeus Fairbanks invented and designed scales and machinery, while Erastus Fairbanks managed the successful business for thirty years. Joseph Fairbanks contributed his talents to marketing and served the company in this capacity for twenty-two years. Eventually, they employed itinerant salesmen and opened sales houses in Boston, New York, and the West Indies. The first salesman was Zelotus Hosmer. Hosmer's nephew, Charles Hosmer Morse, apprenticed for the company as a clerk and accountant in December 1850 at the age of seventeen. Later, Charles worked for his uncle in Boston before advancing to a higher position in New York and then establishing a company sales agency in Chicago. By 1865, Morse had established the Fairbanks business in Cincinnati as Fairbanks, Morse, Co., and in quick succession he established branches in Cleveland, Pittsburgh, and Indianapolis, where he took up the manufacture of letter presses, waybill presses, and warehouse trucks. In 1916, Charles Morse acquired control of the company.[211]

---

[210]"Fairbanks Scales, A Legacy of Pride . . . A Look at How It All Began" (Kansas City: Fairbanks Scales, 2004). The entire history of the Fairbanks family and a comprehensive look at company history is found in Hiram Carlton, *Genealogical and Family History of the State of Vermont—A Record of the Achievements of her People in the Making of a Commonwealth and the Founding of a Nation* (New York and Chicago: The Lewis Publishing Company, 1903), 110–17.

[211]"Fairbanks Scales, A Legacy of Pride . . . A Look at How It All Began," ibid.

It is interesting to note that the E. & T. Fairbanks Co. was a major advertiser in the 1850s and 1860s. One ad in 1861 in the *Nebraska Republican*:

Fairbanks Scales—It is a significant fact, which the public will appreciate, that whenever new scales are put upon the market, as large numbers have been from time to time, during the last thirty years, it seems to be the first and chief aim of the makers to show that they are the same as Fairbanks', or like them, or are improvements upon them, or have taken premiums over them, thus recognizing and showing the strong hold they have upon the public confidence. It is a well-known fact that while most of these scales have, after more or less trial, passed mainly out of use, Fairbanks' have gone steadily forward, increasing in public favor year after year, and now much more generally used than all others, not only in this country, but wherever American commerce has been carried. This could not be so if they were not all that is claimed for them in respect to their durability, as well as convenience and accuracy.[212]

Fairbanks & Co. apparently was well-established in St. Louis, judging from its ad in the *Gazetteer and Business Directory of the New Southwest* published in 1881.[213] The ad refers to Fairbanks & Co. being located at 302 and 304 Washington Avenue, St. Louis, Missouri, and offering Fairbanks' Scales as "The Standard of the World," and Eclipse Wind Mills as "The Strongest Mills Made" and the safest to buy. The ad also indicates that a catalogue of its products was available by mail.

So powerful became the Fairbanks family that Erastus served twice as governor of Vermont. During his second term, President Lincoln made St. Johnsbury the safe repository for the official standard weights of the United States. During the Civil War, the St. Johnsbury factory converted to the manufacture of stirrups, curb bits, artillery harness irons, and brass cavalry trimmings for the Union cavalry. After the Civil War, the management of the company passed from the founders to their sons.

Screwdrivers

Two screwdrivers survived the sinking of the *Bertrand*. One of these has a 5/16 inch bit and measures 10 1/4 inches overall. There is a brass ferrule 5/8 inch wide between the blade and the handle. The nearly

---

[212]*Nebraska Republican*, April 26, 1861, 3.

[213]*Gazetteer and Business Directory of the New Southwest* (St. Louis: United States Directory Publishing Co., 1881), first ad before the index. See also Ronald R. Switzer, "Fairbanks Weighing Devices on the Steamboat *Bertrand*," *Nebraska History* 55, no. 2 (1974): 254–63.

hour-glass-shaped blade measures 5/8 inch wide at its widest point and 3/8 inch wide at the narrowest. The handle is somewhat unusual in that the distal end of the handle is a flattened lozenge 1 3/4 inches wide, tapering to a 5/8 inch diameter neck before widening to an elongated bead measuring 3/4 inches in diameter at mid-point. This screwdriver is stamped "JOHN MERRILL / CAST STEEL."

The second screwdriver is morphologically similar to the first except that it is 15 1/16 inches long and has a 3/8 inch bit. The 2-inch lozenge-shaped pommel tapers to 7/8 inch and then flares to a bolster-shaped section 1 1/8 inches in diameter connected at the blade with a brass ferrule. The hour glass-shaped blade is 5/8 inch wide, tapering to the narrowest mid-point to 1/2 inch. The screwdriver is stamped "JOHN MERRILL / CAST STEEL."

Shingle Hatchet

This piece has a flared hexagonal butt, nearly round cheeks, and a flared blade with a convex bit and a nail puller at the bottom edge of the blade. From butt to bit, the head measures 6 13/16 inches long and has a 3 3/4 inch wide bit and 2 3/4 inches diameter cheeks with a 1/2 inch eye. The flared end of the butt measures 1 1/18 inches square, tapering toward the cheeks to 1 inch square. What is left of the handle is a 1 1/6 inch oval, flaring to 1 1/2 inches at the base of the socket. This hatchet is stamped "#2 / . . . ENTONS / PHILADE."

One hatchet in the collection for which there is no other information is marked "Jenkins & Tongue."

In *Philadelphia and its Manufacturers; A Hand-Book of the Great Manufactories and Representative Merchantile Houses of Philadelphia* by Edwin T. Freedley, there is a copy of a Jenkins & Tongue advertisement which reveals a good deal about this company:

MACHINE KNIVES & EDGE TOOLS.
JENKINS & TONGUE
33 & 35 Richmond Street, Philadelphia
Are prepared, with an experience of twenty years, to work **STEEL** up to its highest capacity as a cutting edge, and to manufacture large cutting instruments and tools requiring a superior edge and temper,—in which **quality** is the chief object.

The great desideratum in a tool is to *retain* a fine edge; for which purpose it must be both *hard* and *tough*. The union of these qualities depends on three conditions, neither of which can be dispensed with, *viz.:* good steel, good forging, and good tempering. A good steel may be tempered well, but if not properly forged it will be brittle.

*** **Knives for Planning and Moulding Machines, Cork Machines, Straw Cutters, etc.; Dyewood and Chipper Knives; Leather Splitting Knives; Papermaker's and Bookbinder's Knives; Boxmakers Bookbinder's and Cardmaker's Shears; Shear Blades; Shipwright's Carpenter's, Wheelwright's, Cooper's Tools, Mill Picks, etc., —MADE TO ORDER AND WARRANTED.**

*** **Planning Machine Knives.** Our experience in this article enables us to guarantee superiority over those in general use. In ordering it is only necessary to send by mail a paper of the exact size of the knife, with the slots marked on it, width of bevel and thickness.

*** **Spoke Lathe Knives.** We pay particular attention to these. Lay a paper on the *back* of the knife and cut out the exact size; also, the position and size of the slot. Round off a card to fit the hollow side, marking the thickness on it, and these may be sent by mail.

*** **Cork Knives.** We have been very successful in making these extremely difficult tools, both for machine and hand work.

*** **Hatchets.** Shingling, Lathing, Claw and broad, of the best cast steel, and warranted as good as any made in the United States.

Jenkins & Tongue
Nos. 33 & 35 Richmond Street, Philadelphia,
Between Front Street and Frankford Road.

Richmond Street begins at 1043 North Front Street. The *red* cars up Third Street cross Richmond near the shop—*sign in sight.*[214]

Shovels

Records indicate there are 274 complete square-end and round-end shovels, and 133 shovel blades of the same shapes in the collection. In addition, there are 105 shovel handles. These were produced by several manufacturers, none of which appear in the author's field notes or laboratory inventories. Photographs appearing here are of a small scoop-type or "California" shovel made specifically for placer mining Oliver Ames, the "Shovel King" made millions of dollars manufacturing this type of shovel for California gold miners.

---

[214]Edwin T. Freedley, *Philadelphia and Its Manufacturers: A Hand-Book of the Great Manufacturers and Representative Mercantile Houses of Philadelphia in 1867* (Philadelphia: Edward Young & Co., 1867), 317.

FIGURE 82. "California" shovels.

Sledgehammers

At least four of the sledgehammers in the cargo are stamped "SIMMONS & CO / COHOES N.Y. / CAST STEEL." The heads range in length from 6 1/4 inches to 6 3/4 inches, and they are 2 1/4 inches to 2 1/2 inches wide at the eye. The ends are tapered and octagonal in cross section.

Sliding Bevel

One sliding bevel is present among the tools. This piece is nicely made with a rosewood handle and inlet brass head and tail pieces. The handle is 1 3/4 inches thick and slightly more than 1 inch wide and bears 1/16 inch thick brass inlays at the square end that are 9/16 inches wide. There is also a 1/16 inch thick brass filler at the inside center of the handle base. The adjustable end of the handle has a rounded brass nose and straight base that is inlet into the wood and secured with two 3/16 inch brass screws on either side. These two cheek pieces are 1 5/32 inches long by 1 inch wide. The 3/4 inch brass thumb screw in the head is 1 13/32 inches long, 3/16 inch in diameter, and has 18 threads to the inch. When fully extended, the tool measures 1 foot 2 3/4 inches long, and the blade is 7 5/8 inches long with a 1/4-inch bevel. The slot in the rounded base is 3/16 inches wide to accommodate the diameter of the thumb screw. There are no manufacturer's marks on this tool.

Tack Hammer

This hammer measures 10 1/6 inches long overall, and the head is 3 3/8 inches long and 11/16 inch wide/thick, with a 9/16 by 11/16 inch face. It has a small claw 7/16 wide opposite the head set transverse to the handle. The handle is 5/8 inch diameter at the head with a larger 7/8 inch hand grip tapering to a 1/2 inch diameter 3/8 inch ferrule. There are no maker's marks.

Trowels

Field notes contain no references to trowels having been found on the *Bertrand*. However, Museum Curator Leslie A. Perry Paterson of the Bertrand Museum and Laboratory at DeSoto National Wildlife Refuge referred to four trowels in the cargo manufactured by W. Rose of West Philadelphia. If one or more of these exist, they were made by the best bricklayer's tool company in the country. William Rose established his business in 1798 making cavalry sabers and officer swords for the United States Army. In 1864, he began specializing in edged tools, knives, and trowels, which were deemed "The World's Finest." W. Rose was acquired by Kraft Tool Co. in 2001, which has striven to uphold the reputation of the Rose tool industry and trademark. In Freedley's *Philadelphia and its Manufacturers* handbook, there is an advertisement for William Rose's trowels:

Wm. Rose & Brothers,
Manufacturers of
Brick, Plastering and Pointing
T R O W E L S,
SADDLERS' ROUND AND HEAD KNIVES,
MOULDERS' HEART AND SQUARE TROWELLS LIFT-
ERS, Etc.

ALSO
PLASTERER'S MITERING TOOLS,
RULES AND MOULDERS, DOUBLE ENDERS.
Established Nearly fifty years, and can safely say have given general satisfaction as to
quality, finish and material, in all articles manufactured by us.
Manufactory—Corner Thirty-Sixth and Green Streets,
PHILADELPHIA.[215]

Whetstones

There are several whetstones in the cargo, most of which were associated with a large crate weighing more than 500 pounds that contained sawmill parts, tools, and other items. Four different kinds of whetstones are represented. One type varies in length from 10 1/2 inches to 11 1/4 inches, is oval in cross section, and appears to be mica schist. The second type is long and rectangular and rectangular in cross section, measuring 11 inches long, 1 1/4 inches wide, and about 3/4 inches thick. This type is of coarser mica schist. The third type is more brick-shaped, being about 6 1/2 inches long by 1 inch thick by 2 1/4 inches wide. The stone is a light-colored, fine-grained silica material, not unlike some of the argillite from the Ouachita Mountains of Arkansas. The fourth type is brick-shaped, and somewhat smaller than the third type, although made of the same material as the latter. This type measures about 5 1/4 inches long by 1 5/8 inches wide by 3/4 inches thick.

Inasmuch as the stones bear no identifying manufacturer's marks, tracing their origin is somewhat speculative. That having been said, it may not be a stretch to assign the first type to the Pike Manufacturing Co. of Littleton, New Hampshire. During the 1860s, Pike was the largest American producer of whetstones. Those made from mica schist were marketed as "Indian Pond" whetstones because the mica schist stone was quarried at nearby Indian Pond, New Hampshire. Types three and four may be products of Chase Brothers of Brooklyn, New York, a firm that made and marketed "Arkansas Stones." Of the others, the only likely source is the Cleveland Stone Co. in Ohio, or its predecessor.

The story of Pike Manufacturing Co. began in 1820, when Hezekiah Huntington began grinding whetstones from material quarried near East Haverhill, downstream from present-day Pike, New Hampshire.

[215]Ibid., 320.

In 1821, Henry (Person) Noyes settled in the foothills of the White Mountains in New Hampshire upstream from Huntington's property, where he discovered a deposit of the finest mica schist and began selling small numbers of roughly cut scythe stones to his neighbors. About 1823, Noyes bought a saw and grist mill from Clark Woodward that had been built about 1800, leased a whetstone quarry at nearby Cutting Hill, and began grinding whetstones.[216]

Two or three years before Noyes's discovery, eighteen- or nineteen-year-old Isaac Pike came from Massachusetts to Haverhill, New Hampshire, where he apparently became involved in timbering and floating log rafts down the Connecticut River to ponds. Although Pike was an enterprising young fellow, how and why he came into the whetstone manufacturing business is unclear. Some have speculated that Pike competed with Noyes until he bought Noyes's mortgage when the latter defaulted. Others believe he worked with Noyes until Noyes died in 1827, after which he married Noyes's widow and continued to make and market sharpening stones under his own name. It is also known that Isaac Pike built another whetstone mill on the Olevarian River sometime after 1825, where water-driven burrstones replaced hand grinding of whetstones. Pike apparently continued to operate his business until he died in 1860, after which his son Alonzo F. Pike ran the business until 1884.[217]

When Alonzo Pike died in 1899, the company incorporated as Pike Manufacturing Co., and in 1891, Alonzo's brother Edwin Pike became general manager. Edwin joined the company in 1860 as a traveling salesman and actively marketed the company's products in Europe and as far west as the Mississippi River in the United States. Edwin Pike is credited with building the company into the world's largest manufacturer and distributor of natural grit whetstones and 1,100 different grit products produced at several mills acquired by Pike Manufacturing Co. In 1889, Pike bought the Cleveland Stone Co. in Ohio, and two years later, he bought Chase Brothers of Brooklyn, New York, which made soft and hard Arkansas stones quarried near Hot Springs in the Ouachita Mountains of Arkansas. In 1893, Pike Manufacturing Co. purchased the Labrador Oilstone Co. of Manlius, New York, giving Pike a complete line of abrasive products. Apparently, other mills were acquired in Vermont and Indiana.[218]

---

[216]Robert L. Topping, "Pike Manufacturing Company," *Outlook Magazine: The Magazine of Northern New Hampshire* (Fall 1985).

[217]Ibid.

[218]Ibid.

Eventually, the Pike Manufacturing Co. became the Norton Pike Division of the Norton Co., which was started at Pike, New Hampshire, in 1858, when Frank B. Norton began combining and molding abrasives with pottery clay at his shop in Worcester, Massachusetts. In 1891, bauxite ore was discovered in Arkansas, and Norton put it to use, making grinding wheels in 1897 under the name Norton Emery Wheel Co. with the trademark "India" stone. Another Norton product was later marketed under the trademark "Crystolon." By 1899, Pike Manufacturing Co. was licensed by Norton Emery Wheel Co. as its sole agent. In 1932, Norton Co. took over the Pike Co. and renamed it the Norton Pike Co. It is likely that the whetstones were wholesaled by R. Campbell & Co. of St. Louis.[219]

Wood Bits/Auger Bits
There are several wood bits in the collection, none of which bear any maker's marks. These have square shanks and were meant for use in a carpenter's brace.

Wooden Mallets
There are five mallets of two types. One resembles a bung mallet, the head of which is 5 1/2 inches long at the top and 4 11/16 inches long at the base or handle. The body is 3 inches wide at the top and 2 3/4 inches wide at the base by 2 15/16 inches tall; the faces are flat. The simple rough handle measures 9 3/4 inches long and 3/4 inch in diameter. The end of the handle has been whittled to a stubby point and may not be original to the tool. No maker's marks are present. No information is available about the second block type mallet, save a photograph taken during conservation efforts.

Mallets have always been relatively cheap tools. As late as 1877, the New York Mallet & Handle Works was selling 4 inch round hickory mallets for $2.50 a dozen.[220]

Building Materials
Although Jerome Pestche included this category in his inventory of the cargo, no building materials were ever brought into the laboratory.

[219]Ibid.
[220]*Pricelist of the New York Mallet & Handle Works, Manufacturers of Caulkers' Tin, Copper & Boilermakers' Mallets Hawsing Beetles, Hausing Caulking Irons, Sledge, Chisel & Hammer Handles, Also Cotton & Bale Hooks, Patented February 13, 1877; A New Combination of Hooks* (New York: 1877), 5.

POWDER AND MUNITIONS

Black Powder

Twenty-one whole and badly crushed black powder kegs of two sizes were recovered from the *Bertrand*. The kegs were marked "LAFLINS, SMITH & BOIES / SAUGERTIES, NEW YORK" and contained FFF black powder. These are described in detail in "Some Unusual Powder Kegs from the Steamer Bertrand."[221]

The best preserved kegs from the *Bertrand* are half-kegs made from white or red oak. They originally held 12 1/2 pounds of powder and measure 9 1/4 inches from head to head and 7 1/4 inches in diameter across the heads. Constructed with twelve to fifteen smooth jointed staves, the ends of which are slightly chamfered, the kegs are somewhat larger in diameter at the middle or "bilge." The staves are 5/16 inches thick and exhibit a "crow" or groove at each end to accommodate the beveled edges of the heads. The end hoops or "chimes" fit flush with the ends of the staves. Each keg has four hoops of 5/8 by 1/16 inch steel, which, when thoroughly tightened, forced the staves to fit snugly against each other and tightly around the heads.

The kegs are unusual in several respects. First, the hoops around the bilge exhibit riveted straps bent to hold wood-covered heavy gauge wire handles. Second, the screw- type pewter bung is at the middle of the keg in the center of a stave directly beneath the handle instead of in the head. Most of the kegs are plain with no markings, but several bear a small letters "w" wood-burned into one head. Finally, most powder companies produced kegs made solely of wood until sometime during the 1860s. Staves and heads were made of white oak or white ash, and the kegs were hooped with hickory, cedar, alder, willow, or chestnut. The oak bungs were usually plug or screw types, and only rarely were cork bungs used. The standard finished product was "liquor tight." During the mid-nineteenth century, powder manufacturers were identified by printed paper labels glued to the heads of their kegs. Sometime during the 1860s, the big firms like DuPont Co. began making kegs of sheet iron, but these did not wholly displace the wooden kegs, and both appear to have been used in subsequent decades. The author has never before seen half-kegs of the type taken from the *Bertrand*.

A few full-size 25-pound kegs were recovered from the *Bertrand* that seem to be typical for the period except that the staves are 13 1/2 inches

---

[221]Ronald R. Switzer, "Some Unusual Powder Kegs from the Steamer *Bertrand*," *Museum of the Fur Trade Quarterly* 10, no. 3 (1974): 3–6.

long instead of the usual 11 1/2 inches. The heads were stenciled "*LAF-LINS, SMITH & BOIES* / SAUGERTIES, NEW YORK – FFF." In addition, a large wooden crate in the cargo containing twenty-four small tin flasks with pewter caps was stenciled "LAFLINS, SMITH & BOIES / CHICAGO . . . ILL. / AMERICAN RIFLE FFF / GUN-POWDER / 24 POUND FLASKS." Based on the stencils, it may be cautiously inferred that the powder in the half-kegs was also produced by Laflins, Smith, & Boies and that the wood-burned "w" on some kegs may be a cooper's mark. Edwards' St. Louis Directory for 1865 lists six coopers whose last names begin with "w," but none have yet been tied to the Laflin powder kegs. These coopers are:

Christopher Wahl	Benedict Whitener
Henry Weigel	Jacob Weigel
Herman Wervers	Louis Wirthram[222]

The wooden crate bearing the flasks measures 20 3/8 inches long by 7 inches deep by 9 3/4 inches wide. Boards were milled to 5/7 inch and 7/8 inch thick. The consignee was Vivian & Simpson, Virginia City.

The story of the Laflin powder empire is lengthy and complex, but its genesis was in the production of saltpeter at a Southwick, Massachusetts powder mill owned by Matthew Laflin. Irish-born Laflin began making powder at a mill on Fish Creek west of Saugerties, New York, in 1832. In 1834, his brother, Luther Laflin, came from Massachusetts and took a half interest in the business under the firm name "L. & M. Laflin." The mill directly employed twenty to thirty men and made from 30,000 to 50,000 kegs of powder annually. Another brother, Winthrop Laflin, of Lee, Massachusetts, who was engaged in paper manufacturing at W. W. & C. Laflin, came to Saugerties in 1837 and built a powder mill on the Cauterskill River under the name L. & M. Laflin, in which Matthew retained half interest. The following year, "L. & M. Laflin" associated with Solomon A. Smith, owner of a mill at Southwick, and the partnership was known as Laflins & Smith, because Winthrop Laflin sold his interest to Matthew Laflin and Solomon Smith. Although the Cauterskill mill shut down in 1840–1841, Joseph M. Boies of Lee, Massachusetts, bought a half interest in the mill, with Laflins & Smith retaining the other half interest. The Cauterskill mill was renamed Laflins, Smith,

[222] Edwards, *Edwards' Annual Directory to the Inhabitants, Institutions, Incorporated Companies, Manufacturing Establishments, Businesses, Business Firms, etc., etc., in the City of St. Louis, for 1865* (St. Louis and New York: Edwards & Co., 1865).

& Boies. As the Saugerties mill and the Cauterskill mill prospered, more facilities were added.[223]

By 1849, Matthew Laflin withdrew from the business and went to Chicago to establish the Laflin trade in the west. By this time, Sylvester H. Laflin (son of Luther Laflin), who had been carrying on the powder trade in St. Louis, bought the interests of Matthew Laflin at the Saugerties and Cauterskill mills and became a general partner in the entire Laflin business. Five years later, in 1854, the Saugerties mill exploded, killing eight workers and causing serious damage to the buildings. Luther Laflin and Solomon Smith declined to rebuild, and Joseph Boies bought a general interest in the mill on the condition that he rebuild it and take complete charge of powder fabrication. Shortly thereafter, the Saugerties and Cauterskill mills were consolidated under one manager as Laflins, Smith, & Boies. Luther Laflin finally withdrew from the company and sold his interest to his sons, Fordyce L. and H. D. Laflin. At this point, the Laflin, Smith, & Boies story moves to St. Louis, where Sylvester H. Laflin took charge of the business while Solomon A. Smith became established in Chicago. Soon Solomon sold his share of the firm to his son, Solomon A., Jr., who kept it until his death.[224]

The following advertisement appeared in a St. Louis newspaper early in 1865:

THE LAUGHLIN POWDER CO.
Manufacturers of
GUN POWDER,
AND DEALERS IN SAFETY FUSE, SHOT, BAR
Lead and Gun Caps. Office 29 Levee and Commercial Street, cor. Of Olive, St. Louis. All kids of Gun Powder constantly on hand. Orders promptly attended to.[225]

By 1864, military activity resulting from the "War of Northern Aggression" had created an enormous demand for gunpowder, and the

[223]James Harrison Kennedy, ed., "Matthew Laflin," *Magazine of Western History, Illustrated* 16, no. 1 (1891): 177–83. In addition, there are two good references dealing with Matthew Laflin and his companies: Nathaniel Bartlett Sylvester, *History of Ulster County, Part Second* (Philadelphia: Everts & Peck, 1880), and a detailed manuscript, Klaus Neuschaefer, "The Smokeless Powders of Laughlin & Rand and Their Fate 100 years after Assimilation by Dupont," Klaus Neuschaefer, http://www.laflinandrand.com. There also is a short description of the Laflin & Rand Powder Company in L. U. Reavis, "The Laflin, Rand Powder Company," *St. Louis, The Commercial Metropolis of the Mississippi Valley* (St. Louis: Tribune Publishing Company, 1874), 208.
[224]Kennedy, "Matthew Laflin," ibid.
[225]"The Laughlin Powder Company," *Daily Missouri Democrat*, April 4, 1865.

company operated on an extensive scale. During this time, the firm bought a set of mills at Plattsville, Wisconsin, and ran them under the name Laflins, Smith, & Co. Those mills were managed by two company employees, Solomon and John Turck. In addition, in 1864, Laflins, Smith, & Boies transferred all of their interests in the powder business to a stock company with paid-up capital of $300,000. The name of the subsequent association was The Laflin Powder Co., and the president throughout its existence was Joseph M. Boies.[226]

Business boomed, so to speak, and the company had to expand if it was to secure more of the powder market. Powder mills at Esopus, Newburgh, Kinston, and Carbondale, Pennsylvania, were purchased by Smith and Rand and The Laflin Powder Co. purchased the Raynor Mills at Scranton, Pennsylvania, operating them as Laflins, Boies & Turck. Soon the Carbondale and Scranton mills were consolidated under the name Moosic Powder Co., with capital of $300,000. Henry M. Boies, the son of Joseph M. Boies, became president of the company.[227]

In 1867, Albert Tyler Rand of the Smith & Rand Powder Co. suggested the two companies unite. In 1869 the companies merged into the Laflin & Rand Powder Co. of New York, with A. Tyler Rand as president, and Joseph M. Boies as general superintendent of all the mills. The company was capitalized at $1,000,000. By 1872, Laflin & Rand joined forces with their rival DuPont to establish the Gunpowder Trade Association as a trust to regulate the powder industry with price controls and to protect sales quotas. It is also known that the two companies merged in a business venture to produce dynamite by establishing the Repauno Chemical Co. in 1880, the Hercules Powder Co. in 1882, and the Eastern Dynamite Co. in 1895. By 1900, Laflin & Rand and Dupont controlled more than two-thirds of the entire explosives industry.[228]

By 1902, Dupont had purchased Laflin & Rand and tried to assume its assets, but in 1912, it became the target of a federal anti-trust suit and was forced to divest itself of a large part of its explosives business. Out of this came the formation of the Hercules and Atlas Powder Companies, with Hercules assuming Laflin & Rand's patents for smokeless powder. The Saugerties and Cauterskill mills were shut down and dismantled in 1874 so the machinery could be moved to the Passaic mills in New Jersey, twelve miles from New York, where new mills were also under

[226]Neuschaefer, "The Smokeless Powders of Laughlin," ibid.
[227]Ibid.
[228]Ibid.

construction at a cost of $350,000. Laflin and Smith both died at Saugerties, but their company lives on to this day.[229]

Joseph M. Bois was born in Blanford, Massachusetts, and worked on a farm in New England until he was twenty-one, whereupon he started mercantiles in Blanford and Westfield. Thereafter, Boies went into partnership with Walter, Winston. and Cutler Laflin in the manufacture of paper at Lee, Massachusetts, under the firm name of W. W. & C. Laflin, between 1826 and 1850.[230] Joseph's wife was a sister of the Laflin brothers.

In 1874, when Sylvester Hall Laflin was the Resident Director of Laflin & Rand Powder in St. Louis, the company published an ad in Reavis's 1874 book that illustrates the broad array of products it sold:

LAFLIN & RAND POWDER COMPANY
Manufacturers Of
ORANGE SPORTING POWDER
MINING AND BLASTING And Dealers In
SAFETY FUSE AND AMMUNITION.
Rend Rock the great Explosive constantly on hand
Office:
218 N. Second Street, St. Louis, MO.

S. H. Laflin, Resident Director[231]

Some very relevant information regarding the construction of wooden powder containers made for E. I. du Ponte de Nemours Co. during the nineteenth century came via correspondence with Norman B. Wilkinson, Director of Research at The Hagley Museum in Wilmington, Delaware:

Materials
Staves: made of white oak, red oak, or white ash; thoroughly seasoned or kiln dried.

1. Heads: or end pieces, made of same kind of wood as staves.

2. Hoops: made of hickory, cedar, alder, willow, or chestnut. Chestnut referred to as best in appearance.

Bunge: made of same wood as staves and heads. Plug or types. Cork bung mentioned rarely.

---

[229]Ibid.

[230]Charles McEwen Hyde and Alexander Hyde, *LEE: The Centennial Celebration and Centennial History of the Town of Lee, Mass.* (Springfield, Mass.: C. M. Hyde and Alexander Hyde, Publishers, Clark W. Bryan & Company Printers, 1878), 290.

[231]L. U. Reevis, *St. Louis, the Commercial Metropolis of the Mississippi Valley*, 176.

Container Sizes

1. Barrel: 100 pounds
21" from head to head
1" chime at each end beyond head
13-3/4" diameter across the head
7" at each end covered with hoops; 9 hoops at each end

2. Half-Barrel: 50 pounds
18" from head to head
1" chime at each end beyond head
13-1/4" diameter across the head
7" at each end covered with hoops, but would estimate about 6" with 7 or 8 hoops at each end

3. Keg: 25 pounds (most commonly used size container)
11 1/2" from head to head
3/4" chime at each end beyond head
9" diameter across head
4 or 5 hoops at each end.

4. Half-Keg: 12 1/2 pounds
9 1/4" from head to head
5/8" chime at each end beyond head
7 1/4" diameter across head
5 hoops at each end

5. Quarter-Keg: 6 1/4 pounds
7 1/2" from head to head
5/8" chime at each end beyond head
5 1/2" diameter across head
5 hoops at each end

Details of Construction

1. Staves: Had to be thoroughly seasoned, otherwise in time shrank and created spaces between them that leaked powder. No reference found to number of staves needed for each size container except for 25-lb. keg (1841) which specified eleven. 25-lb. kegs in museum collection vary in number of staves from ten to thirteen. Widths of staves not always uniform.

Thickness of staves:
25-lb. keg—3/8"
12 1/2-lb. half-keg—5/16"
6 1/4-lb. quarter-keg—1/4"

Thickness of staves of larger size containers not available. Some staves "jointed smooth;" others described as "tongued and grooved." Ends were slightly chamfered. Each stave had a "crow" or groove cut into it at each end equal to length of chime. Beveled edge of head fitted into grooves of staves and was drawn snug when hoops were tightened. Ends of staves were encircled flush by end hoop to prevent ripping of canvas covering during shipping. All barrels and kegs appear to have had slight bulge, or "bilge" in staves. A 25-lb. keg (1841) was 9 1/4" in diameter across the head and 10 1/4" diameter "in the bilge" or across the widest point at middle of container. Standard of finished product—"liquor tight."

2. Heads: Beveled on underside to provide thinner edge to fit into the "crows" or grooves of the staves. Heads to be a scant fraction oversize so that joints of staves around the heads are slightly separated. When hoops are thoroughly tightened staves are forced into snug fit against each other and tight around the head. Hole for bung was cut into head before container was assembled otherwise wood shavings or sawdust would fall into container and mix with powder when packed.

3. Hoops: Hoops variously referred to as hoop poles, split hoops, flat hoops, shaved hoops. Hoops on containers in museum collection appear to be half-round (split hoops) with bark left on. The chime, or end hoop, fitted flush with end of staves to prevent ripping of canvas covering around containers. Series of hoops at each end of container were placed tight against each other with no space between. Hoops were held in place by notching arrangement, with end tucked under. The only use of tacks or nails observed on museum collection containers was to hold the chime or end hoop in place. Here there would be little chance of metal coming into contact with powder.

4. Bungs: Both plug and screw type bungs used: most museum collection containers have screw type. Bung usually found on head but sometimes in side of the larger size containers holding military powder for Navy and Army use.[232]

Brass Priming Tools (31)

Gun Worms

Field notes indicate there were two or three dozen of these tied in a

---

[232]Norman B. Wilkinson, Director of Research, Hagley Museum, Wilmington, Delaware, correspondence dated August 23, 1971. Wilkinson provided information about DuPont powder keg cooperage derived from company correspondence, papers of agents handling cooperage matters, and from an examination of powder containers in the DuPont Company Museum. In possession of the author.

FIGURE 83. Gun worms.

bundle. These are tapered sheet metal, bearing double helix steel screws at the ends.

Howitzer Ammunition

Between 1863 and 1865, the rush to the goldfields of Idaho and Montana flooded the traditional hunting grounds of the Crow and Bannock Indians with miners, settlers, and frontier suppliers. These incursions angered the tribes, and they began exacting tolls for the use of their territory. The newcomers frequently objected to the tolls, either to the military or by using force against the Indians. By the end of 1865, the Indians of the northern Plains were on the verge of all-out war with white settlers, so it was no surprise to find more than 100 rounds of military howitzer ammunition, friction primers, powder, and lead in the *Bertrand*'s cargo. Archaeologists who excavated the *Bertrand* believe there was a twelve-pounder mountain howitzer fixed on its main deck for protection from Indian attacks, accounting for the presence of the howitzer ammunition. Although this was a common practice in the Missouri River trade at the time, the ordinance was stored in the hold, so it seems more likely that it was bound for military garrisons at one or more locations in the territory. In addition, few, if any, existing pictures of steamboats of the period show howitzers mounted on their decks.

Ordnance on the *Bertrand* included smooth-bore mountain howitzer ammunition, brass friction primers, percussion caps, and black powder, in addition to tape primers and rifle cartridges for Maynard rifles. There were no weapons in the cargo, nor was there any indication that weapons were stored on the deck of the steamboat. In addition, if the steamer was armed, the weapons were probably removed when the boat sank. Nothing of this sort appears in any of the accounts of the sinking and subsequent salvage efforts.

The howitzer ammunition is of two kinds: spherical case or "shrapnel" type, and canister type containing minie balls that sprayed the field of fire with deadly results. The spherical iron case shot have external time fuses and charges inside the shells that cause them to explode in mid-flight as they near their targets. It is interesting that both types were shipped as "fixed" rounds, that is, with all the component parts preassembled for ready use. Both perfectly conform to specifications set forth in the United States Army Manual of 1862.[233] They were assembled and packed at the St. Louis Arsenal in February 1865.

Authorized and constructed in 1827, the St. Louis Arsenal was the place of deposit and departure for all kinds of munitions destined for the remote regions of the Upper Mississippi and Upper Missouri Rivers. Most were military stores, but some were articles of merchandise and trade. The arsenal was shut down in 1879 and was later used as a medical depot. The St. Louis Arsenal was one of the largest in the United States and nearly became victim to the secessionist movement at the start of the Civil War. Secretary of War Jefferson Davis adopted a policy of placing arsenals in southern states under the command of men who were sympathetic to the South. These men could be counted upon to surrender the arsenals to the state governments immediately after the states passed ordinances of secession. In 1861, the St. Louis Arsenal was under command of Major Bell and there was no doubt that he would surrender the arsenal to Governor C. F. Jackson upon demand. In a letter to Governor Jackson from State Adjutant General Frost dated January 24, 1861, Frost said "I have just returned from the arsenal, where I have had an interview with Major Bell, the commanding officer of that place. I found the Major everything that you or I could desire. He assured me that he considered that Missouri had, whenever the time came, *a right to claim it as being on her soil*. He gave me to understand that he would not attempt any defense against the proper state authorities."

[233]T. T. S. Laidley, *The Ordnance Manual for the Use of the Officers of the United States Army*, 3rd ed. (Philadelphia: J. B. Lippincott & Co., 1862), 35.

Meanwhile, immediately after Fort Sumter was fired upon, President Lincoln issued a call for 75,000 volunteers, of which Missouri's quota was 4,000. Governor Jackson refused to send a single man, but Frank P. Blair, a strong Unionist of St. Louis, had already begun organizing military clubs. Upon Jackson's refusal to provide volunteers, Blair offered to fill the entire quota from his clubs, whose members had been drilling without arms. Lincoln agreed, and the men were mustered into the United States service and armed from the St. Louis Arsenal. Blair also knew of Major Bell's southern sympathies and urged Lincoln to replace him with a strong Union man, Captain Nathaniel Lyon. Lincoln complied with the suggestion, and it became abundantly clear that the state could not seize the arsenal without a fight. Jackson chose to seize the United States Arsenal at Liberty instead.[234] Subsequently, Captain Lyon with 1,500 troops routed the state militia from its temporary post at Camp Jackson, captured Jefferson City and Boonville, and in so doing prevented the secessionists from seizing the St. Louis Arsenal. This secured St. Louis and the surrounding counties for the Union. It also made it impossible for Missouri to secede.

A complete description of the howitzer rounds from the *Bertrand* including measured drawings and photographs of the munitions and the Boreman fuses and friction primers is found in "Munitions on the Bertrand" in a 1972 issue of *Archaeology* magazine.[235]

Bormann Fuses

Bormann fuses are a Belgian invention that was kept secret until the 1850s, when its details leaked out of the country. They became instantly popular as reliable, easily manufactured, waterproof fuses for use in smooth-bore ammunition. The principle was quite simple. Within a squat threaded cylinder of soft metal was a groove running around the circumference. A channel at the end of the groove connected to the center of the fuse, which had a powder train to the inside of the shell. The top of the fuse was sealed with a thin sheet of tin or soft metal, graduated in seconds and quarter seconds. The fuse was screwed into the shell, and the timing seal was punched or cut at the desired number of seconds before being loaded down the muzzle. Like other time fuses, these were ignited by the main charge behind the projectile. A gunner

[234]C. H. McClure, *History of Missouri* (Chicago and New York: Laidlaw Brothers, Incorporated, Copyright by A. S. Barnes Company, 1920), 147–49.
[235]Ronald R. Switzer, "Munitions on the *Bertrand*," *Archaeology* 25, no. 4 (1972): 250–55.

had to be sure to load the ammunition with the fuse facing forward to avoid having the main charge force the fuse into the shell and having it explode in the barrel of the gun. The Bormann fuse functioned about 75 percent of the time.

Normally, the artilleryman at the limber would select the time the fuse would burn by referring to a "Table of Fire" that was attached to the lid of the limber chest. As an example, a 2-pound charge of mortar powder could project a 19 1/2 pound case shot from a 20-pounder Parrot Gun 620 yards at one degree elevation of the muzzle, when the fuse was set at 1 7/8 seconds time of flight.[236]

Canister Shot

Canister shot is described in detail in "Munitions on the Bertrand" in *Archaeology*, 1972.[237] Meant for use in a 4.62 caliber 12-pounder mountain howitzer, the canisters measure 4.42 inches in diameter, and the rounds weigh 8 pounds, 8 ounces. The canister is slightly tapered to fit the howitzer's tapered powder chamber. A canister is composed of a side-soldered tinned steel sleeve, 8 3/4 inches long, tacked to a tapered wood sabot. The canister is filled with rows of lead balls packed tightly in sawdust, on top of which is placed an iron closure plate. Tabs cut out at the top of the tin cylinder are crimped over the closure plate to secure it in place, and the round is coated with hot beeswax. A powder charge in a wool or linen bag is tied to a grove at the base of the sabot, completing the assembly. There is no fusing on this type of round. These canisters

---

[236]A good number of references cover military ordnance in the 1860s. A few of these are Captain Lawrence A. Bruff, *A Textbook of Ordinance and Gunnery: Prepared for the Use of Cadets of the U. S. Military Academy* (New York: John Wiley and Sons, 1896); Jack Coggins, *Arms and Equipment of the Civil War* (Mineola: New York, Dover Publications, Inc., 1962); Confederate States of America, War Department, *The Ordnance Manual for the Use of the Officers of the Confederate States Army* (Charleston: Evans & Cogswell, 1863); T. T. S. Laidley, *The Ordnance Manual for the Use of Officers of the United States Army*, 3rd ed. (Philadelphia: J. B. Lippincott & Co., 1862); Albert Manucy, *Artillery Through the Ages: A Short Illustrated History of Cannon , Emphasizing Types Used in America* (Washington, D.C.: United States Government Printing Office, 1949); Captain Joseph Roberts, *Handbook of Artillery, for the Service of the United States Army and Militia* (New York: D. Van Nostrand, 1860); Carl P. Russell, *Guns on the Early Frontiers: A History of Firearms From Colonial Times to the Years of the Western Fur Trade* (New York: Regents of the University of California, 1957; rept., Lincoln: University of Nebraska Press, 1980); Light Artillery Board, William H. French, William F. Barry and Henry J. Hunt, *Instruction for Field Artillery: Prepared by a Board of Artillery Officers* (New York: D Van Nostrand, 1864).

[237]Switzer, "Munitions on the *Bertrand*," 254–55.

were packed as twelve fixed rounds per case, and there were twelve cases recovered from the *Bertrand*. The cases are stenciled:

[End]
12, 12 PDR. Mount / HOWITZER / CANNISTERS FIXED /
FEB. 1865
[Sides]
18 FRICTION PRIMERS / FROM ST. LOUIS / ARSENAL

Friction Primers

The dangerous cotton wick linstock used to ignite a cannon charge fuses was superseded during the Civil War by an efficient friction primer. A friction primer was made with a small brass tube that was open at one end. The opposite end was closed and had a small hole about the same diameter as the tube drilled in one side. A short length of tubing was inserted and soldered in the hole. Opposite the short tube, which was filled with friction compound similar to a match head, was a smaller hole for a short length of brass wire with a flattened serrated end. The wire was inserted through the hole into the short tube, which was crimped to hold the flattened end of the wire in place. The long end of the wire was then twisted into a loop, and the head of the primer was sealed shellac before the body of the primer was filled with musket powder. The open end was then sealed with wax.

In use, this waterproof device was placed in the vent hole of the field piece with a lanyard hooked to the loop of wire at the head of the primer. When the lanyard was pulled, the serrated end of the wire ignited the friction compound, which burned to ignite the musket powder in the main tube. When the musket powder flashed down the vent, it set off the main charge. The ammunition was intended for use in Model 1841 twelve-pound brass mountain howitzers adapted from a French version of the gun by the United States in 1836. The first American versions were cast by Cyrus Alger Co. in South Boston, Massachusetts, sometime between October 1836 and September 1837. The earliest of these were mounted on carriages with six wheels that were 36 inches in diameter and with 38-inch long axle trees. Even though these large carriages were unsuitable for use on the American frontier, by the time the Civil War began, the only modification was to increase the diameter of the wheels by two inches.[238]

---

[238]Ibid., 253.

Cyrus Alger was born in West Bridgewater, Massachusetts, on November 11, 1781, and died in Boston on February 4, 1856. This genius inventor became an iron founder early in life and established his business in Easton, Massachusetts. By 1809, he moved to South Boston where he established the iron works that were known as Alger's Foundry, Cyrus Alger & Co., and after 1817, as the South Boston Iron Co. During the War of 1812, Alger's foundry produced a large amount of shot and shell, and his company was well known for its excellent ordinance.[239]

Alger was said to be one of best metallurgists of his time, and he was awarded numerous patents. He devised many improvements in the construction of time fuses for bomb-shells and grenades, and his "Columbiad" was the largest cast-iron gun cast in the United States at the time. His first cannon, produced in 1834 for the United States government, was a rifled brass field piece modeled after the French field howitzer. The Massachusetts firm of Cyrus Alger & Co. was the leading cannon manufacturer when he died in 1856. Leadership of the firm was assumed by his son, Francis, who controlled it until his death in 1864. During the Civil War, the company continued to produce large numbers of weapons for the Union Army and Navy. Most weapons were marked "C. A. & Co.," or more rarely, "C. Alger & Co., Boston, Mass."

Smooth-bore mountain howitzers have a lower muzzle velocity than most artillery and tend to arc their shells onto a target. Because of the limited range of howitzer ammunition, targets were almost always within the line of sight of artillerymen. From a prepared position, the artillerymen tried to have shells explode over the enemy's head, where the air burst would cause more casualties. A twelve-pounder howitzer weighed 1,700 pounds and could propel a 9-pound explosive shell more than 1,000 yards. It was generally mounted on a two-wheeled carriage attached to a two-wheeled limber.[240]

Spherical Shell and Case Shot

An earlier article described the howitzer ammunition recovered from the *Bertrand*, but it was not then known that some of the ammunition was "common shell" and some was "case shot," because the crates indicated the contents were case shot and the rounds looked the same. The

---

[239]Anonymous, "Cyrus Alger," *Edited Appletons Encyclopedia*, Virtualology, http://famousamericans.net/cyrusalger/.
[240]Switzer, "Munitions on the *Bertrand*," 252–53.

only way to discern the difference is to weigh the rounds, the case shot being heavier because of the lead balls within the cases. Both the shells and case shot were intended for use in a twelve-pounder smooth bore howitzer, 4.62-inch caliber. The cases, including the straps securing the iron to the sabots, are 4.52 inches in diameter and weigh 10 pounds, 9 ounces. Artillery was fairly expensive, as a May 1861 article in the *Nebraska Republican* indicates:

> Cost of Artillery—The cost of Dahlgren's great nine-inch iron guns is seven and half cents per pound. As they weigh 9,000 pounds each, the cost of a gun is $645. The eight-inch columbiads weigh about 8,500 pounds; the ten-inch, 16,000 pounds each; both are sold at six and a half cents a pound. Forty-two pounders weigh 8,000 pounds; thirty-two pounders, 3,300 to 3,600 pounds each. **The twelve pounders are sold at five cents, the others at six cents a pound**. Sea coast howitzers of eight and ten-inch bore, weigh from 8,500 to 9,500 pounds each, and are sold art six and a half cents a pound. Siege howitzers of eight-inch bore are much lighter, weighing 2,500 to 3,000 pounds, and are sold at the same rates as those above mentioned. **Brass guns are much lighter, the army pattern twelve-pounders weighing only 4,300 pounds; they are, however sold at forty-six cents a pound**. The Dahlgren brass guns are still proportionately higher priced; the **patent mountain twelve-pound howitzers, weighing 220 pounds are sold at seventy-five cents a pound**.—**Shell sell according to weight, at from four to six cents a pound; shot at three and a half to four cents.**[241]

Case shot was made by casting a hollow spherical iron ball. Musket balls were packed in the sphere, and a grooved stick was inserted in the center of the fuse hole to the bottom of the ball. The case was then placed in a hot sand bath or oven and brought to a high temperature to receive molten sulfur that was poured into the case, filling the interstices between the balls. When the sulfur cooled, the stick was removed from the case. If a Bormann fuse was to be used, a powder charge was inserted in the hole left by the stick, and a stopper and fuse were screwed into place. The stopper was perforated to insure that fire from the fuse could communicate with the internal charge. At some point during the Civil War, the spherical case was filled to the top with sulfur, and a cutter was used to bore out a powder chamber in the case.

A wood sabot was attached to the base of the shell with tin straps, and a powder charge in a linen or wool bag was tied to a groove in the

[241]*Nebraska Republican*, May 22, 1861, 1.

base of the sabot. These were packed twelve fixed rounds to the crate, and there may have been three cases on the *Bertrand*. The shipping cases were stenciled:

[End]
12, 12 PDR. MOUNT / HOWITZER / SHELL FIXED / FEB. 1865
[Sides]
18 FRICTION PRIMERS / FROM ST. LOUIS / ARSENAL

After recovery from the *Bertrand* hold, the shells were drilled and flushed of their black powder exploder charges by U.S. Army ordinance personnel.

Lead Bars

Two hundred and twenty-two lead bars from the *Bertrand*'s hold are stamped "ST. LOUIS SHOT TOWER CO." The bars weigh one pound each and measure 10 3/8 inch long, 1/2 inch wide, and 5/16 inch thick and were probably shipped in cotton bags. This company produced a large amount of shot and lead bar stock used on the western frontier between 1850 and the turn of the century. It has been suggested that the bars may have been cast early in 1865 or late in the preceding year.[242] According to Hanson, changes in ownership of the controlling interest of the St. Louis Shot Tower Co. took place between 1849 and 1893, some of which are reflected in the markings of lead bar stock. Bars marked "St. Louis Shot Tower Co." date no earlier than 1858, and the bars from the *Bertrand* probably date from 1865.[243] In any event, the bar dates can be bracketed between 1858 and 1865.

It is notable that the lead mining and smelting industry was well established on the Mississippi and Missouri Rivers in Wisconsin and Missouri by 1830. Smelters produced lead ingots or "pigs" weighing sixty-five to seventy pounds, making it practical to ship the pigs to fur trading posts where they could be cut into small bars or cast into trade balls by company employees. This reduced labor costs at shot towers and brought down shipping costs. There was less need to bag balls or to bundle and tie bars before packing them in heavy wooden crates for shipping because

---

[242]Ronald R. Switzer, "Lead Bars from the Steamboat *Bertrand*," *Museum of the Fur Trade Quarterly* 6, no. 4 (1970): 5–6.

[243]Charles E. Hanson, Jr., "The St. Louis Shot Tower," *Museum of the fur Trade Quarterly* 3, no. 3 (1967): 2–5.

the pigs could easily be stacked in the holds of boats. However, as the fur trade declined, more balls and bars were shipped directly from shot towers, so it was not unusual to see ready-made items like the ones described in the *Bertrand*'s cargo headed for the western frontier.

Lead Shot (50 pounds)

Although not associated with wooden cases, there were approximately fifty pounds of lead shot of four sizes removed from the cargo. These measure 2, 5, 8, and 17 millimeters in diameter. In all probability these were shipped in cloth nags that had disintegrated.

During this period, lead shot was generally produced at shot towers constructed of brick or stone to a height of 150 to more than 300 feet, with twenty-five or thirty-foot wells at the bottom that held water to quench the molten lead. Lead drop-shot was made by melting pig lead in iron pots to which arsenic was added. The molten lead and arsenic mixture was allowed to steep for several hours to ensure proper mixing of the metals. The lead was taken to the top of the shot tower and again melted before being poured through copper colanders with holes of differing sizes, depending upon the size shot being made. The lead formed perfect globules as it fell from the colander into the water well at the base of the tower. The cooled shot was collected in buckets and taken to the polishing room, where imperfect shot was removed by passing it over several inclined wooden planes. At the bottom of the planes, round shot dropped into a box about 2 inches from the end of the last plane. Imperfect shot, having less velocity than perfect shot, dropped into a box between the end of the last plane and the box receiving the perfect shot.

One of the oldest shot towers of note in the United States was the Philadelphia Shot Tower owned by Thomas W. Sparks, John Bishop, and one other partner. The tower was opened in 1808. It was 140-150 feet tall, tapering to 15 feet in diameter at the top, with a 30 foot deep well at the bottom. In addition to drop-shot, the company produced bar-lead like that found on the steamboat *Bertrand*, as well as buck-shot. By 1812–1815, Bishop, who was a peace-loving Quaker, withdrew from the company, and Sparks began manufacturing bullets and conical balls used in the War of 1812. Sparks carried on the business until his nephew Thomas Sparks became the proprietor in 1855. During the Civil War, the tower supplied shot for the Union army. In 1874. Thomas Spark's son, Thomas W. Sparks, became the sole proprietor and manager. The tower was in operation until 1903.[244]

In 1808. Paul Beck built a taller shot tower on the Schuykill River that remained in operation until after the War of 1812, but competition with the Sparks shot tower forced it to close by 1828. That year Baltimore's Phoenix Shot Tower was engineered and built by Jacob Wolfe to produce drop-shot for pistols and rifles and molded shot for canons. The tower remained in operation until 1892.[245] Other early towers were built at New York in 1821 (Youle's Shot Tower), and Spring Green, Wisconsin (Tower Hill Shot Tower). In addition, the Wisconsin Shot Tower was organized by Green Bay merchant Daniel Whitney as the Wisconsin Shot Co. Another tower was built on a cliff at Helena on the Wisconsin River between 1831 and 1833 by Daniel Whitney and T. B. Shaunce (Wiskonsin Patent Shot); it operated successfully until 1861. Another was constructed at Dubuque, Iowa in 1856. The latter, which was 122 feet high with a 19-foot diameter base and a 12-foot diameter top, apparently was built to break the St. Louis Shot Tower's monopoly, but St. Louis Shot Tower cut its prices and the Dubuque tower went out of business in three years. It was later acquired by the St. Louis Shot Tower and abandoned.

Earlier, in 1807, Thomas Jackson built a tower at Jackson Ferry, Virginia. It was 150 feet tall with 75-foot stacks. Another was built in 1809, at Pittsburgh by John Maclot, and another at Herculaneum (Potosi) in 1810 by Moses Austin. The St. Louis Shot Tower, which was built in about 1830, was owned by Ferdinand and Luther Kennett and James White. By 1836, they had purchased the J. H. Alford Co. warehouse and shot tower at Herculaneum. Four years later, they partnered with John Latty to make shot under the company name F. Kennett & Co.

By 1849, there apparently was another partner in the firm, because the name was changed to Kennett, Simonds, & Co. The *Missouri Republican* for January 31, 1849, contained the following:

KENNETT, Simonds & Co. "WHO WILL KEEP A CONSTANT SUPPLY OF PATENT AND BUCK SHOT AND SMALL BAR

[244]Benson J. Lossing, *The American Centennary: A History of the Progress of Republic of the United States During the First One Hundred Years of Its Existence* (Philadelphia: Porter & Coates, 1876), 159.

[245]J. Dorsey and J. D. Dilts, *A Guide to Baltimore Architecture*, 3rd ed. (Centerville: Tidewater Publishers, 1997), 182. See also "Baltimore: Register Of National Historic Places Travel Itinerary B," "Shot Tower," National Park Service, http://www.nps.gov/nr/travel/baltimore/b29.htm, last modified December 8, 1990.

LEAD ON HAND AND WILL FILL ORDERS UPON SHORT-
EST NOTICE. THE OFFICE OF THE COMPANY WILL BE
KEPT AT THE COUNTING ROOM OF JOHN SIMONDS, 24
WATER ST., ST. LOUIS. JAN 31, 1849"[246]

The St. Louis Shot Tower was capable of producing 2,422,835 pounds of shot and bar lead every five months, 1,994,375 pounds of which was shot of various sizes. The business prospered to the extent that Ferdinand Kennet retired a very wealthy man in 1854.

Not all shot was made at shot towers. After 1830, when the lead industry was well developed, "pigs" of lead weighing 65 to 75 pounds were shipped up and down the Mississippi and Missouri Rivers, and it was not uncommon for port workers to cut up the pigs and mold the lead into trade balls and bar lead in their spare time. Trade balls were cast in gang molds of iron, bronze, or brass, and by 1850, most forts on the Missouri River including Fort Union had several of different sizes of molds. One cargo shipped upriver by Chouteau & Co. in 1831 listed one lead mold for twelve bars of lead at $4.50, and two pigs of lead weighing 140 pounds valued at $4.20, or three cents a pound.

By the time the Civil War began, a good deal of shot was being produced at shot towers, especially those in Baltimore, St. Louis, and Chicago. E. W. Blatchford & Co. of Chicago is known to have stamped customers' names on lead bars as a sales incentive. As late as 1883, the Baltimore and St. Louis Shot Towers were selling 1/2-ounce balls of .52 caliber. Trade in shot prospered on the western frontier well into the early 1900s.

Finally, not all shot was made in the East, as exemplified by the Selby Smelting Works and the Selby Shot Tower in San Francisco. Named after Thomas Henry Selby, these works produced a credible amount of shot in the late 1860s and early 1870s. Selby, another self-made man, was born on May 14, 1820, in New York City, and at age twenty-nine moved to California, where he established a gold rush mercantile in San Francisco. He later built the Selby Smelting Works and Selby Shot Tower. He served as mayor of San Francisco from 1869 to 1871. He died of pneumonia in San Francisco on June 17, 1875, and was interred at the Mountainview Cemetery in Oakland.[247]

[246]*Missouri Republican*, January 1849.

[247]Anonymous, *The Bay of San Francisco, The Metropolis of the Pacific Coast and its Suburban Cities, A History*, Vol. 2 (Chicago: Lewis Publishing Company, 1892), 434.

Maynard Cartridges and Paper Tape Primers

Although not found in large numbers, two of the most interesting arti-facts in the cargo are Maynard cartridges and paper tape primers. An extensive article about these artifacts, "Maynard Cartridges and Primers from the Steamboat *Bertrand*," was written by the author in 1972. What follows is taken directly from that article.[248]

> Ten years later, the now famous French Captain Minie' patented a coni-cal bullet with a sheet iron cup in the base which greatly complemented Greener's invention.[249] Finally, a flat-based projectile known as the Wilkinson system was invented, which obtained the desired expansion in the bore at the instant of firing the weapon. Contemporaneous to the developments in bullets was the invention of percussion caps and their application to the Springfield Percussion Musket in 1842. However, even with these improvements, some of the problems of using muskets seemed insurmountable.
>
> Muskets were neither safe nor easily manipulated saddle guns because they had to be loaded with ramrods. In addition, when tiny brass percus-sion caps were used with muskets, the caps were awkward to handle by troops under fire and were easily dropped, especially in cold weather. About 1845, considerable experimentation was underway to produce breech-loading arms with self-contained cartridges, but gas leaks at the breeches of these early guns made their use questionable. Paper case and linen case ammunition were tried as potential solutions to the problem, but not until the invention of metallic expanding cartridges did breech-loading arms become effective.[250]

In January 1845, Dr. Edward Maynard, a Washington dentist, suc-cessfully applied his talents to the problem of muzzle-loading small arms when he invented a self-contained tape-lock priming system. Meeting with a board of ordnance officers at West Point, he won their support to convert flintlocks to percussion firearms by attaching primer maga-zines of his own design to musket lock plates.[251] These magazines were

---

[248]Ronald R. Switzer, "Maynard Cartridges and Primers From the Steamboat *Ber-trand*," *Military Collector & Historian: Journal of the Company of Military Historians* 24, no. 3 (1972): 85–87.

[249]Edwards, *Civil War Guns*, 15.

[250]Berkley R. Lewis, "Small Arms and Ammunition in the United States Service, 1776–1865," *Smithsonian Miscellaneous Collections* 129 (1968): 119.

[251]Francis Bannerman, *100th Anniversary of the Bannerman Catalogue Military Goods Business* (Blue Point, N.Y.: Bannerman & Sons, Inc., 1966), 78.

designed to contain pelletized primers on paper tapes, also invented by Dr. Maynard. The good doctor described his inventions as follows:

> The detonating material of the "Maynard Primer" is in the form of *little lozenges*, each about one-sixth of an inch wide and one thirtieth of an inch thick. These lozenges were enclosed between two narrow strips of strong paper cemented together and rendered waterproof and incombustible. The single strip thus formed is a little less than one-fourth of an inch wide, is very stiff and firm, and contains four of these lozenges (each of which is a *charge*) in every inch of its length; the charges forming projections, of their shape, on one side, having considerable and equal spaces between them; the other side of the strip being one flat and even surface.
>
> One of these strips, containing fifty or more or less charges, is coiled up and placed in a magazine in the lock, and is *fed out* by the action of the lock, one charge at each time the hammer is raised. When the hammer descends it cuts off and fires the charge fed out upon the vent (or nipple, if one is used) of the gun, thus igniting the powder of the cartridge in the barrel.[252]

The U.S. Ordnance Department in March 1845 paid Dr. Maynard a dollar per gun for the rights to apply his tape lock to 4,000 Model 1840 flintlock muskets. A short time later, some Sharps 1853 models were modified by attaching a Maynard tape lock to the lock plate in front of the hammer. In 1854, Maynard sold the rights to use his design for $50,000 to the government, which in turn contracted with Remington Arms Co. to alter 20,000 additional muskets and .69-caliber smoothbore flintlocks. The United States Army standardized the Maynard primer lock in 1855 and continued its use in both rifles and pistols until about 1860.[253] After 1854, Dr. Maynard improved the tape lock and adapted it for use on several other types of arms. The improved version was forged with the tape magazine in the plate lock. The magazine was closed with a hinged trap door that swung downward when opened.[254]

In 1851, Dr. Maynard patented tipping-barrel, breech-loading carbines with under levers. Modifying the patent in 1857 and again in December 1859, the first patent of his .50-caliber carbines utilized tape primers fed from a magazine on the right side of the breech.[255] This action was already in use on Harper's Ferry Muskets, Springfield Model 1855s,

[252]Lewis, "Small Arms and Ammunition in the United States Service, 1776–1865," 161.
[253]Ibid.
[254]Edwards, *Civil War Guns*, 101–102.
[255]James J. Grant, *Single Shot Rifles* (New York: William Morrow & Company, 1947), 227.

Sharps Carbines, and a few other models. A typical U.S. issue Maynard carbine purchased by the government in 1857 had a nearly symmetrical butt plate with a patch box for two rolls of primer tapes and a fixed rear sight blade set crosswise on a 20- inch barrel. A number of these carbines were also purchased by Jefferson Davis for use by the Confederacy at the beginning of the Civil War.[256]

Another and more common type of .50-caliber Maynard carbine produced in 1863, of which 20,002 were purchased by the federal government in 1864–1865, does not have the Maynard primer magazine and used ordinary musket or rifle caps on the nipples. Very few of either type had sufficiently long barrels to be called rifles.[257]

Dr. Maynard was quite anxious to receive government contracts for his carbines and rifles and, in 1861, the Massachusetts Arms Co., Chicopee Falls, Massachusetts, employed 160 men to make Maynard rifles. Sharpe implies that fire destroyed the factory in 1863, however, Edwards states that, in 1864, with new equipment and a major contract, the Massachusetts Arms Co. had to employ 200 men to make Maynard's arms to keep up with the demands.[258] After the Civil War, the surplus of unfinished carbine actions was used to produce sporting rifles with interchangeable barrels of various lengths. The guns designated Model 1865, were produced in .35, .40, and .50 calibers, and used Maynard cartridges.[259]

Prior to the end of the Civil War, Maynard patented several types of reloadable brass cartridges fitted with extractor cords. In 1865, he patented another brass cartridge composed of a cylinder soldered to a perforated brass closing disk. The pierced center of the wide-rimmed base permitted the flame from the tape primer to enter the case and ignite the black powder charge.

This ammunition was meant for use in the Maynard Model 1865 rifle. Later, this arm was modified for center-fire Berdan primed shells in many calibers, but early primed center-fire cartridges were also a product of Maynard's genius. His first attempt at making a self-contained cartridge came in 1866, when he added a fulminate pellet between the bottom of the case and a copper cover and submitted the projectile for testing to the Army.[260] This improvement greatly reduced the number

[256]Edwards, *Civil War Guns*, 101–102.
[257]Ibid.
[258]Sharpe, *The Rifle in America* (New York: Funk and Wagnalls Company, 1958), 71.
[259]Ibid.
[260]Lewis, "Small Arms and Ammunition in the United States Service, 1776–1865," 132.

of motions required to load and fire the weapons, and increased their efficiency.

Most gun buffs and collectors of Civil War arms are well aware of the numerous contributions of Dr. Maynard to the development of modern repeating weapons and sighting mechanisms. His sporting and gallery rifles were undoubtedly some of the best ever produced in the United States.

Putting aside the history of Dr. Maynard's inventions, 114 rounds of .50-caliber rifle ammunition and eight tinned cans of primer tapes were recovered from the hold of the steamer *Bertrand*. The brass cases of the rifle cartridges are 3.1 cm long, including the basal closing disk, and slightly less than 1.4 cm in diameter. The reloadable cases weigh 5.5 grams. Centrally perforated basal closing disks are 1.9 cm in diameter and about .05 cm thick. The mold-made conical lead bullets are 1.3 cm in diameter and slightly more than 2.3 cm in length, with a .2 cm groove around the base set .2 cm up from the proximal end. The slugs vary in weight from 335 to 487 grains, which would seem to be an inordinately large deviation in weight, even if one allows for deterioration of the metals during burial.

The tape primers match Dr. Maynard's description perfectly. Each roll of primers contains four pellets per inch of tape, and each roll is wrapped in thin brown wood-pulp paper. The rolls are packaged ten per can. The fragmentary tinned cylindrical sheet-metal cans once were about three inches long, including the soldered bottoms and lids. They are about 1 1/8 inches in diameter, including the soldered side seam, and appear to have been covered with some sort of water-proofing paint or preservative. Although eight cans are represented in the collections, only 22 rolls of tape primers and a number of fragments survived the test of water and time.

The now-rare artifacts of the Civil War era described in this paper currently reside at the U.S. Fish and Wildlife's Department's DeSoto National Wildlife Refuge, where they are being preserved by in the Bertrand Conservation Laboratory and Museum. Dr. Maynard's biographic profile is interesting from the historical perspective. Edward Maynard was born in Madison, New York, on April 26, 1813, and at the age of nineteen he entered the United States Military Academy at West Point. Resigning because of illness, four years later Maynard became a dentist and eventually was regarded as one of the most successful practitioners in the country catering mainly to Presidents and Congressmen in Baltimore and Washington, D.C. Maynard's son, George Willoughby Maynard, was born in Washington, D.C., March 5, 1843, and George went on to become a prominent artist. In 1857 Edward Maynard became a professor at the Baltimore College of Dental Surgery.

Although Edward Maynard is known for many firearms-related patents, beginning in 1845 with the percussion priming system and the tipping barrel, lever-operated breech loading rifle in 1851, he stayed true to the practice of dentistry and was Chair of Dental Theory and Practice at the National University in Washington in 1888. During his life Edward Maynard invented a substantial number of dental methods and instruments still in use today. The distinguished Dr. Maynard was awarded top military honors by the King of Prussia, the Great Medal of Merit by King of Sweden, and was offered the position of Court Dentist by Czar Nicholas I of Russia, which he declined. Dr. Edward Maynard died in Washington on May 4, 1891, and is recognized as one of most respected scientists and inventors of his time.

Percussion Caps

Among the munitions recovered from the *Bertrand* were 71 tin boxes each of percussion caps. The copper caps are charged with fulminate of mercury mixed with half its weight of saltpeter and sealed with a drop of varnish. The weight of the charge is 1/2 grain. Packed 100 caps to a can, each can is labeled:

ELEY BROS LONDON / Manufacturers of Sporting Ammunition / PERCUSSION CAPS / E.B. Quality / 100 Caps No. 12

The caps measure 3/16 inches high by 3/16 inches in diameter, and the 1/64 inch thick metal caps are crimped with 28 grooves.

The small round cans are flat on the top and bottom, the tops being of the overlapping type that are slightly larger than the bodies of the cans. The cans are 1 9/16 inches in diameter and 17/32 inches tall without the lids, which are also 17/32 inches in depth. They are of tinned steel, the bottoms of which are soldered on.

The caps were imported, having been produced by Eley Brothers of London, England. This business apparently was started as a cottage industry early in the 1820s by the Eley family of Woodbine Cottage, West End, Hampstead, Middlesex County, England. In July 1828, William and Charles Eley opened an extensive factory in London to supply patent cartridges, which later grew into a major cartridge-making business under the ownership of William Eley in 1838. In 1837, they added percussion caps to their product line. William Eley was killed in an explosion in 1841, and his three sons inherited the business in 1842. They made a major expansion of the company in 1874 by selling shares to the public. Notable among the many ammunition developments of the company were a joint patent with Samuel Colt for revolver cartridges by William Thomas Eley in 1855; the first British centerfire cartridge in 1857; patents for the Boxer priming system in the 1860s; the first bottleneck cartridges for rifles in 1869; and, a brass waterproof shotshell in 1882.[261] Although Eley was not the inventor of waterproof percussion caps, in 1837, he invented his own version of a waterproof percussion cap and added it to the company's line of products. In the 1840s, the company appears to have become Eley Brothers—London when it advertised to sportsmen that it had invented a "perfectly WATER-PROOF PERCUSSION CAP, which they warrant to stand immersion in sea water for several days, and remain uninjured by change of climate for any period."

After the oldest brother, William Thomas Ely, died in 1881, the company had its ups and downs, but still managed to create many innovations in ammunition and smokeless gunpowder. In 1894, the British War Office removed the company from its approved list of suppliers for production of .303 ammunition because much of it had to be returned as unusable. Between 1901 and 1906, the company saw explosions and workforce strikes, but by 1907, it had constructed a shot tower. Nevertheless, it was not equipped to mass produce .303 ammunition during World War I, and after the war, demand for this ammunition slumped. Eley's tried to salvage the company through buy-outs of other firms and partnerships in the 1920s, but closed their Angel Road factory in 1921. Ely Co. survives today mostly because of its many innovations in munitions.

The Quarterly Review for January and April 1858 captures more of the detail of copper percussion cap manufacture:

> **The Manufacture of Percussion-Caps.** The first process in this light and delicate work is the stamping of sheet-copper into pieces of the required form to make the caps. For this purpose the copper is placed beneath the punch of the machine, and immediately it is put into action, small crosses of metal are seen to fall from it into a box in a continual stream, whilst

[261]"History of Eley," Eley Company, London, 2011, http://www.eley.co.uk/history-of-eley.

the sheet itself is transposed by the punching process into a kind of trellis work. These crosses of equilateral arms are now transferred to another machine, which instantly doubles up the four arms, and at the same time so rounds them, that they form a tube just the size of the gun-nipple, and by a third operation of the same machine, a kind of rim is given to the free end, which makes the cap take the form of a hat. This rim marks the difference between the military and the ordinary percussion-cap— the soldier, in the hurry and confusion of battle, requiring this guide to enable him to apply the proper end to the nipple. The metal portion of the cap completed, it is transferred to a man who fills it with detonating powder. As this is a very dangerous process, the artisan upon whom the duty devolves sits apart from the boys, who perform all the other work, for fear of an accidental explosion. To fix the fine dust in the cap, a very pretty machine is employed, which gets through its work with extreme rapidity. The caps are placed in regular rows in a frame work, to which is attached a lever, armed with as many fine points as there are caps in a single row. The motion given by the hand alternately dips these fine points into a tray of varnish, and then into each succeeding line of caps. When the varnish is dry, the powder is fixed and effectually protected from the effects of damp. The caps are now finished, and are ready for the boy who counts and packs them. Machinery is even employed to perform the part of Cocker, and with one gentle shake does the brain-work of many minutes. A frame is constructed, into which fit a number of small trays, each tray being pierced with seventy-five holes. Upon this frame the boy heaps up a few handfuls of caps, and then gives the whole machine a few jerks, and when he sees that every hole is filled with a cap, he lifts out each separate tray and empties it into appropriate boxes. In this manner he is enabled, with extreme rapidity, to count out his parcels of seventy-five caps, the regulation number served to each soldier with sixty rounds of ball-cartridge—the excess of fifteen being allowed for loss in the flurry of action. The British soldier's clumsy fingers are by no means well calculated for handling and adjusting such light articles.[262]

Powder Flasks and Shot Flasks

Field notes indicate there were two cases of screw-type powder flasks in the cargo, each case bearing four dozen 16-ounce flasks. Apparently, twenty-one of these survived. The largest flasks are of the shell design because of the clamshell pattern on the flask body. These shotgun flasks

---

[262]John Murray, *Quarterly Review*, 103 (1858): 232–33.

FIGURE 84. American Flask and Cap Co. brass and pewter powder flasks.

have screw-off tops with five setting adjustable chargers that can be adjusted from 4 to 6 drams. They are made of copper and measure 7 1/4 inches long, 3 3/4 inches wide at the body, and 1 3/8 inches thick. They have four hanger ringlets, blued steel springs on the chargers, and the heavy brass tops are stamped in a curve on the top faces near the charger spouts with "AM. FLASK & CAP CO." One had maroon tassels attached to the hanger ringlets.

The smaller brass flasks are of the Remington style, bearing a hunting scene with a dog and waterfowl on the bodies. These too were made by the American Flask & Cap Co. and have screw-off tops. In addition, at least one badly corroded pewter flask was recovered. It is only slightly smaller than the smaller brass flasks, bears a hunting scene on the body, and has a thumb spring measure on the top of the cap plate marked "American Flask and Cap Co."

Two or three leather shot flasks were present in the cargo. These bear embossed hunting scenes on the bodies and brass lever-operated measures on the caps. The flasks are 8 11/16 inches long, 3 3/8 inches wide at the bodies, and 1 5/16 inches in thickness. The brass measures are stamped

FIGURE 85.
American Flask & Cap Co. leather shot flask.

"AM. Flask & Cap CO." There was some speculation that the leather bodies were made by the Lionberger boot and shoe company in St. Louis.

The American Flask & Cap Co. was organized in 1857 by consolidation with the American Flask Co. of Meriden, Connecticut, and the Walter Hicks Percussion Cap Co. of Haverstraw, New York. The consolidated company had capital stock of $125,000, most of which was owned by the stockholders of the Waterbury Brass Co. of Waterbury, Connecticut. After the consolidation, the machinery at Meriden and Haverstraw was removed and installed in the Manhan Woolen Mills building adjacent to the Waterbury Brass Co. Abram Ives, president of the Waterbury Brass Co., was elected president of the American Flask & Cap Co. and served until 1867, when he sold his stock and was replaced by Calvin H. Carter of the Waterbury Brass Co. Thereafter, into the 1890s, the company had a succession of executive directors. The factory suffered fire and flood damage more than once during its existence. American Flask and Cap Co. and Waterbury Brass Co. functioned as separate entities until March 20, 1865, when the former was consolidated with Waterford Brass.[263] The American Flask & Cap Co. also made dress and corset fittings.

Primer Boxes (6)

---

[263]Joseph Anderson, ed., *The Town and City of Waterbury, Connecticut, from the Aboriginal Period to the Year Eighteen Hundred and Ninety-Five* (New Haven: The Price & Lee Company, 1896), 333.

Priming Cord

Field notes indicate there was about 800 feet of priming cord in coils of 100 to 200 feet each. These were wrapped in woven jute with some hand lettering on the exteriors of the bundles.

Shot Molds

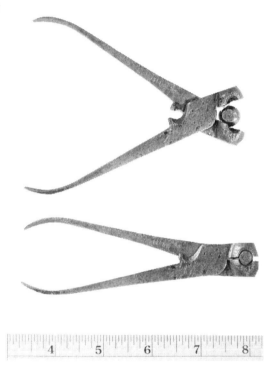

FIGURE 86. Plier-type shot mold.

These three are typical 5-inch plier-type molds made for casting a single ball. They are stamped with the number 110.

MISCELLANEOUS
Artist's Pastels

Book Covers
Bible Cover(s)?

Mitchell's School Geography

One book cover recovered was probably from a book belonging to one of the passengers. Likely owners include the grandchildren of Willard Burroughs, Mary Atchison's daughter Emma, or Anne or Fannie Campbell.

Labeled *Mitchell's School Geography* on the spine, the book was prepared by S. Augustus Mitchell of Philadelphia and published in 1859 by E. H. Butler & Co., New York: Sheldon & Co.[264] This example was likely a revised edition and would have born a title page reading:

MITCHELL'S SCHOOL GEOGRAPHY
NEW REVISED EDITION
A SYSTEM OF MODERN GEOGRAPHY, COMPRISING A DESCRIPTION OF THE PRESENT STATE OF THE WORLD, AND IT'S FIVE GREAT DIVISIONS, AMERICA, EUROPE, ASIA, AFRICA AND OCEANIA, WITH THEIR SEVERAL EMPIRES, KINGDOMS, STATES, TERRITORIES, ETC. EMBELLISHED BY NUMEROUS ENGRAVINGS. ADAPTED TO THE CAPACITY OF YOUTH. ACCOMPANIED BY AN ATLAS CONTAINING THIRTY-TWO MAPS, DRAWN AND ENGRAVED EXPRESSLY FOR THE WORK.

It is no surprise that most of the text in the book was devoted to the United States, its territories, and one district. The frontispiece would have been titled "Stages of Society" and would have shown scenes labeled "Savage," "Barbarous," "Half-Civilized," "Civilized," and "Enlightened." It had 336 pages and sixteen catalog pages advertising textbooks.

Book Edgings

Children's Toys, Blocks, Whistles, Chalk Board, etc.

Recovered from the trunk belonging to Mrs. John Atchison, wife of a banker in the territory, were clothing and toys of her two children, Emma, four, and Charles, five. The child's shoes with metal toe plates probably belonged to Charles. The toys include three sets of wooden blocks, one stamped to portray "Hill's Village School / Hill's Union College," and a small cast-metal horse-drawn cart.

---

[264]S. Augustus Mitchell, *Mitchell's School Geography* (New York: E. H. Butler & Co., 1860).

/ VIVIAN & SIMPSON." Arnold inks were also sold in 32-ounce stoneware bottles.

The bottles are somewhat distinctive in character, and a fair amount is known of the bottle manufacturer. There is a clear set of stamped or impressed markings on each bottle. Near the base the bottle maker is identified as "VITREOUS STONE BOTTLES / J. BOURNE & SON, / PATENTEES / DENBY & CODNER PARK POTTERIES / NEAR DERBY. P. J. ARNOLD / LONDON."

The story of these ink bottles begins in 1806, when a turnpike was being constructed between Alfreton and Derby, England. Near Denby, a rich seam of clay was discovered near a coal deposit on the estate of W. Drury Lowe, Esq., and William Bourne of the nearby Belper pottery works recognized the value of the clay and had it mined and sent to the Belper works for making ink, blacking, and pottery bottles until 1809, when the Denby pottery works was established at Denby by a man named Jager. The Denby Works operated until 1812 when William Bourne's son, Joseph, succeeded Jager. Both the Denby and Belper Works continued to operate simultaneously, and Joseph built a strong reputation for the Denby Works by producing high quality bottles and jars. In 1834, the Belper Works went out of business and Joseph Bourne moved its equipment and workers to Denby, where he had already begun to increase the magnitude of the operations by acquiring the Codner Park Works in 1833. In 1856, the Shipley Works was acquired by Bourne, and in 1861, the Codner Park Works were closed and moved to Denby. In 1836, Joseph Bourne tried his hand at inventing and patented improvements in the size and shape of kilns used in salt glazing.

As the business grew, so did the product line. Denby soon became one of the world's principal suppliers of "Varley's Patented Double V. Insulators," which were marketed to railroads and telegraph companies. The Denby Works eventually held patents for white glazed ink and other bottles in addition to its patents for brown salt glazed vitreous wares. In addition to ink bottles of every shape and size and bottles for ale, ginger beer, porter, and liquid blacking, the company also made spirit and liquor bottles, foot warmers, carriage warmers, medical appliances, mortars and pestles, pipkins, feeding bottles, candle sticks, pork pie molds, hunting jugs, flower vases, wine coolers, water bottles, ewers, cake stands, and cheese stands. Later the company began producing a more artful line of domestic vases and other domestic wares.[266] William Bourne had nine

---

[266]Jewitt, *The Ceramic Art of Great Britain*, 357–59.

children, but only four of his sons survived to carry on the family name. During the 1850s, Joseph Bourne took his son, Joseph Harvey Bourne, into the business under the name Joseph Bourne & Son. Joseph Bourne died in 1860, and his son died in 1869. The company continued to operate for some time afterward.

Arnold's inks were the product of P. & J. Arnold of London. Had the labels on the *Bertrand* ink bottles survived, they would have been quite elaborate, black, white, and red in color, with text reading, "ARNOLD'S / CHEMICAL / WRITING FLUID / WHICH WILL NOT MOULD / The color at first is of a greenish blue / afterwise changing to a deep blue / P. & J. Arnold / CHEMISTS, 126 ALDERSGATE STREET / LONDON." Arnold's blue/black writing fluid was a mixture of sulphate of indigo and gallotannate ink (regular ink), but the company made other inks as well, according to an ad in *The Sidney Mail* newspaper in 1881 that lists blue black writing fluid, blue black copying fluid, black copying ink, office and steel pen ink, crimson and scarlet ink for steel pens, ticketing ink, Japan ink, and ink powders.[267]

Arnold's inks have a considerable history and may have originated as early as 1724, when R. Ford began making gall ink in England. He continued making ink until 1772, when the firm name was changed to William Green & Co. In 1809, the company was succeeded by J. & J. Arnold, who ran it until 1814, when Pichard and John Arnold acquired it and renamed the firm P. & J. Arnold. Located at 59 Barbican in London, the company later moved to the Aldersgate Street location shown on its labels, where it first marketed its blue black ink in 1830. Over time, they manufactured more than thirty varieties of ink. Unfortunately, there is very little detailed information about Arnold's inks, but a bit more can be found in Chapter XXII, "Ink Industry," in David N. Carvalho's *Forty Centuries of Ink, or a Chronological Narrative Concerning Ink and its Background* published in 1904.[268]

Letter Clips

Pencils

Pencils made by two different companies were among the cargo. Graphite

---

[267]*Sidney Mail* (Sydney, Australia), May 1, 1886, 3.

[268]David N. Carvalho, "Ink Industry," *Forty Centuries of Ink, or a Chronological Narrative Concerning Ink and its Background* (New York: Banks Law Publishing Co., 1888; 1904).

VII

End of an Era

THE STEAMBOAT TRANSPORTATION INDUSTRY ON THE Missouri River between the 1840s and the 1860s arose to supply trappers, traders, miners, farmers, and merchants in the West with the necessities for their new lives on the frontier. Although there was considerable freighting of goods overland in competition with or as a supplement to steamboat transportation, speed of delivery and cost per unit drove the development of fierce competition not just between overland freighting companies and steamboat companies, but also among overland freighters and among steamboat companies. This remained the case until 1869, when the first transcontinental railroad was completed, shortening the time required for transport from weeks or months to a few days at less cost per unit. It is also significant that prior to the advent of the railroads, western consumers were at the mercy of merchants and shipping companies. A person on the western frontier could get most of what he or she *needed* at no small cost in most cases, but not always get what he or she *wanted*. He or she had to buy what was available at the mercantiles, and most shopowners would not stock much in the way of luxury goods because they were too difficult and expensive to order and ship and might not sell if the corresponding price was too high. Merchants thought this was a waste of capital. In addition, time was a consideration. A frontier person might have to wait for months to take delivery of common goods or specialty items. A corollary to this mindset was that if it was too heavy per unit to ship by steamboat, it probably would not be shipped. Metal products and some kinds of equipment and tools fell in this category and consequently were always in short supply.

There simply was not enough profit in these items to waste stowage space, so they were shipped overland.

Steamboat transportation shortened delivery time for goods on the frontier, but did not eliminate the need for overland freighting. Shipping by steamboat on the Missouri River was fraught with dangers, expensive to insure, and seasonal in nature. In a good high-water year, steamboats might make it to Fort Benton from St. Louis twice, once in the spring flush that resulted from the melting of ice and snow upriver, and again during the summer when the rains filled the river's tributaries in the north. However, just because the water was high and a boat could make it to Fort Benton, it did not necessarily equate to profit. Company steamboats that were lucky enough to be the first up the river in the spring garnered the highest profits. After a long cold winter in the north that exhausted supplies, the first boats to arrive at their destinations with the largest varieties of goods were assured the greatest profits. In bad years, steamboats were even more at the mercy of the river. Those that could not make it to Fort Benton because of low water, snags, boiler explosions, sand bars, and Indian attacks, were forced to discharge cargos at various places along the Missouri where overland freighters were employed to complete the job of transporting goods to their final destinations. Additionally, as the west became more populated, communities pushed west from Fort Benton, and overland freighting was the only means of extending the supply lines. Thus, for several decades following the 1840s, there was something of a symbiotic relationship between the overland freighters and steamboat companies, even though considerable competition persisted. Extremely heavy freight and machinery was usually shipped overland, while tools, groceries, and clothing were shipped by water. Even after the arrival of the railroads in the 1860s and 1870s, the two coexisted with railroads until more new rail lines were added to the web of western transportation. By the late 1870s, both steamboat transportation and overland freighting of goods were fast reaching the end of an era. The need to get there first with the most had passed. Now freight could be transported to the west year-round and provide a consistent supply of needed goods and equipment.

It should be remembered that Manifest Destiny was not a tide of humanity making one great invasion into the west. Rather, in addition to people moving to the west in great numbers, it was people moving around in the west. The biographies in this book give strong testament to this fact. That having been said, supplying this multi-dimensional emigration over several decades required enormous resources on the part of the transportation industry, not just to supply the first flush of emigrants, but to also supply the ever-growing and shifting populations of western communities. It is quite significant that after the discovery of gold and silver in the western territories, eastern manufacturers and food producers saw an unprecedented demand for their goods. This in turn led to innovations and inventions that made industry more efficient and better able to supply the needs of the country, including western-ers. The eastern states, particularly in the northeast, began to transform themselves into highly industrialized centers, and the industrial age in America exploded. Even so, eastern industry was at a loss to keep up with the needs of the west, and by the time of Civil War, when a large part of the industrial output went into the war effort, it lagged farther and farther behind.

A question to ponder is whether western commerce was the driver of the eastern industrial engine during the middle years of America's "Golden Age." If it was, this phenomenon was caused only in part by the Civil War. The "War of Northern Aggression" solidified the amalgama-tion of industrial interests in the North with the agrarian interests of the South and provided a strong base for marketing goods in the west in exchange for the resources extracted from the growing western ter-ritories and states. Western mining, milling and smelting, agriculture, and lumber pumped hundreds of millions of dollars into the eastern economy after the Civil War. If the gross national product of the nation sagged a bit immediately after the Civil War, that was simply an indica-tion that industry was just catching its breath and readying itself for the next growth spurt. It was a time when strong-willed men of vision used their entrepreneurial boldness to marshal the nation's resources, improve transportation to support a continent-wide market, support technological innovation, and manufacture powerful machines of mass production. Within ten years after the Civil War, the country saw a huge industrial transformation. The grand Centennial Exposition in Philadelphia in 1876 offered a glimpse of the future. There were hydraulic pumps, new farm implements, gear-cutting machines, steam engines, petroleum products, processed foods, and new methods of communication to name a few. Between 1860 and 1890, the values of manufactured goods in the United States grew from two billion to nine billion dollars.

In part, this progress was supported by a large and willing workforce. After the Civil War, the labor market was flooded with cheap immigrant labor, and there were now 4 million emancipated slaves available to work as freemen in competition with the Irish, Scotts, Germans, and Scandinavians who constituted a large part of the workforce in the north and northeast. After the Civil War, the western railroads would still be built largely on the backs of Chinese immigrants, many of whom escaped repression in China to search for wealth and new beginnings in America. America was becoming more urbanized during this period. In 1860, only six million of the country's 30 million people lived in cities of 2,500 residents, but by 1880, fourteen million people lived in cities or urban places compared to thirty-six million who did not.

The steamboat transportation industry had come and gone by 1890, the same year most western historians and the United States government declared the western frontier was sufficiently populated to be "closed." The steamboat era on the Missouri River was a richly fascinating time in America, as reflected in the thousands of boats that were constructed and the hundreds that met their demise in its waters. It was a time when things were being invented and improved and men began investing themselves not just in personal fortunes, but also in the development of their communities. Those who had the vision and skills and who were willing to risk all that they had for new opportunities generally succeeded both in the east and the west.

The story of the steamboat *Bertrand* represents one small chapter in the development of western commerce in the 1860s, but it unquestionably will continue to attract public interest as well as the interest of scientists and historians into the future. It has been my ambition and the ambition of my friend Jerome Petsche over several decades to tell at least a small part of the *Bertrand*'s story. By providing historically documented accounts of the officers, crew, passengers, consignees, cargo, and manufacturers, perhaps we have partly achieved our aim. This book and its journey through time are now at an end.

Bibliography

Adam, Peter S. "Schaeffer Manufacturing Company, History." Schaeffer Oil, History of Schafer Oil—Lubricants. http://www.schaefferoil.com/company/history.html.

An Account of the Past and Present Activities of the Charles Parker Company and the Bradley and Hubbard Division. Meriden: International Silver Company Historical Library, n.d.

Anderson, Joseph, ed. *The Town and City of Waterbury, Connecticut, from the Aboriginal Period to the Year Eighteen Hundred and Ninety-Five.* New Haven: The Price & Lee Company, 1896.

Andreas, A. T. *History of Chicago from the Earliest Period to the Present Time, in Three Volumes.* Vol. 2, *From 1857 until the Fire of 1871.* Chicago: The A. T. Andreas Company, 1885.

"Baltimore: Register of National Historic Places Travel Itinerary B, Shot Tower." National Park Service, U.S. Department of the Interior. Last modified December 8, 1990. http://www.nps.gov/nr/travel/baltimore/b29.htm.

Bannerman, Francis. *100th Anniversary, The Bannerman Catalogue Military Goods Business.* Blue Point: Bannerman & Sons, Inc., 1966.

Barrows, Willard. "History of Scott County, Iowa." *Annals of Iowa* 1, no. 4 (1863): 1–17.

———. "Three Thousand Miles up the Missouri by Willard Barrows, Esq., of Davenport, Iowa." *Boston Review* 6, no. 36 (1866): 188–205.

———. "To Idaho and Montana; Wanderings There; Returning." *Boston Review* 5, no. 26: 422–60.

Bayliss, Derek. "Bower Spring Furnaces in 1858." *The Cutting Edge*, no. 8 (1992). html://www.topforge.co.uk/Magazine/Bower%202.html

Bazelon, Bruce S., and William F. McGuinn. *Directory of American Military Goods Dealers & Makers 1785–1915.* Woonsocket, R.I.: Andrew Mowbray, 1999).

Berman, Nick. "Stanhopes: The World in Miniature." *Knife World* (1990): 33–38.

Biddle, John and Edward C. *McElroys's Philadelphia Directory for 1855: Containing the Names of the Inhabitants, Their Occupations, Places of Business, and Dwelling Houses: A Business Directory, a List of the Streets, Lanes, Alleys, the Banks, &C., &C., Also the Names of Housekeepers and Persons in Business in Bridesburg, Frankford, Germantown, Manayunk, P.A., &C., &C.*. 8th ed. Philadelphia: Edward C. and John Biddle, 1855.

Bigelow, Albert Paine. *Mark Twain, A Biography, 1835–1910, Complete, the Personal and Literary Life of Samuel Langhorne Clemens.* Vol. 1. New York: Harper & Brothers, 1912.

Binkley, Peter, "Historical Outline" and "William's Montana Trip (1865–66)." Wheatley Family History Project. Last modified July 14, 1999. www.wallan binkley.com/wheatly/-Canada.

Boston Directory, 1861. Boston, Mass: Adams, Sampson, & Co., 1861.

Boston Directory, 1865. Boston, Mass: Adams, Sampson, & Co., 1865.

Boston Directory, 1869. Boston, Mass: Adams, Sampson, & Co., 1869.

Boston Massachusetts Business Directory, 1867. Boston: Sampson, Davenport, & Co.

Bowen, A. W. & Co. *Progressive Men of the State of Montana, Illustrated.* Chicago: W. Bowen & Co., 1902.

Boyd, C. E. *Boyd's Philadelphia Business Directory, 1899.* Section M. Philadelphia: C. E. Howe Co., 1899.

Bradfield, Nancy. *Costume in Detail.* Boston: Plays, Inc., 1968.

Brenner, Barbara. *Careers and Opportunities in Fashion.* New York: E. P. Dutton and Company, 1966.

Broehler, Wayne G., Jr. *John Deere's Company, A History of Deere & Company and its Times.* Garden City, Doubleday & Company, Inc., 1984.

Bruff, Captain Lawrence A. *A Textbook of Ordinance and Gunnery: Prepared for the Use of Cadets of the U.S. Military Academy.* New York: John Wiley and Sons, 1896.

Callahan, James Morton, and Special Staff Writers. *History of West Virginia Old and New, Biography, Illustrated.* Vol. 2. Chicago and New York: The American Historical Society, 1923.

Campbell, R. A. and Richardson, *Campbell & Richardson's St. Louis Directory 1863.* St. Louis: R. A. Campbell, 1863.

Carlton, Hiram. *Genealogical and Family History of the State of Vermont—A Record of the Achievements of Her People in the Making of a Commonwealth and the Founding of a Nation.* New York and Chicago: The Lewis Publishing Company, 1903.

Carvalho, David N. "Ink Industry." *Forty Centuries of Ink, or a Chronological Narrative Concerning Ink and Its Background.* New York: Banks Law Publishing Co., 1904.

Chittenden, Hiram Martin. *Steamboat Navigation on the Missouri River: Life and Adventures of Joseph La Barge.* Vol. 2. New York: Francis P. Harper, 1903.

Coggins, Jack. *Arms and Equipment of the Civil War.* Mineola: Dover Publications, Inc., 1962.

Conley, Mark. "The Saw Set Collector's Resource-Bemis and Call." Saw Set Collector's Resource. Last modified December 19, 2010. http://members .acmenet.net/~con12a/saw%20set%20website/weirdstuffbemis.htm.

Conrad, Randall. "The Machine in the Wetland: Re-imagining Thoreau's Plumbago Grinder." *Thoreau Society Bulletin,* no. 253 (2005): 5–8.

Contributions to the Historical Society of Montana; with its Transactions, Officers and Members. Vol. 3. Boston: J. S. Canner and Company, 1900.

Corbin, Annalies. *Material Culture of Steamboat Passengers—Archaeological Evidence from the Missouri River.* Underwater Archeology Series. New York: Kluwer/Plenum Press, 2000.

"Crawford and Other Relatives." Crawford Archives.com. www.crawfordclan .org.

Cunningham, Phyllis C. Willet. *Handbook of English Costume in the Nineteenth Century.* London: Faber and Faber, 1966.

Cushing, Dr. Thomas. *A Genealogical and Biographical History of Allegheny County, Pennsylvania.* Boston: A. Warner & Co., Chicago, 1889; retitled and reprinted, Genealogical Publishing Co., Inc., 1975, 1993, 2007.

"Cyrus Alger." *Appleton's Encyclopedia.* http://famous americans.net/cyrusalger/.

Dacus, Joseph A., and James W. Buel, *A Tour of St. Louis; or, The Inside Life of a Great City—1878.* St. Louis: Western Publishing Company, Jones & Griffin, 1878.

"Daniel B. Smith." Appleton's Encyclopedia (2001). http://famousamericans .net/danielbsmith/Editedappleton'sEncyclopedia.

Davis, William T. "Marshall Dizer." *The Professional and Industrial History of Suffolk County, Massachusetts (1894).* Vol. 3. Boston: The Boston History Co., 1894.

Disston, Jacob S., Jr. "Henry Disston (1819–1878) Pioneer Industrialist Inventor and Good Citizen." Henry Disston—Disston: An Institute. Taken from a publication based on an address given at Newcomb Society dinner, January 17, 1950. http:/www.distonianinstitute.com/ disstonbio.html.

"Dixon Ticonderoga Company." Dixon Ticonderoga Company. http://www .fundinguniverse.com/company-histories/dixon-ticonderoga-company-history/.

Dorsey, J., and J. D. Dilts. *A Guide to Baltimore Architecture.* 3rd ed. Centerville: Tidewater Publishers, 1970.

Dun & Bradstreet Boston. Vol. 71, 50, and 75. 20HH.

Dyer, Walter A. "The Clockmakers of Connecticut, 108–18. *Early American Craftsmen.* New York: The Century Company, 1915.

Eads, James B. "Recollections of Foote and the Gun-Boats." *Century Magazine,* 29 (1885): 419–25.

"Early Industrial Period (1830–1870)." *Massachusetts Historical Commission Reconnaissance Survey Report—Associated Regional Report: Connecticut Valley.* Boston: Massachusetts Historical Commission, 1982.

Edminster, Daniel. "A Brief Historical Profile of The Holmes, Booth & Haydens Company." The Lampworks (2004). http://www.thelampworks .com/lw_companies_hb&h.htm.

Edwards, Richard. *Edwards' Annual Directory to the Inhabitants, Institutions, Incorporated Companies, Manufacturing Establishments, Businesses, Business Firms, etc., etc., in the City of St. Louis for 1865.* St. Louis and New York: Edwards & Co., 1865.

———. *St. Louis Directory 1864–1865.* St. Louis: Richard Edwards, 1865.

Edwards, William B. *Civil War Guns.* Harrisburg: The Stackpole Company, 1962.

Emerson, William Andrew. *History of the Town of Douglas, (Massachusetts), from the Earliest Period to the Close of 1878.* Boston: Frank R. Bird, 1879.

Evans, Jim. "Carpenter and Tildesley, Summerford Works, Willenthal." A Gazetteer of Lock and Key Makers. 2002. http:www.localhistory.scit.wlv .ac.uk/Museum/locks/gazetteer/gaze.htm.

"Fairbanks Scales, A Legacy of Pride . . . A Look at How It All Began." Kansas City: Fairbanks Scales, 2004.

Federal Census, Schedule 1.—Free Inhabitants in Second Ward, City of Winona, 30 June, 1860.

Federal Census for Helena, Montana Territory, 1 June, 1870.

"Federal Period (1775–1830)." *Massachusetts Historical Commission Reconnaissance Survey Report—Associated Regional Report: Connecticut Valley.* Boston: Massachusetts Historical Commission, 1982.

Fletcher, Robert H. "The Day of the Cattlemen Dawned Early." *Montana The Magazine of Western History* 2, no. 4 (1961): 22–26.

"Former U.S. Senator Joseph H. Millard." *Bankers Magazine* 104 (1922): 423–24.

Freedley, Edwin T. *Philadelphia and Its Manufacturers: A Hand-Book of the Great Manufacturers and Representative Mercantile Houses of Philadelphia in 1867.* Philadelphia: Edward Young & Co., 1867.

French, William H., William F. Barry, and Henry J. Hunt. *Instruction for Field Artillery: Prepared by a Board of Artillery Officers.* New York: D. Van Nostrad, 1864.

Gallaher, William H. "Ho! For the Gold Mines of Montana—Up the Missouri River in 1865. The Journal of William H. Gallaher, Parts I and II." *Missouri Historical Review* 57, no. 2 (1963): 156–82.

Garvin, James L. *A Building History of Northern New England.* Lebanon, N.H.: University Press of New England, 2001.

Gazetteer and Business Directory of the New Southwest. St. Louis: United States Directory Publishing Co., 1881. First ad before the index.

Goodman, Florence. "Seth Thomas." Dissertation given by Florence Goodman to the Thomaston Historical Society, Wolcott, Conn., April 10, 2000.

———. "Seth Thomas, His Wolcott Years," *News* (Wolcott Historical Society), (2000–2010).

Gopsill, James. *Gopsill's Philadelphia City Directory, 1869.* Philadelphia: James Gopsill, 1869.

Gorgas, Col. J., Preparer. *The Ordnance Manual for the Use of the Officers of the Confederate States, Army, Confederate States of America, War Department.* Charleston: Evans & Cogswell, 1863.

Goss, Charles Frederick. *Cincinnati: The Queen City, 1778–1912, Illustrated.* Vol. 3. Chicago and Cincinnati: S. J. Clarke Publishing Company, 1912.

Gould, E. W. *Fifty Years on the Mississippi River; Or, Gould's History of River Navigation.* St. Louis: Nixon-Jones Printing Co., 1889.

Grant, James J. *Single Shot Rifles.* New York: William Morrow & Company, 1947.

Hanson, Charles E., Jr. "The St. Louis Shot Tower." *Museum of the Fur Trade Quarterly* 3, no. 3 (1967): 2–5.

Hanson, John Mills. *Conquest of the Missouri,* Chicago: A. C. McClurg, 1907.

Hanson, Kermit E. "Files From the Steamboat Bertrand," *Museum of the Fur Trade Quarterly* 9, no. 4 (1973): 7–11.

Harold, Jeanne M. "Have You Checked Your Pocketknife Lately?" *Cultural Resource Management* 19, no. 7 (1996): 15–16.

Harper's New Monthly Magazine (October 1867).

"Here Was New Land." In the files of Jerome E. Petsche.

Heuring, Elaine, and Jerry Heuring. "Brief History of the Simmons Hardware Company." Archives of the Winchester *Keen Kutter* Diamond Edge Chronicles. The Hardware Kollectors Klub. Last modified April 1, 2010. http://www.thckk.org/history/simmons-hdwe.pdf.

Herndon House Register. RG3034.AM: Herndon House (Omaha, Neb.) Register: 1865–1866, Omaha, Douglas County, Neb.: Hotel—Size: one reel of microfilm containing one volume, March 28, 1865, to June, 1866. Nebraska State Historical Society, Lincoln.

"History of Eley." *Eley Company London.* http:/www.eley.co.uk/about-eley.aspx.

History of Montana 1739–1885. Chicago: Warner, Beers & Company, 1885.

History of St. Louis County. Vol. 2. St. Louis, 1911.

"History of the Joseph Burnett Company." Southborough Historical Society. http://www.soutboroughhistory.org/History/Burnette%.

"History of the Lead Pencil." Early Office Museum. 2011. Earlyofficemuseum .compencil_history.htm.

"Holland Gin as a Medicinal." *Water-Cure Journal and Herald of Reforms; Devoted to Physiology, Andropathy, and the Laws of Life* 14, no. 5 (1852): 117–18.

Hunt, Freeman, ed. *Merchants Magazine and Commercial Review* 18, no. 1 (1848): 562.

Hunter, Louis C. *Steamboats on the Western Rivers: An Economic and Technical History.* New York: Dover Publications, Inc., 1949.

Hyde, Charles McEwen, and Alexander Hyde. *Lee: The Centennial Celebration and Centennial History of the Town of Lee, Mass.* Springfield: C. M. Hyde and Alexander Hyde, Publishers, 1878.

Hyde, William and Howard Conrad. *Encyclopedia of the History of St. Louis: A Compendium of History and Biography for Ready Reference.* Four vol. New York, Louisville, and St. Louis: The Southern History Company, 1899.

Iatarola, Louis M. "The Life and Influence of Henry Disston." *Profile in Tacony History.* Vol. 1. The Historical Society of Tacony, 1994. http://members.aol .com/historictacony2/profile_disston.html.

Jackson, Ron Vern, Gary Ronald Teeples, and David Schaefermeyer, eds. *Illinois 1830 Census Index.* Bountiful: Accelerated Indexing Systems, Inc., 1830.

Jewett, Llewellynn Frederick William. *The Ceramic Art of Great Britain from pre-historic times down to the Present Day Being a History of the Ancient and Modern Pottery and Porcelain Works of the Kingdom and of their Productions of Every Class.* Vol. 2. London: Virtue and Co., Ltd., 1878.

"John Deere—Our Company." Deere and Company. http://www.deere .com/wps/dcom/en_US/corporate/our_company/about_us/history/history .page?%)A%09%09%09.

"John S. Atchison." *Society of Montana Pioneers—Constitution, Members, and Officers, with Portraits and Maps. . . .* Vol. 1, register 131. Helena: Society of Montana Pioneers, 1889.

Johnson, Allen, ed. "Barsotti—Brazer." *Dictionary of American Biography.* Vol. 2. New York: Charles Scribner's Sons, 1929.

Johnson, David F. *Uniform Buttons: American Armed Forces 1784–1948—Descriptions and Values.* Vol. 1. Watkins Glen: Century House, 1948.

Johnson, Lawrence A. *Over the Counter and on the Shelf—Country Storekeeping in America 1620–1920,* New York: Bonanza Books, 1961.

"John T. Murphy Papers 1849–1973." Manuscript Collection 84. Montana Historical Society Archives, Montana Historical Society, Helena.

"Judge James Gallaher and Helen Campbell Gallaher." *Headwaters Heritage History, Diamond Jubilee Edition.* Three Forks, Mont.: Three Forks Area History Society, 1983.

Kennedy, James Harrison, ed. "Matthew Laflin." *Magazine of Western History, Illustrated* 14, no. 1 (1891): 177–83. Kennedy, R. V. *Kennedy's 1860 St. Louis Directory 1860: Including, Also, a Business Mirror, Appendix, Co-Partnership Directory, &c.* St. Louis: R. V. Kennedy & Co., 1860.

Kingsbury, George W., and George Martin Smith, eds. *History of Dakota Territory—South Dakota Its History and Its People. Illustrated.* Chicago: S. J. Clarke Publishing Company, 1915.

Kleber, John E., editor in chief, Thomas D. Clark, Lowell H. Harrison, and James C. Klotter, assoc. eds. *Encyclopedia of Kentucky.* Lexington: University Press of Kentucky, 1992.

Kouwenhoven, John A. "The Designing of the Eads Bridge." *Technology and Culture* 23, no. 4 (1982).

Kreilick, Scott T. "The Ubiquitous Nail: An Annotated Bibliography" (1990). Research paper on file at the Technical Information Center, Denver Service Center, National Park Service.

Kurtz, Jeffry J. "The Old Pioneer—The Journey of John F. Boepple Founder of the Fresh Water Pearl Button Industry." Muscatine, Iowa: The Pearl Button Museum, 2003.

Laidley, T. T. S. *The Ordnance Manual for the Use of Officers of the United States Army.* 3rd ed. Philadelphia: J. B. Lippincott & Co., 1861.

Lancaster, Jane. "Scientifically Managing New England Butt." *Making Time— Lillian Moller Gilbreth—A Life Beyond Cheaper by the Dozen.* Lebanon, N.H.: Northeastern University Press, 2004.

Lass, William A. *A History of Steamboating on the Upper Missouri River.* Lincoln: University of Nebraska Press, 1962.

Lathrop, William Gilbert. *The Brass Industry in Connecticut: A Study of the Origin and the Development of the Brass Industry in the Naugatuck Valley.* New Haven: The Price, Lee & Adkins Co., 1909.

Leeson, Michael A., ed. *History of Montana 1739–1885, A History of its Discovery and Settlement, Social and Commercial Progress, Mines and Miners, Agriculture and Stock Growing, Churches, Schools and Societies, Indians and Indian Wars, Vigilantes, Courts of Justice, Newspaper Press, Navigation, Railroads and Statistics, with Histories of Counties, Cities, Villages and Mining Camps; Also, Personal Reminiscences of Great Historic Value, Views Characteristic of the Territory in Our Own Times, and Portraits of Pioneers and Representative Men in the Professions and Trades. Illustrated.* Chicago: Warner, Beers & Co., 1885.

Leonard, William, ed. *The Book of St. Louisans: A Biographical Dictionary of Leading Living Men of the City of St. Louis.* St. Louis: St. Louis Republic, 1906.

Lewis, Berkley R. "Small Arms and Ammunition in the United States Service, 1776–1865." *Smithsonian Miscellaneous Collections* 129 (1968): 119.

Lewis Publishing Company. *The Bay of San Francisco: The Metropolis of the Pacific Coast and its Suburban Cities; A History, Illustrated.* Vol. 2. Chicago: The Lewis Publishing Company, 1892.

Lippincott, Joshua Ballinger, ed. *Lippincott's Gazetteer of the World. A Complete Pronouncing Gazetteer or Geographical Directory of the World.* Philadelphia: J. B. Lippincott Company, 1893.

Lossing, Benson J. *The American Centenary: A History of the Progress of the Republic of the United States During the First One Hundred Years of Its Existence.* Philadelphia: Porter & Coates, 1876.

Luscomb, Sally. *The Button Collector's Encyclopedia.* New York: Bonanza Books, 1967.

Lytle, William., and Forest R. Holdcamper. *Merchant Steam Vessels of the United States, 1817–1868.* Staten Island: Historical Society of America and University of Baltimore Press, 1975.

Macintosh. "Charles Macintosh and Co.: The History of the Company." http://www.bouncing-balls.com/serendipity/chasmacintosh.htm.

"Major James B. Campbell." *Headwaters Heritage History, Diamond Jubilee Edition.* Three Forks, Mont.: Three Forks Area History Society, 1983.

"Major James B. Campbell." *Progressive Men of the State of Montana, Illustrated.* Chicago: A. W. Bowen & Co., 1902.

"Making Files in Sheffield, Early 1840s." *Penny Magazine Supplement* 16 (1884).

Manucy, Albert. *Artillery through the Ages: A Short Illustrated History of Cannon, Emphasizing Types Used in America.* Washington, D.C.: U.S. Government Printing Office, 1949.

"Mark Twain's Tutor." *Waterways Journal*, March 22, 1902; repr. *Cairo Telegram* (Ill.), March 22, 1902, 80.

Marquis, Albert Nelson, ed. *The Book of St. Louisans: A Biographical Dictionary of Living Men of the City of St. Louis and Vicinity.* Chicago: A. N. Marquis & Company, 1912.

Massachusetts Business Directory, 1856.

May, Earl Chapin. *Principio to Wheeling 1715–1945, a Pageant of Iron and Steel.* New York: Harper and Brothers, 1945.

McClure, C. H. *History of Missouri.* Chicago and New York: Laidlaw Brothers, Inc., 1920.

McDonald, W. J. "The Missouri River and Its Victims." *Missouri Historical Review* 21, no. 2 (1927).

McKearin, George S. and Helen McKearin. *American Glass.* New York: Crown Publishers, Inc., 1971.

McWatters, Mike. "Manufacturers of Regulation Model Enlisted Swords During the Civil War—American Manufacturers." http://www.angefire.com/wa/swordcollector/marks/pagel.html.

Meagher, Thomas Francis. "A Ride through Montana." *Harper's New Monthly Magazine* 35, no. 209: 583–84.

"Mepham Family Papers 1832–1947." Missouri State Archives, Missouri Historical Society, St. Louis. http:www.mohistory.org/files/archives_guides/MephamFamilyPapers.pdf.

Merrick, Captain G. B. "The Old Boats—Additional Information from Men Who Know—Valuable Contributions to River History, Supplementary to Captain Merrick's Narratives —Communications Invited to this Column—Addenda—Addenda." *Saturday Evening Post*, March 2, 1918.

"Millard, Joseph Hopkins (1836–1922)." *Biographical Directory of the United States Congress 1774–Present.* House Document No. 108–222. Washington: Joint Committee on Printing, 2005.

Miller, Joaquin. *An Illustrated History of the State of Montana, Containing a History of the State of Montana From the Earliest Period of its Discovery to the Present Time, Together with Glimpses of it Auspicious Future; Illustrations and Full-page Portraits of Some of its Eminent Men, and Biographical Mention of Many of its Pioneers and Prominent Citizens of To-day.* Chicago: The Lewis Publishing Company, 1894.

Milner, Clyde A., II, and Carroll A. O'Conner. *As Big As the West: Pioneer Life of Granville Stuart.* New York: Oxford University Press, 2009.

Missouri, An Encyclopedia of Useful Information and a Compendium of Actual

Facts, It Contains a Condensed History of the State of Missouri and its Chief City—St. Louis, the Constitution of the United States and of Missouri and an Abstract of the Laws of Missouri; A Reliable History of Pike County: Its Legal, Political, Official, and War History; A Sketch of the Bench and Law; The Medical Fraternity; The Old Ladies of Pike County; Schools; Churches; The Press; Biographical Sketches, Incidents, etc. etc.—Illustrated. Vol. 20. Des Moines: Mills & Co., 1883.

Mitchell, S. Augustus. *Mitchells' School Geography.* New York: E. H. Butler & Co., 1860.

Morgan, George H. *Annual Statement of the Trade and Commerce of St. Louis for the Year 1865 Reported to the Union Merchant's Exchange by George H. Morgan, Secretary.* St. Louis: H. P. Studley & Co., Printers, 1866.

Morris, Charles. "Charles Goodyear, the Prince of the Rubber Industry." *Heroes of Progress in America* (Philadelphia and London: J. B. Lippincott Co., 1919), 171–77.

Moss, James E. "Ho for the Mines of Montana, Up the Missouri in 1865—The Journal of William Gallaher." *Missouri Historical Review* 57, no. 2 (1963).

Murray, John, "Woolrich Arsenal and Its Manufacturing Establishments." *Quarterly Review* 103 (1858).

Neuschaefer, Klaus. "The Smokeless Powders of Laflin & Rand and Their Fate 100 Years after Assimilation by DuPont." Laflin & Rand. 2007. http://www.laflinandrand.com.

"New England Butt Company." The On-line Industrial Sites and Commercial Buildings Survey in a partnership between the Providence Preservation Society and the Providence Plan. 2002. http://loval.provplan.org/pps/detail .asp?UID=NEBC.

"One Hundred Years of Growth, Shapleigh Hardware Company, St. Louis 1843–1943."

Paine, Albert Bigelow. *Mark Twain: A Biography, 1835–1910, Complete: The Personal and Literary Life of Samuel Langhorne Clemens.* 3 vols. New York and London: Harper and Brothers, 1912.

Park, Benjamin, ed. *Appleton's Cyclopedia of Applied Mechanics: A Dictionary of Mechanical Engineering and the Mechanical Arts.* Vol. 2. New York: D. Appleton and Company, 1881.

Partoll, Albert J. "Frank L. Worden, Pioneer Merchant, 1830–1887." *Pacific Northwest Quarterly* 40, no. 3 (1949).

"Past Leaders." Deere & Company. 2012. http://www.deere.com/wps/dcom/ en_US/corporate/our_company/about_us/history/past_leaders/past_leaders .page?%0A%09%09%09.

Payne, Blanch. *History of Costume.* New York: E. P. Dutton and Company, 1966.

Paxton, John A. *The St. Louis Directory, 1821 and Register.* St. Louis: John A. Paxton, 1821.

Perkins, David C., compiler. *Tazwell County Illinois Land Records Index.* Vol. 1. Perkins, Ill.: Tazwell County Genealogical Society, 1838.

Peterson, Harold L. *American Knives*. New York: Charles Scribner's Sons, 1958.

Peterson, Leslie A. *Ironstone Treasures aboard the Steamboat* Bertrand. Chesterfield: The White Ironstone China Association, 1999.

Peterson's Magazine 40, no. 5 (1861).

Petrosky, Henry. *The Pencil: A History of Design and Circumstance*. New York: Knopf Publishing Group, 1990.

Petsche, Jerome E. "Uncovering the Steamboat *Bertrand*." *Nebraska History* 1, no. 1 (1970).

———. *The Steamboat* Bertrand—History, Excavation, and Architecture. Publications in Archeology 11. Washington, D.C.: National Park Service, U.S. Department of the Interior, 1974.

———. "Here Was the New Land." Unpublished draft chapter. N.d.

Phillips, Paul C., ed. *Forty Years on the Frontier as seen in the Journals and Reminiscences of Granville Stuart*. Vol. 2. Glendale: Arthur H. Clark Company, 1967.

Pierce, Bradford K. *Trials Of An Inventor—Life and Discoveries of Charles Goodyear*. New York: Carlton & Porter, 1866.

Pike Industries. "The Pike Manufacturing Company." www.nhnorth.us/pikeindustries.html.

Pittsburgh Patentees 1790–1879. Pittsburgh: Carnegie Library of Pittsburgh, 2009.

"Powder River Land and Cattle Company Records 1911–1944" (inclusive). Collection MC83 of the Montana Historical Archives, Montana Historical Society, Helena.

Pricelist of New York Mallet and Handle Works, Manufacturers of Caulkers' Tin, Copper & Boilermakers' Mallets Hawsing Beetles, Hausing Caulking Irons, Sledge, Chisel & Hammer Handles, Also Cotton & Bale Hooks, Patented February 13, 1877; A New Combination of Hooks. New York: New York Mallet and Handle Works, 1877.

Reavis, L. U. "The Laflin, Rand Powder Company." *St. Louis: The Commercial Metropolis of the Mississippi Valley*. St. Louis: Tribune Publishing Company, 1874.

———. "Nicholas Schaeffer." *St. Louis: The Future City of the World, Illustrated, Biographical Edition*. St. Louis: Gray, Baker and Co. 1875.

Record Group 41, Records of the Bureau of Marine Inspection and Navigation. Washington: General Services Administration, National Archives and Record Service.

"Records of Packs and Cost of Various Items 1855–1866." William Underwood & Co. August 30, 1865. Transmitted to the author by V. A. Fulmer of the Underwood Co., August 22, 1974. In the possession of the author.

Roberts, Captain Joseph. *Handbook of Artillery, for the Service of the United States Army and Militia*. New York: D. Van Nostrand, 1860.

Robinson, Charles, ed. *The Manufactories and Manufacturers of Pennsylvania of the Nineteenth Century*. Philadelphia: Galaxy Publishing Co., 1875.

Russell, Carl P. *Firearms, Traps, & Tools of the Mountain Men.* New York: Alfred A. Knopf, 1967.

——. *Guns on the Early Frontiers: A History of Firearms from Colonial Times to the Years of the Western Fur Trade.* New York: University of California Press, 1957.

Russell, Loris S. *A Heritage of Light, Lamps and Lighting in the Early Canadian Home.* Toronto: University of Toronto Press, 1968.

Russell, Norman. "On American River Steamers." *Transactions of the Institution of Naval Architects.* Vol. 2. London: 1861.

Sanders, Helen F. "Nicholas J. Beilenburg." *History of Montana.* Vol. 2 and 3. Chicago and New York: Lewis Publishing Co., 1913.

Sanders, James U., ed. "John S. Atchinson." *Society of Montana Pioneers— Constitution, Members, and Officers, with Portraits and Maps—Register 131.* Helena: Society of Montana Pioneers, 1899.

Sanders, Walter F. "Francis Lyman Warden." *Contributions to the Historical Society of Montana; with its Transactions, Act of Incorporation, Constitution, Ordinances, Officers and Members.* Vol. 2. Boston: J. S. Canner and Company, Inc., 1966.

Scharf, John Thomas. *History of St. Louis, City and County from the Earliest Periods to the Present Day, including Biographical Sketches of Representative Men.* Vol. 1. Philadelphia: Everts & Co., 1883.

Schell, Herbert S. *History of South Dakota.* Lincoln: University of Nebraska Press, 1961.

Schoeffler, O. E. and William Gale. *Esquire's Encyclopedia of 20th Century Men's Fashions.* New York: McGraw-Hill Company, 1973.

Schweiger, Catherine M. "Techniques for the Analysis of Dyes on Historic Textiles." Master's thesis, University of Nebraska, 1971.

Second Annual Report of the Missouri Board of Agriculture, with an Abstract of Proceedings of the County Agricultural Societies, to the General Assembly of Missouri for the Year 1866. Jefferson City: Emory S. Foster, 1867.

Sellers, James. "Memoir of James Buchannan Eads, 1820–1887." *Papers Read Before the National Academy of Sciences.* Washington: April 1888.

"Shapleigh Hardware Company." Shapleigh Family Association. http://shapleigho .tripod.com/shapleighfamilyassociation/id13.html.

Sharpe, Philip B. *The Rifle in America.* New York: Funk and Wagnalls Company, 1958.

Sheldon, Addison E. ed. "First Hat Factory in Nebraska." *Nebraska History and Record of Pioneer Days* 4, no. 1 (1921).

Short, Lloyd M. *Steamboat-Inspection Service, Its History, Activities, and Organization.* New York: D. Appleton & Co., 1922.

Smith, Roger. "Notes on New England Tool Makers, 1—Edge Tool Makers, Hinsdale, NH, 1840–1900, P. Merrill 1840–1858." Mid-West Tool Collectors Association. http://www.mwtca.org/the-gristmill/sample-articles/ 96-notes-on-new-england-edge-tool.

Spencer, Patricia C. *Images of America: Helena Montana*. Chicago: Arcadia
    Publishers, 2002.
Steel City Founders. "George Wostenholm 1800-1876." Last modified April
    20, 2003. http://www.tilthammer.com/bio/wost.html.
———. "William Butcher 1791-1870." http://www.tilthammer.com/bio/butch
    .html.
St. Louis Directory, 1864. St. Louis, Mo.
Stone, Orra L. *History of Massachusetts Industries*. Vol. 1. Boston and Chicago:
    S. J. Clarke Publishing Co., 1930.
Stout, Tom. *Montana, Its Story and Biography, I*, Chicago and New York: The
    American Historical Society, 1921.
Stuart, Granville. *Montana As It Is; A General Description of its Resources, Both
    Mineral and Agricultural, Including a Complete Description of the Face of the
    Country, its Climate, etc.* New York: Arno Press, 1973.
———. *Pioneering In Montana: The Making of a State, 1864–1887*. Paul C. Phil-
    lips, ed. Lincoln: University of Nebraska Press, 1925.
"Stuart, Granville." *Dictionary of American Biography*. Vol. 18. New York:
    Charles Scribner's Sons, 1936.
Sullivan, Jack. "Ulysses S. Grant His Whiskey History." *Bottles and Extras*.
    Raymore: The Federation of Historical Bottle Collectors, 2007.
Switzer, Ronald R. "The Chemical Differentiation of Dyestuffs in Anthropo-
    logical Specimens." Lecture presented at the University of New Mexico, 1969.
———. "Lead Bars from the Steamboat *Bertrand*." *Museum of the Fur Trade
    Quarterly* 6, no. 4 (1967).
———. "Charles Parker's Britannia on the Steamboat *Bertrand*." *Museum of
    the Fur Trade Quarterly* 7, no. 4 (1971).
———. "Munitions on the Bertrand." *Archaeology* 25, no. 4 (1972).
———. "Tally Ho's from the Steamboat *Bertrand*." *Just Buttons* 30, no. 4 (1972):
    416–26.
———. "Butcher Knives as Historical Sources." *Museum of the Fur Trade Quar-
    terly* 8, no. 1 (1972): 5–7.
———. "Maynard Cartridges and Primers From the Steamboat *Bertrand*."
    Military Collector & Historian: Journal of the Company of Military Historians
    24, no. 3 (1972): 85–87.
———. "Fairbanks Weighing Devices on the Steamboat *Bertrand*." *Nebraska
    History* 55, no. 2 (1974): 254–63.
———. "Small Chinas from the Steamboat *Bertrand*." *Just Buttons* 32, no. 5
    (1974): 135–42.
———. "Some Unusual Powder Kegs from the Steamboat *Bertrand*." *Museum
    of the Fur Trade Quarterly* 10, no. 3 (1974): 3–6.
———. *The* Bertrand *Bottles, A Study of 19th Century Glass and Ceramic Con-
    tainers*. Washington, D.C.: National Park Service, U.S. Department of the
    Interior, 1974.
Sylvester, Nathaniel Bartlett. *History of Ulster County, Part Second*. Philadel-
    phia: Everts & Peck, 1880.

Tariff Hearings before the Committee on Ways and Means of the House of Representatives, 6th Congress, 2nd Session, 1908–1909. Vol. 8—Appendix. Washington, D.C.: United States Government Printing Office, 1909.

Tarbell, Ida M. *The History of Standard Oil Company*. New York: Phillips and Co., 1904.

Tenner, Edward. "Gordon McKay (1821–1903)." *Harvard Magazine* 103, no. 1 (2000): 37.

Thomas, William L. *History of St. Louis County, Missouri*. Vol. 2. St. Louis: S. J. Clarke Publishing Co., 1911.

Thompson, Holland. "The Story of Rubber." *Chronicles of America Series: The Age of Invention, A Chronicle of Mechanical Conquest*. Book 37. New Haven, Yale University Press, 1921.

Thompson, Mark. "Baldwin History." The Society for the Preservation and Study of American Wooden Planes. Last modified May 7, 2001. http://www.woodenplane.org/Bald-History.htm.

Topping, Robert L. "Pike Manufacturing Company." *Outlook Magazine: The Magazine of Northern New Hampshire*. North Woodstock: White Mountain Region Association, 1985.

Toulouse, Julian Harrison. *Bottle Makers and Their Marks*. New York: Thomas Nelson, Inc., 1971.

Treaty with the Iowa, Etc. (September 17, 1836) 7 Stat., 511. Proclamation, February 15, 1837.

Twain, Mark. *Life on the Mississippi*. New York: Harper & Brothers, 1901.

Upham, Hiram. "Uphan Letters from the Upper Missouri, 1865." *The Frontier: A Magazine of the Northwest* 13, no. 4 (1933): 311–13.

Vincent, Benjamin. *Hayden's Dictionary of Dates and Universal Information Relating to all Ages and Nations*. New York: G. P. Putnam's Sons, 1906.

"Virginia City Was Site of First Bank." *Your Banks . . . Historical Sketches of Montana Banks and Bankers*. Helena: Helena Branch of the Federal Bank of Minneapolis, 1946.

Von Sneidern. Erik. "A Brief Rendering of the Disston and Sons History." Online Reference of Disston Saws—Disston Centennial 1849–1940. htttp:www.distonianinstitute.com/ 100anniversary.html.

Voss, Wm. Erik. "American Silversmiths—Luther Boardman." An Ancestry.Com Community (2005). http://freepages.genealogy.rootsweb.ancestry.com/-silversmiths/makers/ silversmiths/120661.htm.

Wager, Daniel E., ed. *Our County and Its People, A Descriptive Work on Onieda County, New York*. Boston: The Boston History Company, Publishers, 1896.

Walke, Henry (Rear Admiral, USN). *Naval Scenes and Reminiscences of the Civil War in the United States on the Southern and Western Waters during the years 1861, 1862, and 1863 with the History of the Period*. New York: F. R. Reed & Co., 1877.

Wallace, John. *The Practical Engineer: A Treatise on the Subject of Modeling, Constructing and Running Steam Engines, Containing Also Directions In Regard To Various Kinds of Machinery Connected With Steam Power, Prepared with Special*

Reference to the Needs of Steamboat Owners, Captains, Pilots and Engineers, and also Connected with Stationary Steam Engines, on Land and Water. 2nd ed. Pittsburgh: W. S. Haven, 1861.

Walton, John Edward. "Up the Missouri River—Memories as a Child." Unpublished manuscript written about 1939. Copy in possession of the author.

"Welcome to Worcester—Worcester Sauce." http:www.birminghamamuk.com/Worcester_sauces.htm.

White, Henry Hall. "The Willington Glass Company." *Antiques Magazine* 40, no. 2 (1941): 99–100.

White, James Terry, ed. "Oakes Ames." *The National Cyclopedia of American Biography Being the History of the United States as Illustrated in the Lives of the Founders, Builders, and Defenders of the Republic, and of the Men and Women Who Are Doing the Work and Moulding the Thought of the Present Time*. Vol. 2. New York: James T. White & Company, 1895.

White, Walter. *A Month in Yorkshire*. London: Chapman and Hall, 1858.

Woodhead, Eileen. *Trademarks on Base-Metal Tableware*. Studies in Archaeology, Architecture and History. Ottowa, Ont.: National Historic Sites, Park Service, Environment Canada, 1991.

Woodward, C. M. *A History of the St. Louis Bridge Containing a Full Account of Every Step in Its Construction and Erection, and Including the Theory of the Ribbed Arch and the Tests of Materials*. St. Louis: G. I. Jones and Company, 1881.

The Worden Company Papers for 1865, No. 277. Helena: Montana State Historical Society, 1865.

Worthen, Dennis B. "Daniel B. Smith, 1792–1883: Patriarch of American Pharmacy." *Journal of the American Pharmacists Association* 48, no. 6 (2008): 808–12.

Young, James Harvey. *The Toadstool Millionaires: A Social History of Patent Medicines in America before Federal Regulation*. Princeton: Princeton University Press, 1961.

Index